**Central and
Southern Laos**
Pages 188–203

Phnom Penh
Pages 46–63

CENTRAL
AND
SOUTHERN
LAOS

• Pakse

• Champasak

**Northern
Cambodia**
Pages 88–103

*South
China Sea*

NORTHERN
CAMBODIA

mpong
om

Kompong
• Cham

nom Penh

OM
H

**Southern
Cambodia**
Pages 104–121

CAMBODIA
& LAOS

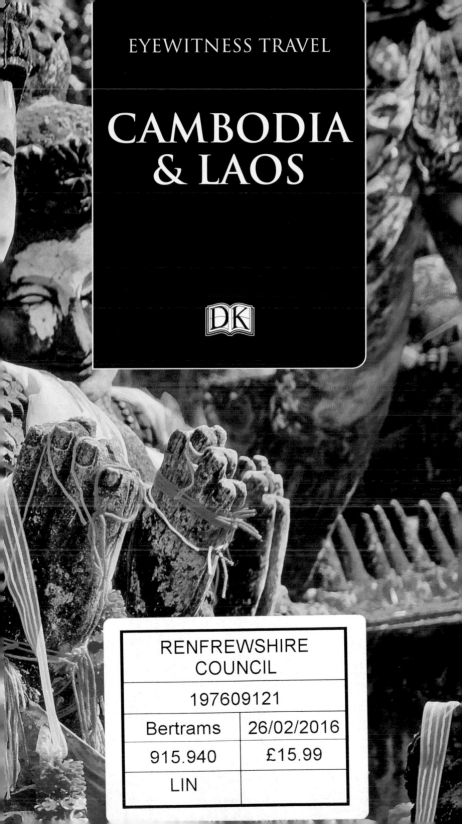

EYEWITNESS TRAVEL

CAMBODIA & LAOS

DK

DK

LONDON, NEW YORK,
MELBOURNE, MUNICH AND DELHI
www.dk.com

Managing Editor Aruna Ghose
Senior Editorial Manager Savitha Kumar
Senior Design Manager Priyanka Thakur
Project Editor Smita Khanna Bajaj
Project Designer Amisha Gupta
Editors Karen Faye D'Souza, Shreya Sarkar
Designer Neha Sethi
Senior Cartographic Manager Uma Bhattacharya
Cartographer Schchida Nand Pradhan

DTP Designer Rakesh Pal

Senior Picture Research Coordinator Taiyaba Khatoon

Picture Researcher Sumita Khatwani

Main Contributors David Chandler, Peter Holmshaw, Iain Stewart, Richard Waters

Photographers Demetrio Carrasco, Linda Whitwam

Illustrators
Chingtham Chinglemba, Sanjeev Kumar, Surat Kumar Mantoo,
Arun Pottirayil, Gautam Trivedi

Printed and bound in Malaysia

16 17 18 19 10 9 8 7 6 5 4 3 2 1

First published in UK in 2011
by Dorling Kindersley Limited
80 Strand, London WC2R 0RL

Reprinted with revisions 2013, 2016

Copyright 2011, 2016 © Dorling Kindersley Limited, London
A Penguin Random House Company

A CIP catalogue record is available from the British Library.

ISBN 978-0-2411-9678-6

Floors are referred to throughout in accordance with
American usage, ie the "first floor" is at ground level.

MIX
Paper from
responsible sources
FSC
www.fsc.org   **FSC™ C018179**

**The information in this DK Eyewitness
Travel Guide is checked regularly.**
Every effort has been made to ensure that this book is as up-to-date as possible
at the time of going to press. Some details, however, such as telephone numbers,
opening hours, prices, gallery hanging arrangements and travel information, are
liable to change. The publishers cannot accept responsibility for any consequences
arising from the use of this book, nor for any material on third party websites, and
cannot guarantee that any website address in this book will be a suitable source of
travel information. We value the views and suggestions of our readers very highly.
Please write to: Publisher, DK Eyewitness Travel Guides, Dorling Kindersley,
80 Strand, London, WC2R 0RL, UK, or email: travelguides@dk.com.

Front cover main image: The monumental Angkor Wat temple complex

◀ Colorfully adorned Buddhas in Xieng Khuan, southeast of Vientiane

Visitors kayaking down the Nam Song,
Vang Vieng

Contents

How to Use this Guide
6

Introducing Cambodia and Laos

Discovering Cambodia
and Laos **10–15**

Putting Cambodia and
Laos on the Map **16**

A Portrait of Cambodia
and Laos **18**

Monks enjoying a quiet moment amid the
stone sculptures, the Bayon

Laos Area by Area

Thongs adorning the inside of Wat Luang Ban Xieng Jai

Cambodia Area by Area

Ornate carvings at the temple complex of Banteay Srei, Angkor

Detail of carving, Wat Xieng Men

Travelers' Needs

Survival Guide

Wat Xieng Thong, Luang Prabang

HOW TO USE THIS GUIDE

This guide helps you to get the most from your visit to Cambodia and Laos. It provides detailed practical information and expert recommendations. *Introducing Cambodia and Laos* maps the two countries and sets them in their historical and cultural context. *Cambodia Area by Area* and *Laos Area by Area* are the main sightseeing sections. They cover all the important sights with maps, photographs, and illustrations. Information on hotels, restaurants, shops and markets, and entertainment is found in *Travelers' Needs*. The *Survival Guide* has advice on everything from travel and medical services, to telephones and internet facilities.

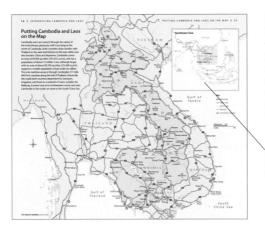

Putting Cambodia and Laos on the Map

The orientation map shows the location of Cambodia and Laos in relation to their neighboring countries. Each country has been divided into four main sightseeing areas. These eight sections form the separate chapters.

A locator map shows where Cambodia and Laos are in relation to other Southeast Asian countries.

Cambodia and Laos Area by Area

Each of the eight sections starts with an introduction and a map. The best places to visit have been numbered on a *Regional Map* at the beginning of each chapter. The key to the map symbols is on the back flap.

1 Introduction
The history, landscape, and character of each area is outlined here, showing how the area has developed over the centuries and what it has to offer the visitor today.

Each region can be quickly identified by its color coding. A complete list of color codes is shown on the inside front cover.

2 Regional Map This map shows the road network and gives an illustrated overview of the region. All the sights are numbered and there are also useful tips on getting around.

Sights at a Glance lists the chapter's sights by category: Places of Worship, National Parks, Museums, and Markets.

5 Street-by-Street Map
This gives a bird's-eye view of the key area covered in each chapter.

A suggested route for a walk is shown in red.

A feature deals with a topic related to that region or place.

3 Detailed Information
All important places to visit are described individually. Addresses, telephone numbers, opening hours, and information on admission charges and wheelchair access, is also provided.

The visitors' checklist provides all the practical information needed to plan your visit.

4 Cambodia and Laos's Top Sights
These are given two or more full pages. An illustrated artwork shows the layout of the site. Parts worth visiting are highlighted.

Stars indicate the sights that no visitor should miss.

6 Town Map
Within each chapter, important towns and cities are described in detail, and numerous sights recommended. A handy map locates the main sights and transport hubs in the town.

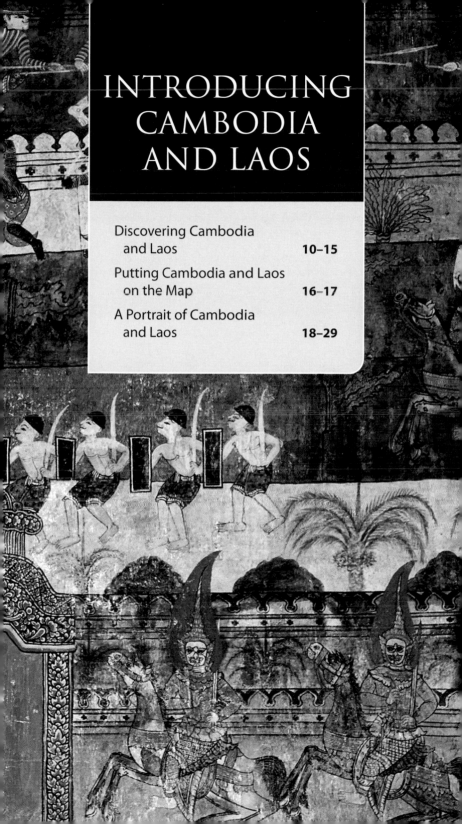

INTRODUCING CAMBODIA AND LAOS

DISCOVERING CAMBODIA AND LAOS

The following tours have been designed to help you get the most out of your trip to Cambodia and Laos, while keeping journey times to a minimum. The two-day tours provide an introduction to the two countries' capital cities – Phnom Penh and Vientiane – and will help you to cover the very best sights, as well as some lesser-known attractions that reveal different sides to the cities.

The next two itineraries are both possible within the space of a week. The first tour takes in some of Cambodia's finest historic sights, including the majestic temples of Angkor. The second will guide you into a little-explored region of northern Laos where intriguing wartime tales, welcoming locals and breathtakingly beautiful mountain scenes are the rewards for enduring long and bumpy bus rides.

The final two-week tour follows the Mekong River as it snakes along the Thai-Lao border and into Cambodia. While some sections of the river are now impassable, much-improved roads make it possible to roughly follow its course – from the former royal capital of Laos, Luang Prabang, all the way south to the bustling heart of modern Cambodia.

Key

━━ Two Weeks along the Mekong

━━ A Week on the Khmer Trail

━━ A Week in Northern Laos

0 kilometers 150

0 miles 150

Two Weeks along the Mekong

- Sample French-Lao cuisine at Luang Prabang's waterfront restaurants

- Go shopping and temple hopping in Vientiane, or take a local cookery class

- Cycle among peeling Colonial buildings in sleepy Savannakhet

- Kick back with a coffee in Champasak, or make a trip to nearby Wat Phu

- Relax by the riverfront on one of 4,000 islands in magical Si Phan Don

- Splash about in Stung Treng, the perfect base for boat trips

- Stock up on souvenirs in Phnom Penh, Cambodia's bustling capital

Li Phi waterfalls in Don Khon, on the Si Phan Don archipelago
Nicknamed the "Devil's Corridor," these rapidly flowing waterfalls cascade across the rocky landscape.

◀ A 19th-century mural showing a triumphal military procession, in Wat Pa Huek, Luang Prabang

Reflection Pool at Angkor Wat
The majestic Angkor Wat is beautifully reflected in the still waters that surround the complex. The best views are from the left of the causeway.

A Week in Northern Laos

- Go tubing, caving, kayaking, or biking in Vang Vieng, where rivers and mountains meet

- Cool off in Phonsavan, then wander among ancient stone urns on the mysterious Plain of Jars

- Experience a little bit of Vietnam in Sam Neua, the bordering town that's renowned for its handwoven colorful textiles

- Head deep into the natural caves of Vieng Xai, where Pathet Lao leaders famously hid from the USA's aerial bombardment

Vang Vieng
Magnificant scenery surrounds the Nam Song River in Vang Vieng, a town that serves as the starting point for a wide range of adventure sports.

A Week on the Khmer Trail

- Get acquainted with Khmer architecture at Banteay Srei

- Climb the monumental stairway at Prasat Prear Vihear for views of the surrounding plains

- Take a trip from Stung Treng to see the ruins of 6th- and 7th-century temples

- Admire pretty French Colonial buildings and wide boulevards in Kompong Cham

- See early examples of intricate bas-reliefs at Sambor Prei Kuk

- Explore the world's largest religious monument, the awe-inspiring Angkor Wat

Two Days in Phnom Penh

Many visitors overlook Phnom Penh in their rush to reach Angkor but Cambodia's sprawling capital offers lots to explore, not least the gilded Royal Palace, the treasure-filled National Museum, and Sisowath Quay's lively after-dark scene.

- **Arriving** Phnom Penh's airport is around 6 miles (10km) west of the downtown area. Take a taxi, tuk-tuk, or motorbike.
- **Moving on** Bus stations for long-distance journeys are dotted around town. Trains bound for Battambang depart from the western end of 108 St.

Day 1
Morning Start your day at the official residence of the Cambodian king, the **Royal Palace** *(pp54–5)*, which was designed to face the rising sun. Before admiring the throne hall, whose roof is adorned with mythical beasts, take in the splendid **Silver Pagoda** *(pp56–7)*, named after the silver tiles that decorate its floor.

Afternoon To escape the heat of the afternoon, visit the **National Museum of Cambodia** *(p52)*, a treasure trove of Khmer art set around a handsome

Interior of the Art Deco Central Market in Phnom Penh

central courtyard. Nearby, the stupa at **Wat Ounalom** *(p52)* is said to contain a hair from the Buddha's eyebrow.

Day 2
Morning For an insight into Phnom Penh's harrowing past, visit the sombre **Tuol Sleng Genocide Museum** *(p53)*, a former school that gained notoriety as the torture headquarters for the Khmer Rouge. At the **Killing Fields of Choeung Ek** *(p60)*, nearby, some 17,000 people were murdered.

Afternoon Back in the center, the **Art-Deco Central Market** *(p53)* is a good place to stock up on clothes and electronics. Wind up your second day with a sundowner at the **Foreign Correspondents' Club** *(p222)*, overlooking the Tonlé Sap River.

Two Days in Vientiane

Although Vientiane is growing fast, it remains one of the world's sleepiest capital cities and is relatively easy to get around. Tick off the main sights and you will still have time to explore smart French-Lao restaurants, glittering temples, and charming antique shops.

- **Arriving** Vientiane's airport is on Luang Prabang Avenue, around 4 mile (6km) west of the centre. Taxis, minivans, and tuk-tuks are on hand for the journey into the center.
- **Moving on** Regional and international buses depart from stations on the edge of the city. Buses to the Friendship Bridge, which connects Laos with Thailand, some 12 miles (20km) east of Vientiane, leave from the Talat Sao bus station.

Day 1
Morning Some of Vientiane's finest temples are within a block or two of the Mekong River, which forms the city's southern boundary. Once the king's personal temple, **Haw Pha Kaew** *(p142)* now serves as Vientiane's museum of art and antiquities. Across the road, **Wat Si Saket** *(p143)* is the city's oldest place of worship, and is surrounded by a weather-blackened cloister housing countless Buddha statues. **Wat Si Muang** *(p142)*, farther east along tree-lined Setthathirat Road, attracts far more worshipers these days, as the wafts of sweet-smelling incense filling the ordination hall attest to.

Afternoon After a morning of temple hopping, relax on Nam Phu Square, where restaurants and cafés surround a gushing fountain. Exhibits at the dusty **Lao National Museum** *(p143)*, a short stroll to the northwest, are often little more than examples of socialist propaganda but there are some intriguing

A shrine in the grounds of Wat Si Saket, Vientiane

Beautiful scenery surrounds the Nam Song River in Vang Vieng

objects, including a large urn from the **Plain of Jars** *(p177)*, and some impressive life-size re-creations of the Khmer lintels of Wat Phu Champasak *(pp198–9)*.

Day 2

Morning The golden stupa that is seen on banknotes around Laos, **Pha That Luang** *(p145)*, glows magnificently in the early morning light. Take your time to wander around the serene temple complex and admire the intricate architecture and dazzling Buddha images.

To see the city from a completely different perspective, take a tuk tuk to **Patuxai** *(p144)*. Built to commemorate the many lives lost during the Lao Civil War, this huge concrete structure is Vientiane's answer to the Arc de Triomphe. From the top, the views of the palm-shaded plaza and Lan Xang Avenue are superb.

Afternoon Stroll down Lan Xang Avenue toward the western end of Setthathirat Road, where you can find antique emporiums selling opium pipes, handmade jewelry and old-style Buddha images. For modern, hand-woven textiles, try Carol Cassidy Lao Textiles on Nokeo Khumman Road. When the sun starts to sink, head down to the Mekong and wander through the lively riverfront Night Market. Sample the street food and explore the many stalls and kiosks, which sell anything from designer handbags to local crafts.

A Week in Northern Laos

With twisting mountain passes, sleepy riverside towns, and creaking, dilapidated buses, Northern Laos is unlike any of the other areas covered in this guide. This week-long tour covers the main sights in the eastern part of the region.

- **Arriving** Vang Vieng is roughly equidistant from Luang Prabang and Vientiane, both of which have international airports. Domestic flights from Vientiane also land at Phonsavan, making it possible to start and end the journey there.

- **Transport** Getting around northern Laos takes time. Buses ply some legs of the route, as outlined below, but for the most part you will be relying on local *songthaew* services.

Day 1 & 2: Vang Vieng

Set amid soaring limestone karsts, the self-styled "tubing capital of the world" has turned over a new leaf. Spend time exploring the surrounding caves and mountain bike trails, or just enjoy a cold Beerlao by the still-magnificent Nam Song River. There are far fewer backpackers here than there once were, which makes it much easier to find a tranquil spot, clamber into a hammock, and admire the idyllic scenery.

Day 3 & 4: Phonsavan and the Plain of Jars

After a long bus ride across the countryside, the capital of Xieng Khuang Province rewards visitors with a cool, welcoming climate. This town, almost wiped off the map by American bombing during the Vietnam War, is the ideal base for trips to the mysterious **Plain of Jars** *(p177)*. Huge craters and heavy stone urns dot the landscape, large parts of which are still off limits due to the huge amount of unexploded ordnance.

Day 5: Sam Neua

The route east from Phonsavan is tortuous but takes in some jaw-dropping scenery. Break your journey in **Sam Neua** *(p176)*, a simple, workaday town known for its hand-woven textiles. The fresh food market by the riverside here sells hearty bowls of *pho* (noodle soup) – it is the perfect way to warm up first thing in the morning, when the air can feel surprisingly chilly.

Day 6 & 7: Vieng Xai

The honeycomb of limestone caves around **Vieng Xai** *(p176)* helped the Pathet Lao survive the largest aerial bombardment in history. On a tour of the vast caves, which housed hospital beds, weaving mills, and even a movie theater, you can hear the stories of the people who hid there. The town itself sits at the foot of epic limestone karsts and is still wonderfully sleepy – it is a far cry from the bustling capital that Pathet Lao leaders envisioned at the end of the war.

Mysterious stone urns at the Plain of Jars, near Phonsavan

A week on the Khmer trail

At one stage the Khmer Empire exerted power across much of Southeast Asia. Most travelers visit Angkor Wat, built at the empire's zenith, but there are many other Khmer and pre-Khmer ruins to discover in Cambodia and Laos, and most of them are blissfully free from crowds.

- **Arriving** Siem Reap's airport, around 22 miles (35km) south-east of the first temple, is served by international flights.

- **Transport** It is essential to rent a car for this route. If you can, rent a car with a driver. It is relatively inexpensive in this part of the world, and far safer than driving yourself. Most know the roads well and can help you to avoid the busiest times of day.

Day 1: Banteay Srei
Around 19 miles (30km) north-east of Angkor Wat, the exquisitely carved temple of **Banteay Srei** (p84) provides a bite-sized introduction to Khmer architecture. Built in the 10th century and dedicated to the Hindu god Shiva, it is on a miniature scale compared with later temples, and sits in fantastically sleepy surrounds.

Day 2: Prasat Preah Vihear
Near the border with Thailand, **Prasat Preah Vihear** (pp96–7) has long been the subject of ownership disputes. Cambodian

Buddha statue at Wat Nokor, near Kompong Cham

soldiers often guard the monument, but do not let that put you off. Set high in the Dangkrek Mountains, this temple enjoys epic views of the plains far below. Its monumental stairway leads to a series of *gopuras* (entrance buildings) and the remains of a central shrine, which now houses a Buddhist temple.

Day 3: Chenla ruins near Stung Treng
For a glimpse back to a time before the Khmer Empire began to flourish, head to **Stung Treng** (p102). Guesthouses here can arrange trips to visit nearby ruins, some of which are thought to date back to the 6th and 7th centuries. The most impressive of the local sites is Prasat Preah Ko, which derives its name (meaning "Sacred Bull"), from the three stone statues of Nandi, Shiva's bull, which face the temple's central towers.

Day 4: Wat Nokor, Kompong Cham
After admiring the French Colonial buildings and wide boulevards in riverside Kompong Cham (p102), make the pleasant cycle ride out to Wat Nokor. It is an unusual mix of old and new, with a modern Buddhist pagoda squeezed inside the walls of a far older shrine.

Day 5: Sambor Prei Kuk
The 7th-century temple complex of **Sambor Prei Kuk** (pp100–1) was at the heart of the Chenla-period capital of Isanapura. The ruins here predate the Khmer temples at **Angkor** (pp64–87) by more than 150 years, but certain artistic techniques – such as intricate bas-reliefs – were already being pioneered.

Day 6 & 7: Angkor
There is no better place to end your tour than **Angkor** (pp65–87), home to some of Southeast Asia's greatest architectural accomplishments. If you base yourself in **Siem Reap** (pp68–9), it's easy to take in the sprawling, partially forested area and its magnificent remains – chief of which is the world's largest religious monument, **Angkor Wat** (pp70–71).

To extend your trip...
Cross the Lao border to visit **Wat Phu** (pp198–9), the most impressive Khmer ruin outside of Cambodia. Its setting, at the foot of a jungle-clad mountain, is perhaps the most beautiful of any Khmer temple.

Elaborate carvings at the temple of Banteay Srei, near Siem Reap

For practical information on travelling around Cambodia and Laos, see pp260–71

Monks line the street as part of the morning almsgiving ceremony in Luang Prabang

Two Weeks along the Mekong

The Mekong runs like a thread through Cambodia and Laos, passing some of the countries' most enchanting cities. While the river itself is not always easy to follow, it still plays an important role in the lives of the communities it flows past.

- **Arriving** Luang Prabang and Phnom Penh both have international airports. If you are arriving into Vientiane, you can simply transfer there – the airport has flights to both Luang Prabang and Phnom Penh.

- **Transport** Overzealous hydroelectric power projects have made parts of the Mekong impassable, so for many sections of this route the only option is to travel by bus or private car. However, short trips out onto the Mekong are easy to organize in most towns, and in Si Phan Don (pp202–3) you will have no choice but to take to the river.

Day 1 & 2: Luang Prabang
Start your journey in the former royal capital of Laos, **Luang Prabang** (pp150–69). Soak up the laid-back vibe at exquisite waterfront restaurants and cafés, and indulge yourself with

a massage at one of the old town's spas. For better or worse, the morning almsgiving ceremony here has evolved into a major tourist attraction. In this daily ritual, orange-robed monks silently line the street to receive gifts of food from local Buddists.

Day 3 & 4: Vientiane
Leave the Mekong behind as you snake through spectacular scenery on Route 13, which passes the backpacker town of **Vang Vieng** (pp174–5). Rejoin the river in **Vientiane** (pp138–49), the nation's capital and home to ancient wats, shopping malls and a good local market (p148).

Day 5 & 6: Savannakhet
Cycle among the sun-scorched Colonial buildings of **Savannakhet** (pp194–5), the Mekong town best known as the birthplace of Revolutionary Party leader Kaysone Phomvihane. Make time for a visit to the city's dinosaur museum (p195) and the four-tiered stupa known as **That Ing Hang** (p195).

Day 7 & 8: Champasak
Sleepy, one-street **Champasak** (p196) hugs a spectacular stretch of the Mekong. Relax in Colonial shophouses converted into guesthouses and cafés, or make the short tuk-tuk or motorbike journey to **Wat Phu Champasak** (pp198–9), a Khmer ruin that is untroubled by Siem Reap's large crowds.

Day 9 & 10: Si Phan Don
Choose a bungalow near the water for a back-to-basics experience among the riverine islands of **Si Phan Don** (pp202–3). Don Det attracts a young crowd while Don Khon, the launching point for dolphin-spotting trips, is sleepier.

Day 11 & 12: Stung Treng
Cross into Cambodia by bus (the river route is now closed), and make a stop in little-visited **Stung Treng** (p102), a former French-Lao outpost that makes a good base for trips into the surrounding countryside. Boat rides and kayaking excursions can be organised here.

Day 13 & 14: Phnom Penh
The Mekong meets the Bassac and Tonlé Sap in Phnom Penh, Cambodia's capital city. A pulsing metropolis compared with other cities on this route, it is the perfect place to finish your trip – shopping, eating, and sightseeing.

> **To extend your trip...**
> Head east from Savannakhet for guided treks into the dense Lao jungle, where there is a good chance of seeing monkeys and hornbills. As an alternative, head to the island of Don Khong in Si Phan Don, which is larger than its neighbors, but easy to explore by motorbike or bicycle.

The beautifully carved That Ing Hang Stupa, Suvannakhet

Putting Cambodia and Laos on the Map

Cambodia and Laos stretch through the center of the Indochinese peninsula, with Laos lying to the north of Cambodia. Both countries share borders with Thailand to the west and Vietnam to the east, while Laos also borders China and Myanmar. Cambodia covers an area of 69,900 sq miles (181,035 sq km), and has a population of about 15 million. Laos, although larger, with an area of about 90,700 sq miles (235,000 sq km), supports a smaller population of just under six million. The only maritime access is through Cambodia's 277-mile (443-km) coastline along the Gulf of Thailand. Historically this made both countries dependent for transport, irrigation, and food on a network of rivers, notably the Mekong. It enters Laos at its northwestern corner and exits Cambodia in the south, en route to the South China Sea.

CHINA

U Thai

Boun Neua

Phongsali

Muang Khua

Muang Sing

Luang Nam Tha

2E

Muang Ngoi

Vieng Phukha

13

3

Nong Khiaw

1C

Huay Xai

2W

Luang Prabang

Vieng Thong

Pak Beng

Luang Prabang

Phonsav

4

7

Muan Khu

Sainyabuli

13

Vang Vieng

5

4

Phong Hong

Pak Lai

13

Vientiane

Wattay

Kaen Thao

Udon Thani

210

MYANMAR

Thaton

11

12

Yangon

105

Phitsanulok

12

Khon Kaen

209

Mawlamyine

1

THAILAND

2

Nakhon Sawan

Chai Nat

219

1

32

Nakhon Ratchasima

2

Dawei

323

24

304

Thm Pok

Bangkok

35

33

Sisophon

69

Ratchaburi

Battambang

Phetchaburi

Chanthaburi

10

Pailin

Hua Hin

3

Myeik

4

Koh Kong

Prachuap Khiri Khan

Gulf of Thailand

Koh Kong Island

Chumphon

Sihanoukvil

Southeast Asia

CHINA

NEPAL
BHUTAN
TAIWAN
BANGLADESH
INDIA
MYANMAR
LAOS
Vientiane
PHILIPPINES
THAILAND
VIETNAM
CAMBODIA
Phnom Penh
SRI
LANKA
BRUNEI
MALAYSIA
SINGAPORE
INDONESIA

VIETNAM

Hanoi

Sam
Neua
Vieng Xai

Muang Kham

Thanh
Hoa

LAOS
Vinh

Paksan
Vieng Thong

Pak
Kading
Lak
Sao

Hin
Bun
Nyommalat

Thakhek
Mahaxai

Xai Bua
Thong
Dong Hoi

Xaibuli
Savannakhet
Sepon
Dong Ha

Muang
Phin
Hué

Danang
Hoi An

Salavan
Lao
Ngam
Muang Tha Teng
Quang Ngai

Ubon
Ratchathani
Muang Lumam

Pakse
Paksong
Attapeu

Champasak
Sanamxai
Kontum

Muang
Khong
Voen
Sai
Quy Nhon

Choam
Khsant
Pleiku

Siem Reap
Melu Prey
Ban Lung
Tuy Hoa

Siem Reap
Stung Treng
Lumphat

Tonle
Sap
CAMBODIA
VIETNAM

Pursat
Kompong
Thom
Kratie
Sen
Monorom
Buon Ma
Thuot
Nha Trang

Kompong
Chhnang

Udong
Kompong
Cham
Dalat

Phnom
Penh
Prey Veng
Phan Rang-
Thap Cham

Takeo
Neak
Luong
Svay Rieng

Chhuk
Angkor Borei
Phan
Thiet

Kampot
Kep
Ho Chi
Minh City

*Gulf of
Tonkin*

*South
China Sea*

Key

— Motorway
— Major road
— Minor road
— Railroad
— International border

0 kilometers   100
0 miles   100

Landscape and Wildlife

With some of the best-preserved rainforests in Asia, Cambodia and Laos are home to rich biological diversity. Laos's mountainous and rugged landscape is typified by soaring outcrops of karst limestone, lush river valleys, and emerald-green paddy fields. Much of central Cambodia is flat, with the terrain defined by the fertile influence of the Tonlé Sap and Mekong rivers. The abundant wildlife in the region includes a number of endangered animals such as the Asian elephant and the tiger. Rare species such as the antelope-like saola and the kha nyou are also found here. The region's rainforests, however, are being steadily depleted by illegal and state-sanctioned logging.

Majestic karst limestone mountains in Vang Vieng, Laos

Rainforest Preserves

Covering thousands of square miles, the rainforests of the two countries include outstanding national parks such as Nam Ha in Laos and Botum Sakor in Cambodia. These largely inaccessible forests harbor a stunning array of wildlife, including various species of birds, mammals, and reptiles.

Mekong River

Forming an entire border between Laos and Cambodia, the 2,710-mile (4,361-km) long Mekong is the world's 12th longest river. It is home to a variety of big fish, including the giant Mekong stingray, measuring up to 14 ft (4 m) across, and the world's largest catfish.

The clouded leopard is known to inhabit the rainforests of Asia. One of the most agile cats, it is a superb tree climber.

Irrawaddy dolphins number fewer than 100 in the Mekong. They live in brackish waters near coasts, river mouths, and estuaries.

The Siamese crocodile is a freshwater reptile typically found around rivers in rainforests. It is critically endangered in the wild.

Frangipani trees, cultivated in tropical and subtropical countries, have evergreen leaves and a strong perfume.

The Malayan porcupine is a common resident of Asian rainforests. A nocturnal species, it is one of the largest rodents in the region.

The dugong, also known as the sea cow, is a marine mammal that is found off the coast of Cambodia.

Tonlé Sap

A combined lake and river system, the Tonlé Sap is not only Cambodia's most intriguing natural feature and its greatest natural resource, it is also the largest lake in Southeast Asia. This floodplain, with its rich biodiversity, is a perfect habitat for waterbirds, aquatic animals, and fish.

Gray-headed fish eagles are mostly found in the north-western part of the lake – the largest gathering of this bird in Asia. Despite its name, the fish eagle mainly feeds on water snakes.

The black-headed ibis often feeds on the banks of the Tonlé Sap. This exotic wader's existence is now under threat due to drainage and loss of habitat.

Fishing cats are common in the lake and depend on its wetlands for prey. They mainly eat freshwater fish, but also catch rats and birds.

Mangrove Forest

The region's mangrove wetlands are vital in protecting its coastline. A nursery for juvenile fish, the mangroves are home to marine organisms, as well as birds. The Peam Krasaop Nature Reserve in Southern Cambodia has some of the best mangroves in the country.

Coastal Forest

Many of Cambodia's most important forest preserves lie along its coastline. These preserves, which include the Botum Sakor and Ream National Park, are home to a wide variety of animals, reptiles, and marine organisms, including pileated gibbons, pythons, king cobras, and dugongs.

Crab-eating macaques are wide-spread in the region. Known at times as the "crop raider," their main diet consists of fruit and seeds.

The loris is found in tropical habitats in Southeast Asia. It is poached for Chinese traditional medicine and the pet trade.

Storks, especially the milky stork and lesser adjutant, are quite rare, but still found in Cambodia's mangrove forests.

The blue-eared kingfisher, one of the ten different species of kingfishers found in Cambodia, lives in coastal forests and hunts for small fish and insects.

The hawksbill turtle is common around the coast of Cambodia. It has a distinctive beaked mouth and a beautifully patterned shell.

Bantengs were probably the ancestors of domestic cattle. Large and graceful, they live in herds and prefer open, dry, deciduous forests.

Peoples of Cambodia

Ethnic Khmers constitute more than 90 percent of Cambodia's population, making it one of the most homogenous countries in the world. At the same time, the country is also home to a number of ethnic minorities, principal among them the Cham, the Chinese, and the Vietnamese. There are at least 20 distinct hill tribes, such as the Kavet, the Tompuon, and the Phnong, who inhabit the mountainous northeast provinces. The majority of the country's population lives in rural areas.

A Phnong woman with her baby, Mondulkiri province

Ethnic Khmers

Traditional Khmer *apsara* dance performers

The Khmers are the dominant ethnic group in Cambodia and are proud to proclaim themselves the descendants of the great civilization of Angkor, the symbol of the nation. They once controlled a large chunk of Southeast Asia that extended into modern-day Thailand and Vietnam. The impact of classic Khmer culture in Cambodia is evident in the revival of several ancient arts such as the *apsara* (celestial dancing girl) dance and the music that accompanies these dances, both of which go back to the glorious traditions of Angkor.

Ethnic Vietnamese

Although official records state that there are only about 100,000 Vietnamese in Cambodia, the actual number may be much higher, making them the largest non-Khmer group in the country. Settled in southeast and central Cambodia, they form the numerous fishing communities around Takeo and the Tonlé Sap Lake. Many Vietnamese are also rice farmers. Phnom Penh has a large population of Vietnamese, many of whose ancestors had been brought over from Vietnam by the French as civil servants.

A Vietnamese man selling vegetables from his boat

Ethnic Chinese

Chinese shopkeepers in Phnom Penh

Cambodians of Chinese or mixed Chinese and Cambodian descent are known as the Khmer Chen. The Chinese controlled businesses and economic interests in Cambodia before the 1975 revolution, but the community was brutally persecuted by the Khmer Rouge, and thousands emigrated. Today, half a million Khmer Chen live in Cambodia and they continue to dominate commerce in the urban centers, particularly banking, moneylending, and the import and export of food products.

Ethnic Cham

Originally from the Champa Kingdom of Central Vietnam, the Cham people, who number at least 250,000, have lived in Cambodia for over 500 years. More than 90 percent of the Cham are Muslims, and are referred to as the Khmer Islam *(see p23)*. Most live in Cham-only villages along the banks of the Mekong River and the Tonlé Sap Lake. Apart from fishing, they are also involved in farming, raising cattle, and growing rice. Cham men wear a sarong called a *batik*, and the women usually cover their heads with a scarf or turban.

Cham men socializing after prayers

Peoples of Laos

Laos is one of the most sparsely populated
countries in Asia, with only six million inhabitants
in a landmass larger than the United Kingdom.
The population is broadly divided into two groups –
the Lowland Lao and the Highland Lao – although
there are as many as 160 recognized ethnic
minorities. There are also small communities of
ethnic Vietnamese, numbering around 140,000,
and Chinese, constituting between 2 and 5 percent
of the population, including rapidly expanding
numbers of migrant workers.

Devout Chinese offering prayers at a temple

Lowland Lao

Forming an estimated 68 percent of the population, most
Lao Loum, or Lowland Lao, can trace their ancestry back to
the Thai tribe that originated in southern China. They live
along the Mekong River and in river valleys across the nation.
Their language comprises five major dialects, all mutually
intelligible. Although nearly all Lowland Lao practice
Theravada Buddhism, they still retain a few rituals related to
animism. They are the most affluent group in the nation,
dominating both government and commerce.

The Lao Loum are known to
be expert silversmiths, creating
intricate pieces of jewelry that
are in great demand.

Skilled wet-rice farmers, the Lao Loum build
houses raised on wooden stilts in order to
protect them from flooded rice paddies. Rice
granaries are often built next to the houses.

Highland Lao

Ethnic minorities in Laos can be categorized into two groups:
the Lao Theung, or Upland Lao, who account for around
23 percent of the population, and the Lao Sung, or Highland
Lao, who comprise 9 percent of the population. These groups
tend to have lower living standards compared with the Lao
Loum, and suffer from discrimination. While the Upland Lao,
such as the Katu, are primarily of Mon-Khmer ancestry, the
term Highland Lao
loosely describes ethnic
groups such as the Yao
and the Hmong who live
at high altitudes.

The Hmong, who number
around 475,000, is the
biggest minority group
in Laos. Hmong men
traditionally wear a black
tunic and black wide-
legged pants, while the
women's clothing differs
with each subgroup.

The Katu live in heavily forested
mountains near the Vietnamese
border and depend on the forests
for their food and livelihood. Katu
women often have facial tattoos.
However, this is a dying tradition.

Religions of Cambodia and Laos

Buddhism is by far the most widespread religion in both Cambodia and Laos, with a majority of the people practicing this faith. Virtually every village has a *wat* (temple), the spiritual heart of the community, where the monks reside. Animist beliefs also remain very strong and most followers believe that the world is influenced by an array of spirits, guardians, and ghosts. Although these traditions are strongest in rural areas, many city dwellers also consult a shaman. There are some followers of Islam in Cambodia, and both countries also have a considerable Christian population.

A young monk reading scriptures at a *wat* in Laos

Buddhism

Theravada Buddhism defines most cultural practices in Cambodia and Laos, and entering monkhood is thought to accrue many benefits. Most men become monks for a short period in their lives, typically between three months and three years, living under a set of strict monastic rules. Women are also allowed to become monks, although it is usually later in life, often after the death of their husbands.

Pha That Luang is one of the most revered Buddhist sites in Laos. The original temple is said to have been built by missionaries sent by King Ashoka in the 3rd century BC, and was rumored to contain a piece of the Buddha's breastbone. The Boun That Luang festival is held here each year.

Buddhism in Cambodia is influenced by Hinduism and animism. These influences are visible not just in rituals and ceremonies, but also in temples such as the Bayon in Angkor Thom *(see pp74–7)*, where statues of the Buddha coexist with those of Hindu gods.

Animist Beliefs

Animism is practiced by the 50 or so ethnic minorities in Laos, who follow varied forms of its rituals and customs. Several Lowland Lao also retain a belief in phi *(spirits), which are associated with numerous aspects of day-to-day life, including health, the house, and nature. Believers show respect to all spirits, except the* mneang phteah *and* mrenh kongveal, *who are considered troublemakers and also capable of causing serious illness.*

Animist customs among ethnic minorities include leaving offerings of food and burning incense sticks to placate spirits. Ancestor worship is important for a number of groups such as the Lao Theung, the Lao Sung, and the hill tribes of Cambodia, including the Khmer Lue.

Spirit houses are shrines to animist spirits. Virtually every household, office, and shop has one since they are believed to act as a safeguard against malevolent forces.

Islam

A majority of Muslims, numbering about 250,000 in Cambodia, and some 500 in Laos, are of Cham origin, although a few are ethnic Malays. Belonging to the Sunni sect of Islam, the Cambodian Chams, who suffered terribly under the Khmer Rouge, live on the coast of Cambodia in fishing communities. The Cham of Laos live mostly in Vientiane.

Headscarves are worn by most Cham women.

Islamic places of worship were ransacked under the Khmer Rouge and an estimated 132 mosques were destroyed. Today, however, many new mosques are being built along the coast of Cambodia.

Khmer Islam, the name given to the Muslims in Cambodia, traditionally practiced a syncretic form of the religion, incorporating animist beliefs. In recent years, however, they have become more orthodox.

Cham villagers on the coast of Cambodia are experiencing a resurgence in Islamic culture and pride.

Other Religions

Christianity, Confucianism, and the Baha'i faith are among the other religions practiced in Cambodia and Laos. There is a substantial, and expanding, Christian population in both countries, along with small numbers of followers of the Baha'i and Confucian faiths. Evangelical and Mormon churches are active in Cambodia, but proselytizing was officially banned in 2007, after missionary groups were accused of trying to convert people by offering free food and clothing.

Confucianism is practiced by many ethnic Chinese in the region. The religion is based on the teachings of the highly revered Chinese sage and philosopher Confucius (551–479 BC), who outlined a code of moral, social, and political ethics that includes loyalty to the state and to the family.

Abdu'l-Bahá was the eldest son and successor of Bahá'u'lláh, the founder of the Baha'i faith. There are around 8,000 followers of this faith in Laos. Vientiane, the capital, houses a National Spiritual Assembly, or elected council, which leads the faith.

Christianity has had a foothold in the region since 1556. There are around 120,000 Christians in Laos, and around 20,000 in Cambodia. Laos officially recognizes three churches – Roman Catholic, Lao Evangelical, and Seventh-Day Adventist – but there are several other denominations as well.

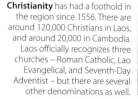

Buddhism in Cambodia and Laos

For many centuries, both Buddhism and Hinduism coexisted in this region. While the early Funan Kingdom was primarily Hindu, it was influenced by Buddhism, which became a secondary religion between the 1st and 6th centuries AD. During the Angkor period in Cambodia, Buddha images flourished alongside representations of Hindu gods such as Shiva and Vishnu. Today, Buddhism is the primary religion in both Laos and Cambodia. A majority of the population follows the Theravada Buddhist sect, which belongs to the Hinayana, or Lesser Wheel School, and is said to closely mirror the original form of the religion. In Laos, the religion continues to be influenced by animist beliefs, and spirit and ancestor worship.

Statue of Seated Buddha at Wat Ong Teu Mahawihan, Laos

Practice of Buddhism

Religious rituals form part of the daily life of most Cambodians and Lao. Visits to wats, the giving of alms, and merit-making – the performance of good deeds as mentioned in the Buddhist doctrine – are performed by all devout Buddhists. Many men also enter monkhood, at least for a brief period.

Traditional saffron robes worn by monks.

Burning incense sticks accompanies virtually all prayer ceremonies. This ritual has been in practice for thousands of years and links prayer with meditation and ritual purification.

Feeding monks forms an important part of the Buddhist New Year celebrations.

Bowing and prostrating before an image of the Buddha, or before a monk, is believed to be an act of humility in Buddhist culture. The act is thought to bring good fortune.

The offering of alms is an ancient Buddhist tradition, born in the early days when monks were wanderers, whose only possessions were a robe and a begging bowl. The tradition continues today and is a meritorious act, thought to bring good *karma* (fate). Solemn almsgiving is conducted at dawn every day when monks leave their monasteries to seek sustenance.

The New Year is a special occasion marked by rituals and *baci sukhuan* ceremonies (see p126). Celebrations last for several days; on the third day, statues of the Buddha, kept in *wats*, are cleansed with perfumed water. This ritual is said to bring happiness and good fortune.

Colorful bunting is used to decorate *wats* during the New Year celebrations.

Banana leaves and flowers, used as offerings in *wats*, are often artistically molded into forms such as that of a stupa.

Prayers being offered

The Phabang is the most sacred image of the Buddha in Laos and is currently housed in the National Musuem Complex in Luang Prabang. On Buddha Day, the image is cleansed with holy water and taken out in a procession to Wat Mai.

Buddhist Symbols

There are several religious symbols in Buddhism, each representing different aspects of the religion. Most of them can be seen in *wats*, stupas, and other religious sites. Symbols such as the Wheel of Law are said to have been used by the Buddha himself.

The Bodhi tree is the tree under which the Buddha achieved enlightenment.

Buddhist Celebrations

Visits to wats, thanksgiving ceremonies, prayers, and other offerings are an essential part of Buddhist celebrations. Most festivals are connected to the Buddhist calendar and may be specific to a particular tradition or ethnic group.

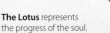

The Wheel of Law, or *Dharmachakra*, is symbolized as an eight-spoked chariot wheel.

The Lotus represents the progress of the soul.

Naga, or serpent, is a dragon-like figure representing wisdom and a protective force for the Buddha.

Visak Bochea, or Buddha Day, is held on a full moon night, usually in May. It is celebrated with traditional processions, among other activities.

Architecture of Cambodia and Laos

Over the centuries, architectural styles in Cambodia and Laos have been shaped by myriad influences, most notably Buddhist and Hindu temple-building traditions and French Colonial construction techniques. In urban areas, a degree of Soviet influence is also evident in the concrete municipal buildings, marketplaces, and apartment blocks. In the countryside, however, tried-and-tested designs have been maintained, and rural buildings continue to use locally sourced materials, such as timber, bamboo, and palm leaves, which are well suited to the tropical monsoon climate.

Floating houses on the Tonlé Sap

Temple Architecture

Up until the 10th century, temples in Cambodia and Laos were made mainly with brick. Khmer ceremonial buildings after this time were constructed using sandstone, usually with a lower section of laterite (moist clay blocks that harden over time). Their elaborate, decorative designs, created by expert stone masons, incorporate religious and spiritual themes, and also reflect historical, military, and dynastical events. Many features of classic Khmer architecture, such as *nagas* (serpents), elaborate pediments, and lintels, were later incorporated into Buddhist buildings in the region. Modern temples in both countries are more similar to contemporary Thai designs, featuring a pointed roof, front veranda, and an elaborate gateway.

A central tower, or a number of towers, crown Khmer temple complexes. The characteristic ogive design is thought to represent a lotus flower bud.

Red sandstone

The lintels are richly carved with religious figures, most often those of the four Hindu gods associated with the cardinal directions.

Banteay Srei *(see p84)* is thought to be the only major Angkor temple not built by a king. Believed to have been dedicated to Shiva, the God of Destruction, the temple is known for the intricacy of its carvings.

Bas-relief on a brick wall, Prasat Kravan

A Buddha figure adorns the center of the richly decorated pediment.

The gilded door depicts scenes from the Buddha's life.

Elaborate arches above the gateway

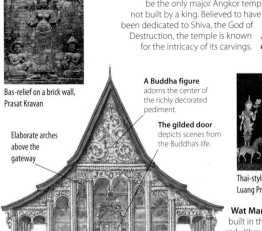

Thai-style stenciling on the facade of Wat Sene, Luang Prabang

Wat Manolom *(see pp166–7)* was originally built in the 14th century on the site of an early Khmer Buddhist mission. The main ordinance hall was reconstructed in 1972 and is a good example of modern Lao temple architecture. Inside the *wat* is a huge bronze Buddha that dates from the 1370s.

Rural Architecture

Houses in rural areas are traditionally wood and bamboo structures, built on stilts to raise the home above seasonal flood waters. The main living quarters of each rectangular two-story building is divided into sections for sleeping and cooking, with a storage area above.

House on stilts near the Mekong River

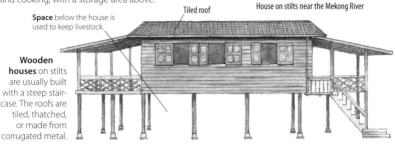

Space below the house is used to keep livestock.

Tiled roof

Wooden houses on stilts are usually built with a steep staircase. The roofs are tiled, thatched, or made from corrugated metal.

Colonial Architecture

The most important architectural reminders of French rule are found in 19th- and 20th-century buildings in Phnom Penh, Vientiane, Battambang, Siem Reap, Luang Prabang, and Kampot. Kep has a fascinating number of Modernist seaside villas – some restored, but most in ruins.

Two-story brick and stucco villas are one of the enduring legacies of Colonial rule, although many have been poorly maintained since independence. Phnom Penh boasts a particularly fine collection of French villas.

Shuttered windows shade the interior from direct sunlight, while the slats allow a breeze to circulate and cool the house.

The Presidential Palace in Vientiane showcases a grand Neo-Classical façade and elegant colonnaded balconies. It was once the home of the French governor of Laos, but is now used for official ceremonies.

Modern Khmer Architecture

Influenced by the clean lines and simplicity of the Modernist movement, New Khmer Architecture, at its height from 1955 to 1972, draws heavily on ancient Khmer temple designs. The National Sports Complex in Phnom Penh, for example, was laid out on an east-west axis, mirroring classic Khmer buildings with *barays* (reservoirs). The most influential architect of this period, Vann Molyvann, created structures such as the startling library at Phnom Penh's Teacher Training College, with its radial roof resembling a farmer's hat. The sharply geometrical building of the National Bank of Cambodia and St Michael's Church in Sihanoukville are also striking examples.

Fan-shaped roof

A stupa-like spire emerges from the roofline.

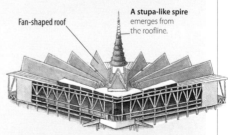

Chaktomuk Conference Hall, designed by Vann Molyvann and completed in 1961, has a stunning facade that is supported by concrete stilts. Renovated in 2000, the Chaktomuk Conference Hall now hosts conferences and performances of traditional music and dance.

The French Legacy

Until the mid-19th century, Colonial interest in Cambodia and Laos was minimal, mainly consisting of sporadic forays by Catholic missionaries in search of conversions. However, continued aggression by Thailand and Vietnam caused King Norodom of Cambodia to invite the French to establish a protectorate in 1863, who eventually made it into a French colony. Laos, too, was steadily absorbed into Indochina. Although the French withdrew from the region in 1954, their legacy remains in the boulevards and Neo-Classical buildings of Phnom Penh, and in the streets of Laos, where coffee is served as *café au lait*.

Pastry shops selling French delights, such as éclairs and profiteroles, were common in the main towns, and some survive even today. In Colonial times they were owned mainly by ethnic Vietnamese.

French Cuisine

The French culinary influence is most evident in popular snacks such as baguettes and croissants. Locals usually eat them for breakfast or as a quick bite, often with a thick layer of pâté, or luncheon meat, and some sliced salad, vegetables, or pickles. Phnom Penh, Vientiane, and other tourist centers have trendy French restaurants, bistros, and brasseries where the partaking of aperitifs, digestifs, and classic French wine continues to thrive.

Baguettes are the most visible reminders of French cuisine. Every town still has a bakery producing these quintessentially French loaves. Vientiane baguettes, made in traditional French style, are particularly good.

The first railroad in Cambodia was laid by the French between 1930 and 1940. It extended from Phnom Penh right up to Poipet on the Thai border.

Economy

French Colonialists concentrated on exploiting the rich natural resources of the region with timber, rubber, corn, and rice being the main items of export. They were also responsible for installing the first roads, railroads, and rubber plantations. Apart from imposing a more efficient taxation system, the French did little to transform the village-based economies of these countries.

Rubber plantations, first established by the French, remain a significant industry in Cambodia even today.

Language and Culture

French heritage also lingers in the language and culture of these countries. There are French-language schools in all major cities, and private institutions offer classes in French. French-language newspapers such as *Le Rénovateur* and *Cambodge Nouveau* are still popular, and establishments such as the Centre Culturel Français (CCF) continue to flourish. In the field of sports, soccer (which was first introduced by the Colonialists) continues to be the most popular game.

A French theater artiste

The Centre Culturel Français in Phnom Penh, Vientiane, and Luang Prabang attempts to revive interest in French culture. It organizes movie screenings, exhibitions, and other cultural events.

French Architecture

Perhaps the most prominent feature of the French legacy is seen in the Neo-Classical architecture of major towns. Although many of the once-grand buildings are now crumbling due to neglect, fiscal constraints, or local distaste for what they once represented, cities such as Phnom Penh, Siem Reap, Battambang, and Kampot have an impressive array of chic Modernist villas, lovely old French quarters, and Colonial facades. The National Museum Complex and the Centre Culturel Français in Luang Prabang represent French-Lao-style architecture.

Serene riverside boulevards, such as Sisowath Quay in Phnom Penh, lined with tall, swaying palms and other foliage, are typically Parisian. They add to the Colonial charm of cities such as Vientiane, Battambang, and Kampot.

Louvered windows not only allow ventilation, but also provide shade from the tropical sun.

Roofs usually boast European-style terra-cotta tiles.

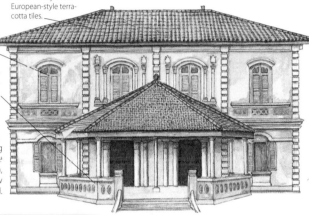

Verandas lined with double doors extend from the front of the house.

Colonial villas, some of the best examples of which are in Phnom Penh, provided cooling tropical retreats for the French. Most of them, however, have now been abandoned.

The interior of the Foreign Correspondents' Club in Phnom Penh is classically French Colonial in design, with a mahogany bar, slim columns, and elegant seating overlooking the Mekong River.

Elaborate stucco detailing adorns many French Colonial buildings.

Official buildings of the Colonial era are recognized by their imposing Neo-Classical facades, which embody the authority of the bygone administration.

Multiple-arch design

Shophouses in Kampot's French quarter, in Cambodia, are typically Colonial. They have shuttered windows with rectangular transoms over the opening, and multiple arches. Most of them, however, are now quite dilapidated and in desperate need of repair.

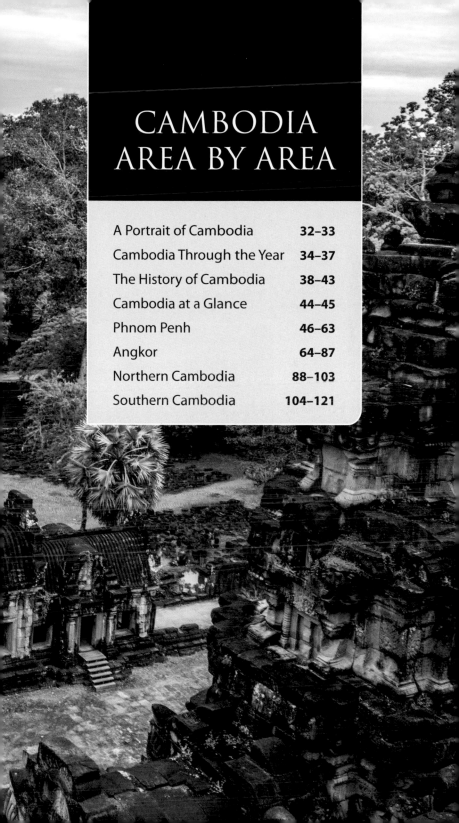

CAMBODIA
AREA BY AREA

A PORTRAIT OF CAMBODIA

Emerald paddy fields, a rich diversity of wildlife, powder-fine beaches, and the magnificence of the temples of Angkor – Cambodia has an alluring mix of romantic escapes and exhilarating outdoor pursuits, as well as world-renowned archaeological wonders. All this, combined with the warmth of its people, has helped to put the country firmly on the tourist map.

Land and Ecology

Covering an area of 69,900 sq miles (181,035 sq km), Cambodia is bordered by Laos to the north, Thailand to the north and west, and Vietnam to the east. To the southwest lie the Cardamom Mountains, rising to almost 5,787 ft (1,764 m), while in the north are the dramatic 1,804-ft (550-m) high Dangkrek Mountains. The most dominant feature of the country, however, is the mighty Mekong River, which runs its course from Tibet and floods the Tonlé Sap during the monsoon, swelling its waters to make it the largest freshwater lake in Southeast Asia. The northeast lays claim to being the wildest and most remote region, with forests and mountains inhabited by tigers and wild elephants. In the northwest, fertile Battambang is nicknamed "the rice bowl of Cambodia." The south, with its archipelago of deserted islands and perfect beaches, is a pleasant tropical retreat and is well worth visiting.

The endangered wild Asian elephant

Cambodia's pristine landscape, forests, and wildlife, however, are under threat from oil-drilling companies and logging. The habitats of the Asian tiger and other endangered species such as the banteng, wild Asian elephant, and Asian golden cat are visibly shrinking. Deforestation is also contributing to the flooding of the Mekong, while gradual siltation threatens the existence of the Tonlé Sap Lake. Fortunately, the government has adopted a number of conservation proposals, and has set up several national parks and other areas to protect wildlife and forest cover.

Politics and the Economy

Cambodia was ranked 156 (out of 174) in the 2014 Corruption Perceptions Index, providing evidence of the limited transparency of its government and the execution of democracy. Official positions are usually achieved not on merit, but on the power of wealth and nepotism. This is also reflected in the fact that Hun Sen,

Visitors relaxing on the beautiful beach at Koh Russie, Sihanoukville

◀ Ruins of Angkor, the ancient capital of Cambodia

leader of the Cambodian People's Party (CPP), has been at the helm of political affairs since 1993, making him the longest-serving prime minister in Southeast Asia. Although a multiparty democracy on paper, there was very little opposition in the way the CPP won 72 percent of the seats in parliament in the June 2012 elections. Criticism of Hun Sen is seldom heard, especially since dissident media has been completely silenced.

Despite such pitfalls, the country is making steady headway, with economic growth at around 5 percent. While oil, rubber, and the availability of cheap labor are fueling this growth, Cambodia has also found a niche as an international garment producer, and tourism remains one of its highest foreign exchange earners.

Angkor Wat, Cambodia's most popular attraction

Society and Religion

According to official records, Cambodia is the most homogenous country in Southeast Asia, with more than 90 percent of its 15 million people ethnic Khmer. The population also includes 100,000 Vietnamese, about half a million Chinese and around 250,000 Cham Muslims, as well as the Khmer Lue – the ethnic minorities that live in the northeast of the country.

Khmer society lays stress on the importance of the family. While elders are respected and obeyed, women are expected to be models of restraint and to treat their husbands with deference. Nevertheless, women are dominant figures in society, providing moral and financial support to the family. Although fidelity is a given for them, it is normal for husbands to have extramarital affairs – a problem that led to the country having the one of the highest incidences of HIV infection in Southeast Asia.

A traditional Khmer *apsara* dancer

While a majority of Khmers today are Buddhists – the religion came from India during the 13th and 14th centuries – Hinduism was the dominant state religion during the Angkor period. Most men spend at least a few weeks in a *wat* (temple) as a monk, learning the teachings of Theravada Buddhism. Most ethnic minorities, however, practice animism, while the Chams are followers of Islam.

Culture and the Arts

Although all traces of Cambodia's culture were erased during the years of the Khmer Rouge, the country now seems to have rediscovered its artistic edge, with exiled artists returning to their roots. Traditional dance, particularly ballet, is also making a glorious return through the University of Fine Arts. Musical instruments such as *khsae muoy* (single-stringed bowed instrument), and *tro khmae* (three-stringed fiddle), used by *apsara* dancers in Angkor, are popular. Cambodia is also renowned for its fine silk weaving, silver-smithing, sculpting, wood-carving, and ceramics made in traditional kilns in Siem Reap.

CAMBODIA THROUGH THE YEAR

Cambodians love a good celebration, and festivals provide the opportunity for family members scattered across the country to reconnect and reassert their sense of togetherness. Many of Cambodia's festivals, such as Bon Chol Vassa and Meak Bochea, are based on lunar cycles. Thus, dates for these festivals change from year to year. While most secular holidays follow the Gregorian calendar, a few, such as Bon Om Tuk, or the Water Festival, date back to the days of Angkor. Apart from being solemn religious occasions, these festivals present rural Khmers with an excuse to return home to visit family. Celebrations are often followed by partying, shows, and fireworks. Cambodia has three seasons – hot, rainy, and cool – which influence several festivals, especially in rural areas, since agriculture is the main livelihood for a majority of the population.

Dramatic dragon dancers entertain revelers during Chinese New Year celebrations

Hot Season (Jan–Apr)

Temperatures increase in February, which is the start of the hot season, and keep rising until April, which is the hottest month. April also marks the end of the harvest. The sweltering heat and high humidity can test visitors' endurance. However, areas such as Ratanakiri and Mondulkiri provinces in the northeast, which have the advantage of higher elevations, enjoy cooler weather.

January–February

Victory Day (Jan 7), nationwide. This holiday commemorates the victory of the Vietnamese over the Khmer Rouge's bloody regime. Celebrations are marked by exhibitions and remembrance services.

Chinese New Year (end Jan/early Feb), all major cities. This exciting, vibrant festival sees the streets thronging with colorful dragon dancers and processions, along with firework displays at every corner. Although this is not a national holiday, it is a widely celebrated festival, and many Chinese commercial businesses shut down for its duration. There is a large population of Chinese in Phnom Penh, along with a significant number of Vietnamese who also celebrate Tet (New Year) at the same time. Wealthy families eager to flaunt their fortunes organize elaborate private firework displays.

Meak Bochea (end Jan/early Feb full moon), nationwide. The name of this festival means Big Prayer and it is one of the holiest and most important ceremonies in the Buddhist religion. Candlelit processions commemorate the 1,250 disciples who gathered to witness the last sermon delivered by the Buddha before his death in northern India 2,500 years ago. Families visit their local wat (temple) during the full moon to venerate the five precepts of Buddhism and the great teacher himself. They light candles and make offerings of food and money in order to gain merit.

March–April

Women's Day (Mar 8), nationwide. This day celebrates the role of women in modern society and highlights issues such as rape, domestic violence, and inequality. This is a vital festival in a country where women are often abused and subjugated. The UNESCO office in Phnom Penh has supported this important day over the past few years by sponsoring the Ministry of Women's Affairs of Cambodia. Parades are held in various parts of the country, and T-shirts highlighting women's rights and displaying messages against domestic violence are distributed. Drama shows and workshops are organized, which are often attended by the prime minister.

Cambodian New Year (Apr 14–16), nationwide. This festival is better known as Chaul Chnam Thmey and lasts for a period of three days. Khmers see it as a time to go wild in a nationwide water fight, as well as applying talcum powder to each other's faces. The festival has its roots in Hinduism, the country's primary religion before the arrival of Buddhism. The best place to be is Wat Phnom (see pp50–51), where free concerts are held

Dancer, Cambodian New Year

Average Daily Hours of Sunshine

Hours

(bar chart showing average daily hours of sunshine by month, with y-axis from 0 to 10 and x-axis labeled Jan Feb Mar Apr May Jun Jul Aug Sep Oct Nov Dec)

Sunshine Chart
Even during the rainy season the sun is hot, particularly in the middle of the day. It is wise to carry bottled water and to eat plenty of fruit to keep energy levels high. The heat and humidity can be debilitating, especially for those not used to tropical weather. A hat and sunscreen are strongly recommended.

at night. The last day of the festival involves worshipers bathing Buddha statues with water and apologizing to monks, elders, and grandparents whom they may have offended during the year. This ritual is known as *pithi srang*. It is also celebrated in a similar fashion in Laos. Visitors are likely to have water thrown at them during this period.

Rainy Season (May–Aug)

This season is characterized by short, intense bursts of rain, which leave the land glistening, and remote roads impassable. This is a good time to explore temples since there are relatively fewer people around.

May–June

Visak Bochea *(May full moon)*, nationwide. The Buddha's birthday, his enlightenment, and admission to Nirvana are celebrated with candlelit processions to the local *wat*, most notably at Angkor Wat *(see pp70–71)*.

International Labor Day *(May 1)*, nationwide. Traditionally a day when workers march for their rights, such as the improvement of minimum wages. Their achievements are also celebrated.

Genocide Day *(May 9)*, nationwide. This day commemorates the many lives lost to the Maoist driven Khmer Rouge. It is a pensive occasion for every Khmer. Without exception, every family was torn asunder by the bloody regime of the Khmer Rouge.

King Sihamoni's Birthday *(May 13)*, nationwide. Although there are no mass celebrations or processions on this day, firework displays take place at the Tonlé Sap lakefront late at night.

Monks walking with lit candles at the Bayon during Visak Bochea

Royal Ploughing Ceremony *(late May)*, Phnom Penh. Also known as Bon Chrat Preah Nongkol, this festival celebrates the first planting of rice for the coming harvest. Locals dress up in colorful traditional attire, and participate in a lively procession. The procession is led by the king and other royals outside the National Museum *(see p52)*, where a sacred ox is fed with a selection of food and drink. A Brahmin priest then predicts the kind of harvest that can be expected, according to what the ox has eaten. This is a significant festival for many Cambodians because their fortunes are linked to the land that they farm. The presence of the king also reaffirms the importance of this ceremony.

Oxen heading the procession during the Royal Ploughing Ceremony

Average Monthly Rainfall (Phnom Penh)

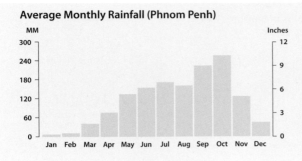

Rainfall Chart
During the monsoon, rains may last for a few hours per day followed by bright sunshine. The heaviest rainfall occurs in the mountains along the coast, and in the southwest where precipitation varies from between 2,500 mm (98 inches) to more than 5,000 mm (197 inches).

July–August

Bon Chol Vassa (*Jul full moon*), nationwide. Held to coincide with the eighth full moon of the lunar calendar, this festival marks the beginning of the three-month Buddhist Lent, a time of fasting and strict meditation. This is also the time for young men to be ordained as monks. Traditionally, the newly ordained monks would spend the entire rainy season within the temple, but nowadays this period can be as little as three weeks.

Cool Season (Sep–Dec)

As the rains retreat toward the end of October and early November, a cool breeze sweeps over the land. The Tonlé Sap, having been rejuvenated, abounds with fish. The best time to visit the country is between November and January, when humidity levels are lower than usual.

September–October

Bon Dak Ben (*Sep–Oct full moon*), nationwide. Dedicated to the spirits of the dead, this is one of the most traditional of Khmer festivals. Influenced by elements of animism, the festival is celebrated over a period of 15 days, beginning on the full moon. Food and drink are offered to monks so that they may assist people in blessing the souls of their ancestors. People throng to temples to listen to sermons and to make offerings of respect to their ancestors. They believe it is vital to keep the spirits of the dead appeased; these spirits are believed to protect the living.
Bon Pchum Ben (*Sep/Oct*), nationwide. This festival of the dead is equivalent to All Souls' Day. Khmers make offerings of

boiled eggs, paper money, food, and drink to the dead in order to avoid being haunted.
Bon Kathen (*variable*), nationwide. Starting at the end of the Buddhist Lent and continuing for a month until the next full moon, this festival marks the emergence of monks from their retreat with offertory robes and slow public processions to the local *wat*. Donations are given in order to receive merit, thereby improving *karma* (fate) for the next life.

Monk collecting alms, Bon Dak Ben

King Sihanouk's Birthday (*Oct 31*), nationwide. This day celebrates the country's influential and mercurial leader, the former king, Sihanouk, who managed to endure both Colonialism – eventually achieving Cambodian independence – as well as the Khmer Rouge. It is believed that understanding his psyche is the key to comprehending the complex soul of Cambodia, and the compromises it has had to make in order to survive. Processions take place in front of the Royal Palace (*see pp54–5*), and many loyal followers of the former king return to Phnom Penh to celebrate.

November–December

Independence Day (*Nov 9*), nationwide. Cambodia's independence from France is marked by processions of elaborate floats in front of the Royal Palace. A special day

Colorful float parades in front of the Royal Palace, Independence Day

Average Monthly Temperature (Phnom Penh)

Temperature Chart
The rainy season, which lasts from May to late October, turns the land an emerald green. This is followed by the cool season in November. Coastal and mountainous areas can get very cool at this time. Temperatures start rising in February and peak in April, which is the hottest month of the year.

Dance performance in front of Angkor Wat, Angkor Festival

Phnom Penh, on the Mekong.
Legends of Angkor Wat Festival (variable), Angkor Wat. This festival of performing arts is held at Angkor Wat. Epic stories of Khmer myth are enacted, accompanied by traditional dances, costumes, and musicians, with the temple providing a stunning backdrop. The royal family often attends the event, which makes for a truly memorable evening.

for all Khmers, fireworks and parades are arranged across the country, and bunting is strung across narrow streets. The main festivities, however, take place at the famous Independence Monument at the junction of Norodom and Sihanouk boulevards in Phnom Penh.

Bon Om Tuk (Nov), nationwide. This three-day event, also known as the Water Festival, celebrates the victory of Angkor over the Chams in the 12th century. It also observes the natural phenomenon of the Tonlé Sap reversing its flow and emptying back into the Mekong River, thus marking the end of the rainy season. (It is the only waterway in the world to reverse its flow at different times of the year.) Along with the Cambodian New Year, it is the most important festival in the Cambodian calendar. Boat races and a carnival atmosphere on the Tonlé Sap attract millions from across the country. More than 400 boats take part in the boat race of Bon Om Tuk, with oarsmen and their vessels coming from far and wide, and bringing with them thousands of supporters from their villages. A smaller festival also takes place around Angkor Wat, but the real heart of the celebration lies in

Boat crews getting ready for the race, Bon Om Tuk

Public Holidays

New Year's Day (Jan 1)

Victory Day (Jan 7)

Meak Bochea (Jan/Feb)

Women's Day (Mar 8)

Cambodian New Year (Apr 14–16)

Visak Bochea (May)

International Labor Day (May 1)

Royal Ploughing Ceremony (May)

King Sihamoni's Birthday (May 13)

Queen Mother's Birthday (Jun 18)

Constitution Day (Sep 24)

Bon Pchum Ben (Sep/Oct)

Coronation Day (Oct 29)

King Sihanouk's Birthday (Oct 31)

Independence Day (Nov 9)

Bon Om Tuk (Nov)

Human Rights Day (Dec 10)

THE HISTORY OF CAMBODIA

From the splendor of the Khmer Empire to the chilling brutality of the Khmer Rouge, Cambodia has had a tumultuous past. For nearly six centuries, between the fall of Angkor and the rise of Communism, the kingdom remained in obscurity, forgotten by the rest of the world. Recent years, however, have seen the nation overcome its former misfortunes. Cambodia is now a developing economy boasting World Heritage sites and a thriving tourist industry.

It is likely that the Khmers originated in China and arrived in what is now Cambodia several millennia ago. Archaeologists have discovered evidence of stone-working people in northwestern Cambodia around 4000 BC. They date the first rice cultivation in the region to around 2000 BC, and bronze working to perhaps a millennium later. At that time, many Cambodians lived in fortified, circular villages, eating rice and fish, and raising domestic animals. Bronze artifacts, found in places such as Kg Chhnang in the heart of present-day Cambodia, prove that they possessed advanced metalworking skills.

The first urban civilization in Cambodia, and what is now southern Vietnam, sprang up both inland and along the coast, where excavations of a port-city have been carried out near the Vietnamese town of Oc-Eo. The rulers of this civilization, known to the Chinese as Funan, established their capital at Angkor Borei and built an extensive canal system, probably used for drainage and transportation. They traded with China and India, and coins from the Roman Empire have been found at Oc-Eo. Unfortunately, no reliable written records from this era have survived.

Between 500 BC and AD 500, Cambodia experienced the process referred to as "Indianization." During this time, elements of Indian culture, such as the Hindu pantheon, Buddhism, language (Sanskrit), a writing system, a centralized administration, and the idea of universal kingship, were absorbed by the Khmer and blended with local customs such as ancestor worship.

The earliest inscriptions in the Khmer language date from the 7th century AD. Between the 5th and 8th centuries AD, several small city-states flourished in central Cambodia and northeastern Thailand. These were known collectively as Chenla. Stone inscriptions from this period reveal the slow unification of principalities under a smaller group of rulers. This was to culminate, in the early 9th century, in the consolidation of power near the present-day city of Siem Reap, by the mysterious "universal monarch", known as Jayavarman II, who established the Khmer Empire.

4200 BC–AD 700 Caves in northwestern Cambodia occupied by stone-working people

200 BC Kingdom of Funan established in southern Cambodia

Roman coin used for trading

AD 600–AD 700 The Chenla period

| 4000 BC | 2000 BC | AD 1 | AD 200 | AD 400 | AD 600 | AD 800 |

2000 BC Cultivation of rice begins in the region

500 BC–AD 500 "Indianization" of Cambodia

1000 BC Bronze casting begins

Jayavarman II

802 Jayavarman II establishes the Khmer Empire

◀ A lithograph by Louis Delaporte, dated 1873, depicting a French expedition into Angkor

Rise of Angkor

Angkor, derived from the Khmer word for city, dominated much of mainland Southeast Asia between 802 and 1431. At the end of the 9th century, King Yasovarman I moved the capital closer to Siem Reap, where it remained for the next 500 years. He named the new city Yasodharapura after himself. Successive kings expanded the empire, building more temples honoring themselves, their forebears, and Hindu deities such as Shiva, the God of Destruction.

Bayon-style statue of Jayavarman VII

Between 1130 and 1150, King Suryavarman II built the spectacular Angkor Wat, which served as an astronomical observatory, his tomb, and a monument to Vishnu, the Hindu Protector of Creation. The might of the Khmer Empire steadily increased, and by the mid-12th century, its rule stretched beyond present-day Cambodia to what is now northeastern Thailand, southern Laos, and southern Vietnam. The powerful empire had trade links with China, but trade was conducted on a barter basis, simply because Angkor never used currency of any kind.

Successive kings, such as Jayavarman VII (r.1181–1218), a Mahayana Buddhist, added to the architectural magnificence of Angkor. He built the walled city of Angkor Thom inside Yasodharapura, and several impressive temples, including the Bayon. But the days of Hindu influence were numbered and in the 13th century most Cambodians converted to Theravada Buddhism (the relatively ascetic religion of the country today), and the construction of stone temples ended.

Decline and Fall of Angkor

In the 14th century, several Theravada kingdoms broke away from the empire and in 1431, Thai armies attacked Yasodharapura. As a result, the city was partially abandoned and the royal capital was moved south, close to Phnom Penh.

The next five centuries, often referred to as the Middle Period, were marked by frequent wars with Thailand, and by the slow, informal expropriation of Cambodian territory in the Mekong Delta by the Vietnamese. Vietnam established a protectorate in Phnom Penh in the 1830s and fought Thai forces sent from Bangkok to dislodge them. In 1849, however, a fragile peace was established between the two warring states.

The Colonial Era

In 1863, France, which had colonized southern Vietnam, offered its protection to Cambodia in exchange for certain economic

A 19th-century lithograph depicting French scholars removing precious artifacts from Angkor

1130–50 Angkor Wat built

1200–50 Conversion of Khmer people to Theravada Buddhism

Angkor Wat

1431 Thais attack; Angkor partially abandoned

| 1010 | 1130 | 1250 | 1370 | 1490 |

Bas-relief, the Bayon

1178–1220 Jayavarman VII builds the Bayon and the walled city of Angkor Thom

Bas-relief depicting Thai mercenaries, Angkor Wat

Prince Norodom Sihanouk at a ceremony celebrating the victory of his political party

privileges. The French protectorate evolved, resulting in its complete control after an anti-French rebellion was suppressed in the 1880s.

The French record in Cambodia, however, was mixed. On the one hand, they established towns, roads, and institutions; the economy flourished, the population doubled, and Cambodia was at peace for the first time in centuries. France also forced Thailand to return the annexed territory, and French scholars restored the Angkorian temples, reconstructing the history of Angkor. On the other hand, France did little to improve education or health, and also imposed high taxes on the locals.

Independence and Revolt

In 1941, the French crowned 19-year-old Prince Norodom Sihanouk the king of Cambodia. France also allowed Japanese troops to be stationed in Cambodia during World War II. In March 1945, the Japanese imprisoned French officials throughout Indochina (Cambodia, Laos, and Vietnam), and urged local leaders to declare independence. Sihanouk did so reluctantly,

welcoming back the French when they returned to power in October 1945. But in 1952, he launched a royal crusade, forcing the French to grant Cambodia its independence the following year. In 1955, however, Sihanouk abdicated the throne to become a full-time politician, founding a political party, Sangkum Reastr Niyum, that won several elections unopposed. The Communist Party, led by Pol Pot (1925–98), had a small following at that time and had little chance of coming to power.

In 1968, the war in Vietnam began to spill over into Cambodia as the US Army bombed Communist supply bases in the country. By this time, local and international pressure had weakened Sihanouk's control and in March 1970, the National Assembly voted to depose him. A pro-American regime, led by Lon Nol, came to power. This event precipitated the Cambodian Civil War. Sihanouk vowed to return, accepting support from North Vietnam, China, and Cambodian Communists. Months of fighting and heavy bombing ensued between Communist and US-backed forces until the former occupied the capital, ending the war in April 1975.

Communist soldiers during the Cambodian Civil War, 1975

		French in Cambodia		1945 French return to power		
			1830–49 Wars between Thailand and Vietnam over Cambodia	1941 Norodom Sihanouk crowned king by the French	1953 France grants Cambodia independence	
						1970–75 Cambodian Civil War
1610		**1730**		**1850**		**1970**
	1593 Thais sack Cambodian capital at Longvaek	1794 Thais annex northwestern quarter of Cambodia	1863 Imposition of French protectorate	1968 War begins between US-backed South Vietnam, and Communist North Vietnam	1970 Sihanouk overthrown in bloodless, pro-American coup	

Pol Pot's Khmer Rouge

On April l7, 1975, Cambodian Communist forces occupied Phnom Penh, welcomed by a population exhausted by five years of civil war. Within 48 hours, however, the victors forcibly evacuated the city, driving over two million people into the countryside to take up agricultural work. The Communists, under Pol Pot, established the government of Democratic Kampuchea (DK), and in order to form a new society "with no oppressors and no oppressed," abolished money, personal property, schools, laws, religious practices, markets, and freedom of movement.

Pol Pot (1925–98) led the Khmer Rouge

Pol Pot, the prime minister of DK, remained hidden during this time, denying DK's Communist affiliations. He wanted the revolution to be seen as uniquely Khmer. In reality, he borrowed many policies and slogans directly from Maoist China.

In 1975, the regime executed thousands of former soldiers and ex-civil servants.

Paranoid about unidentified enemies destroying DK, it also began indiscriminate executions the next year. In the countryside, where the regime irrationally sought to triple rice production overnight, thousands died of malnutrition, overwork, and disease.

When fighting broke out between DK and Vietnam in September 1977, Pol Pot finally came into the open, traveling to China to seek military aid. In a speech delivered before the visit, he claimed that the Communist Party of Kampuchea (CPK), which until then had been hidden to all but its members, had ruled Cambodia since April 1975. As the fighting with Vietnam expanded into a full-scale war, thousands of inhabitants from the eastern parts of Cambodia, suspected of being pro-Vietnamese, were executed. Several DK cadres, including a 25-year-old regimental commander called Hun Sen, sought refuge in Vietnam, where the Vietnamese began recruiting refugees into a "liberation army."

A Democratic State

In December 1978, Vietnam invaded Cambodia with a force of over 100,000 men. Phnom Penh fell in January 1979, and Pol Pot, his colleagues, and thousands of DK troops fled to Thailand. The "three years, eight months, and twenty days" of tyranny, as Cambodians commonly refer to this period, were over, but not before over 1.5 million people had met with unexpected, and often violent, deaths. The Vietnamese

Khmer Rouge fighters celebrating their victory as they enter Phnom Penh, April 17, 1975

1975 Cambodian Communists come to power

1984 Hun Sen becomes prime minister

Khmer Rouge soldier

1989 Vietnamese withdraw military support

1991 Paris Peace Conference establishes UN protectorate over Cambodia

1977 War breaks out between DK and Vietnam

| 1975 | 1980 | 1985 | 1990 | 1995 |

1979 Vietnamese topple DK, establish pro-Vietnamese regime

1993 Coalition government takes office after UN-sponsored elections

1976 Democratic Kampuchea (DK) established, with Pol Pot as prime minister

Paris Peace Conference, 1991

established a friendly regime in Phnom Penh that called itself the People's Republic of Kampuchea (PRK). Hun Sen was named foreign minister. Aged 27, he was the youngest in the world to hold the post.

Protected by 200,000 Vietnamese troops, the PRK moved cautiously to stabilize the country. It re-opened schools, re-introduced money, and allowed the revival of Buddhism. Unfortunately, although the horrors of the Khmer Rouge regime had now become widely known, DK retained Cambodia's seat at the UN, because China, the US, and their allies vigorously opposed the Vietnamese "invasion." This isolated PRK from all except the former Soviet Bloc. As a result, most of the assistance the country needed in order to recover never arrived.

Coronation ceremony of King Norodom Sihamoni, October 29, 2004

Peace At Last

Vietnam withdrew its troops from Cambodia in 1989, and the PRK renamed itself the State of Cambodia (SOC), rejecting Marxism-Leninism. The PRK party structures remained in place, and political opposition was dealt with severely. Over the next two years, Cambodia's fate hung in the balance.

A major international conference held in Paris in 1991, however, decided to establish a temporary UN protectorate over Cambodia to disarm the three Cambodian factions that opposed the PRK – Sihanouk's Funcinpec party, the Khmer Rouge, and the Khmer People's National Liberation Front – to repatriate over

Cambodian soldiers holding portraits of Norodom Sihanouk

300,000 Khmer from Thailand, and prepare the country for general elections. The United Nations Transitional Authority in Cambodia (UNTAC) was the most expensive UN operation to date and accomplished mixed results. It held fresh elections in July 1993, won by the royalists. Sihanouk was crowned king for the second time, with Hun Sen serving as prime minister. Initially, the SOC and DK factions refused to disarm, which forced the victors into an uneasy coalition that lasted until 1997, when the Khmer Rouge finally collapsed.

In the new millennium, foreign investment and assistance poured in, as did millions of tourists. King Sihanouk retired in 2004, succeeded by his son, Norodom Sihamoni. In 2007, the UN established the Extraordinary Chambers in the Courts of Cambodia (ECCC) to try leaders of the Khmer Rouge. Pol Pot was never tried by the tribunal because he died in 1998. Hun Sen's Cambodian People's Party has tightened control over politics and for the first time, the kingdom is at peace and part of the globalized world.

Norodom Sihamoni at his coronation

97 Hun Sen deposes coalition partners; mer Rouge movement ally collapses

2007 International tribunal to try leaders of DK opens in Phnom Penh. Boeung Kak Lake government land-grab in Phnom Penh spurns years of protest

2012 US Secretary of State Hillary Clinton attends ASEAN conference in Phnom Penh

2000   **2005**   **2010**   **2015**

1998 Cambodia joins ASEAN

2004 Sihanouk retires as king and is replaced by his son, Sihamoni

Prime Minister Hun Sen in Phnom Penh

2010 Kang Kek Lew (Comrade Duch) sentenced to 35 years in prison for crimes against humanity by the Khmer Rouge Tribunal

Cambodia at a Glance

Dominated by the Mekong River and the Tonlé Sap Lake, Cambodia's central plains are an incredibly fertile area. The majestic Dangkrek Mountains in the north and the Cardamom Mountains in the southwest form secure habitats for a variety of endangered plants and animals. The country's 277-mile (443-km) long coastline is marked with fine powdery beaches, while the warm tropical waters are dotted with thousands of islands, making a rich contrast with the rugged north. Although the temple complexes of Angkor continue to be Cambodia's primary attraction, towns such as Ban Lung, Battambang, and Sihanoukville also have much to offer.

Angkor Wat *(see pp70–71)* was built by King Suryavarman II in the early 12th century and rediscovered by the French during the 1860s. It is the biggest and best preserved of the numerous temples that were built in and around the ancient city of Angkor Thom.

Siem Reap *(see pp68–9)* serves as an ideal base for exploring the magnificent temples of Angkor, as well as the Tonlé Sap, Southeast Asia's largest freshwater lake.

Sihanoukville *(see pp108–9)* is a bustling town that serves as a gateway to an archipelago of verdant islands and a number of splendid beaches. Boat trips, snorkeling, scuba diving, and windsurfing are on offer here.

Kbal Chhay Cascades *(see pp110–11)*, situated on the scenic Prek Toeuk Sap River, is a favorite picnicking and swimming spot among locals and also visitors, particularly during the rainy season.

ANGKOR
(see pp64–87)

Sisophon

Siem Reap

Battambang

Tônlé Sap

Pursat

Koh Kong

SOUTHERN CAMBODIA
(see pp104–121)

Sihanoukville

Kampot

Kep

Prasat Preah Vihear *(see pp96–7)*, another temple from the Angkor period, was built by seven different Khmer kings. Dramatically located atop the cliffs of the Dangkrek Mountains, this complex is 2,625 ft (800 m) long, with a majestic stairway that ascends through four exquisitely carved Gopuras (gateway towers) before reaching the sanctuary.

Kratie *(see p102)* is a great place to spot the endangered Irrawaddy dolphin, which is found in the muddy waters of the Mekong River.

Stung Treng

Mekong River

Ban Lung

NORTHERN CAMBODIA *(see pp88–103)*

Kompong Thom

Kratie

Sen Monorom

Kompong Cham

Kompong Cham *(see p102)*, a sleepy provincial capital, is home to a number of temples and French-style boulevards.

Phnom Penh

OM PENH *(see pp46–63)*

Svay Rieng

Ban Lung *(see pp102–3)*, capital of the remote province of Ratanakiri in the northeast, awes visitors with its waterfalls, bamboo forests, and crater lakes. An emerging hub for ecotourism, it offers exciting activities such as trekking, kayaking, and elephant rides.

0 kilometers 50

0 miles 50

The Royal Palace and Silver Pagoda *(see pp54–7)* are the most striking landmarks in Phnom Penh. The Royal Palace, built in 1866, is the official residence of the king of Cambodia. The adjoining Silver Pagoda, named for the 5,000 silver tiles that cover its floor, is the most important structure in the complex. Also known as Wat Preah Keo, it houses the sacred Emerald Buddha.

PHNOM PENH

Cambodia's capital city is a sprawling metropolis, abuzz with scooters, tuk-tuks, and luxury 4WDs. A study in contrasts, Phnom Penh has vibrant, colorful markets, which thrive alongside sleek new malls, designer boutiques, shuttered French villas, and Parisian-style cafés dating from Colonial times. The city is also an excellent springboard for visits to other parts of the country.

Due to its strategic position at the confluence of the Tonlé Sap and Mekong rivers, Phnom Penh became the capital of the Khmer Empire in the mid-15th century after it was relocated from Angkor. Phnom Penh, meaning Hill of Penh, derives its name from the legend of an old lady, Penh, who found four Buddha statues washed up on the shore of the Mekong River and set them on a hill. The city traded with Laos and China until the 17th century, when it was reduced to a buffer state between the warring Vietnamese and Thais. The Thais eventually razed the city in 1772. In 1863, Phnom Penh found itself under French rule, which lasted until 1953, when King Sihanouk finally declared independence.

Phnom Penh fell to Pol Pot's black-clad forces on April 17, 1975, the city was emptied of its population, who were driven to the infamous Killing Fields of Choeung Ek. Cambodia was liberated by the Vietnamese in 1979 but it was another ten years before Phnom Penh was finally free to manage its own affairs. Having moved past the uncertainties of the 1980s, the city has reinvented itself with a growth in public works and considerable foreign aid.

Once known as the Pearl of the Orient, the capital is regaining some of its former luster, offering a selection of world-class boutique hotels and international cuisine. Local specialties include *amok* (fish cooked in coconut milk), *kari* (curry), and rice noodle soup. The atmospheric Sisowath Quay, which overlooks the Tonlé Sap River, harbors a wealth of French restaurants, book-shops, and stylish boutiques, as well as dozens of local eateries. Sights well worth a visit include the Royal Palace and Silver Pagoda, the National Museum, and the Tuol Sleng Genocide Museum.

Scenic view of the Mekong River from the tree-lined riverfront, Sisowath Quay

◄ Elaborate exterior of the National Museum of Cambodia, Phnom Penh

Exploring Phnom Penh

A vibrant city, far removed from its harrowing past, Phnom Penh attracts a steady flow of visitors. Designed around a grid system, the capital does not have a distinct city center. The 3-mile (2-km) sweep of the riverfront known as Sisowath Quay is arguably the most attractive area in the city. Lined with popular boutiques and myriad restaurants and bars, the area is liveliest at night. The city's best-known landmarks, the beautiful and sprawling Royal Palace and Silver Pagoda, lie across from the flag-studded promenade of the Tonlé Sap River. A little farther ahead are the terra-cotta pavilions of the National Museum. To the west lies the well-known Central Market with its Mediterranean-style dome and bustling shops. The southern part of the city is home to the Tuol Sleng Genocide Museum and Psar Tuol Tom Pong.

Sights at a Glance

Places of Worship

❸ Wat Ounalom

❹ Wat Phnom

Palaces and Museums

❶ Royal Palace and Silver Pagoda pp54–7

❷ National Museum of Cambodia

❻ Tuol Sleng Genocide Museum

❽ Killing Fields of Choeung Ek

Markets

❺ Central Market

❼ Psar Tuol Tom Pong

Areas of Natural Beauty

❾ Koki Beach

❿ Tonlé Bati

⓫ Phnom Tamao Wildlife Rescue Center

⓬ Phnom Chisor

Phnom Penh International Airport 5 miles (8 km)

CHARLES DE GAULLE BLVD (ST 217)

MONIRETH BLVD (ST 217)

Olympic Stadium

OKNHA TEP PHAN (ST 182)

JOSEP BROZ TITO (ST

OKNHA PEICH (ST 24

PREAH SIHANO

MAO TSE TO

The Royal Palace dominating the skyline, central Phnom Penh

For hotels and restaurants see p210 and pp222–3

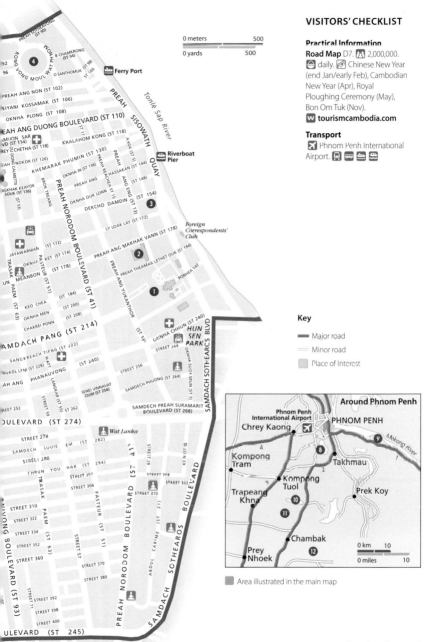

0 meters 500
0 yards 500

Ferry Port

Riverboat Pier

Foreign Correspondents' Club

VISITORS' CHECKLIST

Practical Information
Road Map D7. 🔺 2,000,000.
🚌 daily. 📅 Chinese New Year
(end Jan/early Feb), Cambodian
New Year (Apr), Royal
Ploughing Ceremony (May),
Bon Om Tuk (Nov).
Ⓦ **tourismcambodia.com**

Transport
🛫 Phnom Penh International
Airport. 🚌 🚌 🚌 🚌

Key

▬▬▬ Major road
═══ Minor road
▨ Place of Interest

Around Phnom Penh

Phnom Penh International Airport
Chrey Kaong
PHNOM PENH
Mekong River
Kompong Tram
Takhmau
Kompong Tuol
Trapeang Khna
Prek Koy
Chambak
Prey Nhoek

0 km 10
0 miles 10

▨ Area illustrated in the main map

Getting Around

Phnom Penh does not have a comprehensive public
transportation system. There are no public buses or even a train
service. The best way to get around the city is in a tuk-tuk or
moto, although areas such as Sisowath Quay are best explored
on foot. Metered taxis, a relatively recent addition to the city, are
reasonably priced, though not always easy to find. Those who like
to cycle can also move around the city on a hired bicycle.

For keys to symbols see back flap

Street-by-Street: Riverfront

Phnom Penh's riverfront is distinguished by its Gallic architecture – stucco-fronted, ocher-colored villas, and shuttered townhouses – while the surrounding area is home to many embassies, a number of old municipal buildings built under the French in the 19th and early 20th centuries, and several Chinese-style shophouses. The capital's scenic riverside promenade, Sisowath Quay, is the hub of the city's nightlife, with a variety of restaurants, lively bars, and boutiques. Other interesting places in the area include the Royal Palace and Silver Pagoda, the National Museum, and Psar Kandal – all within walking distance.

Visitors enjoying a quiet meal at one of the riverside restaurants

The palace's grounds and ornamental gardens are studded with stupas and statues of the royal family.

❶ ★ Royal Palace and Silver Pagoda
Built in the mid-19th century with French assistance, the Royal Palace is home to the current monarch, King Norodom Sihamoni. The adjoining Silver Pagoda houses the highly revered statue of the Emerald Buddha.

ST 184

Silver Shops
Owned by Cham Muslim silversmiths, who are noted for their fine filigree work, the silver shops sell exquisite belts, jewelry, betel pots, and other souvenirs.

SAMD

Key

— Suggested route

0 meters	100
0 yards	100

Foreign Correspondents' Club (FCC)
The FCC's walls are adorned with atmospheric war photographs. Comfortable leather sofas line the walls of the elegant bar and restaurant, which offers excellent food and impeccable service. The views of the river from the club are spectacular.

For hotels and restaurants see p210 and pp222–3

❸ Wat Ounalom

The seat of Buddhism in Cambodia, Wat Ounalom, has had a tragic history. Today, its attractions include a statue of its murdered religious leader, Samdech Huot Tat, and the stupa behind the main building, which contains a hair from the Buddha's eyebrow.

Locator Map
See Phnom Penh City Map

Psar Kandal is a dry goods market selling everything from electronics to pirated DVDs. Visitors will also find vendors offering fried crickets, a local delicacy.

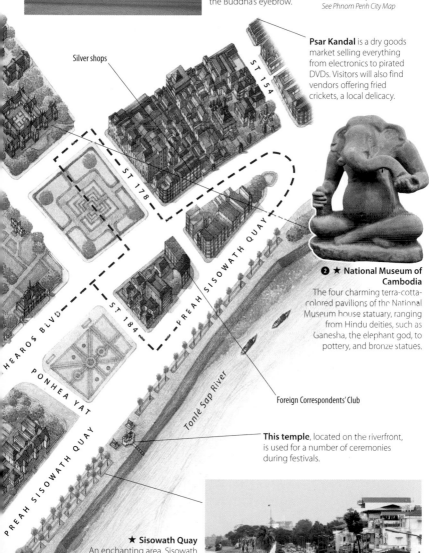

Silver shops

ST 154

ST 178

PREAH SISOWATH QUAY

ST 184

CHEAROS BLVD

PONHEA YAT

PREAH SISOWATH QUAY

Tonlé Sap River

❷ ★ National Museum of Cambodia

The four charming terra-cotta-colored pavilions of the National Museum house statuary, ranging from Hindu deities, such as Ganesha, the elephant god, to pottery, and bronze statues.

Foreign Correspondents' Club

This temple, located on the riverfront, is used for a number of ceremonies during festivals.

★ Sisowath Quay

An enchanting area, Sisowath Quay is favored by visitors for its lively bars and the wide variety of international cuisine on offer. It also serves as a starting point for river festivals and boat cruises down the Tonlé Sap River.

Imposing terra-cotta exterior of the National Museum of Cambodia, Phnom Penh

❶ Royal Palace and Silver Pagoda

See pp54–7.

❷ National Museum of Cambodia

Sts 178 and 179 (entrance is on corner of Sts 13 & 178). **City Map** E2. **Tel** (023)-211-753). **Open** 8am–5pm daily. 🚫 last ticket sold at 4:30pm. 📷 📹 inside the museum. 📷 W **cambodia museum.info**

Housed in four majestic terra-cotta pavilions enclosing an enchanting, landscaped courtyard, the National Museum of Cambodia houses the country's greatest display of Khmer statuary. Exhibits range from prehistoric to present-day items, and include Indian sculptures such as a striking eight-armed statue of Vishnu, a Hindu god, and a magnificent cross-legged

sandstone statue of the 12th-century king, Jayavarman VII. In the courtyard is a stone statue of Yama, the God of Death. The museum also has an excellent collection of local pottery, and bronze statues from the Funan and Chenla periods *(see p39).*

A small shop at the entrance sells books on Cambodian history and archaeology, as well as an assortment of souvenirs.

Stone statue of a *garuda*

❸ Wat Ounalom

Samdech Sothearos Blvd. **City Map** E2. **Open** dawn to dusk daily.

Built in 1943, Wat Ounalom is the headquarters and home of the Buddhist *sangha* (order) in Cambodia. In the early 1970s, more than 500 monks lived here. Tragically, the Khmer Rouge

murdered the then leader, Samdech Huot Tat, for his religious convictions, and threw a statue of him into the Tonlé Sap River. The statue was recovered after the expulsion of the Khmer Rouge and is now on view on the second floor of the temple. Outside is a beautifully detailed stupa said to contain a hair from the Buddha's eyebrow. There is also an extensive Buddhist library in the main temple, although the building is currently under renovation. Visitors to the temple should be wary of self-styled guides who insist on showing them around for a price.

❹ Wat Phnom

Norodom Blvd, N of St 102. **City Map** D1. 🚫 **Open** dawn to dusk daily. 🎎 Cambodian New Year.

Built in 1373 to house the Buddha statues found by Duan Penh – who laid the foundations of the shrine – on the shores of the Tonlé Sap River, this temple, at a modest 89 ft (27 m), is the highest point in the city. Today, it has something of a carnivalesque atmosphere with flashing altar lights and elephant rides.

Visitors enter this vibrant house of worship through an easterly *naga* stairway, passing beggars, hawkers, and dogs and cats fed by the monks. The temple's walls are adorned

Sculptured *nagas* flanking the staircase leading to Wat Phnom

with *Jataka* (stories from the former lives of the Buddha) murals, although many have been blackened by smoke from the incense offerings. There is a shrine dedicated to Duan Penh behind the *vihara* (temple sanctuary). Nearby, a couple of shrines of Taoist goddesses are popular with the locals, who make offerings of cooked chicken and raw eggs here.

❺ Central Market

E of Monivong Blvd, N of St 63. **City Map** D2. 🚌 **Open** dawn to dusk daily. ♿ 📷 📱

Known locally as Psar Thmei, which actually means New Market, this fabulous ocher-hued Art Deco building was erected by the French in 1937 on former swamp ground. Its immense central dome is on a scale similar to Hadrian's Pantheon in Rome. Offering a variety of products under one roof, this one-stop shop is any visitor's delight.

The food section here is packed with fresh fruits and vegetables, as well as delicacies such as peeled frogs and fried insects. Four wings radiate from the main building where vendors hawk gold and silver jewelry, watches, electronic goods, Buddha statues, clothes, and fresh flowers. The market is comfortable to visit at midday as the corridors of merchandise are surprisingly cool.

Imposing design of the dome at Central Market, Phnom Penh

Locally made cotton clothes on sale at Psar Tuol Tom Pong

❻ Tuol Sleng Genocide Museum

St 113. **City Map** C4. **Open** 8am–5:30pm daily. 📷 📱 📱

Hidden down a peaceful side street bordered with bougainvillea, this memorable, if disturbing, museum was originally a school that was turned into the Khmer Rouge torture headquarters. Tuol Sleng Prison, also known as S-21, was the largest detention center in the country, and subjected 17,000 men, women, and children to torture en route to the Killing Fields of Choeung Ek (*see p60*); most did not get that far. When Vietnamese forces liberated Phnom Penh in 1979, they found only seven people still alive at S-21, each having survived because of their skills as an artist or photographer.

The prison has now been converted into a museum; its former cells and gallery are covered with thousands of haunting photographs of subjects before and after torture. There is an interesting exhibition on the second floor of the main building, which gives important details on the main instigators of the murderous regime, as well as photos, diaries, and poems written by those affected. The balconies on the upper floors are still enclosed with the wire mesh that prevented prisoners from jumping to an early death.

Despite allegedly being haunted, today the place plays host to young footballers on its lawns, and a colony of bats in one of the stairwells.

❼ Psar Tuol Tom Pong

S of Mao Tse Toung Blvd. **City Map** C5. **Open** dawn to dusk daily. ♿ 📷 📱

Also known as the Russian Market because of the many Russians who shopped here during the 1980s, this market is perhaps the best place for visitors looking for good bargains. Under the sweltering tin roofs is a smorgasbord of handicrafts, fake antiques, silk scarves, and musical instruments. Also on sale is a huge selection of fake designer clothing, as well as genuine items made in local factories. They are sold here at a fraction of their international prices.

Wire mesh enclosing the balconies, Tuol Sleng Genocide Museum

❶ Royal Palace and Silver Pagoda

Bearing a striking resemblance to the Grand Palace in Bangkok, Thailand, the Royal Palace, with its gilded, pitched roofs framed by *nagas* (serpents), is one of the most prominent landmarks of Phnom Penh. Built in the mid-19th century in the classic Khmer style, the Royal Palace is the official residence of Cambodia's reigning monarch, King Sihamoni. Known as Preah Barom Reachea Vaeng Chaktomuk in the Khmer language, the palace was built with French assistance on the site of a former temple, on the western bank of the Tonlé Sap River, and is designed to face the rising sun. Parts of the complex are closed to the public.

Pavilion of Napoleon III in the grounds of the Royal Palace

Main Entrance

A tour of the Royal Palace begins at the main entrance, situated in the eastern part of the complex. The ticket counters are located here and visitors can also hire English-speaking guides for a few dollars. Visitors should be dressed in clothes that cover the arms, shoulders, and legs. Suitable items of clothing can also be hired from here.

Silver Pagoda
See pp56–7.

Pavilion of Napoleon III

A former French villa, this pavilion was built in Giza, Egypt, by Napoleon III for his wife, Empress Eugénie. Presented to King Norodom I (r.1860–1904) in 1876, it was entirely dismantled, shipped to Phnom Penh, and re-erected in the grounds of the Royal Palace. The pavilion stands out from all other structures in the complex due to its Colonial design and the exquisite iron fretwork of its balconies.

The pavilion was refurbished in 1991 with assistance from the French government. Today, photographic exhibits, as well as a collection of royal memorabilia, such as busts, gifts from visiting dignitaries, glassware, and royal clothing, are on display inside.

Royal Treasury

A tall, narrow pavilion, whose upper story, or Hor Samritvimean, houses regalia that was used in royal coronation ceremonies. Its highlights include the Great Crown of Victory and the Victory Spear, as well as the Sacred Sword. The lower floor is home to some minor regalia and utensils.

Throne Hall

Built in 1917 and inaugurated by King Sisowath in 1919, the Throne Hall is known locally as Preah Thineang Dheva Vinnichayyeaah, meaning the Sacred Seat of Judgement. Its design is heavily influenced by Bayon-style architecture *(see p73)*, evident from its cruciform shape and triple spires. The central spire is crowned by an imposing 194-ft (59-m) high tower. The roof is adorned with *nagas* (serpents) and *garudas* (mythical beasts that are half-man, half-bird). Today, the Throne Hall is used for coronations, and for extending a formal welcome to visiting diplomats.

The Throne Room, accessed from a door to the east, is painted in white and yellow to symbolize Hinduism and Buddhism, respectively. It is an excellent example of the harmonious fusion of the two religions, which was encouraged by the 12th-century monarch, King Jayavarman VII. Its ceiling is adorned with a beautiful mural depicting the *Reamker*, the Khmer version of the Hindu epic, *Ramayana*. A lotus-patterned

Intricately detailed façade of the Throne Hall

Royal Palace and Silver Pagoda

List of Sites

① Main Entrance
② Silver Pagoda
③ Pavilion of Napoleon III
④ Royal Offices
⑤ Banquet Hall
⑥ Royal Treasury
⑦ Throne Hall
⑧ Victory Gate
⑨ Royal Waiting Room
⑩ Dancing Pavilion
⑪ Royal Residence

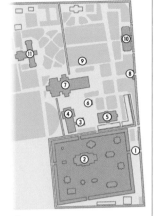

0 meters 100
0 yards 100

Key

 Area illustrated (see pp56–7)

VISITORS' CHECKLIST

Practical Information
City map E2.
Samdach Sothearos Blvd.
Main entrance. **Open** 7:30–11am & 2–5pm daily. hired at main entrance. Throne Hall. Note: Royal Residence is closed to the public; Throne Hall is closed during royal receptions.

carpet, donated by China in 1933, perfectly complements the lotus bud floor tiles in the room. The Throne Room also houses the majestic thrones of the king and queen of Cambodia. While the king's throne is small and sits at the front, the queen's is taller and built on a golden stage adorned with *nagas*. There are three stairways running from the queen's throne – two for the Brahmin priests who tend to her during the king's coronation, and the third for the queen herself.

Victory Gate
Set on the eastern end of the complex, the Victory Gate leads directly to the Throne Hall. Once used only by the king and queen, it is now also used by visiting dignitaries.

Royal Waiting Room
Situated to the right of the magnificent Throne Hall, Hor Samranphirum, or the Royal Waiting Room, is used by the king and queen while waiting for their ceremonial elephants on Coronation Day. Posts to tether the beasts are visible on the east side of the building, as are the platforms used by the king and queen to mount the elephants for the coronation procession.

Dancing Pavilion
Located near the Victory Gate, the Dancing Pavilion, or Chan Chaya Pavilion, was originally built in 1914 with wood. It was traditionally used by Cambodian kings to view parades and to enjoy

performances of classical Khmer dances. A balcony to the east of the pavilion was used for viewing parades along Sotheavos Boulevard, beyond the royal grounds.

Today, the Dancing Pavilion is used for royal celebrations, and royal (as well as state) banquets. The building was memorably used to celebrate the coronation of King Sihamoni in October 2004.

Royal Residence
Built in the mid 20th century, during the reign of King Sisowath Monivong, by well-known Khmer architect Okhna Tep Nimith Khieu, the Royal Residence is also known as the Khemarin Palace, or the Palace of the Khmer King. It currently houses the present monarch, King Sihamoni, whose presence in the capital is indicated by the blue royal flag, which flies at full mast. The Royal Residence is off limits for visitors.

Next to this beautiful building stands the royal guesthouse known as Villa Kantha Bopha, which was built in 1956 and is used only to house foreign guests.

View of the elegantly lit exterior of the Dancing Pavilion at night

Silver Pagoda

Near the easy-going riverfront of Phnom Penh, the 19th-century Silver Pagoda lies within the same complex as the Royal Palace, and is a prominent jewel of the city's squat skyline. The Silver Pagoda is a short walk from Sisowath Quay. With its intricately curled golden roofs and tropical gardens, it is a beautifully calm oasis away from the rush of the city.

The gilded gateway at the northern entrance to the Silver Pagoda

Royal Pavilion
The Dhammasala, which is also known as the Royal Pavilion, is an open hall used by the royal family as a reception area, as well as by Buddhist monks to recite religious texts.

Chedi of Suramarit
This stupa holds the ashes of former king, Suramarit, and his queen, Kossomak – grandparents of the current ruler, King Sihamoni.

South Entrance

KEY

① **Phnom Kailassa** contains a stylized Buddha's footprint gifted by Sri Lanka.

② **Scale model of Angkor Wat**

③ **The Mondap** is a small library housing sacred texts written on palm-tree fronds. Also of interest is a statue of a bull's head wreathed in flowers, and an exquisite stained-glass window.

④ **Dome-shaped chedis** are shrines or stupas containing the ashes of the dead.

★ **Buddha's Footprints**
The Keong Preah Bath houses the Buddha's footprints. This shrine is especially popular with Cambodians, and is surrounded by fortune-tellers.

For hotels and restaurants see p210 and pp222–3

★ **Murals in the Gallery**
The inner compound wall of the complex is beautifully ornamented with vivid frescoes of scenes from the *Reamker* – the Khmer version of the Hindu epic, *Ramayana*.

★ **Wat Preah Keo**
Named for its centerpiece, a Baccarat crystal Buddha, Wat Preah Keo (Temple of the Emerald Buddha) is also famous for a golden, life-sized Buddha and miniature Buddhist statuary.

North Entrance

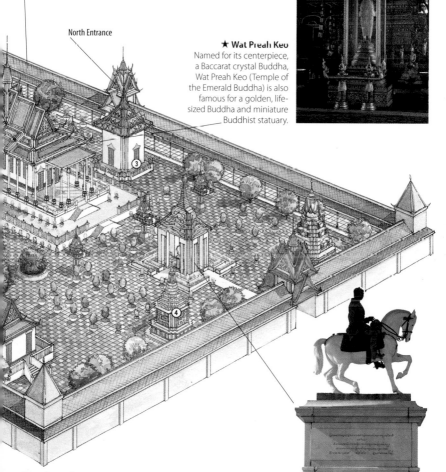

The Complex
Also known as Wat Preah Keo, the Silver Pagoda is named for its floor, which is inlaid with more than 5,000 solid silver tiles. The name also describes the complex that houses the Buddha's Footprints, the Mondap library, the Reamker murals, and a number of royal family shrines.

Equestrian Statue
King Norodom (r.1860–1904) and Napoleon III were firm friends – this statue of Norodom in full Napoleon III regalia is a parody of the French emperor on his steed.

The stunning Silver Pagoda in the Royal Palace complex ▶

🔵 Killing Fields of Choeung Ek

5 miles (8 km) S of Phnom Penh.
Open 7am–5:30pm daily. 🚗 📷 ♿

A former longan orchard, this deceptively peaceful setting was the scene of one of the most disturbing acts of violence in contemporary history.

Signpost identifying the tree against which babies were killed, Killing Fields of Choeung Ek

Some 17,000 men, women, and children kept as prisoners in the torture chambers of Tuol Sleng Prison, also known as S-21 *(see p53)*, were brought here to be killed, often by blunted hoes to conserve bullets. Of the 129 communal graves, 49 have been left intact, and it is still possible to chance upon bone fragments and bits of clothing. Signposts close to the graves tell visitors about the number of people buried there; another one marks a macabre tree, against which babies were flung by their ankles and killed.

In 1988, however, a fittingly dignified pavilion was erected within the complex in memory of the 9,000 people found here. Through the glass panels of the pavilion one can see some 8,000 skulls arranged according to age and sex. A museum in the corner of the grounds offers detailed background information, not only on the founders of the Khmer Rouge, but also on its victims, who included doctors, politicians, and actors.

🔵 Koki Beach

Off National Hwy 1, 9 miles (14 km) E of Phnom Penh. 🚌 from Central Market. 🚌 **Open** dawn to dusk daily. ♿ 📷 📱

A romantic picnic spot on a tributary of the Mekong River, Koki Beach is popular with young Khmers, who come here on weekends. The clean sands, stilted huts with thatched roofs, and calm setting make it an ideal place to relax and unwind. Visitors can venture on inexpensive boat trips along the river, or swim close to the sandy beach, where a few people can usually be found braving the waters. There is always plenty of food to be bought from the local vendors who sell a selection of grilled fish, chicken, and fresh coconuts. The beach is also lined with makeshift restaurants specializing in local food. However, it is best to agree on the price of dishes before settling down to eat.

Justice for Victims of the Khmer Rouge

Conceived in 1997 and finally set up in 2007, the Extraordinary Chambers in the Courts of Cambodia (ECCC) is a UN-backed tribunal located near Phnom Penh's airport. The first organization of its kind to bring the leaders of Khmer Rouge to justice, the ECCC is an independent tribunal comprising international monitors. Designed to be fair and open, these trials aim to relieve the burden still felt by survivors of the holocaust. The proceedings have been affected by lack of funding and alleged corruption, along with some resistance by Prime Minister Hun Sen, who fears that reopening the wound could spark a fresh civil war.

The first accused to be tried by the tribunal was "Duch," head warden of Tuol Sleng Prison. On July 26, 2010, Duch was sentenced to 35 years in prison for war crimes and crimes against humanity. Only senior leaders of the Democratic Kampuchea, the state formed by the Khmer Rouge, are being tried.

Trials in the Extraordinary Chambers in the Courts of Cambodia are usually not on camera, and can be witnessed by the public except in some special cases. The courtroom is designed to provide additional seating for onlookers, with a glass partition separating them from the area where the accused and judges are seated.

⑩ Tonlé Bati

Off National Hwy 2, 19 miles (30 km) S of Phnom Penh. 🚌 **Open** dawn to dusk daily. ♿ ✏ 🖼

Another popular weekend haunt, Tonlé Bati is a peaceful lake with stilted huts bordering its acacia-shaded shoreline. It is frequented by locals who find it an ideal spot for a quiet picnic or fishing trip. Adding further appeal are the nearby ruins of **Ta Prohm** and **Yeay Peau**, two beautifully preserved temples built in the late 12th century under King Jayavarman VII.

Ta Prohm's main sanctuary has five chambers, each containing a Shiva *lingam* (phallic symbol), as well as a number of bas-reliefs depicting several *apsaras*. On weekends, the temple grounds play host to musicians and fortune-tellers catering to visitors. Located a short distance from Ta Prohm, Yeay Peau is named after King Ta Prohm's mother. Both sites show signs of damage by the Khmer Rouge.

⑪ Phnom Tamao Wildlife Rescue Center

Off National Hwy 2, 25 miles (40 km) S of Phnom Penh. 🚌 from Central Market, then tuk-tuk. **Open** 8.30am–5pm daily. 🐾 ✏ ♿ 🖼 🗓

Opened in 1995, the Phnom Tamao Wildlife Rescue Center is the largest zoo in the country. Covering 10 sq miles (26 sq km) of protected forest, of which only a small part is in use, the zoo serves as a rehabilitation

Crumbling ruins of Phnom Chisor, overlooking the plains below

center for animals, many of them endangered, rescued from the illegal wildlife trade. A haven for wildlife enthusiasts, the center cares for, and protects, several rare birds and animals that usually inhabit inhospitable parts of the country, and are therefore almost impossible to observe in the wild.

These well-nurtured animals are kept in a variety of enclosures, the largest of which houses a group of Malayan sun bears who willingly accept fresh coconuts from visitors. Other exotic species found here include the world's greatest collection of pileated gibbons and the Siamese crocodile. The center also has several elephants that have been taught to paint, and many fully grown Asiatic tigers.

Asiatic tiger, Phnom Tamao

These are best viewed in the afternoon, when they usually come out in their enclosures.

⑫ Phnom Chisor

31 miles (50 km) S of Phnom Penh. 🚌 from Central Market, then tuk-tuk. **Open** dawn to dusk daily. 🚴

An 11th-century sanctuary formerly known as Suryagiri, the temple of Phnom Chisor is set upon the eastern side of a solitary hill affording wonderful views of the plains below. Within its crumbling interior stand a few surviving statues of the Buddha, while the carvings on the wooden doors depict figures standing on pigs. Best visited in the early morning or late afternoon, when it is cooler, the temple is reached by climbing almost 400 stairs – the path taken by the king of Cambodia 900 years ago. Directly below the summit is the sanctuary of Sen Ravang, the pond of Tonlé Om, and beyond it the Sen Ravang temple, all forming a symbolic straight line to sacred Angkor.

Nearby stand two deteriorating brick *prasats* (towers) of the 10th-century temple Prasat Neang Khmau. Beside them is an active pagoda where another ancient *prasat* may once have stood.

Bas-relief depicting *apsaras* in various postures at Ta Prohm, Tonlé Bati

ANGKOR

The ancient capital of the great Khmer Empire, Angkor is without doubt one of the most magnificent wonders of the world, and a site of immense archaeological significance. Located in dense jungle on the hot and torpid plains of northwestern Cambodia, its awe-inspiring temples transport visitors back to an enchanting and mysterious ancient world of grandeur and glory.

Often referred to as the eighth wonder of the world, Angkor, the ancient capital of Cambodia, is a remarkable place. For nearly six centuries, between AD 802 and 1431, it was the political and religious heart of the Khmer Empire, an empire that extended from the South China Sea almost to the Bay of Bengal.

The Khmer Empire was founded at the beginning of the 9th century AD by Jayavarman II (r.802–850), who proclaimed himself *devaraja* (god-king) of the land. He built a gigantic, pyramidal temple-mountain representing Mount Meru, the sacred mythical abode of the Hindu gods. This structure laid the foundations of Angkor's architecture. In the following centuries, his successors shifted the capital from Roluos to Angkor, built magnificent temples such as Phnom Bakheng, Angkor Wat, Banteay Kdei, and Ta Prohm, as well as the bustling city of Angkor Thom.

Today, the remains of the metropolis of Angkor occupy 77 sq miles (200 sq km) of northwestern Cambodia, and although its wooden houses and magnificent palaces decayed centuries ago, the impressive array of stone temples still stand. Set between two *barays* (reservoirs), Angkor today contains around 70 temples, tombs, and other ancient ruins. Among them is the splendid Angkor Wat, the world's largest religious complex.

One of the most important archaeological sites in the world, Angkor attracts millions of visitors each year, providing a substantial boost to Cambodia's economy. Other sites in the area include the rapidly developing town of Siem Reap. With its tree-lined boulevards and gentle pace, Siem Reap is the gateway to the temples of Angkor, which lie only 4 miles (6 km) north of the town.

Monks enjoying the stunning sunset over Angkor Wat from the top of Phnom Bakheng

◄ Ancient statues outside the elaborate Banteay Srei temple, Angkor, Siem Reap province

Exploring Angkor

Set among dense green forests and neat rice paddies, the massive monuments of Angkor are the most remarkable architectural masterpieces in Southeast Asia. Located north of Siem Reap town, in Siem Reap province, the vast Angkor Wat complex, with its imposing towers, and the great city of Angkor Thom, with its impressive causeway and the gigantic smiling faces of the Bayon, are breathtaking sights, especially at sunrise or sunset. Farther north are the smaller yet unique temples of Preah Khan and Preah Neak Pean. To the east of Angkor Thom is the magical Ta Prohm, with large trees growing through the temple walls. Farther out, the pink sandstone structure of Banteay Srei lies to the northeast, while to the southeast are the temples of the Roluos Group, the oldest in Angkor.

Sights at a Glance

Towns, Cities, and Villages

1. *Siem Reap pp68–9*
15. Chong Kneas
17. Kompong Phhluk
18. Kompong Khleang

Historical Sites

2. *Angkor Wat pp70–71*
3. *Angkor Thom pp74–7*
4. Phnom Bakheng
5. Preah Khan
6. Preah Neak Pean
7. East Baray
8. Pre Rup
9. Srah Srang
10. Banteay Kdei
11. *Ta Prohm pp82–3*
12. Prasat Kravan
13. Banteay Srei
14. Roluos Group

National Parks and Preserves

16. Prek Toal Bird Sanctuary

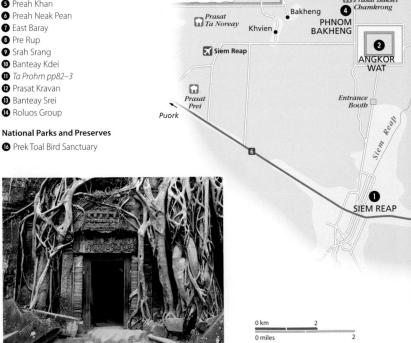

The tree featured in the movie *Lara Croft: Tomb Raider*, Ta Prohm

For hotels and restaurants see pp210–11 and pp223–5

Tuk-tuks plying the well-trodden road between
Siem Reap and Angkor

Getting Around

The temples at Angkor require both time and
motorized transport to visit. It is possible to visit the
main sites by motorcycle, but the most comfortable
way to travel in this hot and dusty area is in an air-
conditioned car with a driver. In Colonial times, the
French defined two circuits, both starting at Angkor
Wat, which are still used today. The 11-mile (18-km)
"small circuit" takes at least a day and covers the central
temples of the complex, continuing to Ta Prohm,
before returning to Angkor Wat via Banteay Kdei.
The "great circuit," a 17-mile (27-km) route, takes in the
small circuit as well as the outer temples, going past
Preah Neak Pean to Ta Som, before turning south to
Pre Rup. This takes at least two full days.

Key
- Urban areas
- Archaeological sites
- Major road
- Minor road

Exquisite carvings of *apsaras* at the
Bayon, Angkor Thom

Area illustrated in the main map

For keys to symbols *see back flap*

❶ Siem Reap

Siem Reap literally means Siam Defeated, referring to the Khmer sacking of the great Thai city of Ayutthaya in the 17th century. Until recently, this French Indochinese town with its Colonial buildings and tree-lined boulevards was little more than a staging post for visitors on their way to the temples of Angkor and the Roluos Group. Today, however, it is fast becoming a destination in its own right, with quality restaurants serving excellent French-influenced cuisine, upscale boutique hotels, and a new airport. The locals have been quick to ride the tourist wave by opening an increasing number of souvenir stores, tour agencies, and massage vendors.

🏛 Cambodia War Museum
Tel (088)-848-7351. **Open** 8am to 5.30pm daily. 🐾 🎫 ♿ 🅿
W warmuseumcambodia.com

This museum offers visitors an insightful view of the perils that Cambodia faced during the last three decades of the 20th century. The story of Cambodia's "war years" is told through a unique collection of war apparatus and rare photograhs.

🏛 Angkor National Museum
968 Charles De Gaulle Blvd.
Tel (063)-966-601. **Open** 8:30am–6:30pm daily (to 6pm Apr–Sep).
🐾 🎫 ♿ 🖥 🅿
W angkornationalmuseum.com

Opened to the public in 2007, the Angkor National Museum is housed in a sprawling building with well-manicured lawns. The museum comprises eight galleries, each containing a wealth of ancient Angkorian artifacts. On arrival, visitors first head to the screening of a documentary on the marvels of Angkor entitled *Story Behind The Legend*. The next stop is Gallery 1, with its stunning exhibition of 1,000 Buddha images in wood, stone, and precious jewels.

Brightly lit restaurants and bars along the popular Pub Street

The subsequent galleries focus exclusively on subjects such as the pre-Angkorian period, Khmer kings, and Angkor Wat. A mall with a shopping center is attached to the museum.

❶ Psar Chaa and Around
Corner of Pokambor Ave. **Open** dawn to dusk daily. ♿ 🚻 🖥 🅿

Once the mainstay of the town's vendors, today Psar Chaa faces competition from shops lining the surrounding streets. Never-theless, the market continues to be a popular stop for both locals and foreign visitors who come for its reasonable prices and variety of goods. Popular products include wood-carvings, lacquer-ware, silverware, and groceries.

Nearby is the carefully restored old French Quarter and the atmospheric Pub Street. This lively area, aptly named for the numerous restaurants and pubs lining its length, comes alive at night with loud music, *apsara* dance performances, and crowds of visitors sauntering up and down the street.

🏛 Les Chantiers Écoles
Stung Thmey St. **Tel** (063)-963-330.
Open 7am–5pm daily. 🎫 ♿ 🖥 🅿
W artisansdangkor.com

A school set up in the early 1990s for under-privileged children, Les Chantiers Écoles is located down a tiny side street. Here, children are taught stone carving, lacquer-making, silk painting, and wood sculpting. Visitors can walk through the workshops with a guide who explains the stages of each intricate craft; the tour takes about an hour. Artisans d'Angkor, the school's shop, is also located in the same complex and sells products made by the students.

Those keen to see the process of silk farming can head for the Les Chantiers Écoles Silk Farm, 10 miles (16 km) northwest of Siem Reap. The tour takes three hours. Bus rides from Les Chantiers Écoles are available.

🏛 National Center for Khmer Ceramics
Charles De Gaulle Blvd. **Tel** (063)-963-330. **Open** 8am–6pm. 🎫 ♿ 🅿
W khmerceramics.com

A non-profit, non-government organization, the National Center for Khmer Ceramics was established to re-introduce Khmer's ancient pottery tech-niques to the country. The center also provides valuable job opportunities to the people of Siem Reap province, which,

Outstanding display of Buddha images in Gallery 1, Angkor National Museum

For hotels and restaurants see pp210–11 and pp223–5

despite the considerable wealth accrued from visitors to nearby Angkor Wat, is still the poorest in Cambodia. Students are taught for free and are encouraged to set up their own studios on completion of the course. They learn to work with clay, and master the potter's wheel and kilns, faithfully modeled on an ancient Khmer design. Guided tours of the center are generally given by one of the trainees, and those interested can also try their hand at the potter's wheel. The center also has a lovely souvenir shop, which sells some of the finished ceramics made on-site. Afterwards, visitors can relax in the center's charming, shady tropical gardens.

Ceramic pot, National Center

🏛 Tonlé Sap Exhibition

2 miles (3 km) N of town center. **Open** 8am–5:30pm daily. ♿
Krousay Thmey, an NGO that supports orphans, has set up the informative Tonlé Sap Exhibition on the outskirts of Siem Reap. This exhibition offers an insight into the ecology of the Tonlé Sap, the largest freshwater lake in Southeast Asia. The lake and its marine-rich waters feed over 3 million people and provide

75 percent of the country's annual fish stocks. The displays, which feature models, nets, illustrations, and a range of fishing equipment, focus on the varied wild-life of the lake, as well as its floating villages and the people who live in them. Visitors can pamper their tired muscles at the end of the day by opting for a traditional massage at the adjoining NGO, Seeing Hands, which has been set up to help the blind.

🏛 Cambodian Cultural Village

6 Airport Rd, Khum Svay Dang Kum, Krus Village. **Tel** (063)-963-098. **Open** 8am–7pm daily. 🚫📷♿📷📷
🌐 **cambodianculturalvillage.com**

Hugely popular with the Cambodians, the Cambodian Cultural Village is an interesting hour's diversion for international visitors who want to learn about Cambodia's diverse demography, religion, and architecture. There are Cham (Muslim), Khmer (Buddhist), and Phnong and Kroueng (animist) houses, as well as floating villages in the complex. There are also miniature replicas of famous contemporary buildings in Cambodia, and wax renderings of national historical

figures. A variety of shows, such as *apsara* dances, fishing ceremonies, and a lion dance, provide a brilliant insight into the country's ancient traditions.

Traditional dance performance at the Cambodian Cultural Village

Siem Reap Town Center

① Angkor National Museum
② Psar Chaa and Around
③ Les Chantiers Écoles
④ National Center for Khmer Ceramics
⑤ Tonlé Sap Exhibition
⑥ Cambodian Cultural Village
⑦ Cambodia War Museum

Key

🟦 French Quarter

❷ Angkor Wat

The largest religious monument in the world, Angkor Wat literally means the City which is a Temple. Built during the 12th century by King Suryavarman II, this spectacular complex was originally dedicated to the Hindu god, Vishnu. The layout is based on a *mandala* (sacred design of the Hindu cosmos). A five-towered temple shaped like a lotus bud, representing Mount Meru, the mythical abode of the gods and the center of the universe, stands in the middle of the complex. The intricate carvings on the walls marking the temple's perimeter are outstanding and include a 1,970-ft (600-m) long panel of bas-reliefs, and carvings of *apsaras* (celestial dancing girls). The outermost walls and the moat surrounding the entire complex symbolize the edge of the world and the cosmic ocean, respectively. Angkor Wat, unusual among Khmer temples, faces the setting sun, a symbol of death.

Detailed carvings on the outer walls of the central sanctuary

★ **Central Sanctuary**
Towering over the complex, the central sanctuary is a steep climb. Its four entrances feature images of the Buddha, reflecting the Buddhist influence that eventually displaced Hinduism in Cambodia.

★ **Apsaras**
The carvings of hundreds of sensual *apsaras*, each one different from the next, line the walls of the temple. Holding alluring poses, they are shown wearing ornate jewelry and exquisite headgear.

View of Towers
The five towers of Angkor Wat rise through three levels to a grand central shrine. The entire complex is surrounded by thick walls. The view of the temple from the giant pool to the left of the causeway is stunning – particularly at sunrise – with its five towers reflected in the still water.

VISITORS' CHECKLIST

Practical Information
Road map C6. 4 miles (6 km) N of Siem Reap. *i* Khmer Angkor Tour Guide Association, Siem Reap, (063)-964-347. **Open** 5:30am to sunset daily (ticket office from 5am). 1-, 3- and 7-day passes for Angkor. **w** khmerangkor tourguide.com

Transport
✈ Siem Reap. **Taxi** from Siem Reap. Hotels offer group tours.

★ **Gallery of Bas-Reliefs**
The southern section of the western gallery depicts several scenes from the Hindu epic *Mahabharata*. The intricate bas-reliefs here feature images of hundreds of brave, weapon-bearing warriors engaged in furious combat during the Battle of Kurukshetra.

The Causeway
The wide pathway leading to the temple's main entrance on the west side affords a spectacular view of Angkor Wat's grand exterior. Balustrades carved in the form of *nagas* (serpents) once lined both sides of the avenue.

KEY

① **The library** provides views of the upper levels of Angkor Wat.

② **Bas-reliefs in the southern gallery** depict images of King Suryavarman II, who initiated the construction of Angkor Wat.

③ **The Terrace of Honor** was used by the king to receive ceremonial processions and foreign dignitaries.

④ **Hall of Echoes**

Architecture of Angkor

Angkor-period architecture generally dates from Jayavarman II's establishment of the Khmer capital near Roluos in the early 9th century AD. From then until the 15th century, art historians identify five main architectural styles. The earliest, Preah Ko, is rooted in the pre-Angkorian traditions of Sambor Prei Kuk (see pp100–1), to Angkor's east, and the 8th-century temple style of Kompong Preah, relics of which are found at Prasat Ak Yum by the West Baray. Khmer architecture reached its zenith during the construction of Angkor Wat.

Pink sandstone library building in the inner enclosure of Banteay Srei

Preah Ko (AD 875–90)

The Preah Ko style was characterized by a simple temple layout, with one or more square brick towers rising from a single laterite base. The Roluos Group (see pp84–5) saw the first use of concentric enclosures entered via the gopura (gateway tower). Another innovation was the library annex, possibly used to protect the sacred fire.

This well-preserved guardian figure is carved from sandstone and set in the outer brick wall of a sanctuary tower at the 9th-century Lolei Temple.

The eastern causeway of Bakong runs straight from the main *gopura* to the high central tower. This structure is raised on a square-based pyramid, rising to a symbolic temple-mountain.

Bakheng to Pre Rup (AD 890–965)

The temple-mountain style, based on Mount Meru, evolved during the Bakheng period. Phnom Bakheng (see p80), Phnom Krom, and Phnom Bok all feature the classic layout of five towers arranged in a quincunx – a tower on each side, with a fifth at the center. The Pre Rup style developed during the reign of Rajendravarman II (r.944–68). It continues the Bakheng style, but the towers are higher and steeper, with more tiers.

Phnom Bakheng impressively exemplifies the Bakheng style. It was the state temple of the first Khmer capital at Angkor, and dates from the late 9th century. It rises majestically through a pyramid of square terraces to the main group of five sanctuary towers.

Pre Rup's carved sandstone lintels are more finely detailed than in earlier styles. Distinguished by its size, and the abrupt rise of its temple-mountain through several levels to the main sanctuary, it is speculated that the structure may have served as a royal crematorium – *pre rup* means turn the body.

Banteay Srei to Baphuon (AD 965–1080)

Represented by the delicate and refined Banteay Srei *(see p84)*, this eponymous style is characterized by ornate carvings of sensuous apsaras and devadas (dancers). By the mid-11th century, when Khmer architecture was reaching its majestic apogee, this style had evolved into the Baphuon style, which is distinguished by vast proportions and vaulted galleries. The sculpture of the period shows increasing realism and narrative sequence.

The five-tiered Baphuon *(see p74)* was the state temple of Udayadityavarman II (r.1050–66). The structure was described by 13th-century Chinese traveler Zhou Daguan as "a truly astonishing spectacle, with more than ten chambers at its base."

Banteay Srei, constructed between AD 967 and 1000, is known for its fine craftsmanship, evident in the exquisite detail of the bas-reliefs and carved stone lintels.

Angkor Wat (AD 1080–1175)

Art historians generally agree that the style of Angkor Wat *(see pp70–71)* represents the apex of Khmer architectural and sculptural genius. The greatest of all temple-mountains, it also boasts the finest bas-relief narratives. The art of lintel carving also reached its zenith during this period.

Bas-reliefs of Suryavarman II in the west section of the southern gallery portray the king seated on his throne, surrounded by courtiers with fans and parasols. Below him, princesses and women of the court are carried in palanquins. In another fine bas-relief, the king is shown riding a great war elephant.

An aerial view of Angkor Wat makes the vast scale and symbolic layout of the complex very clear. Every aspect of Angkor is rich with meaning, the most apparent being the central quincunx of towers rising to a peak, representing the five peaks of the sacred Mount Meru.

Bayon (AD 1175–1240)

Considered a synthesis of previous styles, Bayon – the last great Angkor architectural style – is still magnificent, but also characterized by a detectable decline in quality. There is more use of laterite and less of sandstone, as well as more Buddhist imagery and, correspondingly, fewer Hindu themes.

Bas-reliefs depicting scenes of battle at the temple of the Bayon in Angkor Thom *(see pp74–7)* provide a remarkable record of contemporary wars between the Khmer Empire and the Kingdom of Champa, which resulted in the victory of Khmer King Jayavarman VII in 1181.

The South Gate of Angkor Thom is surmounted by a large, four-faced carving of the *devaraja* (god-king), Jayavarman VII. He is depicted as the Bodhisattva Avalokitesvara, gazing somberly in the four cardinal directions for eternity.

❸ Angkor Thom

Remarkable in scale and architectural ingenuity, the ancient city of Angkor Thom, which means Great City in Khmer, was founded by King Jayavarman VII in the late 12th century. The largest city in the Khmer Empire at one time, it is protected by a wall 26 ft (8 m) high, about 7.5 miles (12 km) long, and surrounded by a wide moat. The city has five gates – four facing the cardinal directions, and an extra one on the east side – all bearing four giant stone faces. Within the city are several ruins, the most famous of which is the Bayon, an atmospheric temple at the center of this complex.

Exploring the Complex

The fortified city of Angkor Thom is spread over an area of nearly 4 sq miles (10 sq km). Of the five gateways into the city, the most commonly used is the South Gate, from which a pathway leads straight to the Bayon temple. Beyond this lie the ruins of many other striking monuments, including Baphuon and Phimeanakas.

South Gate

The imposing South Gate is the best preserved of the five gateways into Angkor Thom. Its approach is via an impressive causeway flanked by 154 stone statues – gods on the left side, demons on the right – each carrying a giant serpent.

The South Gate itself is a massive 75-ft (23-m) high structure, surmounted by a triple tower with four gigantic stone faces facing the cardinal directions. The gate is flanked by statues of the three-headed elephant Erawan, the fabled mount of the Hindu god, Indra.

The Bayon
See pp76–7.

Massive smiling stone face gazing into the distance, South Gate

Baphuon

Believed to be one of the grandest of Angkor's temples, Baphuon was built by King Udayadityavarman II in the 11th century. A Hindu temple, its pyramidal mountain form represents Mount Meru, the mythical abode of the gods. A central tower with four entrances once stood at its summit, but has long since collapsed.

The temple is approached via a 656-ft (200-m) long raised causeway and has four gateways decorated with bas-relief scenes from Hindu epics such as the *Mahabharata* and *Ramayana* (*Reamker* in Khmer). Inside, spanning the western length of Baphuon, is a huge Reclining Buddha. Since the temple was dedicated to Hinduism, this image was probably added later, in the 15th century. The temple has undergone intensive restoration, and is now fully open to the public.

Phimeanakas

This royal temple-palace was built during the 10th century by King Rajendravarman II, and added to later by Jayavarman VII. Dedicated to Hinduism, it is also known as the Celestial Palace, and is associated with the legend of a golden tower that once stood here, and where a nine-headed serpent resided. This magical creature would appear to the king as a woman, and the king would sleep with her before going to his other wives and concubines. It was believed that if the king failed to sleep with the serpent-woman, he would die, but by sleeping with her, the royal lineage was saved.

The pyramid-shaped palace is rectangular at the base, and surrounded by a 16-ft (5-m) high wall of laterite enclosing an area of around 37 acres (15 ha). It has five entranceways, and the stairs, which are flanked by guardian lions, rise up on all four sides. There are corresponding elephant figures at each of the four corners of the pyramid. The upper terrace offers great views of the Baphuon to the south.

Preah Palilay and Tep Pranam

Two of the lesser, yet still impressive, structures at Angkor Thom, Preah Palilay and Tep Pranam are located a short distance to the northwest of the Terrace of the Leper King.

Preah Palilay dates from the 13th or 14th century and is a small Buddhist sanctuary set within a 164-ft (50-m) square laterite wall. The sanctuary, which is partially collapsed, is entered via a single gateway,

Visitors climbing the stairs leading to the top of Phimeanakas

Angkor Thom

List of Sites

① South Gate
② The Bayon
③ Baphuon
④ Phimeanakas
⑤ Preah Palilay and
Tep Pranam
⑥ Terrace of the Leper
King
⑦ Terrace of Elephants
⑧ North and South
Khleang

| 0 meters | 500 |
| 0 yards | 500 |

Key to Map

■ Area illustrated (see pp76–7)

VISITORS' CHECKLIST

Practical Information
Road map C6. **Tel** (063)-964-347.
1 mile (2 km) N of Angkor Wat; 5
miles (8 km) N of Siem Reap. **Taxi**
from Angkor Wat. 🚹 Khmer Angkor
Tour Guide Association, Siem Reap,
Open 5am–6pm daily. 🎫 1-, 3-
and 7-day passes for Angkor.

Terrace of Elephants

Built by King Jayavarman VII, this
structure is more than 950 ft
(300 m) long, stretching from
the Baphuon to the connecting
Terrace of the Leper King. It has
three main platforms and two
smaller ones. The terrace was
primarily used by the king to
view military and other parades.
It is decorated with almost life-
sized images of sandstone
elephants in a procession,
accompanied by mahouts.
There are also images of tigers,
serpents, and Garuda – mythical
beasts mounted by Vishnu.

North and South Khleang

These two essentially similar
buildings are located to the
east of the main road running
past the Terrace of Elephants.
The North Khleang was built by
King Jayavarman toward the
end of the 10th century, and
the South Khleang was constructed by King Suryavarman I
during the early 11th century.
The main architectural features
of the Khleangs are their
sandstone lintels and elegant
balustered stone windows.
Unfortunately, the original
function of the buildings is as yet
unknown. Khleang, which
means storehouse, is a modern
designation, and is considered
misleading.

and rises to a tapering stone
tower. A 108-ft (33-m) long
causeway leads to a terrace to
the east of the sanctuary, which
is distinguished by fine *naga*
(serpent) balustrades.

Nearby, to the east, lies Tep
Pranam, a Buddhist sanctuary
built in the 16th century.
This was probably originally
dedicated to the Mahayana
school. Used as a place of
Theravada worship now, it
features a big sandstone
Buddha image, seated in the
"calling the earth to witness"
mudra (posture).

Terrace of the Leper King

This small platform dates from
the late 12th century. Standing
on top of this structure is a
headless statue known as the
Leper King. Once believed to be
an image of King Jayavarman VII,
who, according to legend,
had leprosy, it is in fact a
representation of Yama, the God
of Death. This statue is, however,

Restoration in progress at the Terrace of the
Leper King

a replica – the original was
taken to Phnom Penh's National
Museum *(see p52)*.

The terrace is marked by two
walls, both beautifully restored
and decorated with exquisite
bas-reliefs. Of the two, the
inner one is more remarkable,
and is covered with figures of
underworld deities, kings, celestial
females, multiple-headed *nagas*,
devadas, *apsaras*, warriors, and
strange marine creatures.

The exact function of this
terrace, which appears to be
an extension of the Terrace of
Elephants, is not clear. It was
probably used either for royal
receptions or cremations.

Intricately carved and sculpted bas-reliefs and elephant figures, Terrace of Elephants

The Bayon

Located in the heart of Angkor Thom, the Bayon is one of the city's most extraordinary structures, epitomizing the "lost civilization" of Angkor. Shaped like a pyramid, this symbolic temple-mountain rises on three levels, and features 54 towers bearing more than 200 huge, yet enigmatic stone faces. It is entered via eight cruciform towers, linked by galleries that were once covered, and which are gradually being restored. These galleries have some of the most striking bas-reliefs found at Angkor, showcasing everyday scenes as well as images of battles, especially those against the Cham.

Row of gods lining the path to Angkor Thom's South Gate

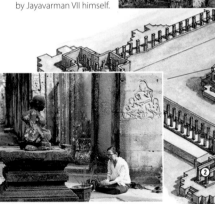

★ Enigmatic Faces
The temple's central towers are decorated with four massive, mysteriously smiling faces gazing out in the cardinal directions. These are believed to represent the all-seeing and all-knowing Bodhisattva Avalokitesvara, as personified by Jayavarman VII himself.

The Western Gallery
A statue of the Hindu god Vishnu, thought to date from the time of the founding of the temple, is installed in the southern section of the western gallery, one of the many galleries surrounding the Bayon. Devotees burn incense sticks before this statue.

KEY

① **Library**

② **South Gate**

③ **Outer Enclosure**

④ **Central Tower**

⑤ **Bas-reliefs of a Khmer circus**

⑥ **Inner Enclosure**

★ Bas-Reliefs in the Southern Gallery
Carved deep into the walls, the bas-reliefs in the southern gallery feature images from everyday life in 12th-century Angkor. These include depictions of a cockfight, meals being cooked, festival celebrations, and market scenes.

For hotels and restaurants see pp210–11 and pp223–5

★ **Southern View of the Bayon**
From a distance, the Bayon appears
to be a complicated, almost erratically
structured temple. On closer inspection,
however, its 54 majestic towers and
216 eerie stone sculptures take a more
definite shape – their architectural
grandeur inspiring the visitor with
a sense of awe.

Detail of Devada
The *devada* (dancer)
differs from the sensual
apsara and could be
either male or female.
A *devada* is portrayed
in less alluring poses.

East
Entrance

Khmer Army in Procession
The bas-reliefs in the eastern gallery
provide scenes from the struggle
between the Khmers and the Cham,
which has been recorded in
painstakingly fine detail. Here, the
Khmer king, seated on an elephant,
leads his army into battle.

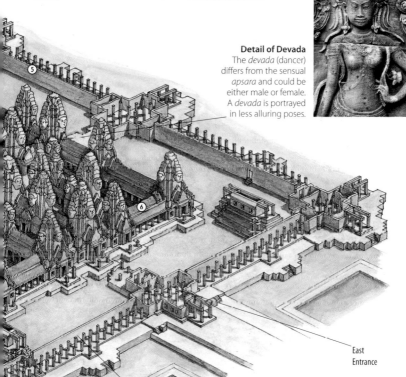

The roots of a giant banyan tree engulf part of Ta Prohm temple, Angkor ▶

Visitors waiting to see the sunset over Angkor Wat, Phnom Bakheng

➍ Phnom Bakheng

Road Map C6. 550 yards (500 m) S of Angkor Thom. **Open** dawn to dusk daily. 🗺 1-, 3- & 7-day passes for Angkor. 🗃

Famous for its sunset views of Angkor Wat, the Tonlé Sap, and the Bayon, the ancient Hindu temple of Phnom Bakheng surveys the surrounding plains from the top of a 220-ft (67-m) high hill. Built by King Yasovarman I, the Bakheng complex is one of the region's first examples of Mount Meru-style temple architecture. The complex was once surrounded by 109 towers spread around its six tiers; however, most of them have now collapsed.

➎ Preah Khan

Road Map C6. 0.5 miles (1 km) NE of Angkor Thom. **Open** dawn to dusk daily. 🗺 1-, 3- & 7-day passes for Angkor. 🗃

Named for the sacred sword owned by the 9th-century King Jayavarman II, the Preah Khan temple complex was built by Jayavarman VII (r.1181–1218). It is believed to have functioned as his temporary capital while Angkor Thom was being

restored after it was sacked by the Cham in 1177. It also served as a monastery and religious college with more than 1,000 teachers. An inscribed stone stela found here in 1939 indicates that the temple was based at the center of an ancient city, Nagarajayaciri – *jayaciri* means sword in Siamese. Originally dedicated to the Buddha, this temple was later vandalized by Hindu rulers who replaced many Buddha images on the walls with carvings of numerous Hindu deities.

Today, the complex extends over a sprawling 2 sq miles (5 sq km), and is surrounded by a 2-mile (3-km) long laterite wall. The central sanctuary is accessible through four gates set at the cardinal points. One of the main highlights is the Hall of Dancers, named for the *apsara* bas-reliefs that line the walls. The premises also has a massive *baray* (reservoir). The most notable temple in the complex is the Temple of the Four Faces. Similar to Ta Prohm *(see pp82–3)*, Preah Khan is

Statue of a hermit in prayer, Preah Khan

home to many great trees whose roots cover and, in places, pierce the laterite and sandstone structures over which they grow. Unlike Ta Prohm, however, the temple has undergone extensive restoration by the World Monuments Fund, and many of the trees have now been cut down.

➏ Preah Neak Pean

Road Map C6. 3 miles (5 km) NE of Angkor Thom. **Open** dawn to dusk daily. 🗺 1-, 3- & 7-day passes for Angkor. 🗃 🖥 🖼

This monument – a shrine dedicated to Avalokitesvara – is set within the center of a cruciform arrangement of sacred ponds. Around the shrine's base coil a couple of snakes, giving the temple its name – Entwined Serpents. Located in the now dry North Baray, the temple is built around a central artificial square pond measuring 230 ft (70 m), which is surrounded by four smaller ponds. The central pond represents the mythical Lake Anvatapta, which is located at the summit of the universe, and is responsible for giving birth to the four great curative rivers, each represented by a different gargoyle at each corner of the central pool. The east head is that of a man, the south a lion, the west a horse, and the north an elephant. When the temple was functioning, sacred water would be diverted through their mouths into the smaller pools and used to heal devotees.

Intricately detailed bas-relief of *apsaras* in the Hall of Dancers, Preah Khan

❼ East Baray

Road Map C6. 1 mile (2 km) E of
Angkor Thom. **Open** dawn to dusk
daily. 🏛 1-, 3- & 7-day passes for
Angkor. ⬛ ⬛ ⬛

The second largest of
Angkor's *barays*, East Baray
measures 4 miles by 1 mile
(6 km by 2 km), and was built
by King Yasovarman I in the
9th century. Watered by the
Stung Treng, it held nearly
13 billion gal (50 million cu m)
of water and may have been
10 ft (3 m) deep. While some
believe that its purpose was
symbolic, representing the
sea surrounding Mount Meru,
others contend its purpose was
for irrigation – with a population
of about one million, it would
have been essential to produce
three rice harvests a year.

On an island in the middle
of the *baray* is the **Oriental
Mebon** temple, built by
Rajendravarman II in honor
of his parents. Surrounded by
three laterite walls, the temple
gradually rises to a quincuncial
arrangement of towers dotted
with holes that would have

Towering lotus-shaped structures, Pre Rup

supported stucco decorations.
At ground level its stairways
are flanked by sandstone lions,
and at its corners are four well-
preserved sandstone elephants.

❽ Pre Rup

Road Map C6. 3 miles (5 km) E of
Angkor Thom. **Open** dawn to dusk
daily. 🏛 1-, 3- & 7-day passes for
Angkor. ⬛ ⬛ ⬛

Dedicated to the Hindu god
Shiva, Pre Rup has five lotus-
shaped towers. Thought to have
been a crematorium, its name
means Turning of the Body,
which relates to a religious rite
of tracing the deceased's outline
in his or her ashes.

❾ Srah Srang

Road Map C6. 3 miles (5 km) E of
Angkor Thom. **Open** dawn to dusk daily.
🏛 1-, 3- & 7-day passes for Angkor. ⬛

To the west of Pre Rup lies
the great reservoir of Srah
Srang, or Royal Bath. Built in

the 7th century and measuring
1,312 ft by 2,625 ft (400 m by
800 m), it was used exclusively by
King Jayavarman V and his wives.
On the western side of the lake is
a landing platform flanked by two
sandstone lions and balustrades
bearing a large *garuda* on the
back of a three-headed serpent.
The lake is best visited at
sunrise, when water buffalo
graze in its shallows, and local
children congregate for a swim.

❿ Banteay Kdei

Road Map C6. 3 miles (5 km) E of
Angkor Thom. **Open** dawn to dusk
daily. 🏛 1- 3- & 7-day passes for
Angkor. ⬛

Built in the late 12th century,
Banteay Kdei, meaning
Citadel of the Cells, lies west
of Srah Srang. This Buddhist
temple has four entrances,
each guarded by *garudas*.
One of the highlights of
this temple is the Hall of
Dancers, located in the
central corridor.

Picturesque view of the lake from the
landing platform, Srah Srang

Barays

Integral to Khmer architecture, the *barays* provided a
twofold function: firstly, as a religious symbol of the
Sea of Creation, and secondly, as a vital means of irrigation
to ensure a bounteous crop. The most notable reservoirs
in Angkor are the East Baray and West Baray. The latter was
built in the 11th century and covered an area of 7 sq miles
(18 sq km), making it the largest *baray* ever constructed.
With a maximum depth of 23 ft (7 m), it could contain
32 billion gal (123 million cu m) of water, and still support
several species of fish. Both reservoirs feature man-made
islands with temples.

Vast expanse of water channels, West Baray

⓫ Ta Prohm

Perhaps the most evocative and mysterious of all the temple structures at Angkor, Ta Prohm (which means Ancestor of Brahma) was a wealthy Buddhist monastery built during King Jayavarman VII's reign (r.1181–1218). During the Colonial period, the French started an archaeological restoration of the temple, making a deliberate attempt to maintain the structure as they found it, by limiting restoration and cutting down little of the surrounding dense jungle. As a result, the temple buildings remain smothered by the roots of giant banyan trees, preserving the atmosphere that 19th-century explorers must have experienced.

Bas-reliefs depicting dancing *apsaras* at the eastern entrance

Waterfall Tree
Named for the cascading appearance of its roots down the wall of the inner gallery, this strangler fig tree has encompassed its host, and dominates the temple's masonry.

★ **Face Tower**
The four stone faces on Gopura-5 are believed to represent Jayavarman VII. Seen above the west entrance, they are reminiscent of the huge faces carved into the Bayon *(see pp76–7)*.

To West Entrance ↙

KEY

① **Central Sanctuary**

② **Tomb Raider Tree**

③ **The Hall of Dancers**, located in a sandstone building, features rows of intricate *apsara* bas-reliefs.

④ **Galleries**, many of which are crumbling and not suitable for exploration, are linked by narrow passageways, and in turn connect the *prasats* of the structure.

Dinosaur Carving
A narrow stone column in the complex has ornate circles that enclose various animal reliefs. One such carving depicts what seems to be a stegosaurus. No one has been able to explain the presence of this mysterious carving.

VISITORS' CHECKLIST

Practical Information
Road map C6. **Tel** (063)-964-347.
1/2 mile (1 km) E of Angkor Thom.
Khmer Angkor Tour Guide
Association, Siem Reap, **Open**
dawn–dusk daily.
1-, 3- and 7-day passes for
Angkor.

★ Crocodile Tree
On the easternmost gopura of the central enclosure is the
strangler fig known as the Crocodile Tree. Every year its roots
spread further across the complex.

To East
Entrance

★ Tomb Raider Tree
This striking strangler fig enjoyed a
moment of screen time as Angelina Jolie
appeared from the doorway below it
in one of the most dramatic scenes
of *Lara Croft: Tomb Raider*.

Lara Croft: Tomb Raider

Long before she became half of a
Hollywood power couple, Angelina
Jolie was delighting teenagers who
played the seminal strategy game,
Tomb Raider. With her sultry looks,
passable English accent, and lithe
figure, she seemed the perfect choice
to bring the long-running video game
character to the screen. A couple of

Angelina Jolie in *Tomb Raider*

scenes in the movie were shot in Cambodia, and it is here that Jolie's global
social conscience seems to have been sparked. She remains a firm patron of
Cambodia, a UN ambassador, and a champion of children's causes.

Bas-relief of a goddess adorning a brick wall at Prasat Kravan

⓬ Prasat Kravan

Road Map C6. 2 miles (3 km) SE of Angkor Thom. **Open** dawn to dusk daily. 1-, 3- & 7-day passes for Angkor.

Dating from the 10th century, Prasat Kravan was built by high-ranking officials during the reign of Harshavarman I. It is located at a slight distance from the capital, Angkor, since only royals could build temples close to the city's center. Comprising five brick towers, it is one of the smaller temples in the Angkor complex and is dedicated to Vishnu.

The temple, whose name means Cardamom Sanctuary, after a tree that stood here, is particularly remarkable for its brickwork and bas-reliefs, the only such known examples of Khmer art. No mortar was used in its construction, only a type of vegetable compound. Partly restored in the 1960s, the bricks, added by Conservation Angkor, are marked with CA. These brick carvings represent Vishnu, his consort Lakshmi, his eagle mount (Garuda), a *naga* (serpent); and a number of other divine attendants. The doorways and lintels of all five towers are made of sandstone. The southernmost tower has a fine image of Vishnu riding his eagle mount, while the northernmost tower has an image of Lakshmi. The central tower has a raised stone that was used to receive water for purification rites.

⓭ Banteay Srei

Road Map C6. 20 miles (32 km) N of Siem Reap. **Open** dawn to dusk daily. 1-, 3- & 7-day passes for Angkor.

Located at the foot of the Kulen Mountain, the remote temple complex of Banteay Srei, meaning Citadel of Beauty, is ornamented with exquisitely detailed carvings. Executed in pink sandstone, the complex was built in the second half of the 10th century by Yajnavaraha, one of King Rajendravarman's counselors and the future guru of King Jayavarman V. Therefore, unlike most other monuments in Angkor, it is not a royal temple. Granted land along the Stung Siem Reap, Yajnavaraha commissioned the temple to be built here. What separates this miniature scaled temple from so many others in Angkor is the fact that most of its surface area has been elaborately decorated; little wonder that it is often described as the jewel of Khmer art.

Discovered in 1914, four of its *apsaras* were famously snatched by the future French minister of culture, Andre Malraux – who served under President Charles De Gaulle – in 1923. The statues were recovered and returned soon after.

Rectangular in shape, and enclosed by three walls and the

Ancient statue in Banteay Srei

remains of a moat, the central sanctuary contains ornate shrines dedicated to Shiva. The intricately carved lintels reproduce scenes from the Hindu epic, *Ramayana*. Representations of Shiva, his consort Parvati, the Monkey God – Hanuman, the divine cowherd – Krishna, and the Demon King – Ravana are all beautifully etched. Also exceptional are the elaborate and finely detailed figures of gods and goddesses carved into the niches of the towers in the central sanctuary. The male divinities carry lances and wear simple loincloths. By contrast, the goddesses, with their long hair tied in buns or plaits, are dressed in loosely draped traditional skirts, and almost every inch of their bodies is laden with gorgeous jewelry.

⓮ Roluos Group

Road Map C6. 7 miles (12 km) SE of Siem Reap. **Open** dawn to dusk daily. 1, 3- & 7-day passes for Angkor.

The Roluos Group, a group of the earliest temple monuments to have been built in the Angkor region, borrows its name from the small town of Roluos, 8 miles (13 km) east of Siem Reap. The temples mark the site of Hariharalaya, the first Khmer

View of the red sandstone entrance, Banteay Srei

capital established by Indravarman I (r.877–89). Three main complexes can be found here. To the north of Highway 6, en route to Phnom Penh from Siem Reap, is **Lolei**. Founded by Yasovarman I (r.889–910), this temple stands on an artificial mound in the middle of a small reservoir, and is based on a double platform surrounded by a laterite wall. The four central brick towers have surprisingly well-preserved false doors and inscriptions.

To the south of Lolei stands **Preah Ko**, meaning the Sacred Bull. Built by Indravarman I, to honor his parents as well as Jayavarman II (the founder of the Khmer Empire), this temple was dedicated to the worship of

A well-preserved, carved lintel and lion statue at Bakong, Roluos Group

Figures and lintels carved out of sandstone at Lolei, Roluos Group

Shiva. The main sanctuary consists of six brick towers resting on a raised laterite platform. Close by are three statues of the sacred bull Nandi, for whom the temple was named, which are in a remarkably good condition. The motifs on the lintels, false doors, and columns are also well preserved. They include *kala* (mythical creatures with grinning mouths and large bulging eyes), *makara*, (sea creatures with trunk-like snouts), and Garuda. The temple sits resplendent in its serene rural setting.

Beyond Preah Ko, the huge mass of **Bakong**, by far the largest of the Roluos Group, is well worth a visit. Originally dedicated to Shiva in AD 881,

the temple has since become a place of worship for Buddhists. More than 1,000 years ago, it was the central feature of Hariharalaya, as a temple-mountain representing Mount Meru, the mythical abode of the gods. Approached by a pathway that is protected by a seven-headed *naga*, and flanked by guesthouses for pilgrims, the mount rises in four stages, the first three of which are flanked by stone elephants at the corners. At the summit rests the square central sanctuary, with four levels and a lotus-shaped tower rising from the middle. The mount is surrounded by eight massive brick towers that feature finely carved sandstone decorations.

Motifs of the Temple-Mountains

Life in the great kingdom of Angkor revolved around religion. Hinduism brought with it two cults – those of Vishnu and Shiva. The god-kings of Angkor sought to symbolize and re-create Mount Meru (*see p70*) with their temple-mountains. They decorated these temples with a rich medley of legends, symbols, and motifs, which can be found in almost all the temples of the period.

The lotus was considered an agent of purification.

Nandi, the sacred bull, is the mount of Shiva and is his principal devotee.

Apsaras are celestial dancing girls commonly found on bas-reliefs in Angkorian temples.

The flame motif, often seen near sacred steps and doorways, was intended to purify those who entered the temple precincts.

Garuda, Vishnu's eagle mount, the mythical half-man half-bird, is the nemesis of the *naga*.

Asuras, or demons, feature in representations of the Churning of the Ocean of Milk bas-reliefs.

Painted storks nesting among the trees, Prek Toal Bird Sanctuary

⓯ Chong Kneas

Road Map C6. 9 miles (15 km) S of Siem Reap. 🚌 🚤 *i* Gecko Environment Center (063)-832-812. **Open** dawn to dusk daily. 🖥 **jinja.apsara.org/gecko** 🖉 🖉 🖻 🖼

By far the most accessible floating village from Siem Reap *(see pp68–9)*, and the most commercial, Chong Kneas is typical of the villages found on the Tonlé Sap Lake. Inhabited by a mix of Vietnamese and Khmer people, this atmospheric settlement can be reached either by road from Siem Reap or by boat. The road trip, passing lush paddy fields and an ancient temple atop Phnom Krom, takes about 30 minutes from the town center. Although less intriguing than the Kompong Khleang, Chong Kneas is worth a visit for its floating market, clinic, catfish farm, school, and

restaurants. Also an exciting highlight is the Gecko Environment Center's educating exhibition on the ecology and problems relating to the management of the Tonlé Sap's biodiversity. Boats to Chong Kneas and other distant villages can be hired from Siem Reap, but prices are usually quite high.

Passenger ferry, Chong Kneas

⓰ Prek Toal Bird Sanctuary

Road Map C6. 19 miles (31 km) S of Siem Reap. 🚤 from Chong Kneas. **Open** dawn to dusk daily. 🖉 🖉

Widely regarded as the most important breeding ground for large waterbirds in Southeast Asia, Prek Toal Bird Sanctuary covers 120 sq miles (311 sq km) on the northwestern tip of the Tonlé Sap Lake. Of the three designated biospheres on the lake, Prek Toal is the best known, and is easily accessible from Siem Reap. The seasonally flooded forest abounds with numerous endangered birds, such as the lesser and greater adjutants, milky and painted storks, black-headed ibis, spot-billed pelican, and gray-headed fish eagle. An ideal day trip for ornithologists and wildlife enthusiasts, Prek Toal is best visited during the dry season (Feb–Apr) – the time when migratory birds congregate in this preserve in large numbers.

Visiting the sanctuary can be an expensive expedition, although the price includes transport to and on the lake, entrance to the biosphere, meals, and guided tours. Trips can be arranged usually through a guesthouse or a tour operator. Visitors can also make their own arrangements, which would include hiring a taxi to the Chong Kneas dock, from where a boat to the Prek Toal Environmental Research Station can be hired. Those keen on witnessing the spectacular sunrises and sunsets can stay overnight at the research station, although they will have to pay for accommodations and food.

Locals ferrying goods to and fro at the floating market, Chong Kneas

Lake Ecosystem

Situated in the very heart of the country, the dumb-bell shaped Tonlé Sap is Cambodia's most prominent feature, and the largest freshwater lake in Southeast Asia. During the dry season, the lake withers to a diminutive 965 sq miles (2,500 sq km), but when the monsoon arrives it swells to a colossal 4,633 sq miles (12,000 sq km). The lake's ecosystem supports the surrounding floodplain with more than 200 species of fish, several types of waterbirds, and reptiles such as crocodiles and turtles. Thousands of fishermen and their families live in floating villages dotted around the lake. The Tonlé Sap provides Cambodia with more than half of its annual supply of fish.

Picturesque stilted pagoda and houses, Kompong Khleang

One of the floating villages, Tonlé Sap Lake

⑰ Kompong Phhluk

Road Map C6. 10 miles (16 km) SE of Siem Reap. 🚌 from Chong Kneas. **Open** dawn to dusk daily. 🛢 🖼 📷

The atmospheric journey through the wetlands of the Tonlé Sap Lake to reach this village on stilts is a memorable experience. With its floating tethered animal pens, pagoda, fishermen, and gentle pace of life, Kompong Phhluk offers an authentic insight into life on the great lake. Visitors can take in the activities of a typical village – local women selling vegetables on the decks of long-tail boats and school children returning home with the aid of a paddle and boat. Tired sightseers can stop for refreshments at a stilted restaurant that serves local food. It is also possible to visit the vast blue of the Tonlé Sap Lake on a boat, and follow up with a swim in the gnarled, flooded forest – an eerie but exhilarating experience because swimmers must wade through inky darkness. Alternatively, visitors can go out on to the lake in a canoe on their own. The village can be reached either from Roluos, 3 miles (5 km) to the north, or Chong Kneas, although it is easier to take an organized tour.

⑱ Kompong Khleang

Road Map C6. 22 miles (35 km) E of Siem Reap. 🏛 20,000. 🚌 from Chong Kneas. **Taxi** from Dam Dek. **Open** dawn to dusk daily.

Despite being the largest floating settlement on the Tonlé Sap Lake, Kompong Khleang receives only a small number of visitors, giving those who venture here an authentic experience of waterside living. In the wet season, the water levels of the lake swell to within a few feet of the 33-ft (20-m) high houses on stilts, before receding back into the marshy ground.

Similar to Kompong Phhluk, Kompong Khleang is a permanent community, its economy wholly dependent on fishing. In several ways, however, this floating village is even more astounding than Kompong Phhluk – everything floats here, from the school to the general store. Even the pharmacy and the petrol station are afloat.

An island situated in the center of the village has a small, brightly painted pagoda with a macabre depiction of heaven and hell. There is also a flooded forest located next to the village. Kompong Khleang can usually be reached by boat from Chong Kneas. During the dry season, however, visitors are advised to hire a taxi, or moto, from nearby Dam Dek.

Visitors taking a tour of the flooded forest, Kompong Phhluk

NORTHERN CAMBODIA

The geographically diverse and remote region of Northern Cambodia shares borders with Thailand to the north and Laos to the northeast. Today, improved highways enable visitors to reach previously unexplored regions. From the spectacular UNESCO-protected temple of Prasat Preah Vihear to the endangered Irrawaddy dolphin in Kratie, a visit to the north will delight any traveler.

The earliest known evidence of human settlement in the region dates back to 4300 BC, when hunter-gatherers inhabited caves in the northwest. Between the 6th and 7th centuries, Chenla rulers built several temples in the region. Northern Cambodia was overrun by invading Thai forces on numerous occasions during the 16th and 17th centuries. The Thai armies used the region as a gateway to the rest of the country in their quest to pillage the Khmer Empire. In the late 18th century, parts of the northwest were annexed by the Thais, and finally returned to Cambodia in 1946. In the 20th century, Khmer Rouge forces passed through the region as they retreated north from Phnom Penh, ahead of the Vietnamese Army.

Battambang, the country's second-largest city, is fast emerging as a popular tourist destination. Known for producing the nation's finest rice and oranges, the city also has crumbling French Colonial villas, shophouses, and a riverfront promenade. The nearby ruins of Wat Banan and Banteay Chhmer make for excellent day trips.

The remote northeastern provinces of Ratanakiri and Mondulkiri, where tourism is still in its infancy, receive few visitors. However, both have many ethnic minority villages, scattered wild elephants, waterfalls, and beautiful grassy landscapes. Yaek Lom Lake, a beautiful crater lake with inviting verdigris water, is a perfect picnic spot.

The northeast has a few excellent ecolodges and eco-trekking organizations, while farther south the town of Kratie is renowned for its sunsets and the Irrawaddy dolphin. The temple ruins of Sambor Prei Kuk and Koh Ker are well worth a visit. The region is also known for its stone handicrafts, and silk items such as *kramas* (scarves) and shirts.

Rich woodlands bordering the Mekong River on the sandbar island of Koh Trong, Kratie

◄ Ancient ruins of Sambor Prei Kuk temple, Kompong Thom province

Exploring Northern Cambodia

Although some provincial roads in Northern Cambodia remain dusty and unpaved in parts, the region's natural beauty more than makes up for this drawback. The city of Battambang, renowned for its unique, one-track bamboo train, can be reached by improved highways or via a picturesque boat ride from Siem Reap. The temple ruins of Prasat Preah Vihear, Koh Ker, and Sambor Prei Kuk make for interesting diversions, while the province of Kompong Thom, with its emerald paddy fields, is home to the unusual Phnom Santuk and the Santuk Silk Farm. A visit to the far-flung provinces of Ratanakiri and Mondulkiri, which offer rolling hills, volcanic lakes, and lush green forests, is also a rewarding experience.

A statue of Buddha carved into rock, Phnom Santuk

Jungle-covered ruins of Koh Ker

Getting Around

Traveling in the north can be difficult, particularly in the northeast. It is best to avoid visiting this region during the rainy season since safe road conditions can never be guaranteed. However, in the northwest, highways have improved dramatically. Taxis and tuk-tuks can be hired to reach sights that are off the beaten track. Ferries and riverboats ply rivers such as the Stung Sangker and Mekong. Dirt-bike tours are gaining popularity in the north and are a great way to tackle demanding roads.

For hotels and restaurants see pp211–12 and pp225–6

Sights at a Glance

Towns and Cities
- **1** Battambang
- **6** Choob
- **12** Kompong Thom
- **16** Kompong Cham
- **17** Kratie
- **18** Stung Treng
- **19** Ban Lung
- **21** Sen Monorom

Sites of Interest
- **15** Santuk Silk Farm

Places of Worship
- **3** Wat Ek Phnom
- **4** Wat Banan
- **14** Phnom Santuk

Historical Sites
- **2** Killing Caves of Phnom Sampeau
- **5** Kamping Poy
- **8** Banteay Chhmer
- **9** Banteay Tuop

- **10** *Prasat Preah Vihear pp96–7*
- **11** Koh Ker
- **13** Sambor Prei Kuk

National Parks and Preserves
- **7** Ang Trapeng Thmor Reserve

Areas of Natural Beauty
- **20** Yaek Lom Lake
- **22** Bonsraa Waterfall

Key

- —— Major road
- —— Minor road
- === Untarred road
- – – Dirt track
- ==== Railway line
- ▬▬ International border
- — Provincial border
- △ Peak

| 0 km | 50 |
| 0 miles | 50 |

A row of French Colonial shophouses, Battambang

For keys to symbols *see back flap*

❶ Battambang

Road Map C6.180 miles (290 km) NW of Phnom Penh. 140,000.

Cambodia's second largest city and a provincial capital, Battambang lies a short distance southwest of the Tonlé Sap Lake. Sitting by the Stung Sangker and surrounded by beautiful, verdant countryside, the city has been under Thai influence for much of its history, and was not returned to Cambodia until 1907.

The impact of the French Colonial administration on the city is evident from the number of Colonial villas and shophouses still surviving today, hidden down side streets and by the riverside. In the center of town stands Psar Nath, a sprawling mustard-hued Art Deco market that was built in 1936 and is well worth a visit. The most charming area of the city is by the river, south of this bustling market. The **Battambang Provincial Museum** located here houses an eclectic Angkorian and pre-Angkorian collection of statuary, pottery, and traditional musical instruments. Battambang is only now finding an identity as a tourist destination, with a number of excellent cafés and Colonial-style hotels starting to open for business. The natural beauty of the rural countryside surrounding the city must not be missed.

A row of statues at the Provincial Museum, Battambang

Environs

One mile (2 km) northwest of the city, **Phare Ponleu Selpak** is a multi-arts center for orphans and disadvantaged children. A visit to its circus school offers a glimpse into the salvaged lives of these children, many of whom become performers with the troupe. Evening performances take place five times a week.

🏛 **Battambang Provincial Museum**
St 1, Kamkor Village, Svay Por Commune. **Tel** (053)-730-007. **Open** 8–11am & 2–5pm Mon–Fri.

Phare Ponleu Selpak
NH5, Anhchanh Village, O'Char Commune. **Tel** (053)-952-424.
Ⓦ phareps.org

French Colonial buildings on the riverfront, Battambang

Battambang's Bamboo Trains

Noris (bamboo trains) are indigenous to Battambang province and seem to have developed in response to a lack of local public transport. A cheap and effective way for locals to travel, they were created from flatbed mine sweepers that were used in the Civil War of the 1970s. *Noris* have no brakes and are assembled on the track, which is often warped. It is worth traveling by these trains for the experience.

A bamboo platform is mounted on a steel frame with wheels a few inches from the track, making up the train's structure. Power is supplied from a motorcycle engine and belt drive housed at the rear axle.

Running on a single track, the bamboo trains are ideal for transporting produce and livestock. When trains heading in opposite directions meet, the one with the lighter load is removed to let the other pass.

❷ Killing Caves of Phnom Sampeau

Road Map B6. 7 miles (11 km) SW of Battambang. **Open** dawn to dusk daily.

Halfway up Phnom Sampeau – a hill with several temples at its summit – and belying a peaceful rural scene, the Killing Caves of Phnom Sampeau tell yet another brutal tale of the atrocities perpetrated by the Khmer Rouge. The caves bore witness to the cruelty of the regime, during which victims were bludgeoned to death before being thrown from a skylight in the roof of the cave. There was one cave for male victims and another for women. The largest cavern is festooned with the victims' clothes. A glass memorial located in the cave displays the bones and skulls of the deceased. Next to it is a statue of a golden Reclining Buddha. Nowadays, local children hang around the base of Phnom Sampeau hoping to show visitors around the caves and summit in exchange for a small tip.

❸ Wat Ek Phnom

Road Map C6. 7 miles (11 km) N of Battambang. **Open** dawn to dusk daily.

The journey to Wat Ek Phnom takes visitors through dense forest, lush rice fields, and bucolic villages dotted with houses where rice paper (used to wrap spring rolls) is made. After it is made, the circular paper is dried on mesh boards

Carving depicting the Churning of the Ocean of Milk, Wat Ek Phnom

in the sun. Built in the 11th century, during the reign of King Suryavarman, this partially collapsed Angkorian temple comprises finely carved *prasats* (towers) mounted on a platform. The root-strangled ruins have been looted, although the lintel above the eastern entrance to the central tower has survived. It depicts the Churning of the Ocean of Milk by the gods and *asuras* (demons), a Hindu myth (*see p96*).

Close to the temple is a small, peaceful pond that is covered with lily pads. There are several large trees providing shade around the ruins, with a number of alfresco cafés that make for an excellent lunch venue. Opposite Wat Ek Phnom is a modern pagoda of the same name.

Reclining Buddha and glass memorial, Phnom Sampeau

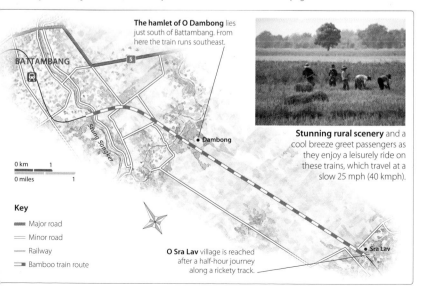

The hamlet of O Dambong lies just south of Battambang. From here the train runs southeast.

BATTAMBANG

Stung Sangker

● Dambong

0 km 1

0 miles 1

Stunning rural scenery and a cool breeze greet passengers as they enjoy a leisurely ride on these trains, which travel at a slow 25 mph (40 kmph).

O Sra Lav village is reached after a half-hour journey along a rickety track.

● Sra Lav

Key

▬▬ Major road

═══ Minor road

—— Railway

▭▭ Bamboo train route

Crumbling ruins of Wat Banan, resembling the layout of Angkor Wat

❹ Wat Banan

Road Map C6. 17 miles (27 km) S of Battambang. **Open** dawn to dusk daily. 🐾 🚗 🖥

Reminiscent of Angkor Wat in terms of layout, this mountain-top temple on Phnom Banan is reached by a flight of 358 steps. Flanked by *naga* balustrades, the stone steps lead to five 11th-century *prasats*, which, despite having been looted in the past, are mostly upright. The views from the top are some of the best in the province, and thirsty visitors can buy drinks from vendors at the summit. Local children often trade hand fans in exchange for a tip.

From the temple, visitors can descend a narrow staircase to explore a group of three caves, with the help of local guides. Flashlights are essential since the caves are very dark. Visitors must be warned that one of the caves is still unmined and not safe to enter. The caves can also be quite a tight squeeze.

❺ Kamping Poy

Road Map B6. 17 miles (27 km) W of Battambang. **Open** dawn to dusk daily.

Yet another poignant reminder of the brutal Khmer Rouge, Kamping Poy, also known as Killing Dam, stretches for some 5 miles (8 km) between two hills. More than 10,000 people, forced into slavery under the regime, lost their lives from malnutrition and execution, building what is now a largely worthless dam. It is believed that the dam was built in an attempt to re-create the irrigation system of ancient Angkor, although the scheme proved to be a failure. Today, there is nothing left of the site except for the sluice gates. The dam is now used by locals as a picnic spot. Visitors can hire a boat, rowed by local boys, to the middle of the lake, but prices can often be exorbitant.

❻ Choob

Road Map C6. 55 miles (89 km) W of Siem Reap. 🏔 5,000.

Located toward the northwestern border with Thailand, the small village of Choob is worth a visit for its renowned sculptors, who sit by the roadside with their wares. Choob's sculptors are celebrated throughout the country for their craftsmanship and are often commissioned by temples to make huge, elaborate sandstone statues that can take months to complete. The village is a great place in which to buy magnificent souvenirs such as miniatures of *apsaras* or myriad statues of the Buddha.

Stone carving, Choob

❼ Ang Trapeng Thmor Reserve

Road Map C6. 62 miles (100 km) NW of Siem Reap. **Tel** (012)-520-828. **Open** dawn to dusk daily. 🐾
🌐 samveasna.org

Based around a water storage reservoir – built in 1976 by slave labor under the control of the Khmer Rogue – this wetland bird

Azure waters ideal for a boat trip, Kamping Poy

For hotels and restaurants see pp211–12 and pp225–6

sanctuary occupies 19 sq miles (49 sq km). A mixture of grassland, forests, and paddy fields, the area was officially declared a Sarus Crane Reserve by royal decree in 2000. The sarus crane is an extremely rare and elegant bird depicted on bas-reliefs at the Bayon *(see pp76–7)*. Besides being a feeding ground for 300 sarus cranes, Ang Trapeng has more than 200 other species of birds, 18 of which have been classified as globally threatened. In addition to the birds, visitors may chance upon the large fruit bats that inhabit semi-submerged trees on the edge of the reservoir. The very fortunate may also see the rare eld's deer.

It is possible to tour the reserve on a boat, but visitors must first register at the Wildlife Conservation Society Office in the adjacent village. While most people visit the reserve on a day trip from Siem Reap, overnight stays can also be organized through the Sam Veasna Center in Siem Reap.

Delicate stone carving on a wall, Banteay Chhmer

❽ Banteay Chhmer

Road Map C5. 80 miles (130 km) N of Battambang. **Open** dawn to dusk daily. 🚌 📷

Across a causeway, through a tumbledown gate, lies one of the largest and most mysterious complexes of the Angkor period. Banteay Chhmer, along with its satellite shrines and vast *baray* (reservoir), was constructed in the late 12th century during the reign of Jayavarman VII. Like the

Landmine Alert

Landmine danger sign

Along with neighboring Laos, Cambodia is one of the most heavily mined places in the world. According to some estimates, the country has between 4 and 10 million mines. Unexploded Ordnance (UXO) from aerial bombs dropped by the US during the late 1960s and early 1970s poses further danger. With China's demand for scrap metal, impoverished and uneducated Khmers often take unnecessary risks to earn a few extra dollars by excavating these "sleeping" bombs. As a result, some 40,000 Khmers, many of them children, live as amputees today. However, only certain areas of the country are affected, with 70 percent of accidents occurring in the northwest (the last refuge of the Khmer Rouge forces). Since 1999, after the last fires of Khmer Rouge resistance were extinguished, no more mines have been laid. That same year, Cambodia ratified the Mine Ban Treaty.

Buddhist-influenced Bayon, it features the enigmatic faces of Avalokitesvara and is well-known for the intricacy of its carvings. However, unlike the Bayon, Banteay Chhmer is rarely overrun with visitors, giving those who do come here a very different temple experience. Often, except for a few families who live and farm around these overgrown ruins, there is no one else here.

The temple complex is surrounded by two moats, with the outer moat measuring 1 mile (2 km) on each side. These moats are now dry and have been converted into rice paddies by local farmers. The complex also has several ceremonial walkways, collapsed towers, and courtyards, typical of other Angkorian structures. Among the highlights are the vast bas-reliefs on the outer walls, depicting life 900 years ago – including processions of elephants and scenes of conflict with neighboring Champa. Visitors can arrange for homestays with the locals, which gives them a chance to admire the temple at sunrise and sunset.

❾ Banteay Tuop

Road Map B5. 74 miles (121 km) N of Battambang. **Open** dawn to dusk daily. 📷

Built in the 12th century, about the same time as Banteay Chhmer 6 miles (9 km) to the north, Banteay Tuop (or Army

View of *prasats* rising above the paddy fields, Banteay Tuop

Fortress) is believed to have been a tribute to the army of King Jayavarman VII after it defeated the Cham. Originally adorned with five *prasats*, the complex now has only four because one collapsed after looting by petty thieves. The remaining towers, however, are in good condition, and some of them feature timber from the 12th century.

Transport to Banteay Tuop can be problematic because there are no local buses. Visitors traveling from Banteay Chhmer can ask for a *moto* ride from the market – the round trip takes about two hours. Hired taxis are also available for the trip. Banteay Tuop is best visited at dusk; sunsets here are particularly spectacular.

⑩ Prasat Preah Vihear

Set high on a cliff in the Dangkrek Mountains, close to the Cambodia-Thai border, Prasat Preah Vihear, or Sacred Shrine, enjoys the most spectacular setting of any ancient Khmer temple. Offering breathtaking views across the lush green plains below, this UNESCO World Heritage Site is believed to have been built on the site of a 9th-century sanctuary dedicated to Shiva, the Hindu God of Destruction. The greater part of the complex was constructed during the reigns of King Surayavarman I (r.1002–50) and Surayavarman II (r.1113–50), the great builder of Angkor Wat. The earliest surviving parts of the temple, however, date from the 10th century. Following the decline of Hindu worship in the Khmer Empire, the temple was dedicated to Buddhism.

Monumental Stairway
A steep stone staircase, the Monumental Stairway comprises 162 steps rising 394 ft (120 m) to the First causeway of Nagas.

To Second Gopura

★ Churning of the Ocean of Milk
At the northern entrance to the third *gopura* is a bas-relief that portrays the Hindu myth of creation, depicting Vishnu creating the Universe.

Upper Level
This level comprises the impressive third and fourth gopuras, and a causeway lined with nagas (serpents) leading to the Central Shrine, which is flanked by galleries offering superb views over the temple complex and the plains far below.

KEY

① **Second causeway of Nagas**

② **Bas-relief of Yama,** the God of Death, riding a buffalo and resting on Kala, the Demon of Time.

③ **The Third Gopura** is an imposing cruciform-shaped structure.

④ **The East Gallery** offers great views over the Cambodian plains below.

⑤ **The West Gallery** is believed to have functioned as a scriptural library.

A Question of Ownership

Long claimed by both Thailand and Cambodia, Prasat Preah Vihear was finally declared Cambodian property by the International Court of Justice in 1962. Despite this, many Thais argue that the decision was unjustified and impractical – Preah Vihear was difficult to access from Cambodia, though now access from either side is via a smooth, surfaced highway. The dispute flared up again after UNESCO declared the temple a World Heritage Site in 2008. Gunfire in the recent past reportedly damaged more than 60 stones of the complex. Occasional skirmishes still occur. Investigate the current status before visiting, and be aware of the risks.

Cambodian soldiers guarding the complex

First Gopura
The lintels, crenellated stone eaves, and square pillars of the First *Gopura* (gateway tower) are in relatively good condition. In the past, it was a resting place for pilgrims.

VISITORS' CHECKLIST

Practical Information
Roas map C5. 162 miles (260 km) NW of Kompong Thom.
Open 8am–4pm daily.

Transport
Taxi from Tbeng Meanchey, then moto.

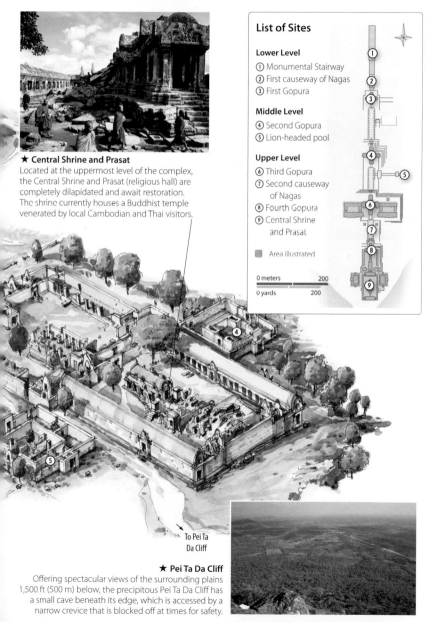

★ Central Shrine and Prasat
Located at the uppermost level of the complex, the Central Shrine and Prasat (religious hall) are completely dilapidated and await restoration. The shrine currently houses a Buddhist temple venerated by local Cambodian and Thai visitors.

List of Sites

Lower Level
① Monumental Stairway
② First causeway of Nagas
③ First Gopura

Middle Level
④ Second Gopura
⑤ Lion-headed pool

Upper Level
⑥ Third Gopura
⑦ Second causeway of Nagas
⑧ Fourth Gopura
⑨ Central Shrine and Prasat

☐ Area illustrated

0 meters   200
0 yards   200

To Pei Ta Da Cliff

★ Pei Ta Da Cliff
Offering spectacular views of the surrounding plains 1,500 ft (500 m) below, the precipitous Pei Ta Da Cliff has a small cave beneath its edge, which is accessed by a narrow crevice that is blocked off at times for safety.

Floating homes on the tranquil Tonlé Sap Lake ▶

Impressive seven-tiered pyramid of Prasat Thom rising out of a clearing in the jungle, Koh Ker

⓫ Koh Ker

Road Map C6. 81 miles (130 km) NE of Siem Reap. **Open** dawn to dusk daily. 🅿

Hidden in the forests of Preah Vihear province, enigmatic Koh Ker is finally on the visitor map thanks to improved roads and mine clearance. It was built during the reign of King Jayavarman IV (r.928–42), who had moved the capital of Angkor here for a brief period. Not long ago, it was one of the most inaccessible and heavily mined Angkorian temples. Today, visitors can safely reach and explore these ruins on a day trip from Siem Reap.

The complex has more than 100 temples with 42 significant structures. The most impressive of these is Prasat Thom, a 131-ft (40-m) high, 180-ft (55-m) wide, seven-tiered sandstone pyramid. Complete with a steep central stairway, it offers dramatic views of the Kulen Mountain and the Dangkrek Mountains to the southwest and northwest, respectively. A giant *garuda* (a mythical beast that is half-man, half-bird) statue sits atop the summit. To the southwest of Prasat Thom lies the huge Rahal Baray, into which the Stung Sen has been diverted to irrigate Koh Ker. Prasat Krahom, the second largest temple in the complex, is notable for its graceful lintel carvings, and its *naga*-flanked causeway. Also of interest are the temples Prasat Thneng and Prasat Leung, both of which lay

claim to the largest *Shiva lingas* (phallic-like shapes used to represent Shiva) in Cambodia. The complex is best visited as part of an organized tour from Siem Reap. The site is patrolled and maintained by the Apsara Authority's Community Heritage Patrol.

⓬ Kompong Thom

Road Map D6. 93 miles (150 km) SE of Siem Reap. 🚌 🚉 66,000. 🛈 Prachea Thepatay St. 🏠 daily.

Situated at the heart of Cambodia along the banks of the Stung Sen, this busy artery town enjoys trade from the traffic en route to Siem Reap or Phnom Penh. Its original name was Kompong Pos Thom, derived from *posthom* meaning two snakes who, according to legend, lived in a cave here and were worshiped by the local Buddhist population. The cave's location has since been

forgotten; however, relics of the recent past, namely the pre-Angkorian temple monuments of Sambor Prei Kuk, are increasingly drawing more visitors to this town, as is the quirky mountain temple of Phnom Santuk. The countryside surrounding Kompong Thom is picturesque, with buffalo lazing in roadside pools, and villagers riding their livestock-drawn carts across their farmlands. Visitors should look out for the home-made effigies outside houses, which are believed to ward off evil spirits.

⓭ Sambor Prei Kuk

Road Map D6. 19 miles (31 km) NE of Kompong Thom. **Taxi** from Kompong Thom. 🚗 🅿 ♿ limited access. 🖉 🖵 📷

Located east of the Tonlé Sap Lake in Kompong Thom province, this 7th-century complex of temples was

Ancient ruins of Preah Yeay Poun, Sambor Prei Kuk

constructed during the reign of King Isanavarman I in the Chenla period (see p39). Spread over a large area of semi-cleared jungle, the ruins are all that remain of the ancient capital of Isanapura. There are three main complexes here – Preah Sambor (North Group), Preah Tor (Central Group), and Preah Yeay Poun (South Group). The sun-dappled, rectangular-shaped Lion Temple, guarded by a lion at its entrance, is one of the highlights of these ruins.

Unique to Sambor Prei Kuk are its many octagon-shaped prasats (towers). Despite being choked by the roots of strangler fig trees, some of these towers are in excellent condition, with lintels, columns, and pilasters displaying intricate carvings. Large bas-reliefs rendered in brick also represent some of the earliest attempts in this style – amazingly, Sambor Prei Kuk was pioneering new forms of artistry 150 years before the mighty Angkor. Visitors can hire trained guides, who can be found near the café, to show them around the ruins for a fee. School children often try and tag along to practice their English. A cursory walk through the ruins will take about an hour. Given the low volume of foot traffic, and the welcome shade provided by the forest, these are rewarding and atmospheric ruins to visit, and can easily be covered in a day trip from Siem Reap.

Woman spinning raw silk into thread, Santuk Silk Farm

jungle and past a resident colony of macaques. The complex at the summit has a gilded, white-walled central temple. A number of Buddha statues have been carved into the rock face, including a few Reclining Buddhas, all of which are over 33 ft (10 m) in length. Various interconnecting cement bridges between small shrines, statues of horses and deities, and a sculpture workshop add to the appeal of the place. There is also an active monastery whose friendly monks like to chat with visitors.

Lion guardian, Sambor Prei Kuk

The views from the summit are stupendous and are a welcome change from the infinite flatness of the lush rice plains. It is recommended that visitors take regular breaks and carry plenty of water should they decide to walk up the road.

⓯ Santuk Silk Farm

Road Map D6. Hwy 6. 11 miles (18 km) SE of Kompong Thom. **Tel** (012)-906-604. **Open** 7–11am & 1–5pm Mon–Sat. 🎨 ♿ 📷

Just outside the village of Kakaoh, and opposite the start of the road that leads to Phnom Santuk, is the Santuk Silk Farm run by ex-Vietnam War veteran Bud Gibbons, and his wife. Visitors can view the various life stages of the silkworm – from egg to caterpillar to cocoon. Cocoons provide the base for the thread, which is then spun and woven into attractive kramas (scarves) by 15 local girls housed in a cooperative on site. The kramas can be bought from a shop on the farm. Several mulberry trees dot the farm, the leaves of which are fed to the silkworms. Lunch can be provided, but the organizers need to be informed in advance.

⓮ Phnom Santuk

Road Map D6. 11 miles (18 km) E of Kompong Thom. **Taxi** from Kompong Thom. **Open** dawn to dusk daily.

Rising to a height of 679 ft (207 m) above lush paddy fields, Phnom Santuk is the most sacred mountain in Kompong Thom province. It is approached via a stone pathway of 809 steps, flanked by gaudily rendered statues, and a number of fairly insistent beggars. Alternatively, visitors can drive up a steep road that snakes through thick

Reclining Buddha carved out of rock, Phnom Santuk

Sandstone and laterite ruins of Wat Nokor, Kompong Cham

⓰ Kompong Cham

Road Map D7. 75 miles (120 km) NE of Phnom Penh. 🚗 1,915,000. 🚌 from Phnom Penh. 🚤 🚤 **Taxi** from Phnom Penh. 🚤 daily.

Sitting on the west bank of the Mekong River, the city of Kampong Cham takes its name from the exiled Cham people who, pursued by the Vietnamese, settled here in the 17th century. Although it is Cambodia's third largest city, capital of its most populous province, and something of a transport hub for the rest of the northeast, Kompong Cham retains a small-town appeal. The city has a number of run-down French Colonial buildings, and the design of the city's grid system has a Gallic feel, with wide boulevards, statue-dotted squares, and a pleasant riverside promenade. By night, the city's streets glow with ornate lampposts and illuminated fountains. The 12th-century Wat Nokor, 1 mile (2 km) west of the city center is an interesting site.

Environs

Located 12 miles (19 km) north of town, the 6th-century **Han Chey** temple is a remnant of Angkorian architecture.

⓱ Kratie

Road Map D6. 43 miles (70 km) NE of Kompong Cham. 🚗 79,000. 🚌 🚤 🚤 daily.

Once an isolated backwater and only navigable by boat, Kratie now enjoys decent road links with the Lao border, Kompong Cham, Stung Treng, and Phnom Penh, making it a major crossroad both for foreigners and local trade. However, this Mekong-bordered town, formerly administered by the French, is still a sleepy place with a thriving local *psar* (market), a handful of dilapidated Indochinese villas that were spared US bombing, and an easy riverside atmosphere. Once a Khmer Rouge stronghold, it is now renowned for its beautiful sunsets and sightings of the endangered Irrawaddy dolphin some 9 miles (15 km) north near the village of **Kampie**. An estimated 70–85 of the bulb-nosed, small-finned dolphins live in the clay-brown stretch of the Mekong between Kampie and Laos. This village can be reached on a hired tuk-tuk or *moto*; the route follows a beautiful riverside stretch, past houses on stilts inhabited by rural families. From here, it is possible to hire a boat to go out on to the river. Sightings, though not guaranteed, are more than likely.

Just across the water from Kratie is **Koh Trong**, a sandbar island in the middle of the Mekong. Here, visitors will come across a floating village and an old stupa. The fortunate ones may also spot the rare Mekong mud turtle. Also worth a visit is the beautiful 19th-century temple Wat Roka Kandal, 1 mile (2 km) south of town. Wicker handicrafts, which are made locally, are available here.

Wooden dolphin souvenir, Kampie

⓲ Stung Treng

Road Map D6. 87 miles (140 km) N of Kratie. 🚗 25,000. 🚤 🚤 daily.

Once a Lao-French admini-stered outpost, the town of Stung Treng is now on the tourist map thanks to a new bridge and a cross-country road. Ironically, these make it easy to pass through the town without breaking the journey. Much of Stung Treng province's traffic still moves by water; the province is criss-crossed by several rivers including Tonlé Kong, Tonlé Sepok, Tonlé San, and the mighty Mekong River, which passes some 6 miles (10 km) east of Stung Treng town. The town and surrounding countryside have much to offer visitors, with a number of riverine sunset trips operating at inflated prices, and the Chenla period ruins of Prasat Preah Ko, a short distance away. Homestay and trekking options are also developing.

⓳ Ban Lung

Road Map E6. 93 miles (150 km) NE of Stung Treng. 🚗 25,000. 🚌 ℹ️ Highland Tour (088)- 988-8098. 🚤 daily. 🌐 **tourismcambodia.com**

The country's northernmost region, Ratanakiri province is often referred to as the Wild East, of which Ban Lung is the provincial capital. The town's nickname, *dey krakhorm*, meaning red earth, derives from the red dust that settles

View of the Mekong River from the town of Kratie

For hotels and restaurants see pp211–12 and pp225–6

on everything from people's faces to the leaves of trees, giving the place a surreal autumnal feel. Ban Lung is best visited between November and February when the rains have stopped and the dust has not yet become a nuisance. During the wet season, from July to September, the town's roads become quite impassable.

Ban Lung is little more than a transportation and accommodations hub for the many riches that lie on its fringes. These include waterfalls, bottle-green crater lakes, minority villages, and ethnic animist cemeteries. Two-day treks in the **Virachey National Park**, 31 miles (50 km) to the north of Ban Lung, are recommended. A number of eco-trekking organizations are starting to take shape here. Elephant rides to local waterfalls, of which Ka Tieng is the most impressive, can be organized by most guesthouses.

⑳ Yaek Lom Lake

Road Map E6. 3 miles (5 km) E of Ban Lung.

Believed to have been formed some 700,000 years ago, this volcanic, bottle-green crater lake is the main attraction around Ban Lung. The lake is ringed by thick green jungle and when viewed aerially, it forms a near perfect circle. The area is peaceful and a visit here makes for a memorable day with morning swims and wooden jetties to sunbathe on. The visitors' center can provide information on Ratanakiri's ethnic minorities, a number of whom live near Ban Lung. Many of these tribes believe the lake to be an especially sacred place and, according to their legends, monsters inhabit its clear waters. An easily navigable path runs around the lake and can be walked in an hour. Admission to the lake is administered by the local Tompuon tribe, with the money being used toward improving the condition of

Visitors enjoying the beautiful scenery and cool waters, Yaek Lom Lake

their villages. Visitors can reach the lake either on foot or by tuk-tuk from Ban Lung.

㉑ Sen Monorom

Road Map E6. 230 miles (370 km) NE of Phnom Penh. 7,000. from Phnom Penh. Phnom Penh. daily.

Capital of Mondulkiri, the largest of Cambodia's provinces, Sen Monorom is a picturesque little place often referred to as "the Switzerland of Cambodia" due to its grassy landscape, rolling hills, and two large lakes. Covering a very small area, this sparsely populated town has a marketplace and a few guesthouses. The area is rich in river valleys, waterfalls, and teal-green deciduous forests, and is also home to tigers, bears, and a number of smaller endangered animals. However, illegal logging in the past 15 years and an increase in plantations have decimated the forests, driving

A house in an ethnic Phnong village, Sen Monorom

these animals farther inland, much to the dismay of wildlife conservationists.

Among the other attractions around Sen Monorom are one- and two-day treks in and around the ethnic Phnong villages, famous for their elephants. Visitors can learn the art of elephant training here, with the help of the Elephant Valley Project. Motorcycles are available for hire in Sen Monorom, but visitors should bear in mind that the roads are undeveloped and there are very few road signs.

㉒ Bonsraa Waterfall

Road Map E6. 22 miles (35 km) E of Sen Monorom. Taxi from Sen Monorom. **Open** dawn to dusk daily.

Accessed via a toll road from Sen Monorom, the Bonsraa Waterfall is now easy to reach and lies 22 miles (35 km) west of the Vietnamese border. This double-tiered waterfall, plunging some 115 ft (35 m) into dense jungle, is the country's most famous and dramatic cascade. The upper tier of the waterfall is 33 ft (10 m) in width and although the thundering water is very powerful, the lower, narrower tier with an 82-ft (25-m) drop, is much more spectacular. To see it from the bottom of the falls, visitors can cross the river and follow a crooked path weaving down a precipitous stairway. Motos can be hired from Sen Monorom to travel to the falls and back.

SOUTHERN CAMBODIA

The most relaxed, lush part of the country, Southern Cambodia is blessed with dazzling white-sand beaches and richly forested national parks. Faded Colonial architecture, lively beach bars, and beautiful virgin islands are on offer in this sparsely populated region. Visitors can engage in a variety of activities, from jungle treks and boat trips to snorkeling and diving.

Stretching from the Thai border in the southwest to Vietnam's Mekong Delta frontier in the southeast, Southern Cambodia is a region of myriad attractions. In the north are the relatively inaccessible Cardamom Mountains, a supremely biologically diverse range. Until the late 1980s these mountains were one of the last strongholds of the Khmer Rouge, whose presence, coupled with the difficult terrain, deterred loggers. The amazing variety of wildlife in the Cardamom Mountains includes elephants, sun bears, tigers, pangolins, Siamese crocodiles, and primates.

The biggest draws of the area are its pristine beaches and virgin islands. Sihanoukville, with its mix of ramshackle buildings and fancy hotels, continues to draw visitors despite its lack of urban planning. The town's fine-sand beaches and turquoise waters are a haven for watersports enthusiasts. A number of tour operators and diving companies,

which can assist travelers with planning activities, operate in the town. Several uninhabited and sparsely populated islands lie just off the coast of Sihanoukville and make for excellent day-trip options. Apart from tourism, the main sources of income in the coastal areas remain agriculture, fishing, and salt production.

The region is also home to several wildlife preserves. Ream National Park envelops a vast swath of coastland, with mangrove forests and coral reefs, in contrast to the expansive pine forests of Kirirom National Park. The rainforest preserve of Botum Sakor National Park is home to elephants and hornbills, while Bokor National Park's old French hill station has been renovated with a hotel complex. Other attractions include the tiny town of Kep, with its crumbling Modernist buildings, and the captivating temple ruins of Phnom Da in Takeo province.

Brightly colored fishing boats and houses on stilts lining the wharf, Kampot

◀ Food huts on tropical Koh Rong island, off the coast of Sihanoukville

Exploring Southern Cambodia

A heady combination of beaches, islands, and national parks makes Southern Cambodia a delight to explore. Koh Kong, near the Thai border, is beginning to establish itself as an ecotourism center, with picturesque waterfalls, forests, and mangrove preserves. In the south, bustling Sihanoukville has some of Southeast Asia's most gorgeous beaches and pristine offshore islands. Kampot, which lies to the east of Sihanoukville, is an important town with a delightful river setting and an atmospheric French quarter, and serves as an ideal base for trips to Bokor National Park. Tiny Kep, a former French resort, still retains a quiet rustic feel, while Takeo province is home to the ancient temple of Phnom Da, which is accessible only by boat from Angkor Borei.

Lush mangrove forests, Botum Sakor National Park

For hotels and restaurants see p212 and pp226–7

Getting Around

The road system in Southern Cambodia has improved greatly. All the main routes are well paved and generally in good condition, although all are single-lane highways. The bus network is reasonably efficient and since distances are not long, journeys are not too tiring. Shared taxis supplement buses, particularly on the Sihanoukville–Kampot route. These usually stop to allow travelers to take pictures en route. Car-rental agencies are common in Sihanoukville, and motorcycle rental companies operate in most towns. Boats are available to offshore islands and riverside towns, and to explore parks and temple ruins such as Phnom Da.

A busy street in the provincial town of Svay Rieng

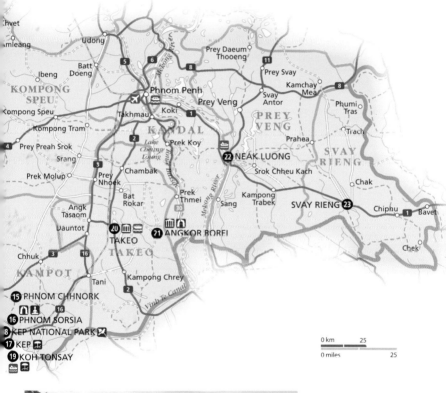

Verdant forests surrounding the rocky ledges of Tatai Waterfalls

Key

— Major road
— Minor road
=== Untarred road
– – Dirt track
— Railway line
▬▬ International border
— Provincial border
△ Peak

For keys to symbols *see back flap*

❶ Sihanoukville

With its stunning white-sand beaches and azure waters, Sihanoukville is Cambodia's principal beach resort. Spread across three districts, the town encompasses a large port zone, and was named after the former king, Sihanouk. Locals, however, still refer to it by its old name, Kompong Som. Although the town is of no real architectural interest, it is now the focus of large-scale international investment, and visitors will find excellent facilities including banks, restaurants, bars, Internet cafés, and upscale hotels. There are regular flights to Sihanoukville from Siem Reap.

Palm-fringed pool at the impressive Sokha Beach Resort, Sokha Beach

Entrance to Cambodia Casino, one of many casinos beyond the Victory Beach area

🚉 Victory Beach

2 miles (3 km) NW of town center.
The pretty, white-sand bay of Victory Beach is located directly below Victory Hill. Its southern end is also known as Lamherkay Beach. Victory Beach is about 984 ft (300 m) long, and its western orientation means that it is perfectly aligned to view sunsets. Late night venues in the area include a number of casinos. These are mostly found around Victory Hill and the Golden Lion area.

Located about 1 mile (2 km) offshore is Koh Pos, or Snake Island, which is easily accessible by boat.

🚉 Independence Beach

2 miles (3 km) SW of town center.
Another lovely tropical bay, Independence Beach gets its name from the renovated Independence Hotel on the hilltop directly north of this stretch of coastline. It is a privately owned space, with fine, pale sand and clear water, ideal for swimmers. Visitors can either buy a drink or two from the hotel's beach café to avoid paying an entrance fee, or head straight to the southern section of the beach, a small part of which is open to all. However, the beach here is crowded with street vendors selling trinkets and fruits.

🚉 Sokha Beach

1 mile (2 km) SW of town center.
With shimmering white sand and the sea a surreal shade of turquoise, Sokha Beach is certainly worth a visit.

The crescent-shaped stretch of sand runs for about 1 mile (2 km) between two small wooded bluffs. Directly behind the beach is the sprawling Sokha Beach Resort (see p212), which officially owns this stretch. Visitors who want to linger have to pay an entrance fee, which includes use of the resort's pool. The beach has deck chairs and snack stalls operated by the resort.

🚉 Occheuteal Beach

1 mile (2 km) S of town center.
This beach is the main tourist hot spot in Sihanoukville, and is the closest to the hotel strip. The beach's northern end is heavily built up. The small rocky cove here, known as Serendipity Beach, is the most pleasant part of Occheuteal Beach, despite there being no sand. It is home to upscale bungalows as well as some of the town's best-known bars and restaurants. In contrast, the southern end is far less developed.

This casuarina-lined beach plays host to sunbathers and watersports enthusiasts

Idyllic Sokha Beach, part of the Sokha Beach Resort

For hotels and restaurants see p212 and pp226–7

who can rent tubes, banana boats, and jet skis to enjoy in the warm water. A strip of shack-like bar-restaurants along the beach also offer cheap beer deals and seafood specials.

Unfortunately, the beach suffers from erosion, which is a serious problem here because most buildings have been built too close to the water. Visitors may come across some unpleasant sights, such as sand bags, owing to the rapid development taking place. However, halfway down the beach, there is a pleasant stretch of white sand and shallow water.

☲ Prek Treng Beach

4 miles (6 km) NW of town center. Located north of the port, Prek Treng Beach is a fairly deserted, long, thin crescent of sand with shallow blue water. Visitors are advised to bring their own drinks and snacks since there are no facilities available. At high tide, this beach is quite narrow and the shoreline is rocky in places.

☲ Otres Beach

4 mile (6 km) SE of town center. Immediately south of Occheuteal, behind a small headland, Otres Beach is a wonderful golden stretch of

Peaceful stretch of sand and water, Prek Treng Beach

VISITORS' CHECKLIST

Practical Information
Map C7. 112 miles (180 km) SW of Phnom Penh. 62,000. corner of Sopheakmongkol & 109 Sts, (034)-933-894. daily.

Transport
Taxi

sand, lined with graceful casuarina trees. The beach itself is narrow, but it is about 2 miles (3 km) long and dotted with sun loungers, which visitors can use in exchange for a drink or a snack. Although much of the land here has been bought by developers, for now the place is still pristine.

There are a number of small-scale bungalow operations, which offer inexpensive accommodations right on the beachfront, with very little traffic to disturb the peace. The beach is not served by public transport but can be reached by rented cars or tuk-tuks from the town center, or on foot from Occheuteal Beach.

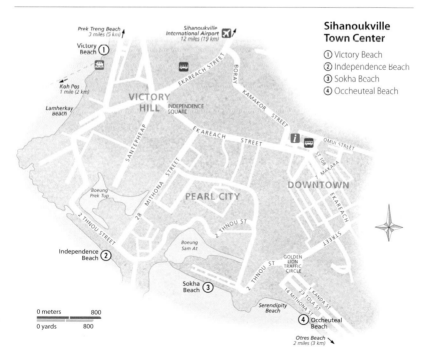

Sihanoukville Town Center

① Victory Beach
② Independence Beach
③ Sokha Beach
④ Occheuteal Beach

❷ Ream National Park

Road Map C7.12 miles (19 km) SE of Sihanoukville. 🚌 🚐 **i** Park HQ (016)-767-686. **Open** 7am–5pm daily. 🏊 🚤

Encompassing 82 sq miles (212 sq km) of coastal land, the varied landscape of Ream National Park includes white-sand beaches, mangrove forests, and the Prek Toeuk Sap Estuary. The park's marine section comprises the islands of Koh Thmei and Koh Seh, as well as some offshore coral reefs. Thmor

Thom, a fishing community consisting of 200 inhabitants, is also located inside the park.

The park is particularly rich in birdlife with a recorded list of over 150 species that includes the Indian pied hornbill, sea eagle, gray-headed fish eagle, and storks. Its forests are home to sun bears, deer, snakes such as pythons and the king cobra, macaques, silver langurs, and pangolins. Closer to the Prek Toeuk Sap river, visitors may chance upon monkeys and several kinds of kingfisher skimming the water. In the

rainy season, it is also possible to catch sight of the endangered Irrawaddy dolphin.

Most visitors explore the national park on a boat trip along the river, which passes through lush mangroves and forests on its way to the sea. Boat trips are an excellent way to view wildlife on the riverbanks. The river also offers opportunities for swimming close to its beaches. Jungle hikes can be organized with national park rangers who speak English; it is not possible for visitors to hike on their own.

❸ Kbal Chhay Cascades

Road Map C7.11 miles (18 km) N of Sihanoukville. **i** Sihanoukville (034)-933-894. 🚤 📷 🏠

The Kbal Chhay Cascades are popular among domestic tourists who come here to see the

Colorful coral reefs in the waters off Ream National Park

Sihanoukville's Islands

Located offshore from the beaches of Sihanoukville (*see pp108–9*), this group of 20 or so idyllic palm-fringed islands offers a good day-trip option from the mainland. There are several hotels on Koh Samloem and Koh Rong as well as more basic guesthouses. While a few islands are completely uninhabited, tiny communities inhabit others, surviving by fishing and farming.

Koh Rong, the largest island in the group, has beautiful unspoiled beaches, perfect for strolls. Its calm waters are home to a variety of marine life.

Koh Rong Samloem, with its white-sand beaches, clear turquoise waters, and excellent snorkeling, is a tropical paradise. The island also has a dive school, known as Eco Sea Dive, and various accommodation options.

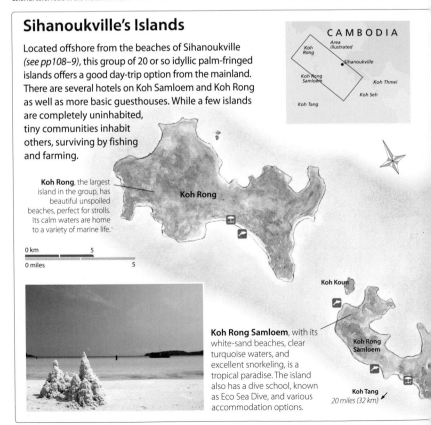

CAMBODIA

Area illustrated

Koh Rong

Sihanoukville

Koh Rong Samloem

Koh Thmei

Koh Seh

Koh Tang

Koh Rong

0 km 5
0 miles 5

Koh Koun

Koh Rong Samloem

Koh Tang
20 miles (32 km)

Water gushing over rocky ledges, Kbal Chhay Cascades

famous falls; Kbal Chhay featured in the Cambodian movie *Chao Pos Keng Kong* (The Giant Snake). The falls offer the chance for a refreshing dip. Upstream there are rocky ledges and sandy coves for sunbathing. However, the water flow reduces toward the end of the rainy season and the swimming is not so good.

On Sundays, the place is busy and litter is a problem. Facilities include snack and souvenir stalls, picnic platforms, and changing booths. Visitors can also reach the falls by *motos* and motorcycles.

❹ Koh Rong

Road map B7. 19 miles (31 km) W of Sihanoukville. 🏔 500. 🚤 from Sihanoukville Serendipity Beach Pier.

This is the second largest island in Cambodia and is rapidly growing into a popular tourist destination. The island offers access to some of the finest dive sites in the region, and Tui Beach has a good concentration of hotels, guesthouses, and restaurants. Several hotels have their own dedicated speed boat to transport visitors to the island.

❺ Kirirom National Park

Road Map C7. 68 miles (110 km) NE of Sihanoukville. **Open** 7am–5pm daily. 🚲 🚗 🛴 🍴 🅿

This intriguing national park occupies a remote plateau about a two-hour ride inland

from Sihanoukville. It lies at an elevation of about 2,296 ft (700 m), making the climate here far less oppressive than on the coast, and Kirirom's extensive pine forests reflect the temperate altitude. Visitors can take advantage of ranger-guided walks to **Phnom Dat Chivit**, or End of the World Mountain, from where the view of the Elephant and Cardamom mountain ranges to the west is spellbinding. Ox-cart rides and gentle hikes to pretty waterfalls are also popular and there is a great web of forest trails. Wildlife here includes elephant, tiger, pileated gibbon, banteng, gaur, and sun bear, although sightings are rare.

The park has a basic guest-house with a restaurant, offering fine views over the forest, particularly at sunset. There is also an upscale resort with manicured lawns that is popular with weekenders from Phnom Penh.

Diving off the coasts of Koh Rong Samloem, Koh Tas, and Koh Tang offers great views of coral reefs, home to marine life such as lionfish, seahorses, and whale sharks.

VISITORS' CHECKLIST

Practical Information
Koh Pos is 1 mile (2 km) W of Sihanoukville. 🅸 island trips run by tour operators and guesthouses in Sihanoukville.

Transport
🚤 to Koh Rong Samloem from Serendipity Beach, Sihanoukville. 🆆 **speedferrycambodia.com**

Sihanoukville

Koh Pos

Koh Pos is a highly desirable site for property development, though progress is often stalled.

Koh Tas

Koh Ta Kiev, blessed with pristine white-sand beaches and fascinating marine life, is a great place for snorkeling. A jungle camp and trekking facilities are also available on the island.

Koh Preus

Koh Ta Kiev

Koh Russie

Koh Thmei
9 miles (15 km)
Koh Seh
13 miles (21 km)

Koh Russie, or Bamboo Island, has a lovely fine-sand beach on its west coast. The east coast, although not as inviting as the west, is frequented by day-trippers.

❻ Koh Kong

Road map B7. 137 miles (220 km) NW of Sihanoukville. 🏛 30,000. 🚌 🚢

The dangers posed by the Khmer Rouge, coupled with the difficult journey through the Cardamom Mountains, led to Koh Kong being neglected for years. Accessible only by sea and air until 2001, its fortunes are now changing thanks to a road that links the town to the NH4 and to the rest of the country. The town has built up its accommodations and dining options to cater for the increased influx of tourists from Thailand – the border is just 6 miles (10 km) away. Koh Kong is a good base for ecotourism – trips up jungle-fringed rivers and through mangrove forests can be organized from here.

About an hour upriver from Koh Kong, **Koh Por Waterfall** has a gorgeous rainforest setting. There is safe swimming below the falls, but visitors should be careful above the main drop because currents can be strong after heavy rain. Between December and June, hiking is possible on trails along the riverbank.

Environs
Near the Thai border, **Koh Kong Safari World**, with its numerous shows featuring a variety of animals, can be a fun excursion for the family.

🐾 **Koh Kong Safari World**
4 miles (6 km) NW of town center. **Tel** 016-800-811. **Open** 9am–5pm daily. 🗺 🌐 kohkongresort.com

Dense mangrove forest, Peam Krasaop Nature Reserve

❼ Tatai Waterfalls

Road map C7. 12 miles (19 km) E of Koh Kong. 🚢 from Koh Kong.

Set amid lush green jungle, the picturesque Tatai Waterfalls lie upstream from the bridge spanning the Tatai River. During the rainy season, the falls have powerful rapids, while the dry season presents opportunities for dips in rocky pools. Visitors can reach the falls by kayak, hiking trails, or boat, as well as by *motos* that can be hired from Koh Kong. Nearby, along the near-pristine Tatai River, are two excellent ecolodges.

❽ Peam Krasaop Nature Reserve

Road map B7. 4 miles (6 km) S of Koh Kong. 🚗 ♿ 🚻 📷 🏛

Covering 93 sq miles (240 sq km), Peam Krasaop Nature Reserve is one of the most important mangrove

environments in Southeast Asia. The mangroves not only protect the coastline from erosion but also support a wealth of flora and fauna. The extensive mud flats here provide a crucial habitat for invertebrates, and a rich feeding ground for waders such as the spotted greenshank and Asian dowitcher. Concrete walkways have been constructed through the forest, allowing visitors a closer look at the wildlife, which includes mud crabs, storks, and cranes. The preserve is also home to pangolins, monkeys, bats, and deer. Fishermen have also reported occasional sightings of saltwater crocodiles. A 49-ft (15-m) high lookout tower in the settlement of Boeng Kayak, at the main gateway to the preserve, offers excellent views of the estuary and mud flats. Boats can be hired for trips into Koh Kong Bay at the entrance gate, and early morning trips might provide the best chance to spot the Irrawaddy dolphin.

❾ Koh Kong Island

Road map B7. 16 miles (26 km) S of Koh Kong. 🚢 from Koh Kong. 🏖

A tropical paradise as yet unspoiled by development, Koh Kong Island features beaches lined with coconut palms and other vegetation. Its transparent waters and pale, powdery sands form seven perfect beaches, although Beach Three, backed by a lovely lagoon, is the one to head for. This is a blissfully peaceful environment, an idyllic virgin beach where only the wind, the waves, and birdsong interrupt the silence. Several species of sea turtle nest here, but visitors are unlikely to encounter them as they usually arrive at night. Snorkeling is good, with excellent visibility and clear views of schools of mirror fish.

There is no regular transport to Koh Kong Island. Visitors will need to organize a boat trip from Koh Kong, and register at the island's police checkpoint before traveling to the beaches. The traveling time to Beach

Lush green jungles surrounding the ecolodges on the Tatai River

For hotels and restaurants see p212 and pp226–7

Crystal-clear water and fine-sand beach, Koh Kong Island

Three by speedboat is 75 minutes. Long-tail boats, on the other hand, take around 2 hours and 45 minutes. It is advisable to carry insect repellant because sandflies can be a nuisance here.

⑩ Cardamom Mountains

Road map C7. 73 miles (119 km) SE of Koh Kong. 🚌 from Koh Kong. 🚌 📷 🖼 Wildlife Alliance **Tel** (023)-211-604. Chi Pat **Tel** (035)-675-6444.

The largest wilderness in mainland Southeast Asia, the Cardamom Mountains cover an area of 3,900 sq miles (10,100 sq km). Two regions in these mountains have been declared protected the Central Cardamom Reserve, which extends across an area of 1,549 sq miles (4,013 sq km), up to Pursat province; and the Southern Cardamom Reserve, covering 557 sq miles (1,443 sq km) east of Koh Kong. These mountains sustain several distinct forest environments and a wide variety of wildlife. Lower elevations, which are dominated by dry forests and deciduous trees, support large numbers of mammals, including the elephant, tiger, and sambhar deer. This region is also one of the last remaining homes of the Siamese crocodile. Rainforests at higher altitudes are prime territory for endemic species such as the Cardamom banded gecko. Around 1,400 bird species have also been recorded here. However, the rise of activities such as hunting, illegal logging, and land

clearance are putting tremendous pressure on these habitats. Renowned environmental activist Chut Wutty was shot and killed in 2012 while guiding journalists to report on deforestation in the Cardamoms.

Koh Kong tour operators can help visitors to plan trips to the foothills of the Southern Cardamoms. An ecotourism program has been established at Chi Phat village, 13 miles (21 km) upriver from the riverside port of Anduong Tuek, 61 miles (98 km) south of Koh Kong. It offers mountainbiking, hiking, and bird-watching. Wildlife Alliance, an NGO working for environmental conservation, organizes boat trips to the Chhay Tameas rapids, 4 miles (6 km) from Chi Phat. The remote park station at Thma Bang, a 2-hour drive west of the Tatai River, also has basic accommodations.

Rhinoceros hornbill

⑪ Botum Sakor National Park

Road map C7. 63 miles (102 km) S of Koh Kong. 🚌 🚌 📷 Sihanoukville (034)-933-894. **Open** 7am–5pm daily. 📷

Occupying the bulbous peninsula between Koh Kong and Sihanoukville, the Botum Sakor National Park encompasses 707 sq miles (1,832 sq km) of coastal land and low-lying rainforests, grasslands, and mangroves. The park is home to the elephant, fishing cat, sun bear, leopard, and pileated gibbon. Leopards and elephants are rarely spotted but there is still plenty to see, particularly reptiles and amphibians such as tree frogs, and birds such as the white-bellied sea eagle. The park has been a bone of contention between developers and environmentalists, with the former eyeing the fine sandy beaches on the western peninsula. Environmentalists argue that these plans are contrary to Botum's status as a national park, and hence disastrous for its wildlife. Despite this, large areas of mangroves have been logged.

There is limited road access to the park, but hikes and boat trips can be organized from the park headquarters, 2 miles (3 km) west of Anduong Tuek. These boat trips pass through mangrove forests teeming with mud crabs and kingfishers.

Visitors hiking through the jungle trail, Cardamom Mountains

Lone fishing boat on the tranquil seashore of Ream National Park ▶

Scenic riverside view of Kampot with the Bokor Mountain Range in the background

⑫ Kampot

Road Map C7. 66 miles (106 km) E of Sihanoukville. 🏔 36,000. 🚌 🚢 🛥 daily.

With a sultry, unhurried air, little traffic, and some fine cafés, Kampot is one of the most atmospheric towns in Cambodia. Nestled along the Kampot River, the town's riverside promenade is a delight at sunset, as fishermen cast their lines and locals enjoy a drink against a backdrop of the Bokor Mountain Range.

Kampot's central area is quite compact and easily explored on foot. Its French Colonial buildings, although in an advanced state of decay, remain impressive. An ideal starting point is the riverbank close to the old bridge, which

Fishing boat, Kampot

was badly damaged during the Khmer Rouge years. Visitors can then head southeast to the renovated market with its incredibly steep pitched roof. Many of the shops and houses around here show clear Colonial influence – louvered windows, terra-cotta tiles, and fine balconies. An interesting stop is the **Kampot Traditional Music School**, south of the town center, where disabled students learn traditional dance and music. Alternatively, visitors can head for the Provincial Training Center, located in a compound behind the main post office, which trains women in textile weaving. The center aims to teach them a trade that will give them a sustainable income, although there is not

enough demand for their products. Visitors can help by buying a silk length or a cotton *krama* (scarf).

Those staying longer can also visit some of the sights around town. About 2 miles (3 km) south of Kampot, on the road to Kep *(see p118)*, are impressive salt fields, with some 1,000 pans. The prepared salt is collected at harvest time by hundreds of locals. About 2 miles (3 km) farther along the same road lies the small Khmer Muslim fishing village of **Kabalromih**, an important boat-building center located on the fringes of a large mangrove swamp.

Kampot Traditional Music School
Plauv Ekareach, 1 Ousaphear Khum Kampong Kandal. **Tel** (033)-932-992). **Open** 8–11am & 6:30–9pm Mon–Fri. W kcdi-cambodia.com

⑬ Tek Chhouu Falls

Road Map C7. 5 miles (8 km) NW of Kampot from Kampot. 🗺 🚻

A popular picnic spot, the Tek Chhouu Falls are a series of rapids best visited after the rainy season. Families come here to sit on little bamboo platforms beside the rapids and take in the view of the Kampot River. There are natural pools, good for swimming, and rocky shelves, ideal for sunbathing. The **Tek Chhouu Zoo**, en route to the falls, is great for children.

🐾 **Tek Chhouu Zoo**
Tel (011)-768-470. 🌿

Healing with Music

Traditional Khmer music and art were nearly annihilated during the Khmer Rouge regime. Musicians and artisans were murdered, while those who managed to survive fled the country. Today, however, these forms of art are not only making a comeback, but also helping Cambodians to get over their past with "art therapy." Non-government organizations, such as Catherine Geach's Kampot Traditional Music School and Arn Chorn-Pond's Cambodia Living Art, not only work on the revival of these lost traditions, but also use music to heal victims of the Khmer Rouge.

Students learning to play an instrument, Cambodia Living Art

⑭ Bokor National Park

Road Map C7. 26 miles (42 km) N of Kampot from Kampot. 🚪 🚻

One of Kampot province's main tourist attractions, Bokor National Park covers 610 sq miles (1,581 sq km) of primary rainforest, grasslands, and deciduous forest. Although illegal logging has decimated large tracts of the park's southern section, Bokor remains home to the Indian elephant, tiger, leopard, pangolin, Asiatic black bear, Malayan sun bear, pilleated gibbon, slow loris, and pig-tailed macaque. Fortunate visitors may also chance upon any of the 300 bird species that inhabit the park, such as the gray-headed fish eagle and the spot-bellied eagle owl.

Besides a variety of birds and animals, Bokor's attractions have included the atmospheric **Bokor Hill Station**, which featured in the 2002 Matt Dillon movie *City of Ghosts*. Located atop the 3,543-ft (1,080-m) high Phnom Bokor, the station was an abandoned French summer post from the 1920s, and included the remains of a once-magnificent four-story hotel and casino. Now renovated by the Sokha group, the old hotel and casino has been reopened and makes a welcome stop for lunch or coffee after a long drive around the mountain and through the chilly fog. On clear days, there are stunning views over Kampot to the Gulf of

Seventh-century brick temple of Shiva, Phnom Chhnork

Thailand, although this is a rarity as the summit is usually blanketed in mist. Close by lie the ruins of an old **Catholic Church**, which has withstood years of warfare and occupation by the Khmer Rouge. Although the church's interior is now gutted and the stonework is encrusted with orange lichen, the altar is still largely intact.

Yet another intriguing spot is the **Bokor Palace**, also known as the Black Palace, located 6 miles (10 km) east of the Bokor Hill Station. Once the royal residence of King Sihanouk, its wasted shell is a reminder of the palace's former grandeur – the marble floors, tiled bathrooms, and fireplaces are still intact.

Most organized tours to the park also include a visit to the pretty **Popokvil Waterfall**, located 3 miles (5 km) northeast of the hill station. This two-tiered waterfall, which is separated by a shallow pool that can be paddled through, is usually not deep enough to swim in. However, it is a peaceful place to spend some time, engulfed by the swirling mist and cool air.

⑮ Phnom Chhnork

Road Map C7. 5 miles (8 km) NE of Kampot. **Open** 8am–5pm daily. 🚗 🚻

Situated on a small hill that rises from the pancake-flat plain east of Kampot, Phnom Chhnork is a renowned cave-temple.

Approached by a walk through muddy rice paddies, the temple is reached by ascending a flight of stone steps, which lead to the cave containing an evocative 7th-century Funan brick temple dedicated to Shiva, the God of Destruction. This temple is accessible by a hired *moto* or tuk-tuk from Kampot.

Stalagmite shaped like an elephant head, Phnom Sorsia

⑯ Phnom Sorsia

Road Map C7. 11 miles (18 km) E of Kampot **Open** 7:30am–5pm daily. 🚻

A religious hill complex, Phnom Sorsia consists of a garishly painted Buddhist temple, and a karst outcrop riddled with caves. A staircase leads up to the temple, to the left of which is the first cave with a stalagmite resembling an elephant's head, giving the cave its name – Rung Damrey Sor, or **White Elephant Cave**. Farther east lies **Bat Cave**, filled with thousands of bats. The walk up to the summit leads to a stupa and scenic views.

Stately remains of the old Catholic Church, Bokor National Park

Charred remains of a once splendid Colonial villa, Kep

❶❼ Kep

Road Map C7. 109 miles (175 km) S of Phnom Penh. 🏠 4,500. 🚌

Once known as Kep-sur-Mer, the town of Kep was an upscale resort for the rich and influential of French Indochina in the 1930s. Today, it is little more than an overgrown village in a scenic location, surrounded by a lofty forested headland, and the sea on three sides. A profusion of greenery and thick tree cover add to the easy appeal of the town. In recent years it has become Cambodia's most successful micro-resort, with a new range of ecolodges and guesthouses mushrooming across town.

The town was overrun by the Khmer Rouge in 1975, who torched most symbols of Colonial prosperity, leaving behind blackened shells of the once sprawling buildings and villas. Despite their devastation, Kep's Modernist concrete villas remain the town's best-known attractions. Although disheveled and ruined, these structures are charred reminders of a more prosperous time, and are certainly worth a visit.

Visitors will also find the town's beaches a pleasant distraction. **Kep Beach**, located on the edge of the Kep peninsula, is about 1 mile (2 km) long and strewn with pebbles. The dark gray sand is quite unlike the Caribbean vision of paradise, and is dotted with sun loungers. The bay's waters are extremely shallow and quite safe for children, although adults may have to wade a long way out for a decent swim. **Coconut Beach**, a short distance east of Kep Beach, is popular with locals.

The region's most renowned dish, the delicious and spicy Kep pepper crab (*see p219*), is served in every restaurant on the strip known as Crab Market, north of town, and is definitely worth a try. There are several pepper farms nearby where visitors can see the vine-like plant, and also buy the famous and pungent Kep peppercorn.

The hill behind Kep offers fine views. Those keen to hike can follow a track through the jungle, accessed from behind the Veranda Natural Resort.

❶❽ Kep National Park

Road Map C7. 1 mile (2 km) NW of Kep 🚌 from Kep.

One of the smallest protected preserves in Cambodia, Kep National Park occupies the hilltop directly behind Kep town. A 5-mile (8-km) long trail loops around the hillside,

Visitors lazing around on a busy beach, Koh Tonsay

passing through an evergreen forest, and takes about 3 hours to hike. En route, visitors will come across views of Kampot and Angkoul Beach, and a pagoda, before arriving at Sunset Rock, which offers fine vistas over the sea to Koh Tonsay. Unfortunately, farmers have encroached on the park's lower reaches and wildlife sightings are rare. The park is reached by a 4WD vehicle from the bottom of the hill.

❶❾ Koh Tonsay

Road Map C7. 4 miles (6 km) S of Kep. 🚌 from Kep. 🏊 ☐ 🏠

A beautiful wooded island just offshore from Kep, Koh Tonsay, or Rabbit Island, is so called because its profile is said to resemble that of a rabbit. The island is inhabited by around 200 people who make a living by fishing, and by harvesting coconuts and seaweed (for Chinese cosmetics). It is possible to walk around the entire island in just a couple of hours.

The main attraction here is a lovely sheltered beach with a narrow strip of golden sand – great for swimmers. There are about half a dozen bungalow operations in Koh Tonsay, all offering similar, simple wood-and-thatch huts, most without private bathrooms. Several of them have restaurants with well-stocked bars. Visitors can also make trips to the islands of nearby Koh Pos and Koh Svai.

Restaurants on stilts lining the waterfront in Crab Market, Kep

For hotels and restaurants see p212 and pp226–7

Flora and Fauna of Coastal National Parks

Cambodia's coastal parks are incredibly diverse, comprising a wide variety of flora and fauna. In the Cardamom Mountains, the rainforests stretch right down to the sea and some of the best-preserved mangrove estuaries in Asia are also on this coastline. Shallower waters contain rich seagrass beds – the diet of dugongs and green turtles. Many of Cambodia's 77 offshore islands have reefs, which are home to hundreds of varieties of coral and fish. These ecosystems, however, are under severe threat and many species are endangered because of loss of habitat and deforestation, illegal wildlife trading, destructive fishing, and poaching. Farming and forestry concessions, even inside national parks, have led to the removal of wildlife territory, and land being cleared for wood chip production.

Coconut palms provide vital income and sustenance for coastal communities who use almost every part of the tree.

Casuarina is a graceful coastal pine, flourishing even in windswept locations.

Flora

Coastal Cambodia contains some of the richest forest environments in Southeast Asia. At lower altitudes, the dense tropical rainforests can soar to a height of almost 164 ft (50 m).

Marine seagrass forms an essential part of the diet of green turtles and dugongs.

Hawksbill turtles are found in shallow waters along the coast where sponges (which are their main diet) are also common.

Seahorses are a unique variety of fish. They flourish in the shallow waters off Sihanoukville.

Hermit crabs are quite common in Cambodian waters, particularly in sheltered areas around the mangrove forests.

Whip coral is characterized by long brush-like strands in a variety of colors. Growing in reefs, it provides a habitat for several species of fish.

Fauna

The coastal waters of Cambodia are quite shallow, not more than 199 ft (60 m) deep. The extensive reefs are rich in variety, consisting of hard and soft corals, and teem with marine life such as crabs, fish, and turtles – a haven for scuba divers.

The white-tip reef shark is a shark that grows up to about 5 ft (1.5 m) in length. It is seldom aggressive, unless provoked.

Lakefront promenade bordered by coconut palms, Takeo

⑳ Takeo

Road Map D7. 48 miles (77 km) S of Phnom Penh. 🏛 42,000. 🚌 🚤 *i* St 4, Takeo (032)-931-323.

A provincial capital, Takeo is located on the fringe of a vast flood plain that forms a vital wetland area. Although not on the tourist map, Takeo's broad streets are visited by those en route to the impressive early Khmer temple of Phnom Da, not far from town. As a result, the town has several facilities, including modest hotels, Internet cafés, and a couple of banks with ATMs. There are not many impressive sights here, although the lakeside promenade has a certain charm, including a dilapidated pier. The Provincial Museum, a short distance from the lakefront promenade, is also worth a visit for its local archaeological exhibits. Visitors could also try the town's culinary specialty,

bong khorng (giant prawns fried with garlic and lemon juice), which is served in several restaurants and street stalls.

㉑ Angkor Borei

Road Map D7. 13 miles (21 km) E of Takeo. 🏛 14,000. 🚤 from Takeo.

A highly enjoyable boat ride from Takeo takes visitors to the small riverside settlement of Angkor Borei, one of the oldest pre-Angkorian sites in Cambodia. This scruffy, isolated town was earlier known as Vyadapura, capital city of the ancient Hindu kingdom of Funan, which rose to prominence between the 1st and 6th centuries AD. The town's unpaved streets and general air of poverty provide little evidence of its illustrious past:

7th-century statue from Phnom Da

it was once a key center of Hindu civilization and culture. Many of its residents are ethnic Vietnamese – the border with Vietnam is just a few miles to the east – and visitors will be able to catch a glimpse of fishermen wearing conical hats, typical of Vietnam's rural folk.

The **Takeo Archaeological Museum**, located on the canal bank, is a reminder of the area's former glory. This interesting museum has a small, eclectic collection of artifacts from the region, including Funan-style ceramics that date back 2,000 years, *lingas* (phallic-like symbols), a 6th-century Standing Buddha, a 12th-century sandstone statue of Lakshmi, Hindu Goddess of Wealth, and ancient images of the Hindu gods Shiva and Vishnu.

Environs
Situated 2 miles (3 km) south of Angkor Borei, **Phnom Da** is an exquisite, partially ruined temple. Standing on the summit of an isolated hill, it has exceptional views over lush, green paddy fields stretching across to Vietnam 5 miles (8 km) away, and over the wetlands to Takeo.

Phnom Da's ruins, rising to a height of 59 ft (18 m), are approached by 142 steps leading up the hill, and visitors are usually guided by bare-footed local children. The temple's red-brick foundation

Façade of Takeo Archaeological Museum, Angkor Borei

For hotels and restaurants see p212 and pp226–7

dates from AD 514, and its intricate carvings have been weathered by centuries of rainfall, while the walls are cracked and penetrated by plants. Despite its dilapidated condition, there still remains much to admire – carved pillars, bas-reliefs of *nagas*, and an imposing stone doorway. However, most of the carvings have been taken away to museums in Phnom Penh and Angkor Borei. Below the temple are several cave shrines that are still used for religious offerings and prayers of good fortune.

🏛 **Takeo Archaeological Museum**
Riverbank, Angkor Borei.
Tel (012)-201-638. **Open** 7:30am–4pm daily. 🐾 ♿

🏯 **Phnom Da**
🚌 from Angkor Borei.

Stone steps leading to the temple ruins of Phnom Da, Angkor Borei

㉒ Neak Luong

Road Map D7. 39 miles (63 km) SE of Phnom Penh. 🚹 24,000. 🚌 from Phnom Penh. 🚌 🚤

Located on the east bank of the Mekong, Neak Luong is a busy transit town with a devastating history. During the Vietnam War, the town was bombed by a US B-52, which dropped a 20-ton (18 tonne) load on the town center, resulting in the deaths of almost 150 people. This incident is depicted in the opening sequence of the 1984 British movie, *The Killing Fields*.

Today, travelers along Highway 1 on their way to the Vietnamese border and Ho Chi Minh City regularly pass through Neak Luong. The riverside used to be dominated by car ferries, which would wait by the ports to shuttle people and cargo across the Mekong River. A 121-ft- (37-m-) high bridge, funded by Japan, opened here in April 2015, which means the ferries are now a less popular option.

The town also has a huge, bustling market where locals peddle fruit and a variety of fried snacks such as crickets. Other than this, there is little reason for visitors to stay in Neak Luong.

㉓ Svay Rieng

Road Map D7. 70 miles (113 km) SE of Phnom Penh. 🚹 23,000. 🚌 from Phnom Penh.

A provincial capital roughly half way between Phnom Penh and Ho Chi Minh City in Vietnam, the town of Svay Rieng is bypassed by most travelers, except those desperately in need of a meal or a drink. The Vietnamese border at Bavet is a short journey from here.

Bombing of Neak Luong

On August 6, 1973, American B-52s accidentally destroyed Neak Luong in an attempt to arrest the advance of the Khmer Rouge to Phnom Penh. The 20-ton (18 tonne) load dropped on the town led to the deaths of almost 150 civilians. This incident was immortalized in the movie *The Killing Fields* (1984), where US journalist Schanberg, played by Sam Waterston, and his Cambodian fixer Dith Pran, arrive in Neak Luong after reports of the bombing. They find a devastating scene – a smoldering town and bloodied survivors who beg Schanberg to photograph their misery. Days later, the US Congress called a halt to the bombardment known as Arclight. Journalists, including John Pilger, argue that this bombing campaign was a key factor in driving people to support the Khmer Rouge.

A moving scene from the 1984 film *The Killing Fields*

Ferry chartering visitors and cargo across the Mekong, Neak Luong

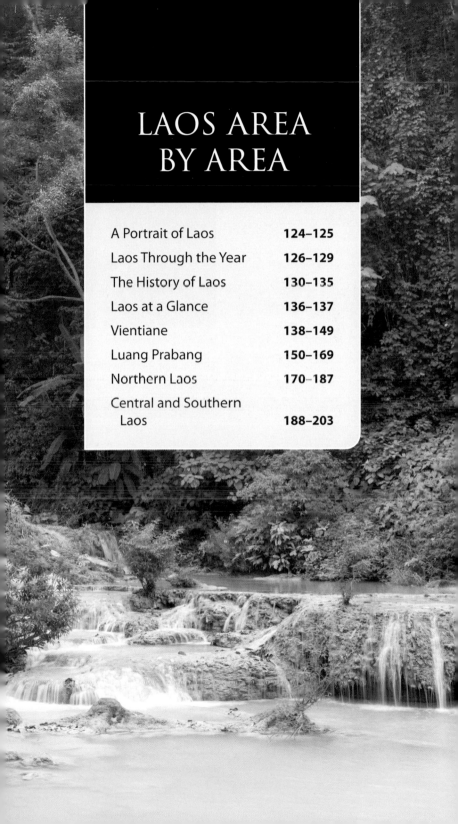

LAOS AREA
BY AREA

A PORTRAIT OF LAOS

A land of rich social and ethnic diversity, Laos displays French, Vietnamese, Thai, and Chinese influences in its distinct cultural mosaic. Its great geographical variety also harbors a wealth of native flora and fauna. This natural beauty, coupled with splendid Buddhist architecture and welcoming people, makes a trip to Laos a memorable experience.

Land and Ecology

Laos touches the temperate northern perimeter of Southeast Asia and extends deep into the heart of the tropical Mekong River valley. The rich lands in between are home to a range of flora, from tall, pale hardwoods and montane evergreen forests to shrub and bamboo undergrowth. Its fauna includes such endangered species as the Laotian black gibbon and the Asiatic tiger. The network of rivers that feed into the great Mekong provide fish, water for crops, and transport for people and goods. However, many of these resources are under threat from activities such as logging. The government has addressed this issue by establishing 20 National Protected Areas, covering 10 percent of the land area. Laos has also recently established itself as an eco-tourism destination with trekking and rafting as ideal ways to economically benefit local populations while conserving the environment.

Monks offering prayers in front of Buddha statues

Politics and the Economy

Ruled by a monarch until 1975, Laos became a Communist state when the Lao People's Democratic Republic (Lao PDR) came to power. The new government chose to isolate the country from the rest of the world with the exceptions of its Socialist neighbor Vietnam and the Soviet Bloc. However, since 1989, the policy of Jintanakan Mai (New Thinking) has reduced the role of the government in the economy and allowed free enterprise to re-emerge. Today, the economic prospects of the country are improving, and economic growth averages 7 percent annually. A rising urban middle class, with no ties to the Communist elite, are now buying cell phones, motorcycles, and cars. At the same time, many young Lao are leaving their villages for work in the cities and sending money home. There is also increased foreign investment with hydro-electric power projects, mining, and tourism leading the economic advances in the country. Visible signs of growth can be seen in Vientiane, where there has been a big increase in the number of hotels for the western market. On the roads, foreign cars are far more common.

Sprawling urban landscape, Pakse

◄ View of the multitiered Tat Kuang Si Falls, Luang Prabang province

Society and Religion

The effects of modernization have not been far reaching, with a majority of the population still continuing an agrarian existence based on the land, the seasons, and the family. Within the family, the culture is both patriarchal and hierarchal, with senior members owing support and protection to the juniors, who reciprocate with respect and loyalty. At the same time, women are considered secondary to men in traditional Lao society. Even though women constitute a majority of the workforce, fewer girls are sent to school, although such norms are now beginning to change.

The impact of the Communist Revolution notwithstanding, Lao society remains rooted in the traditions of Theravada Buddhism, whose tenets remind its followers of the impermanence of their existence, and the pitfalls of desire and acquisition. Even those residents of Laos who follow other faiths, such as the largely Christian Vietnamese, the Muslim South Asians, and animist minorities, are subtly enjoined to follow the culture, if not the religion, based on Buddhist beliefs. Religion therefore, forms an essential part of society, reflected in the daily almsgiving ceremony to Buddhist monks. The almsgiving always takes place early morning with food, incense, and flowers offered to the monks.

Flooded rice fields in Vang Vieng

Culture and The Arts

As in the case of religion, Lao traditional culture and art has proved resilient in the face of Communist assault. Many manifestations of the country's culture, music, dance, architecture, and literature have their roots in Buddhism. Lao music and dance is inevitably similar to that of neighboring Thailand, and to a lesser extent, Cambodia. The hypnotic flute called *khuy* is accompanied by a reed-driven pan pipe known as the *khene*, with a back beat provided by drums and *lanats* (xylophones). Music usually accompanies dances, such as performances of *Phra Lak Phra Lam*, the Lao version of the Hindu epic, *Ramayana*. This didactic tale is portrayed in temple art, both in murals and in the bas-relief panels usually found on the doors and windows. Laos's expertly handwoven textiles, in both cotton and silk, are uniquely designed, with each highland minority creating its own style of textile. The country is also well-known for its silversmiths, who are adept at creating exquisite jewelry, notably the intricate belts that accompany the handwoven *pha sins* skirt of traditional Lao women's attire. One of the most promising developments in the country has been the increase in the number of shops featuring the work of Lao artisans.

Man playing Lao *lanat*

Weaver in Ban Xang Hai village, near Luang Prabang

LAOS THROUGH THE YEAR

The Lao word for festival, *boun*, refers to the Buddhist act of merit-making *(see pp24–5)*. Indeed many festivals in Laos are related to the Buddhist religion, although some celebrate specific rural events such as the harvest, planting, or the onset of the rains. Laos officially uses the Gregorian calendar, but several festivals are celebrated according to the traditional Lao calendar, based on solar and lunar calculations.

However, events often fall on different days in different parts of the country. In addition to these, Lao people also celebrate festivals that are specific to a locality, such as Boun Wat Phu Champasak, which is celebrated at Wat Phu near the town of Champasak, and Boun That Luang, which is celebrated in Vientiane. Most temples also hold an annual fair, although the date varies from temple to temple.

Hot Season (Mar–Jun)

Probably the most difficult time of the year, the hot season is often dusty or humid, although places at higher altitudes such as the Xieng Khuang plateau are cooler. This is followed by the rice harvest season in which the Lao people await the coming of the rains, marking the beginning of the agricultural cycle.

Revelers celebrating Boun Pi Mai, the Lao New Year, Vientiane

March

Lao Women's Day *(Mar 8)*, nationwide. Public holiday and day off for all female employees.
Boun Pha Vet *(end Mar/early Apr)*, nationwide. Celebrations include performances of the Buddhist Jataka tales, accompanied by traditional music in village temples, general merrymaking, and sermons delivered by the temple's abbot. It is an auspicious time for Lao men to enter monkhood.

April

Lao New Year *(Apr 14–16)*, nationwide. Known as Boun Pi Mai in Lao, the impressive New

Year celebrations last for up to four days and are celebrated with an abundance of water.

The first day of the festival is celebrated by building stupas of sand along river banks or in temples, commemorating an act of piety by an Indian king who was an early follower of the Buddha. On the second day, in Luang Prabang, three red-faced figures representing the guardian spirits of the city,

Phu Noe, Na Noe, and Sing Keaw Sing Kham, parade through the streets, make offerings at the river, and are ritually fed by the locals. Traditional beauty pageants are held in the evening. The third day is celebrated with more water throwing and *baci sukhuan* ceremonies at home. Devotees in Luang Prabang climb up Mt Phou Si to make merit at the That Chomsi stupa. On the fourth day, the sacred Phabang statue is carried in a solemn procession from the National Museum to Wat Mai, where it is ritually cleansed. The festival ends with a performance of *Phra Lak Phra Lam*, the Lao version of the *Ramayana*, in the National Museum Complex.

May–June

International Labor Day *(May 1)*, nationwide. Parades are organized by socialist groups, and sports competitions are held in Vientiane.

The Baci Sukhuan Ceremony

This ceremony is central to Lao culture. *Baci sukhuan* (pronounced basee sookuan) refers to a calling of the spirits. It involves tying strings to the wrists of the person to whom it is dedicated. The ceremony is held at birth, marriage, before or after a trip, when a new job starts, or any other significant event in a person's life. Its aim is to concentrate the spiritual forces, which is believed to help the person face the next part of their life with vigor.

A man getting *baci* strings tied to his wrist, *baci sukhuan* ceremony

Average Daily Hours of Sunshine

Hours

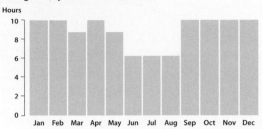

Sunshine Chart
Even during the rainy season, most days have some sunshine. The tropical sun can be very fierce, and adequate precautions against sunburn and sunstroke should be taken. A sun hat, sunscreen, and sunglasses are highly recommended items. Drinking plenty of water is essential.

Boun Visakha Busaa *(May full moon)*, nationwide. This Buddhist festival commemorates the Buddha's birth, death, and enlightenment. It is celebrated at *wats* with sermons and chanting during the day, and candle-lit processions during the evening.

Boun Bang Fai *(mid May)*, nationwide. Better known as the Rocket Festival, this pre-Buddhist fertility event occurs at the height of the hot season and implores the gods to send the rains by launching homemade rockets skyward. Elaborately decorated bamboo rockets are built by villagers who carry them in a procession before launching them. The celebrations continue for two entire days.

Rainy Season (Jul–Sep)

Culturally, this is a time of repose and reflection, with a lull in agricultural activity.

Rockets being fired on the occasion of Boun Bang Fai

During this season, all Buddhist monks are required to remain in their temples and concentrate on spiritual development. It is also the traditional time for Lao men to make merit by temporarily entering into monkhood.

July

Boun Khao Pansa/Khao Watsa *(early Jul)*, nationwide. This festival marks the beginning of the Buddhist Rains Retreat, often referred to as the Buddhist Lent. During this time, devout Buddhists strictly observe the precepts of their faith. Locals visit temples to give alms and listen to chanting and sermons.

August–September

Boun Haw Khao Padap Din *(Aug full moon)*, nationwide. During this somber festival dedicated to the deceased, prayers are offered for the spirits of dead family members. People present rice cakes to monks who are believed to act as intermediaries, transferring merit to the departed. This is also an occasion for traditional boat races in Khammuan province and Luang Prabang. Races take place on the Nam Khan in Luang Prabang.

Boat crews in elaborately carved boats racing each other, Suang Heua

Average Monthly Rainfall (Vientiane)

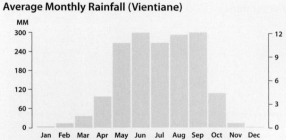

Rainfall Chart
Rainfall is not evenly distributed. Places in the north, such as Xieng Khuang, Phongsali, and parts of Luang Nam Tha province, and the Bolaven Plateau in the southeast get over 120 inches (3,000 mm) annually, but Vientiane and Luang Prabang get 67 inches (1,700 mm).

Locals carrying a prize-winning boat to the Mekong during Lai Heua Fai

Cool Season (Oct–Feb)

This season is perhaps the best time of the year in Laos, when there is a welcome coolness in the air and a substantial drop in temperature. The northern areas of the country, however, are considerably colder, almost brutally so for the locals. This time of year is a period of agricultural transition. Numerous festivals occur over the course of these months, often in celebration of the harvested crop, or in preparation for the next agricultural cycle.

October–November

Boun Ok Pansa/Ok Watsa
(early Nov), nationwide. Held three full moons after Boun Khao Pansa, this festival marks the end of the monastic Rains Retreat and the beginning of the cool season. Monks are presented with new robes and other supplies. Candle-lit processions are held in all *wats* in the evening.
Boun Fai Payanak *(Nov full moon)*, Pak Ngum district. Held at the end of the Rains Retreat, this event occurs once at this full moon and then again in May.

Red, round fireballs, said to represent *naga* spirits, emerge from the Mekong River, moving upward. Locals gather along the riverfront to watch this fascinating phenomenon.
Boun That Luang *(Nov full moon)*, Vientiane. The celebrations actually begin at Wat Si Muang, where the city pillar is located. Here, respects are paid to Sao Si, the guardian goddess of Vientiane. The crowds then move to Pha That Luang, where offerings are made to gathered monks, and a procession with representatives of all the country's various ethnic groups gathers around the stupa. There are candle-lit processions and spectacular firework displays. An international trade fair set up nearby also draws local shoppers.
Lai Heua Fai/Boun Nam *(variable)*, nationwide. Also known as the Boats of Light Festival, this event resembles Loy Krathong in Thailand and Diwali in India. Candle-lit processions are followed by participants proceeding to a nearby river to mount their candles on small bamboo-leaf

boats laden with flowers, which are then set adrift.
In every *wat* in Luang Prabang, a large boat is constructed from bamboo strips and decorated with hundreds of small lanterns. These boats are taken to Wat Xieng Thong and after a winner is declared, the boats are set adrift in the mighty Mekong River.
Suang Heua *(variable)*, nationwide. Boats are carried to a nearby river and raced. The boats are believed to lure the naga river spirits back into rivers from the rice fields. The races provide one of the most spectacular sporting sights in the region.

December

Lao National Day *(Dec 2)*, Vientiane. Military parades and political speeches to commemorate the victory of the Communist government in 1975.

Ethnic Lao participating in a parade at That Luang, Vientiane

Average Monthly Temperature (Vientiane)

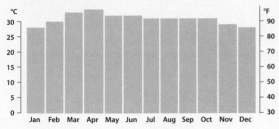

Temperature Chart
With the exception of the cool season (October–December), most parts of Laos are hot. During the rainy season (May–September), humidity adds to the discomfort. During all periods except the hot season, elevated regions are cool and temperatures can fall to below freezing at night.

That Ing Hang Festival *(early Dec)*, Savannakhet. An important Buddhist worship site, That Ing Hang hosts a major temple fair attended by devotees from across the country. The door to the inner sanctum of the stupa is opened only at this time, and male devotees make merit with offerings. A trade fair, musical and dance performances, and sports competitions are held.

International New Year's Day *(Dec 31)*, nationwide. The event is celebrated with baci sukhuan ceremonies at home, and large parties, including New Year's Eve countdowns among the urban elite in the capital, Vientiane.

Hmong New Year *(variable)*, Xieng Khuang province. The Hmong ethnic minority also celebrate their New Year with grand feasts. Women dress in their traditional finery and teenagers engage in an unusual courting ritual, which involves tossing a ball between various rows of enthusiastic boys and girls.

January

Boun Khun Khao *(end Jan/early Feb)*, nationwide. This rural festival is particularly important to rice farmers since it celebrates the successful harvest of their crop. At the local temple, unhusked rice is piled into pyramid-shaped mounds and blessed by the gathered monks. This ceremony is followed by a lavish feast and traditional music, and is a way for farmers to offer thanks to the land.

February

Vietnamese Tet/Chinese New Year *(end Jan/early Feb)*, Savannakhet and Vientiane. Colorful dragon dance troupes pass through the streets to the accompaniment of firecrackers, drums, and gongs. All businesses close for three days.

Lao Elephant Festival *(mid Feb)*, Sainyabuli. This festival is held to raise awareness of the need to conserve the environment of the Asian elephant. There are processions, demonstrations, and opportunities to learn more about this great mammal.

Boun Makha Busaa *(Feb full moon)*, nationwide. An important religious event culminating on a full moon night. There are candle-lit processions where the faithful circle the temple

Hmong girl in traditional dress

compounds. Boun Khao Chi, also known as Rice Cake Festival, commemorating the harvest, is also celebrated.

Boun Wat Phu Champasak *(Feb full moon)*, Wat Phu Champasak, Champasak province. This temple fair attracts visitors from across the country. Pilgrims make offerings at holy sites in the *wat*. Kickboxing and cockfighting take place on the last day.

Boun That Sikhot *(Feb full moon)*, south of Thakhek, Khammuan province. In February, this sleepy town on the Mekong river holds a popular riverside festival that attracts visitors from all over Khammuan province. The usual collection of Buddhist items are sold here, and there are plenty of food stalls. At the heart of the town is a temple, and all things pertaining to the temple, from books to incense, can be bought here.

Public Holidays

New Year's Day (Jan 1)

Pathet Lao Day (Jan 6)

Army Day (Jan 20)

Lao Women's Day (Mar 8)

Lao People's Party Day (Mar 22)

Lao New Year (Apr 14–16)

International Labor Day (May 1)

Children's Day (Jun 1)

Boun Khao Pansa (early Jul)

Lao Issara Day (Aug 13)

Liberation Day (Aug 23)

Freedom from France Day (Oct 12)

Boun Ok Pansa (early Nov)

Lao National Day (Dec 2)

Elephant procession during the Lao Elephant Festival

THE HISTORY OF LAOS

The borders of present-day Laos date from the 20th century, but the region has been populated for thousands of years. Its Lao-Tai-speaking people, although relatively recent arrivals, have an expansive and distinguished history. The stage of many wars and empire builders, Laos has been politically stable since 1975, and is now attracting hundreds of thousands of visitors each year.

Evidence of human settlement in the Laos area reaches as far back as 500 BC, when a megalithic culture flourished in Northern Laos, around a site called the Plain of Jars. Southern Laos was ruled for a time from Champa, a coastal kingdom in what is now Vietnam, until the Cambodia-based Angkorian Empire took control of this territory. Angkorian influence eventually extended as far north as present-day Vientiane, and more tentatively, to Luang Prabang.

Laos was initially populated by Austro-Asiatic groups such as the Mon-Khmer-speaking people. The Lao themselves began arriving in the first millennium AD. These immigrants belonged to the Lao-Tai linguistic group, who originated in moun-tainous southern China and came seeking richer soil, a warmer climate, and escape from the expanding Han Chinese. Over the centuries, those who stayed in the mountains largely retained their animistic beliefs and tribal organization, and those who ventured into the lowlands came into contact with Mon-Khmer people, accepting the latter's methods of agriculture, statecraft, religion, and writing, while keeping some of their own languages and elements of social organization. In the late 13th century, the Khmer Empire weakened, and a number of Tai-speaking, Theravada Buddhist kingdoms sprang up along the Mekong River.

The Lan Xang Kingdom

In the 14th century, the Lao kingdom Lan Xang (Million Elephants), centered on Luang Prabang, came into being. Its founder, the semi-legendary Fa Ngum, was an ethnic Lao who spent much of his life as an exile in the Angkorian court. In the 1340s, he was sent north with a 10,000-man army to negotiate with vassal cities and keep them from falling under Ayutthayan control. Instead, Fa Ngum broke away from Angkor in a series of campaigns and, in 1353, founded Lan Xang. Over the next few years, he gained the allegiance of principalities around the Mekong, and extended his kingdom into what is now northeastern Thailand.

Fa Ngum was deposed by his son, Un Heuan, for obscure reasons. His successor then set about consolidating his power through army recruitment, and by marrying into the royal families of Ayutthaya and Chiang Mai.

500 BC Modern-day Champasak (Southern Laos) ruled by Champa kingdom; megalithic culture in the Plain of Jars, Northern Laos

AD 900–1300 Most of Laos is subordinate to the Khmer Empire at Angkor

1431 Ayutthayan armies sack Angkor, causing the demise of the Khmer Empire

500 BC	AD 1	500	1000	1500

Stone jars excavated at the Plain of Jars

1353 Fa Ngum founds Theravada Buddhist Lao kingdom of Lan Xang

1374 Un Heuan replaces Fa Ngum as ruler of Lan Xang

◀ Gold relief at Wat Mai Suwannaphumaham, built in the 14th century during the Lan Xang Kingdom

The 16th and 17th centuries were a golden age for Lan Xang. The first Westerners in Laos, visiting in the 1640s, left accounts of a peaceful and prosperous kingdom, a hospitable population, and a capital richly ornamented with religious buildings. A Dutch merchant noted that Buddhist monks in Vientiane were "more numerous than the armies of the German Emperor." However, by 1700, the kingdom had broken into four semi-independent principalities, forced to pay tribute to Ayutthaya.

Siamese troops with artillery on elephant back advancing into Laos to combat French expansion

Siam and Vietnam

Luang Prabang was sacked by the Burmese army in the latter half of the 18th century, and Vientiane was sacked by the Siamese army in the early 19th century. Siam was a kingdom based in Thonburi, across the river from Bangkok. It soon became the paramount state in the region, and Lan Xang effectively disappeared. For most of the 19th century, the lowland areas were dependent on Siam, and Vietnam controlled much of the mountainous north. The key figure in this period of Lao history was Chao Anou, a nobleman who became the king of Vientiane under Siamese protection in 1804. Fifteen years later, after he gained control over the southern principality of Champasak, Anou mounted a military campaign against Bangkok in an effort to establish an independent Lao kingdom. The campaign was a disaster: the Siamese army burned down Vientiane and moved its population into Siam. Anou was captured and taken to Bangkok,

Wat doors with elaborate carvings

where he died. For the remainder of the century, the Siamese court maintained tight control over Lao populations on both sides of the Mekong, while the newly empowered Nguyen dynasty in Vietnam took over much of what is now Northern Laos.

French Rule

In the late 1850s, France expressed imperial interests in Indochina by taking possession first of southern Vietnam, and then of Cambodia. By 1885, the French had annexed central and northern Vietnam. Eight years later, after threatening Siam with full-scale war, France was able to peaceably acquire the territory east of the Mekong, that is, most of present-day Laos. Thus, in 1907, Laos was formally united for the first time since 1700, under French rule. Three of its four principalities were ruled directly, without princes, and the fourth (Luang Prabang), by a powerless and cooperative monarch.

Crest of the Dutch East India Company

1637–49 Reign of King Surinyavongsā, considered the Golden Age of Lan Xang

1700 Lan Xang broken into four semi-independent principalities that pay tribute to the Kingdom of Ayutthaya

1600　　　**1650**　　　**1700**　　　1750

1563 Vientiane made capital of Lan Xang in an effort to escape Burmese threats

1641 Gerritt van Wuysthoff, a representative of the Dutch East India Company, is among the first Europeans to arrive in Laos

Buddha at Wat Si Saket, built by Chao Anou

A pioneer in developing Franco-Lao relations was the adventurous geographer Auguste Pavie, who had convinced the Lao upper class that being protected by France would be preferable to submitting to open-ended Siamese control. As a result, France's Colonial burden, such as it was, was lightened by a friendly elite, and the mildness of French economic intervention. During this period, Laos contained only seven percent of Indochina's people, generated one percent of its foreign trade, and in the 1930s, employed fewer than 500 French administrators. Throughout the Colonial period, the kingdom was overwhelmingly rural – less than two percent of the population lived in provincial towns. Vietnamese immigrants dominated the civil service as well as the small commercial sector.

King Sisavang Vong (1885–1959)

Early 20th Century

The idea of independence for Indochina did not arise until World War II, when parts of the region had openly gone into revolt. When France fell to Germany in 1940, the French and Lao were defenseless against the irredentist claims of the pro-Japanese regime in Bangkok. After a brief war, aimed primarily at regaining provinces lost in 1907, Thailand (as Siam had renamed itself in 1939) took over those parts of Laos that lay

west of the Mekong. Stung by the territorial loss, and fearful of further claims, the French proclaimed Laos to be a unified protectorate in 1941. However, in March 1945, the Japanese military imprisoned French civil servants and soldiers throughout Indochina and made local rulers declare independence. The Lao king, Sisavang Vong, the most loyal ruler in the region, refused to do so for a month.

Japan's surrender at the end of World War II created a power vacuum in Indochina. In Laos, this gave rise to three conflicting camps: a pro-French royalist faction led by the king, the Lao nationalists who as the Lao Issara (Free Lao) formed a government in exile in 1945, and Vietnamese Communists recruited from the Vietnamese population and supported by quasi-independent northern Vietnam. These groups maneuvered against each other in what they hoped would soon be an independent kingdom. Their dispute revealed deep fissures within the different parts of Laos, between Communists and non-Communists, and within the Lao elite.

French steamer on a Mekong tributary in Southern Laos, late 19th century

| 1771 Burmese armies sack Luang Prabang | 1828 The Siamese army burns down Vientiane | 1941 Thailand annexes Lao territory west of the Mekong after the Franco-Thai war |

1782 Siam seizes power in Vientiane · 1885 French annex central and northern Vietnam · 1893 French seize Lao territories east of Mekong

1800 · **1850** · **1900**

1804 Chao Anou becomes king of Vientiane · 1907 Franco-Siamese treaty establishes current borders of Laos

1945 Encouraged by the Japanese, the Lao king reluctantly declares independence

Postcard from French-Colonial Laos

Struggle for Independence

Foreign and domestic nation builders in Laos were thwarted in their efforts to unify the country by embedded habits of regionalism, rivalries among the Lao elite, poor communications, and by the devastation of the First Indochina War and the Vietnam War. When Laos was drawn into the First Indochina War, few of its people had strong political ideas. Those who did were either members of the Vietnamese-dominated Indochinese Communist Party (ICP), or were associated with the nationalist movement called Lao Issara. Supported by the Francophobic authorities in Thailand, Lao Issara had formed an interim government.

In 1946, the French returned in force, establishing a new Kingdom of Laos with Sisavang Vong as its ruler. The French hoped that the gesture would unify its protectorate and set it on the road to eventual independence. In 1950, they

Prince Souvanna
Phouma (1901–84)

awarded Laos partial independence, keeping control over the nation's defense and foreign affairs. Four years later, following the Geneva Conference, Laos obtained full independence.

In this postwar era, two Lao princes played important political roles. Prince Souvanna Phouma worked for Lao Issara until 1949, when he returned to Laos, and was often prime minister of Laos in later years. His half-brother, Prince Souphanouvong, broke with Lao Issara in 1949 and joined the Vietnamese-led resistance movement known as Pathet Lao.

The Vietnam War

The Geneva Conference stipulated that Pathet Lao troops would be stationed in two provinces of Northern Laos bordering Vietnam, pending a demobilization which never occurred. Fissures soon developed between these Communist enclaves and successive pro-Western, or neutralist, governments in Laos. In 1960, a fight broke out between the Pathet Lao and the poorly trained Lao army. In an effort to establish stability in the kingdom, a second Geneva Conference was held in 1961–2, where the warring parties pledged to support a neutral Laos. However, the agreement was soon subverted by both the US and North Vietnam. From 1964 onward, eastern Laos was subjected to intensive aerial bombardment – a largely unsuccessful US effort to disrupt the extensive North Vietnamese supply lines known as the Ho Chi Minh Trail. In Northern Laos, surrogate forces paid by the US fought Pathet Lao forces backed by

Pro-Communist demonstrators marching against US Imperialism in the streets of Vientiane

1950 France grants Laos partial independence

1954 Following the first Geneva Conference, Laos gains full independence

1964 US begins bombing Communist targets in Laos

Carrying supplies along the Ho Chi Minh Trail in Laos

1955

1965

1975

1954–75 Vietnam War

1973 Cease-fire between the US and North Vietnam

1975 Lao King Sisavang Vatthana abdicates; the LPRP takes over peacefully in Vientiane

1946–54 First Indochina War

1961–2 Second Geneva Conference supports a neutral government in Laos

US artillery and Lao refugees crossing the border into South Vietnam, 1971

North Vietnam. Efforts to establish a neutral government in Vientiane came to nothing. After a cease-fire between the US and North Vietnam in 1973, fighting subsided In Laos.

Communism and Stability

Once Vietnam was unified under the Communists and Cambodia had fallen to the Khmer Rouge *(see p42)*, a Communist Lao state was only a matter of time. The last king of Laos, Sisavang Vatthana, abdicated in December 1975, and on the following day the Lao People's Democratic Republic (LPDR) was formally established. The Lao People's Revolutionary Party (LPRP), an offshoot of the Indochinese Communist Party (ICP), led the new state.

The Communists who took power in 1975 have never been seriously challenged, but the early years of the new regime were hard for people unsympathetic to Marxism-Leninism. Many were herded into "re-education" camps and many more sought refuge in Thailand. Over the years, the LPRP displayed extraordinary survival skills and rarely resorted to popular repression. Vietnamese guidance was welcomed,

especially from 1975 to 1990. In the late 1980s, as the Cold War ended, Vietnam withdrew most of its forces and the LPRP relaxed its top-down economic policies. Market forces re-emerged, Buddhist practices revived, tourism picked up, and relations warmed with Thailand. Symbolically, a bridge across the Mekong, the first in Lao history, was completed in 1994. Laos joined the Association of Southeast Asian Nations (ASEAN) in 1997.

In the 21st century, Laos exchanged the patronage of Vietnam for the corporate protection of ASEAN and the benefits, such as they are, of globalization, which include massive investment in the country and the assurance of a less impoverished future.

The Thai-Lao Friendship Bridge across the Mekong

1988 Vietnamese troops officially withdraw from Laos as the Cold War draws to a close

1997 Laos joins the Association of Southeast Asian Nations (ASEAN)

Choummaly Sayasone, President of the Lao People's Democratic Republic

1995

2005

2015

1994 Inauguration of the first bridge spanning the Mekong River

Flag of Laos, officially, the Lao People's Democratic Republic

2006 Choummaly Sayasone elected General Secretary of the Lao People's Revolutionary Party

Laos at a Glance

Owing to its geographical expanse, Laos encompasses amazingly diverse terrains. Much of the country is covered by steep, verdant mountain ranges, which gradually give way to plateaus and mixed deciduous forests. The mighty Mekong River dominates the topography of the land and runs through nearly its entire length. Vientiane, the capital city, has many beautiful Buddhist temples, while the ancient royal capital of Luang Prabang is home to the Phabang, the country's most sacred Buddha image. The south is renowned for a magnificent inland archipelago, a counterpoint to the remote mountainous regions of the north.

Wat Xieng Thong *(see pp162–3)*, located at the tip of the Luang Prabang peninsula at the confluence of the Mekong and the Nam Khan rivers, is an exquisite Buddhist temple. It has great historical significance as the coronation venue of Lao kings.

U Thai

Phongsali

Muang Sing

Lunag Nam Tha

Muang Ngoi

NORTHERN LAOS
(see pp170–187)

Huay Xai

Luang Prabang

LUAN· PRABAI
(see pp150–

Boat Tour on the Mekong

Vang Vieng

VIENTIA
(see pp138–

Pak Lai

Vientiane

Vang Vieng *(see pp174–5)* draws numerous visitors due to its signature activity of tubing on the Nam Song. Surrounded by stunning mountain scenery, the limestone karst cliffs are perfect for spelunking. Other attractions include rock climbing and kayaking.

Xieng Khuan *(see p148)*, also known as Buddha Park, is home to a collection of enigmatic statuary made by a Lao holy man, Luang Phu Bounleua Soulilat. Sculptures range from Hindu gods to mermaids and a giant Reclining Buddha.

A Boat Tour on the Mekong *(see pp186–7)* offers splendid views of the region's striking karst limestone mountain slopes, pastoral life, and herds of wild elephants. Boat tours beginning at Huay Xai, the last border town before Thailand, offer an ideal way to explore the area.

Plain of Jars *(see p177),* named after the hundreds of giant stone urns left behind by an ancient megalithic culture, remains an archaeological enigma. The area witnessed intense bombing during the Vietnam War *(1954–75).*

Sam Neua   Vieng Xai

Ban Khong

Muang Kham

nonsavan

Paksan

Lak Sao

CENTRAL AND SOUTHERN LAOS *(see pp188–203)*

Thakhek

Sepon

Savannakhet

avannakhet *(see pp194 5)* is charming riverside town that connected to Thailand by e Thai-Lao Friendship Bridge.

Salavan

Pakse   Paksong

Attapeu

0 kilometers   100

0 miles   100

Muang Khong

Wat Phu Champasak *(see pp198–9),* the largest archaeological site in the country, offers superb examples of Khmer architecture. The Buddhist Lao, who revere the site, have added their own religious iconography to the temple.

Si Phan Don *(see pp202–3)* is an inland archipelago on the Mekong River just north of the Cambodian border.

The Bolaven Plateau *(see p200)* is home to several ethnic minorities such as the Katu, who cultivate rice and other temperate crops such as coffee.

VIENTIANE

The capital of Laos, Vientiane is also Asia's smallest capital.
The city's plan of intersecting streets and boulevards dates
from the early 20th century; these are lined with fine examples of
Buddhist and Colonial-era architecture. Once a sleepy backwater,
today Vientiane is in the midst of a revival, and the city's chic restaurants
and boutiques attract many local and international visitors.

Located on a bend in the wide Mekong
River, the capital city of Laos has survived
numerous changes over the centuries.
More than 1,000 years ago it was a Khmer
trading post. In the 16th century it
became the capital of the Lao kingdom,
but was ultimately destroyed by the
Siamese in 1828. The French Colonialists
appropriated the country as part of
their Indochinese empire in the late
19th century, and Vientiane was chosen
to be their administrative capital. During
the Cold War (1945–91), it was flooded
with refugees while the rest of the country
witnessed intense bombing, and the city
suffered throughout its time as a Soviet-
era Socialist backwater.

Vientiane has undergone rapid changes
during the last couple of decades. The
strict Communist stance of the country
was relaxed after the collapse of the Soviet
Union in 1991, and new business ventures
sprung up around the city. Many Lao
exiles also returned to reclaim
properties they had abandoned as they
fled the Communist regime, and they
are now re-establishing homes and
businesses here.

The religious architecture of Vientiane
is splendid and its numerous *wats* are
positively vibrant with worshipers. The Lao
National Museum has world-class exhibits
covering Lao history from prehistoric
times until the more recent Communist
Revolution of 1975. The Buddhist art on
display at Haw Pha Kaew is the best in the
country. The city's restaurants and hotels
offer Lao and Western cuisine, at reasonable prices, and are often located in
restored French Colonial buildings. While
the riverfront along Fa Ngum Road is
being redeveloped, which will result in a
riverside park, visitors looking for peace
and quiet can head upstream, west of
Khun Bulom Road, where they can enjoy
a drink at sundown by the Mekong.

A French-style restaurant with alfresco dining near Nam Phu Square, Vientiane

◀ One of the four archways of the Patuxai monument, Vientiane

Exploring Vientiane

A few of the most interesting places in Vientiane, such as the Haw Pha Kaew, Wat Si Saket, and Wat Ong Teu Mahawihan, lie between Samsenthai Road and the Mekong River. The lively Talat Sao, where visitors can buy an array of items, is located near Lan Xang Avenue, which leads to the French-inspired Patuxai monument, while Setthathirat Road has numerous cafés, boutiques, and restaurants. Closer to the river border with Thailand is the Xieng Khuan (Buddha Park), with its huge collection of statues. Visitors keen on the outdoors can head to Phu Khao Khuay NPA, where they can enjoy hikes and nature walks.

A sandstone sculpture at Xieng Khuan

Sights at a Glance

Places of Worship
1 Wat Si Muang
3 Wat Si Saket
4 Wat Ong Teu Mahawihan
8 Wat Sok Pa Luang
9 Pha That Luang

Museums
2 Haw Pha Kaew
5 Lao National Museum
10 Kaysone Phomvihane Memorial Museum

Sites of Interest
7 Patuxai
11 Lao Experiences

Market
6 Talat Sao

Areas of Natural Beauty
12 Xieng Khuan
13 Phu Khao Khuay National Protected Area

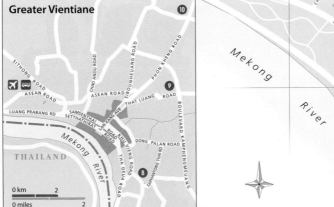

Greater Vientiane

THAILAND

Mekong River

0 km   2
0 miles   2

■ Area illustrated in the main map

Getting Around

Most of the main sites in Vientiane are within comfortable walking distance of each other, but bicycles are available for rent from a number of guesthouses and rental shops across the city. This is a good option for those who want to avoid walking in the tropical heat. Motorcycles offer another way of traveling around the city and can be rented for a few dollars per day. Tuk-tuks can be found outside tourist spots and hotels, or can be flagged down on roads. For journeys to areas around Vientiane, taxis or buses are better options.

VISITORS' CHECKLIST

Practical Information
Road Map B3. 🗺 300,00. *i* Lao National Tourism Administration, Lan Xang Ave, (021)-212-251 Ext 103 or 101, info@tourismlaos.org. 🕐 daily. 🎏 Boat Racing Festival (Oct), Boun That Luang (Nov).
w tourismlaos.org

Transport
✈ Wattay International Airport.
🚉 🚌

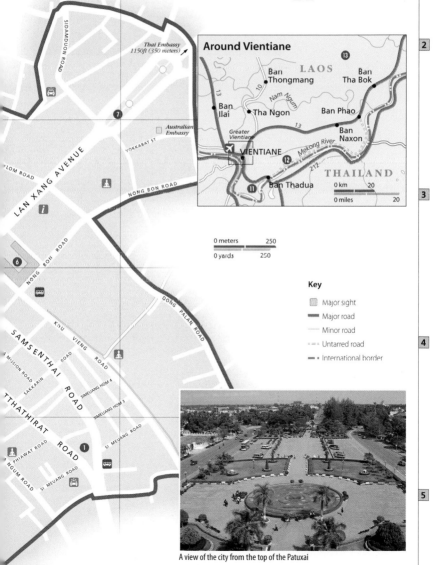

Around Vientiane

A view of the city from the top of the Patuxai

Key

- ◻ Major sight
- ▬ Major road
- — Minor road
- === Untarred road
- ▬ International border

● Wat Si Muang

Convergence of Setthathirat & Samsenthai Rds. **City map** D5. **Open** 8am–3pm daily.

One of the best-known temples in Vientiane, Wat Si Muang houses the *lak muang*, or city pillar, which was installed here by King Setthathirat in 1563 after he moved the Lao capital from Luang Prabang to Vientiane. The temple was razed by the Siamese when they sacked the city in 1828 and later rebuilt.

Today, the temple is a vibrant place of worship and considered particularly auspicious by devotees who come here to perform a variety of rituals. The current *sim* (ordination hall) dates from 1915 and is divided into two chambers. Inside the front chamber, devotees are blessed by a monk with holy water and a *baci* string *(see p126)* is tied to the wrist. After this, worshippers with a particular wish lie face downward before what was once a Buddha image, but is now only a melted lump, having been damaged when the Siamese set the temple on fire. The ritual involves lifting the image three times above the head while expressing the wish. The inner sanctum of the temple houses the city pillar, now gilded and wrapped with a sacred cloth.

Manicured gardens leading up to the main entrance, Haw Pha Kaew

Devotees offering prayers in the main *sim*, Wat Si Muang

An offering, Wat Si Muang

Incense is burned here and candles are lit as offerings to the city spirit. The blackened ceiling of this chamber is testament to the number of offerings made here.

Behind the temple are the laterite remains of an ancient Khmer religious site, next to which a statue of Vientiane's guardian goddess, Sao Si, is located. Legend has it that when the city pillar was installed, Sao Si jumped beneath it to appease malevolent spirits and to bring good fortune to the city. Today, worshippers make fervent offerings to commemorate her sacrifice. East of the temple compound stands a statue of King Sisavang Vong (r.1904–59), holding a copy of the country's first legal code. The statue, a gift from the Soviet Union, was installed here in 1974. Although the royal family perished in prison camps in the northeast, the statue was spared.

❷ Haw Pha Kaew

Setthathirat Rd. **City map** C4. **Open** 8am–noon & 1–4pm daily.

The original structure of this temple-turned-museum was destroyed by the Siamese in 1828. It was reconstructed under the supervision of the Lao prince Souvanna Phouma, a French-trained engineer and later prime minister of the country during the French Colonial period. Once the exclusive temple of Lao kings, Haw Pha Kaew is no longer a functioning Buddhist temple, but a national museum of splendid Buddhist art.

Ironically, it is named after a precious piece of religious art, the Pha Kaew (Emerald Buddha), which is no longer here. Made of jade, it is as important an icon as the Phabang *(see p155)* in Luang Prabang. However, it was seized by the Siamese in 1779, and has remained in Wat Phra Kaew in Bangkok ever since. A signboard, both in Lao and English, expresses the Lao peoples' indignation at this act. However, this well-traveled talisman actually originated in India and spent much time in Thailand until King Setthathirat took it from Chiang Mai when the Lao kingdom of Lan Xang ruled northern Thailand.

Today, the main attraction of this impressive museum is the magnificent collection of bronze Buddha images on a terrace surrounding the building. These have been collected from various temples in the country. Artifacts inside the building include smaller Buddha images, Khmer stelae, bronze frog drums, and a large Seated Buddha image. The beautifully landscaped gardens of the museum offer a verdant respite from the heat of central Vientiane.

❸ Wat Si Saket

Setthathirat Rd. **City map** C4.
Open 8am–noon & 1–4pm daily. 🖼

The oldest *wat* in Vientiane, Wat Si Saket was spared the destruction wrought by the Siamese when they burned the rest of the temples in the city. Wat Si Saket was built in 1818 for King Anouvong, popularly known as Chao Anou, and it was here that Lao nobility swore loyalty to him. Anouvong turned against his original allies, the Siamese, and lost his capital – and his life – as a result.

The architectural feature that makes this temple unique is the cloister, or covered gallery, surrounding the central *sim*. The inner walls of the cloister are filled with more than 2,000 Buddha images arranged in symmetrical niches facing the *sim*. The *sim* itself has an exquisite five-tiered roof, which was restored by the French twice, resulting in a ceiling with a rather European finish. A carved wooden *hao thian* (candle holder) lies near the altar. One of the highlights of this enchanting ancient collection of Buddhist art is a *hdang song nam pha*, a *naga*-headed trough. It is kept in the covered gallery and used for pouring holy water over the Buddha images during the Lao New Year *(see p126)*.

Exhibits of historical significance on display, Lao National Museum

❹ Wat Ong Teu Mahawihan

Setthathirat Rd. **City map** B3.
Open 8am–5pm daily.

The *wat*'s name, meaning Temple of the Heavy Buddha, derives from the 19-ft (6-m) tall bronze Buddha statue, dating from the 16th century, which is kept within the *sim*. The site is significant because it is believed to have been used for religious purposes since the 3rd century. A few Khmer stelae are housed in a *sala* (open-sided hall) within the complex. Monks from all over Laos come to study in the school that is housed in the *wat*. Visitors can strike up an enlightening conversation with these erudite young men. The school is directed by the Hawng

Intricate detail of façade, Wat Ong Teu Mahawihan

Sangkhalat (Deputy Patriarch) of the Lao monastic order.

❺ Lao National Museum

Samsenthai Rd. **City map** B3.
Open 8am–noon & 1–4pm daily.
🖼 🖼 🖼

Once known as the Lao Revolutionary Museum, and derided by foreigners for its Socialist Realism and overt propaganda, the Lao National Museum is gradually being revamped. It now offers fascinating exhibits, well displayed and illuminated, with informative captions in English. The museum traces the history of the country from prehistoric times to the present.

The displays, showcasing artifacts from both the Lao Pako archaeological site and the Plain of Jars *(see p177)*, as well as Khmer- and Buddhist-era exhibits, are excellent. The Buddhist-era room features a rare Thai Lue Buddha image, which resembles an animist icon. The life-sized re-creations of the Khmer lintels of Wat Phu Champasak *(see pp198–9)* are impressive, as are the original Hindu artifacts from the temple, including Shiva and Ganesha statues. The modern-era exhibits mainly comprise photographs of revolutionary heroes, which are interesting relics of those times, while the displays of cluster bombs dropped by the Americans are chilling. The second floor has a display on minority cultures.

Covered cloister with niches containing Buddha images, Wat Si Saket

Brightly colored souvenirs on sale, Talat Sao

❻ Talat Sao

Corner of Lan Xang Ave & Khu Vieng Rd. **City map** D3. **Open** 8am–6pm daily. ▨ ▯ ▩

Clearly referring to a bygone era when it functioned as a wet market for the housewives of Vientiane, Talat Sao, meaning Morning Market, has long since been transformed into an interesting complex of shops. A large portion of the structure dates from the 1960s, and has shops selling electronic goods, such as refrigerators, as well as other home appliances, catering mainly to local needs. Visitors will also find shops selling handicrafts, antiques, jewelry, and 24-karat gold ornaments. Other items of interest include textiles, particularly the beautiful handwoven silk and cotton *pha sins* (wraparound) worn by Lao women, which make attractive souvenirs. Accompanying the *pha sins* are magnificent hand-worked silver belts and silver ornaments such as bracelets and earrings. Bargaining is *de riguer* for anything bought here, and antiques and gemstones are best left to those with sound knowledge of such items, since fakes abound. However, some of the reproduction antiques, generally from Vietnam, are quite attractive. These items are usually priced and sold as reproductions, though visitors should be wary of buying overpriced pieces. There is a

small air-conditioned mall on the southwestern side of the market, and a major hotel and retail construction project has transformed the market's structure, although the goods on offer have remained the same.

The food court on the third floor of the mall, where delicious local cuisine is available, is an ideal stop for weary shoppers. Visitors eager to experience an authentic Lao market selling fresh local produce such as vegetables, flowers, meat, and tobacco can stop by Khua Din, which lies to the east of Talat Sao, just past the bus station.

❼ Patuxai

Lan Xang Ave. **City map** D2. **Open** 8am–5pm daily. ▨ for tower only. ▩

At first sight, the Patuxai, which means Victory Gate, brings to mind the Arc de Triomphe in Paris. The monument was constructed in 1964 to commemorate the lives lost during the course of the Lao Civil War, fought between 1953 and 1975. It is made of concrete, which is rumored to have been donated by the Americans for the

construction of a new airport. The arch is adorned with the typically Lao mixture of Buddhist and Hindu iconography, along with bas-reliefs of *apsaras* facing fierce demons from the Hindu epic, *Ramayana*.

A spiral staircase leads to the top of the monument. En route visitors will pass dozens of souvenir shops that specialize in T-shirts. Once at the top, visitors are rewarded with excellent views across Lan Xang Avenue toward the Mekong River. The Patuxai is best visited early in the morning in order to avoid the heat, and the crowds brought by tour buses.

Vibrant reliefs adorning the ceiling of the Patuxai

Types of Tuk-Tuk

Three types of tuk-tuk ply the streets of Vientiane. The first is the tourist tuk-tuk, which visitors will usually find waiting in queues outside tourist hotspots. Although hiring one of these should not be expensive, drivers generally quote very high prices and

Colorful jumbo tuk-tuk

also produce laminated fare tables to prove the legitimacy of their demands. The second is the wandering tuk-tuk, which can be hailed from anywhere, although it is best not to do so from near a queue of the tourist tuk-tuks. Prices are negotiable and cheaper than those demanded by tourist tuk-tuk drivers. Lastly, there is the jumbo, which charges a set price and follows a fixed route. These are the cheapest and can be boarded from tuk-tuk stations. It is worth traveling by one of these vehicles for an interesting local experience.

A wandering tuk-tuk plying the streets of Vientiane

Gilded structure of the Lao national monument, Pha That Luang

🔞 Wat Sok Pa Luang

Off Khu Vieng Rd. **City map** A5.
Open 8am–3pm daily.

A visit to this simple *wat*, located in a quiet outer suburb, presents an interesting alternative to visiting the grand temples that line the streets of Vientiane. The compound of the *wat*, whose name means Forest Temple, is filled with shady trees. Just outside the entrance to the *wat* is a house offering traditional massages as well as herbal saunas that are available in the afternoons, every day of the week. The temple also offers courses in Vipassana, which is a type of Buddhist meditation.

🔞 Pha That Luang

That Luang Rd. **City map** B4.
Open 8am–noon & 1–4pm daily.
Boun That Luang (Nov).

This important religious monument, whose name means The Great Stupa, is also the symbol of Lao nationhood. Its image appears on the currency as well as the national seal. Excavations have indicated the existence of a Khmer site here dating from around the 12th century, long before the Pha That Luang was erected in its present form. King Setthathirat ordered its construction when he moved

Carving at Wat Sok Pa Luang

the Lao capital from Luang Prabang to Vientiane in the mid-16th century. After the Siamese razed the city in 1828, the site was abandoned, and bandits seeking gold and jewels later destroyed the edifice. The French rebuilt it in the 1930s with the aid of drawings made by French explorers who had visited the abandoned site in 1867.

Today, the That Luang lies in a large compound behind a statue of King Setthathirat, and is flanked by two Buddhist temples. The main stupa reaches 148 ft (45 m) above ground level, and is surrounded by three platforms of decreasing size, each of which is surrounded by rows of smaller stupas and lotus petal-shaped crenulations. A cloister on the outermost wall contains both

Lao and Khmer Buddha images. Boun That Luang, held here in November *(see p128)*, is among the most important festivals in Vientiane, and lasts for several days.

🔟 Kaysone Phomvihane Memorial Museum

NH13, Ban Sivilay, Muang Saythani.
City map B4. **Open** 8am–noon & 1–4pm daily.

Located on the main road south of Vientiane, this museum is divided into two parts. The first is a grandiose memorial to the late president and founding father of Communist Laos, Kaysone Phomvihane, and the second is the actual house in which he lived after the Communists seized power in 1975. The memorial is a huge, well-kept hall that includes a scale model of the late president's childhood home in Savannakhet *(see p194)*, and various revolutionary memorabilia. More interesting, however, is his home, which is located on what was once a US military and CIA base, which the Pathet Lao occupied after its former occupants were ousted. It is a modest, single-story bungalow and has been kept exactly as it was when Kaysone Phomvihane resided here, with his library, work table, and other personal items on display. The house is a short distance from the memorial hall, but staff are happy to guide visitors there.

Bronze statue of Kaysone Phomvihane in front of his memorial

Buddhist statuary at the Xieng Khuan Buddha park, southeast of Vientiane ▶

Giant Reclining Buddha amid several smaller statues, Xieng Khuan

⓫ Lao Experiences

Full Moon Café, Rue Francois Ngin, Riverfront Precinct, Vientiane.
Tel (020)-5569-9429.
Open daily (experiences should be reserved at least a day in advance).
📧 🔳 lao-experiences.com

The Vientiane-based Full Moon Café offers visitors an insight into the culture of the country through its culinary programs. There are options to take a Lao food-tasting tour or a full cooking workshop in the garden of the café. The tasting tour involves a trip to a fresh food market with a Lao Experiences guide who will explain the essential ingredients of Lao cooking, and guide you around the market where authentic Lao ingredients can be tasted. The cookery classes focus on Lao specialties such as

sticky rice pancakes and Mekong River Fish in banana leaf, as well as the preparation of a traditional fish sauce. The tasting tour and the cooking classes can be combined at a discounted rate.

For anyone interested in food, an independent visit to a local day market is a must. Markets are where most Lao go to buy food and the stalls here are full of colorful vegetables, buckets of live fish, and a variety of hanging meat.

⓬ Xieng Khuan

Thadeua Rd, 16 miles (26 km) SE of Vientiane. 🚌 from Vientiane.
Open 8am–5pm daily. 🏍 🔳

Also known as Buddha Park, Xieng Khuan is located in a pleasant meadow next to the Mekong, and is surrounded by

shady trees. This collection of ferro-concrete statuary far exceeds the standard Hindu-Buddhist syncretism that can be seen in most Lao temples. The sculptures are products of the vivid imagination of the Lao guru Luang Phu Bounleua Soulilat. Inspired by the teachings of a Hindu holy man whom he met in a cave in Vietnam, Luang Phu proceeded to create this collection based on his own visions. Luang Phu was not popular with the Communists, and in 1975 he left Laos to create a similar collection of statuary in a park directly across the river in Nong Khai, Thailand, the main stupa of which is visible from here.

Made by amateur artists under Soulilat's direction, this eclectic collection ranges from an enormous Reclining Buddha to statues of Hindu gods, holy men battling with crocodiles, enormous insects, and vestal virgins dancing on giant cobras. Particularly interesting is the large spherical structure at the front of the park, which can be entered through the gaping mouth of a 10-ft (3-m) tall demon head. Inside are staircases leading to three different levels said to represent hell, earth, and heaven. They finally emerge at the top of the structure which overlooks the park. Nearby is a riverside café, which provides a cool and relaxing stop for visitors.

Family stand at Vientiane day market

For hotels and restaurants see p213 and pp228–9

⑬ Phu Khao Khuay National Protected Area

30 miles (48 km) NE of Vientiane. 🚌 from southern bus terminal to Ban Tha Bok. 🚢 ⓘ National Tourism Administration, Vientiane, (021)-212-251. 🖉 📷 ⓦ **trekkingcentrallaos.com**

Boating down a river, Phu Khao Khuay National Protected Area

Covering an area of more than 770 sq miles (2,000 sq km), Phu Khao Khuay, meaning Buffalo Horn Mountain, is the closest National Protected Area to Vientiane, and is excellent for visitors who do not have the time or opportunity to see nature preserves farther afield. The area's wildlife includes the tiger, Asiatic black bear, sun bear, clouded leopard, elephant, and a plethora of smaller mammals and bird species. Many wild orchids and other flora are also found here. Trekking, boat trips, swimming, nature walks, and village homestays are some of the activities and experiences on offer. It is also possible to observe wild elephants.

The entrance to Phu Khao Khuay NPA is off Route 13 going north from Vientiane at kilometer 92, just before the village of Ban Tha Bok. Here, a turnoff on the left signposted to Long Xane leads to the NPA. Although visitors can explore the area independently using a rented motorcycle or car, it is best to employ local guides as their knowledge of the area will make the trip much more interesting. Independent guides are available in Ban Hat Khai, but language remains a challenge. Green Discovery (see p245) in Vientiane offers tours to the elephant observation tower near the village of Ban Na, and other parts of Phu Khao Khuay. Vientiane Orchidées (see p245) organizes treks that combine boat travel and nature walks, focusing on the many species of wild orchid that flourish in the NPA. Both companies offer one-day and several-day trips from Vientiane.

Bright yellow orchid

Ban Hat Khai

5 miles (8 km) NE of Ban Tha Bok. The village of Ban Hat Khai is an ideal place from which to take boat tours and trekking trips deep into Phu Khao Khuay, particularly to the spectacular 328-ft (100-m) high cliff of Pha Luang. Some 3 miles (5 km) north of Ban Hat Khai lies the beautiful Tat Xai waterfall, which is a popular picnic spot for residents of Vientiane. Although not as impressive, the Tat Leuk waterfall, located 3 miles (5 km) west of Ban Hat Khai, has a natural pool at its foot that is excellent for swimming. The visitors' center here can arrange treks and provide information on the conditions of all the trails and rivers in the area, which change with the seasons. Visitors can also rent tents and other basic camping equipment from the visitors' center for a small fee.

Ban Na

4 miles (6 km) SW of Ban Tha Bok. A typical Lao village with lush paddy fields, Ban Na is a great stop for visitors keen to observe wild elephants. The elephant observation tower at Pung Xai, 4 miles (6 km) from here, is located next to a salt lick and is favored by these majestic beasts. Those lucky enough may get a chance to view the herd in its natural environment should their visit coincide with the herd's

Key

△ Peak
▬ Major road
═ Minor road
= = Dirt track
▬ • Park boundary
▬ • International border

0 km — 5
0 miles — 5

Pha Luang
328 ft (100 m)

Tat Xai

Ban Hat Khai

Tat Leuk

Ang Nam
Leuk

Pung Xai

Ban Na

Ban Tha
Bok

THAILAND

Phu Sang
5,464 ft (1,666 ft)

Phu Khao Khuay △
3,408 ft (1,039 m)

Vientiane
30 miles (48 km)

For keys to symbols see back flap

LUANG PRABANG

Nestled amid verdant mountains on the banks of the Mekong, Luang Prabang is as enticing for its natural beauty as for the resplendent golden facades of its many *wats*. This is a city of amazing contrasts, where solemn Buddhist monks appear perfectly at home among stylish hotels and restaurants. The city's Colonial heritage, reflected in its architecture and cuisine, adds to its charm.

Located on a compact peninsula formed by the confluence of the Mekong and its tributary, the Nam Khan, Luang Prabang is the former royal capital of Laos. In 1353, Fa Ngum, a Lao prince who had been exiled to the Khmer capital of Angkor, returned and established the first Lao kingdom here. He named it Lan Xang Hom Khao, meaning Kingdom of a Million Elephants and the White Parasol, aptly reflecting the kingdom's military power and royal status. Shortly thereafter, Fa Ngum's Khmer benefactors sent the sacred Phabang, a golden Buddha image, from Sri Lanka. It is from the Phabang that the city has taken its current name. Although the country's administrative capital was moved to Vientiane in 1545, Lao royalty continued to reside here until the Communist takeover in 1975. Over the next decade and more, the city plunged into desolation as thousands of people, including businessmen, academics, and royalty, left it to escape the Communist regime. Luang Prabang finally reopened to the world after the fall of the Soviet Bloc in the 1990s.

In 1995, the city was designated a UNESCO World Heritage Site, and today it remains the uncontested cultural capital of Laos. Its university attracts hundreds of students from the ethnically diverse northern provinces, and numerous hotels, restaurants, and shops have been established to cater for the steady influx of tourists. The locals, however, continue a traditional lifestyle with farming and small-scale trading being two of the primary methods of making a living.

Luang Prabang's main attractions include its many *wats*, which are best explored on foot. Beyond the urban center, in the surrounding countryside, lie several rustic village temples, caves, and waterfalls. Boat tours are also a great way to explore the undiminished beauty of the area.

Robed Buddha images lining a gold stenciled wall in the Chariot Hall, Wat Xieng Thong

◀ View over the lush Nam Khan river, Luang Prabang

Exploring Luang Prabang

The heart of Luang Prabang, also known as the Old Town, lies on a peninsula between the Mekong and the Nam Khan. All sights of interest, most hotels, and restaurants are located on this promontory or immediately to its south. At the center of this area lies the landmark Mt Phou Si, site of the much-revered stupa, That Chomsi. Close to the city's commercial hub is the National Museum Complex, the former home of Lao royalty. The enchanting Night Market, a great place to pick up exquisite handicrafts made by ethnic minorities, is also close by. The northeastern end of the peninsula is dominated by beautiful and ancient *wats*, with the magnificent Wat Xieng Thong situated at its tip. The refreshing Tat Sae and Tat Kuang Si Waterfalls are a short distance away from the city.

A pleasant outdoor café, frequented by travelers

Around Luang Prabang

Ban Pak Lung

LUANG PRABANG

Ban Xom

Xieng Ngeun

Ban Huay Hia

Mekong River

Nam Khan

13N

13NE

22 23 24 25 26

0 km 5
0 miles 5

Area illustrated in the main map

Mekong

Wat Xieng Men

Cross River Ferry

SUVANBANLANG

SOTIKA KUMAN RD

VONG ROAD

SISAVANG

CHAO FA NGUM

KITSARAT

CHAO SISOUPHON

Dara Market

SAMSENTHAI

BUNKHONG

WAT THAT LUANG ROAD

NORADET

PHOTHISARAT

PHU VAO ROAD

MANOMAI ROAD

MANOMAI RD

PHU VAO ROAD

VISUNALAT R

SETTHATHIR

NAVIENGK

1 3 4 5 6 7 8 19 20

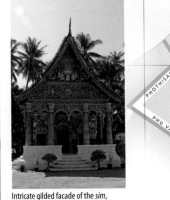

Intricate gilded facade of the *sim*, Wat Pa Phai

A B C

Tree of Life mosaic on the rear wall of the *sim*, Wat Xieng Thong

Getting Around

The Luang Prabang peninsula has four streets that run parallel to each other. These streets are intersected by numerous small lanes running perpendicular to the two rivers. Street names can get a little confusing since the same road is sometimes referred to by different names. However, street names are often irrelevant as directions are given by the nearest landmark or the neighborhood. Fortunately, all sights are located close to each other and can easily be covered on foot. Tuk-tuks ply the regular routes in Luang Prabang and can be hired for sightseeing within the city, as well as for sights around it.

Key

- Major Sight
- Major road
- Minor road
- Untarred road
- Ferry route

Sights at a Glance

Towns and Villages
23 Ban Phanom and
    Mouhot's Tomb
24 Ban Xang Khong

Places of Worship
1 Mt Phou Si and That Chomsi
2 Wat Siphoutabath
4 Wat Mai Suwannaphumaham
7 Wat Xieng Mouan
8 Wat Choum Khong
9 Wat Pa Phai
11 Wat Nong Sikhunmuang
12 Wat Sene
13 Wat Si Boun Huang
14 Wat Khili
16 *Wat Xieng Thong pp162–3*
17 Wat Aham
18 Wat Visounarat
19 Wat Manolom

20 Wat That Luang
21 Wats on the West Bank
22 Santi Chedi

Museums
3 Traditional Arts and Ethnology
    Center
5 National Museum Complex
10 School of Fine Arts

Historical Site
15 UNESCO Maison du
    Patrimoine

Market
6 Night Market

Areas of Natural Beauty
25 Tat Sae Waterfalls
26 Tat Kuang Si Waterfalls

*Wat
Tham
Xieng Maen*

*Wat
Long
Khun*

Wat Chom Phet
21

River

KHEM KHONG
15
16

13
14

SAKKARIN ROAD
12

KINGKITSARAT

11

10

Nam Khan

ROAD

Luang Prabang
International Airport
2 miles (3km)

SISATHTANAK

CHAO XOUMPHOU

0 meters   250

0 yards   250

Street-by-Street: Old Town

The southern end of the Luang Prabang peninsula has several attractions: the Mekong and Khan rivers, a vibrant morning market, and religious and secular architecture. The National Museum Complex, which lies between the Mekong and Mt Phou Si, was constructed by the French between 1904 and 1909 as a residence for King Sisavang Vong. It can be reached by a staircase lined with frangipani trees. The *wats* here range from the rustic Wat Siphoutabath to the splendid Wat Mai Suwannaphumaham. This area also has an assortment of shops, boutique hotels, art galleries, cafés, and restaurants.

Mekong River

SOTIKAKUM

SUVANBANLANG

SISAVANG VONG ROAD

❽ Wat Choum Khong
Two Chinese gods guard the entrance to this temple, which was completed in 1856. The temple is surrounded by a verdant garden, ideal for relaxing. The *sim* is encircled by sculptures of the Buddha in various poses.

❺ ★ National Museum
A unique blend of French and Lao architectural styles, this building houses the sacred Phabang statue. Of equal interest is the throne room with its glass mosaics, as well as the royal artifacts on display.

0 meters 50
0 yards 50

❹ Wat Mai Suwannaphumaham
Elaborate gilded bas-reliefs, which depict scenes from the *Phra Lak Phra Lam*, the Lao version of the *Ramayana*, adorn the front veranda of this *wat*.

Wat Xieng Mouan has a UNESCO-sponsored school on its premises that teaches young monks the arts associated with temple decoration, such as stenciling and lacquerwork.

Locator Map
See Luang Prabang City Map

⑨ Wat Pa Phai
Located in a tree-filled compound, this simple temple is noted for its ornate decoration. The front doors and the surrounding area are not only gilded, but also covered with multi-colored glass mosaic tiles.

Wat Siphoutabath

Shophouse Cafés
Several Colonial-era shophouses line Sisavang Vong Road. These now serve as cafés and restaurants, and are ideal places to relax and observe local street life.

Key

— Suggested route

The Phabang
This 32-inch (83-cm) tall golden Buddha image stands with raised palms in a pose symbolizing protection. The Phabang has bestowed its name on the city. It is also believed to confer spiritual protection on the Lao nation, and Buddhist legitimacy on the country's rulers. A Cambodian king presented it to King Fa Ngum, the founder of the Lan Xang Kingdom. The statue was stolen and, later, returned twice by Siamese kings. It now rests within the National Museum *(see p158)*.

Devotees carrying the Phabang statue

❶ ★ Mt Phou Si and That Chomsi
A flight of 328 steps leads to the top of Phou Si, which means Sacred Mountain in Lao. The simple Buddhist stupa at its summit, That Chomsi, is visible across Luang Prabang and also provides great vistas of the city.

❶ Mt Phou Si and That Chomsi

Sisavang Vong Rd. **City map** C3.
Open 8am–6pm daily. 🎫

Meaning Sacred Mountain in Lao, Mt Phou Si is perhaps the best-known landmark in Luang Prabang. The hill, and the 79-ft (24-m) high **That Chomsi** (a four-sided stupa), on its summit, are visited by locals on the first day of the Lao New Year *(see p126)*.

There are three sets of stairs leading to the summit – one from the National Museum *(see p158)*, where the entry fee is collected, another from the Nam Khan's side, and a third that winds up from behind Wat Siphoutabath. Visitors will find a couple of old temples on the lower slopes of the hill as they make their way up the 328 steps leading to That Chomsi. The stupa, dating from 1804, is more impressive when seen from afar; the adjacent *sim* is rather basic. There are resting places en route but the stunning views of the city from the top certainly make the climb worthwhile.

Elegant Thai-style architecture of Wat Siphoutabath

❷ Wat Siphoutabath

Phou Si Rd. **City map** D3.
Open 8am–3pm daily.

This Thai-style temple, constructed in 1851, takes its name from the stylized Buddha footprint located above the

Ethnic crafts on display, Traditional Arts and Ethnology Center

temple on the path to Mt Phou Si. In the same compound as Wat Siphoutabath is another temple, Wat Pa Khe, whose name is sometimes used to refer to the whole complex. Of particular interest are the bas-relief carvings of Dutch merchants on the doors and window shutters of the two temples. Well executed and in typical Lao style, they are depicted wearing tricorn hats with feathers, tall boots, and with a parrot on each shoulder. The window shutters show a long-haired Westerner with a dog at his feet.

❸ Traditional Arts and Ethnology Center

Between Dara Market and Mt Phou Si.
City map C4. **Tel** (071)-253-364.
Open 9am–6pm Tue–Sun. 🎫 📷 by prior arrangement. 📖 🏠
🌐 **taeclaos.org**

This privately run museum, housed in the restored home of a French judge, at the base of Mt Phou Si, offers an excellent insight into the ethnic cultures of Laos. The museum focuses on the preservation and interpretation of traditional arts, crafts, lifestyles, and culture. Its permanent collection displays more than 200 objects from 17 minority groups. These include clothing, religious artifacts, and household objects, as well as jewelry.

The museum's fair-trade shop sells handicrafts made by local artisans at competitive prices. There is also an excellent café serving food and drinks, with great views of the distant mountains.

❹ Wat Mai Suwannaphumaham

Sisavang Vong Rd. **City map** C3.
Open 8am–3pm daily.

Among the most important *wats* in Luang Prabang, Wat Mai Suwannaphumaham has an opulent exterior covered in red, black, and gold stencil. Inaugurated in 1788, the *wat's* construction took almost 70 years. While restorations have taken place several times, it is one of the few temples in Luang Prabang to have survived in its original form. The *wat* is revered because it was, for decades, the home of the Pha Sangkharat, the most senior monk in Laos. It is also important because the sacred Phabang statue *(see p155)*, the guardian talisman of Luang Prabang, was kept here between 1894 and 1947.

The structure of the *wat* is influenced by both the Luang Prabang style and vernacular architecture. Its *sim* has an impressive five-tiered roof with gilded bas-reliefs on the front veranda. Vivid scenes from the epic *Phra Lak Phra Lam* cover some panels, along with scenes of Lao village life.

Detailed gold stenciling, Wat Mai Suwannaphumaham

Lao Temple Architecture

A *wat* complex usually consists of several buildings in addition to the main ordination hall or *sim*. The *sims* in Lao *wats* differ from place to place and are constructed with variations in the style and design of the roof. While the *sims* of Luang Prabang-style *wats* are noted for their multi-tiered roofs, which almost reach the ground, the Vientiane style features tall and narrow roofs. The Xieng Khuan style, on the other hand, is known for low, single-tiered roofs. The primary decorative color of Lao *wats* is gold, symbolizing the light of the sun. Stencils, bas-reliefs, mosaics of colored glass or tiles, and painted murals are all used, both to create geometric patterns, and to depict religious teachings. Syncretism, or the mixing of various faiths and cultural beliefs, abounds in these places, and elements of both Hinduism and animism are easy to find.

Monks' quarters

A *that* (stupa) contains relics of the Buddha.

Hor tai is the temple library housing sacred scriptures.

The *sim* is the main building of a *wat*, where devout worship takes place and monks are ordained.

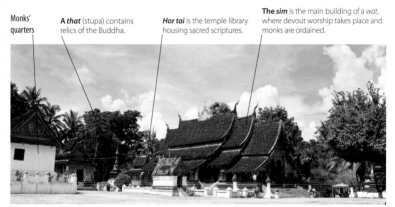

Wat Complex

The layout of a wat complex reflects its diverse functions, which are not limited to worship. It is common to find schools, community centers, and health clinics here. All wats are surrounded by an exterior wall, and all buildings, except the library, are built on the ground, not on stilts.

Hor kang houses the *wat's* ceremonial drums. These drums are usually sounded to awaken the monks at dawn, and to call them for morning and evening prayers.

Decorative Elements

A variety of murals, carved wooden panels, stencils, gilded statuary, and glass mosaic tiles are used to adorn wats.

Murals are usually hand-painted or stenciled. They depict popular tales from the *Jataka* and the *Phra Lak Phra Lam*, the Lao version of the epic *Ramayana*.

Dok heuang pheung is the triangular gable area above the front door of the *sim*.

Dok so faa are metallic roof decorations, often depicting parasols or pagodas.

So faa are roof finials that point upward, often in the shape of a *naga* (serpent).

5 National Museum Complex

Sisavang Vong Rd. **City map** C3. **Open** 8:30am–11:30am & 1:30pm–3:30pm Wed–Mon.  inside the museum.

Cuban royal palms bordering the path to the National Museum

The former home of Lao royalty, the National Museum Complex lies between the Mekong River and Mt Phou Si. Designed by French architects, the palace in the complex was constructed for King Sisavang Vong (r.1904–59), who had then recently ascended the throne. When the monarchy was overthrown in 1975, the country's Communist rulers converted the palace into the National Museum.

The attractive double cruxiform-shaped single-story building is a mixture of Lao and European styles. The walkway is lined with Cuban royal palms that frame a gable above the main entrance. This gable is decorated with a bas-relief of a three-headed elephant protected by a parasol, surrounded by intertwined *nagas* (serpents) – the symbol of the Lan Xang Hom Khao Kingdom. In the background, a graceful spire resembling a Buddhist stupa points skyward. The most sacred of Luang Prabang's

Statue of King Sisavang Vong

religious icons, the Phabang, is currently housed in a room in the front wing of the palace. However, its final resting place, **Wat Ho Pha Bang**, near the main gate, is in the process of being re-constructed.

Upon entering the National Museum visitors will pass through the former king's reception room, which houses murals painted by French artist Alex De Fautereau in the 1930s. These are idyllic representations of life in old Luang Prabang. The impressive throne room is painted red and covered with mosaics depicting Lao rural life, similar to those in the Red Chapel at Wat Xieng Thong (see pp162–3). The effect is even more dazzling in this massive but enclosed

chamber. Behind the throne room lie the private quarters of the royal family, where many of their personal belongings, such as a collection of records and a wind-up phonograph player, are displayed. The furniture in both the king's and queen's bedchambers has been left intact. The atmosphere is familial and far from grandiose. The final stop inside the palace is a hall reserved for diplomatic gifts, notably some moon rocks and a plaque from US President Richard Nixon. This hall also contains two large portraits of King Sisavang Vatthana and Queen Kampoui, painted by a Soviet artist.

A large statue of King Sisavang Vong stands to the left of the main gate and the Royal Ballet Theater behind. Here, evening dance performances of the *Phra Lak Phra Lam* epic are performed three times a week at 6pm.

6 Night Market

Sisavang Vong Rd. **City map** C3. **Open** 6pm–10pm daily.

Every evening, Sisavang Vong Road, the main commercial street of peninsular Luang Prabang, closes to traffic and becomes an open-air market offering a wide variety of colorful local handicrafts, among other things. Textiles predominate, especially the intricately woven Lao silk and cotton. Particularly popular is the interesting geometric appliqué

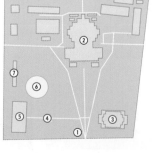

National Museum Complex

List of Sites

1. Main Gate
2. National Museum
3. Wat Ho Pha Bang
4. King Sisavang Vong Statue
5. Royal Ballet Theater
6. Lotus Pond
7. Royal Barge Shelter

Key to Map

☐ Buildings
☐ Lawns

0 meters 100
0 yards 100

work – fashioned into everything from bedspreads to bedroom slippers – which the Hmong minority has made famous. Silverware, imitation antiques, ceramics, hand-woven baskets, and mulberry paper products are all on offer. Lao beer T-shirts and Lao rice whiskey, as well as scorpions and snakes suspended in bottles make for an intriguing browse. The goods are not of the quality found in upscale boutiques, but the prices reflect this fact, and good-natured bargaining is expected. At the southern end of the market, superb baguette sandwiches await hungry shoppers.

Vendors selling a variety of textile products, Night Market

❼ Wat Xieng Mouan

Sotika Kuman Rd. **City map** C3. **Open** 8am–3pm daily.

The construction of this temple was ordered by King Chantarath (r.1851–72) in 1853 to house some particularly melodious temple drums which he had acquired. Consequently, the original name of the temple meant Monastery of the Melodious Sounds. For reasons lost in time, the name has changed to mean Monastery of the Amusing City. A school on the premises of the temple, inaugurated by UNESCO with a grant from the Norwegian government, aims to preserve traditional art forms in Laos. Novice monks produce various forms of traditional arts and crafts, such as stenciling, woodcarving, lacquerwork, and cement sculpture. These products are on display in a small exhibition hall within the premises. The *sim* of the temple features a veranda encircling the entire building, with impressive columns in the front. The drums that inspired the temple's construction are kept in a temple of their own in the front left corner of the compound.

❽ Wat Choum Khong

Sotika Kuman Rd. **City map** C3. **Open** 8am–3pm daily.

Located next to Wat Xieng Mouan, Wat Choum Khong is accessible via a passage that connects the two compounds. It was originally constructed in 1843, though the temple has been restored several times since, most recently with the help of students from the school in Wat Xieng Mouan. According to legend, the *wat* takes its name from an image of the Buddha, which was cast here from a bronze *khong* (gong). A variety of modern but attractively styled Buddha images depicting the various *mudras* (hand positions) used in classical Buddhist statuary have been placed among the rows of shrubs and trees within the garden of this temple, which is particularly verdant and well kept. The ordination hall of the *wat* is in classic Luang Prabang style, with a heavily gilded lintel above the center of three elaborate front doors, eaves with curved brackets, and recessed windows.

Ornate peacock motif on the door to the *sim*, Wat Pa Phai

❾ Wat Pa Phai

Off Sisavang Vattana Rd. **City map** C3. **Open** 8am–3pm daily.

The name of this *wat* means Bamboo Forest Monastery, but the origin of this appellation is unclear. The original date of its construction is also debatable, placed either at 1645 or 1815. There is a Siamese influence on the architectural style of the *wat*, apparent from the narrow base and high, steep roof lines. The main feature is the ornate pediment surrounding the doorway to the *sim*. It resembles those seen in temples in Chiang Mai, Thailand, because it is decorated with a protruding peacock motif festooned with colored glass mosaic tiles. This archway rises in three successive levels, and *nagas* mingle with birds in flight. The door panels depict a leaping figure of Rama holding a staff, trouncing the head of a lion. Around this doorway are murals depicting scenes of village life in a simple, artistic style.

Elaborately decorated exterior of the main *sim*, Wat Xieng Mouan

Carved *naga* balustrades adorning the staircase, Wat Nong Sikhunmuang

⑩ School of Fine Arts

Sotika Kuman Rd. **City map** D3.
Tel (071)-212-047. **Open** 8am–4pm daily. 🖼

Signposted in French as the École des Beaux Arts, this charming single-story building in a tree-filled compound dates from the 1920s, and is an excellent example of the Colonial architecture of the period. With an aim to promote traditional Lao art, the School of Fine Arts offers a four-year certificate program for students who have completed their secondary education. Specialized courses include painting, sculpture, graphic art, ceramics, metalwork, traditional drawing, and lacquerwork. There is also provision for an 18-month internship (post-graduation) in a student's hometown. The school plays a major role in ensuring the continuation of traditional art and craft in Laos. There is also an exhibition center in the complex that displays and sells beautiful paintings, carvings, and sculptures made by the students.

⑪ Wat Nong Sikhunmuang

Sotika Kuman Rd. **City map** D3.
Open 8am–3pm daily.

Originally constructed with wood in 1729, during the reign of King Inta Som, Wat Nong Sikhunmuang was completely destroyed in a fire in 1774. The only surviving piece of the original temple is a bronze statue of the Buddha known as Pha Sao Ong Sanesakid. The statue was originally brought here by a local merchant whose raft grounded mysteriously near the temple after a harrowing journey downriver from Thailand.

The current structure, restored by Thai artisans in the 19th century, is rather contemporary, and painted in bright colors. Of architectural interest is the elaborate roof referred to as *dok so faa (see p157)*; its 15 parasols suggest a royal connection since parasols are symbolic of royalty in Laos. Staircases on either side of the temple are adorned with *naga* balustrades. This temple attracts many Buddhist visitors, particularly during festivals, because of the Pha Sao Ong Sanesakid. Now housed in the *wat's sim*, this sacred statue is said to be endowed with special powers to grant the wishes of supplicants.

⑫ Wat Sene

Sakkarin Rd. **City map** D2.
Open 8am–3pm daily.

This Thai-style temple's name refers to an initial donation of a 100,000 *kip* (*sene* in Lao) to start the construction work. It was built in 1714, and restored in 1957 to commemorate the 2,500th year of the Buddhist era. Located prominently on Sakkarin Road, the central road of Luang Prabang, this is the first in a series of temples that line the street for about 656 ft (200 m). With a stunningly beautiful exterior of bright red and gold, the *wat* is well-known as the storage space for two of the largest and most attractive boats used in the annual Suang Heua boat racing festival *(see p128)*. The *sim* is similarly painted a brilliant red, and covered with stencils depicting a menagerie of mythical animals. The interior of the *wat* is also intricately decorated. A smaller chapel at the front of the *wat* houses a Standing Buddha image and an immense drum and gong used to signal the *wan sin* (holy days) of Buddhism. An adjacent upright carved stone tablet portrays a stylized footprint of the Buddha.

Stenciled figures, Wat Sene

The Thai-style red and gold facade of Wat Sene

The impressive UNESCO Maison du Patrimoine, an excellent example of Laos's Colonial heritage

⑬ Wat Si Boun Huang

Sakkarin Rd. **City map** D2.
Open 8am–3pm daily.

Located just up the street from Wat Sene, after passing Wat Sop, this temple has a tree-lined lawn that is more inviting than the cemented floors of most of the present-day temple compounds in Luang Prabang. Multi-hued bougainvillea, frangipani, and palm trees provide not only shade, but also add a splash of color to the leafy compound.

This temple is said to have been constructed during the reign of King Sotika Kuman (r.1749–68). The four columns in front of the veranda of the relatively small *sim* carry lotus petal capitals. Notable here is the gable above the superbly decorated doors depicting a Buddhist symbol known as the *Dharmachakra*, or the Wheel of Law, which symbolizes rebirth. The roof of the *wat*, typical of the Luang Prabang style, has only two tiers, but its edge is lined with elegant and understated replicas of classical temple roof finials, known as *so faa*.

⑭ Wat Khili

Sakkarin Rd. **City map** D2.
Open 8am–3pm daily. 🎎 Lai Heua Fai (Nov).

This *wat* is a rare example of the ornate style of temples built in the mountainous Xieng Khuang province. Its full name, Wat

Souvanna Khili, can be translated to mean Monastery of the Golden Mountain. It was built in 1779 by Prince Chao Kham Sattha, who hailed from that region. Its construction is said to have established a good relationship between the two rival principalities of Xieng Khuang and Luang Prabang.

The Xieng Khuang style of *sim* is characterized by a wide and low profile. The front wall of Wat Khili's *sim* is decorated with six beautiful Tree of Life mosaics – smaller versions of the now famous mosaic on the back of Wat Xieng Thong's *sim* (*see pp162–3*). The *wat's* window shutters are ornately carved with human-like forms believed to be that of Prince Siddhartha, later known as the Buddha, while the gables above are alive with bas-reliefs of zoomorphic phantasmagoria. Near the front of the *wat*, a somewhat incongruous two-story building

Elaborately carved door with gold stencil, Wat Si Boun Huang

blending Colonial and traditional Buddhist styles of architecture, is an interesting addition to the complex.

⑮ UNESCO Maison du Patrimoine

Sakkarin Rd. **City map** E2.

Located at the far northern end of the Luang Prabang peninsula, the UNESCO Maison du Patrimoine is an imposing but graceful structure that provides a contrast to the Buddhist temples and simple residences that characterize the neighborhood. This two-story building, dating from 1932, was once the Customs House of the ruling French Colonial government. From here, duties were levied on all Lao exports, the most lucrative of which was opium. This attractive building now belongs to the Lao government, and is the headquarters of UNESCO consultants who advise local authorities on urban conservation, and on the administration of the World Heritage Site status that was bestowed on Luang Prabang in 1995. Now referred to as La Maison du Patrimoine, or Heritage House, the large windows and high ceilings of the building present an excellent example of Colonial-era architecture. Although the place is not open to the public, visitors are welcome to take a leisurely stroll through the large and well-kept garden surrounding the building.

⑯ Wat Xieng Thong

Considered by the locals to be the most important symbol of their country's religious heritage, Wat Xieng Thong, meaning Gold City Monastery, is notable for the brilliant colored-glass mosaics that adorn the exterior of several of the main buildings within the temple complex. These mosaics depict standard Buddhist iconography, such as lotus blossoms, as well as scenes from Buddhist scriptures and the daily lives of the Lao people. The *sim* was built in 1560 by King Setthathirat, and the temple enjoyed royal patronage until 1975. It has served as a coronation venue for several Lao kings.

Mosaics depicting fishermen and Buddhist monks, Red Chapel

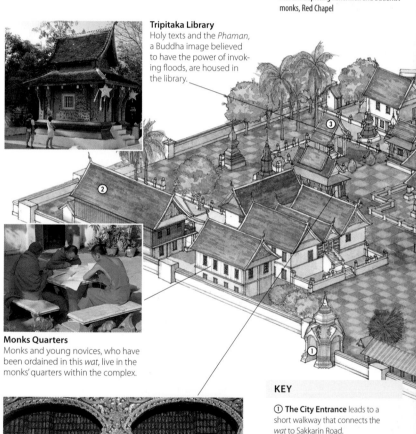

Tripitaka Library
Holy texts and the *Phaman*, a Buddha image believed to have the power of invoking floods, are housed in the library.

Monks Quarters
Monks and young novices, who have been ordained in this *wat*, live in the monks' quarters within the complex.

★ Red Chapel
Christened La Chapelle Rouge by the French, the Red Chapel has red exterior walls with glass inlay work depicting religious and rural scenes. It also houses an expertly sculpted bronze Reclining Buddha.

KEY

① **The City Entrance** leads to a short walkway that connects the *wat* to Sakkarin Road.

② **Meditation Hall**

③ **Sitting Buddha Pavilion**

④ **Boat Shelter**

⑤ **The Elephant Head Fountain** spouts lustral water that is collected by devotees to wash Buddha images in their homes.

⑥ **Chedis** (stupas), which usually contain Buddhist relics, dot the enclosure.

★ **Sim** (Ordination Hall)
Apart from its sweeping roof lines, the *sim* has a carved, gilded Wheel of Life bas-relief with green mosaic lotus buds atop newel posts framing the entrance. The side walls have a rich gold and black motif with stencils depicting *apsaras* and lions, while the back wall has a stunning Tree of Life mosaic.

Riverside Entrance

VISITORS' CHECKLIST

Practical Information
City map D2.
Between Sakkarin Road and the Mekong River. **Open** 8am–4pm daily.

Drum Pavilion
The massive drum inside this pavilion is sounded on special prayer days and at festivities such as the boat races.

Boat Shelter
The boats built here have led many boat crews to success in the annual boat races held during the Lao New Year and Suang Heua (*see p128*).

★ **Royal Funerary Carriage House**
An elaborately carved and gilded structure, the Royal Funerary Carriage House contains the impressive 39-ft (12-m) high gilded chariot that transported the remains of King Sisavang Vong to his cremation.

Golden exterior of the opulent Wat Mai Suwannaphumaham, Luang Prabang ▶

Elegantly sculpted stupas in front of the entrance to Wat Aham

⑰ Wat Aham

Phommathat Rd. **City map** C4.
Open 8am–3pm daily.

This *wat* is situated outside the main peninsular grid of the Old Town, across the street from a charming residential neighborhood of winding lanes. There are two huge banyan trees located in the temple grounds, said to house the spirits of the guardian deities of the city, Phu Noe and Na Noe. The shaggy-haired and red-faced effigies representing these spirits are kept in the grounds of the temple, and are carried at the head of a procession during Lao New Year. The green compound also houses an attractive *sim* with statues from the *Phra Lak Phra Lam* epic guarding its front doors. The Corinthian-style columns of the *sim* are artistically decorated with lotus buds, while the gable on the back of the *sim* is decorated with murals depicting the Buddha addressing his followers.

Mythical guardian, Wat Aham

⑱ Wat Visounarat

Phommathat Rd. **City map** C4.
Open 8am–3pm daily.

Originally constructed in 1512, this temple was named after King Visounarat, during whose reign it was built, making it the oldest surviving Buddhist place of worship in the city. Located adjacent to Wat Aham, and connected to it by an arched passageway, the temple is also known as Wat Visoun. The door panels on the *sim* depict Hindu deities, and a gilded screen inside portrays a battle from the Hindu epic, *Ramayana*. In front of the temple's *sim* lies one of Luang Prabang's most famous landmarks, *that makmo*, meaning watermelon stupa. Officially, however, it is referred to as *that phatum*, meaning lotus stupa, named for its bulbous, hemispherical shape. The original stupa was razed by Chinese Black Flag Haw marauders in 1887 and was rebuilt in 1898 under the patronage of King Sakkarin Kamuk. In 1914, it was struck by lightning and revealed a cache of gold, bronze, and crystal Buddha images that the marauders had missed. These treasures are now on display at the National Museum Complex (see p158).

⑲ Wat Manolom

Manomai Rd. **City map** C5.
Open 8am–3pm daily.

Located on the site of an earlier temple raised by King Fa Ngum, the founder of the Lan Xang Dynasty, Wat Manolom is situated in a quiet residential area 1 mile (2 km) west of the center of the Old Town area of Luang Prabang. It was the first home of the sacred Phabang statue for almost 11 years. The current *sim* was built in 1972 and has an intricately engraved door at the northern entrance,

Monks walking past the watermelon stupa, Wat Visounarat

flanked by a pair of lions. A revered statue of the Buddha, made of bronze, 20 ft (6 m) high and weighing 2 tons (2000 kg), which had been badly damaged by Chinese Black Flag Haw marauders in 1887, is now housed inside the *sim*. This long-eared statue is distinctly Thai-Sukhothai in style. Inside the *wat* compound is a group of gold stupas resembling the famous Pha That Luang *(see p145)* in Vientiane.

⑳ Wat That Luang

Wat That Luang Rd, Near Phu Vao Rd. **City map** B5. **Open** 8am–3pm daily.

Built in 1818, this temple is one of the most important in Luang Prabang, and is located fairly close to Wat Manolom. The *wat* houses the ashes of King Sisavang Vong (r.1904–59), whose funeral chariot is kept in Wat Xieng Thong *(see pp162–3)*. That Luang means royal stupa, and the *dok so faa* ornamentation with the 15 parasols on the roof of the *sim* denotes the temple's royal status. The *sim* is noteworthy for its gold and silver-lacquered door panels depicting various divinities. An elegant stupa, now weathered black, adjoins the *sim*. The members of Luang Prabang's royalty gather here on October 29 each year to commemorate King Sisavang Vong.

Faded murals adorning the front entrance, Wat Long Khun

㉑ Wats on the West Bank

West Bank of the Mekong River. **City map** D2. 🚢 from Wat Xieng Thong or behind the National Museum Complex. **Open** 8am–3pm daily. 📷

As spectacular as the temples of the Old Town of Luang Prabang are, it is worthwhile to deviate from the usual routine by visiting the relaxing and informal rural *wats* on the West Bank of the Mekong River. Most are within walking distance of

each other across the Mekong from Wat Xieng Thong. It is easy to negotiate a round trip with a boatman – you can usually find one on the steps leading to the river outside the temple.

The first of the *wats*, **Wat Long Khun**, meaning the Monastery of the Happy or Blessed Song, was where prospective kings of Laos would meditate for three days before their coronation at Wat Xieng Thong. The front of its *sim* is decorated with interesting but faded murals depicting Chinese gentlemen in elaborate costumes. The interior of the *sim*, with its somewhat garish linoleum flooring, exudes a welcoming simplicity missing

Carved peacock, Wat Xieng Men

in some other temples in Luang Prabang. The tree-filled *wat* complex is a great place to relax and absorb the rural atmosphere.

A short distance upstream from Wat Long Khun lies the small, abandoned cave-shrine called **Wat Tham Xieng Maen**. Local boys volunteer as guides to and around the inside of the small cave. A path downstream along the river from Wat Long Khun will, after a short distance, lead to the bottom of a hill from where a steep flight of steps leads up to **Wat Chom Phet**. This *wat* is more renowned for its spectacular views of the surrounding area than for being of any real architectural or cultural interest.

The last stop, **Wat Xieng Men**, is about 2 miles (3 km) downstream from this group of temples. Although it can be reached on foot, it is easier to go by boat. Built in the second half of the 16th century, the *wat's* small but well-proportioned *sim* has an elaborate three-tiered roof, with separate eaves covering the front veranda. The portico above the front door is intricately decorated as are both the exterior and interior columns. The current *sim* was constructed in the 1920s but artifacts from an earlier building on this site have been preserved, including an embroidered cloth believed to be more than 300 years old.

The exquisite three-tiered roof of Wat Xieng Men on the Mekong's West Bank

Devotees offering prayers in front of Buddha statues, Santi Chedi

❷ Santi Chedi

3 miles (5 km) E of Luang Prabang.
Open 8am–5pm daily.

Built in 1988 with donations
from affluent Lao living
abroad, Wat Phra Pone Phao,
popularly known as Santi
Chedi (Peace Pagoda), is a
forest meditation retreat.
A particular favorite with most
visitors to Luang Prabang, this
golden, bell-shaped stupa is
visible from various spots in
the city, although Mt Phou Si
(see p156) offers the best views.
Located on a hilltop along the
banks of the Nam Khan, the
chedi also offers excellent
views of the city, particularly
from the upper story of the
outer terrace, which is definitely
worth climbing. En route to
the terrace, visitors will pass
walls decorated with brightly
colored murals, painted in
natural colors. In addition to the
standard *Jataka* tales which
recount the lives and deeds of
the Buddha, these murals

portray, in intricate detail, the
punishments awaiting sinners
in hell.

❷ Ban Phanom and Mouhot's Tomb

4 miles (6 km) E of Luang Prabang.
from Luang Prabang. **Open** 9am–
5pm daily.

Settled during the reign of
King Sisavang Vong, Ban
Phanom is populated by people
of the Thai Lue ethnic group,
who traditionally inhabit the
areas around Luang Nam Tha
and Muang Sing. The Thai Lue
were required to serve the
palace as weavers and dancers,
since their women are famous
for both these skills. Although
the dance traditions eventually
disappeared, the weaving of
both cotton and silk continues
today. The women sell their
goods either from their homes
or at the village crafts' center.
The prices and quality of goods
are on a par with those sold in

Luang Prabang's Night Market
(see pp158–9), although visitors
are advised to bargain a little
before buying anything.

About 3 miles (5 km) beyond
Ban Phanom, along the Nam
Khan, and approached by an
unpaved but well-marked road,
lies the tomb of the French
explorer Alexandre-Henri
Mouhot. The first Westerner
to visit Luang Prabang, Mouhot
is often referred to as the
"discoverer" of Angkor Wat,
as it was his vivid description
(published in English after the
French showed little interest in
his journals) that spread the
word about the glories of
Angkor in Europe. Mouhot later
traveled to Luang Prabang from
Thailand and spent three
months here, before contrac-
ting malaria and dying in 1861,
at the young age of 35. His
tomb was discovered in 1990
and restored by representatives
from his home-town in France.
The simple, whitewashed tomb,
which is surrounded by large
trees, has a small statue of the
explorer erected nearby and
is a must-see for any visitor
to Luang Prabang.

Displaying a selection of locally woven
cloth, Ban Phanom

❷ Ban Xang Khong

3 miles (5 km) E of Luang Prabang.
Open 9am–5pm daily.

A picturesque village nestled on
the banks of the Mekong River,
Ban Xang Khong is a haven for
traditional Lao art and craft.
The village was originally known
for its intricate weaving of textiles
by artisans who live and work in
houses scattered along the dirt

Henri
Mouhot

Alexandre-Henri Mouhot (1826–61)

An enterprising adventure-seeker, Henri Mouhot
began his career teaching in Russia, experimented
with the early photographic techniques of Louis
Daguerre, studied botany, and finally set off in search
of exotic destinations in Asia. After his visits to Angkor,
he traveled to Luang Prabang, which, like many other
foreigners, he found extremely pleasing, describing it as
"a little paradise." Mouhot also described the Mekong
River as possessing "almost an excess of grandeur," and
noted that it appeared navigable – this inspired the
early French Colonialists in Indochina to search for an
ultimately unsuccessful river route to China.

road running parallel to the river. Today, however, local artisans have also taken to producing attractive *sa* paper, which is made from the bark of the mulberry or *sa* tree. The bark of the tree grows back, making it a renewable resource. Visitors can not only watch local men and women at work, but also take advantage of great shopping opportunities – products can be bought directly from the workers. Prices here are not necessarily cheaper than those in the Night Market, but the environment is more relaxed and the lighting better for viewing the intricately woven pieces of cloth and paper.

Ban Xang Khong can also be reached by crossing one of the seasonal bamboo bridges running across the river from Luang Prabang, or via the permanent old bridge – on foot or on a two-wheeler.

🌀 Tat Sae Waterfalls

11 miles (18 km) SE of Luang Prabang. **Tel** (020)-429-0848 (for tour bookings). tuk-tuk from Luang Prabang. 🚌 from Ban En. **Open** 9am–5pm daily. 🖼 🖼

Located on a tributary of the Nam Khan, the beautiful Tat Sae Waterfalls are often compared with the more spectacular Tat Kuang Si Waterfalls a little farther away. The falls' milky waters rush over natural limestone formations, falling into clear

Picnickers enjoying the beauty of the spectacular Tat Kuang Si Waterfalls

turquoise colored pools that are ideal for swimming and bathing. However, the falls are less powerful than Tat Kuang Si, and in the dry season are reduced to a mere trickle. Nevertheless, it continues to be a popular spot for visitors and locals alike.

The area is usually quite busy on the weekend, although there are not too many people here on weekdays. There are several other attractions in the vicinity, which include a zip line tour that takes adventure-seekers above the forest canopy and falls, as well as an exciting elephant trek in the surrounding hills and dense forest.

The Tat Sae Waterfalls can easily be reached by taking the road to the village of Ban En, 10 miles (16 km) south of Luang Prabang, followed by a short

boat ride down the charming Nam Khan river.

🌀 Tat Kuang Si Waterfalls

20 miles (32 km) SW of Luang Prabang from Luang Prabang. 🚌 from Luang Prabang, then tuk-tuk. **Open** 9am–5pm daily. 🖼 🖼 🖼 🖼 🖼

The multitiered Tat Kuang Si Waterfalls are a pleasant alternative for visitors looking for something more than the numerous *wats* that Luang Prabang has to offer. The water gushes over limestone formations collecting in azure pools at the base of the falls.

The lower levels of the falls are great for a picnic, with food vendors offering the usual grilled fish or chicken. A trail ascending to the left of the falls leads to a much quieter set of pools above the 197-ft (60-m) high main falls. A second trail leads to more pools and a cave. Visitors are advised to be careful while climbing, since the mist from the falls not only keeps the area green, but also slippery.

Tat Kuang Si is accessible either by road, or by boat along the Mekong followed by a short tuk-tuk ride. The falls are ideal for a day trip from Luang Prabang, although organized tours often propose half-day excursions, usually in the afternoon, when it is warmer and very pleasant.

Lower levels of the picturesque Tat Sae Waterfalls enclosed within green, leafy environs

NORTHERN LAOS

Spectacular mountain scenery, remote riverside settlements, a broad mosaic of minority cultures, places of historical significance, and the opportunity to trek off the beaten path – Northern Laos offers all this and more to the discerning traveler. From the sobering wartime sites on the Plain of Jars and Vieng Xai to tubing and rock climbing in Vang Vieng, a visitor is often spoiled for choice.

Northern Laos may seem isolated, but in fact it lies at a political and geographical crossroad, sharing borders with Thailand, Myanmar, Vietnam, and China. This strategic geographic location has resulted in periods of turbulence in its history. While the region benefitted from regular cross-border trade with the Thais and the Vietnamese, it also had to endure hostility, not only from its trading partners, but also from the Burmese who periodically invaded Laos during the 16th century. Westerners, such as the French and the Dutch, have coveted the resources and river routes of Northern Laos, and its location as a strategic buffer zone cost it dearly during the 19th century.

Lying at an average altitude of more than 3,000 ft (1,000 m), Northern Laos is noticeably cooler than the rest of the country and offers a diverse topography. The rivers, which were the main means of transport through the rugged mountains of the region, also provide livelihoods through fishing. The region is inhabited by more than two dozen ethnic minorities, including the Hmong, Mien, and Akha, who make a living by cultivating crops such as corn and rice, and making handicrafts such as hand-woven textiles and silver jewelry.

Today, the region's many wonders, from its charming towns to thickly forested hills and mountains, are slowly opening up to tourism, and visitors will find an enchanting array of places and activities to choose from. National Protected Areas (NPAs), such as the Nam Ha NPA and the Bokeo Nature Reserve are home to an amazing variety of animals, and are a haven for wildlife enthusiasts. Adventure sport enthusiasts will find Vang Vieng an exciting town, with plenty of activities such as spelunking, kayaking, and rock climbing on offer. The mysterious Plain of Jars site is also well worth a visit.

A local fruit and vegetable market selling fresh produce, Muang Sing

◀ Vast paddy fields near the district of Boun Neua, Phongsali province

Exploring Northern Laos

A trip to Northern Laos can be a delightful experience with a wide variety of activities to indulge in – from adventure sports to visits to beautiful Buddhist temples. While the capital, Vientiane, is well known for its *wats* and memorials, Vang Vieng is Northern Laos's adventure capital. Phonsavan and the mysterious Plain of Jars to the east are also popular attractions. Another exciting option is a boat or road tour from Huay Xai to the former royal capital Luang Prabang, which can be an interesting excursion. In fact, boat tours either on the Mekong between Huay Xai and Luang Prabang, or on the beautiful stretch of the Nam Ou between Luang Prabang and Phongsali, are defining moments of any visit to Northern Laos.

A monk at prayer in the ornamented *sim* of Wat Nam Kaew Luang, Muang Sing

Sights at a Glance

Ban Lantuy
Nyai

U Thai

Ban Sop

Boun Ne

Ban Cha Up

Bun

MUANG SING ⓭

17A

13N

LUANG NAM THA

LUANG NAM THA ⓬

⓾ ⓫ **BAN NAM**

13B

NAM HA NATIONAL PROTECTED AREA

Ban Namha

Ban Ko N

⓮ 🞬 **BOKEO NATURE RESERVE**

Ban Namngeun

Udor

BOKEO

Ban Ta Fa

Ban Pung

Muang Beng

P. Pha 6,398 (1,950

Ton Pheung

Huay Xai

Ban Dan

UDOMXAI

2W

No

Pak Tha

Pha Udom

Ban Navang

Pak Beng

BOAT TOUR ON THE MEKONG ⓯

Nam

Ban Huay Sanei

Ban Tha Suang

Phu Vaysom 5,919 ft (1,8

Xieng Hon

SAINYABULI

4B

Ban Pa

Muang Ngoen

Muang Nan

Ban Nam

Doi Lo 6,814 ft (2,077 m)

Sainyabuli

Ba Va

Phiang

Ban Nampuy

Nam Puy

Feuan

Ban Namo

Ban Suvannaphun

Ban Muangk

Pak Lai

Ban Namxong

Ban Buamthon

Ban Nakok

Kaen Thao

The Mekong River between Luang Prabang and Pak Beng

Key

━━ Major road

══ Minor road

═ ═ ═ Untarred road

– – Dirt track

▬▬ International border

▬▬ Provincial border

△ Peak

Getting Around

The road network in Northern Laos is much better today, but covering a number of sights still means long road trips. Transport facilities have improved with luxury buses plying the roads, although minivans, more comfortable and in better condition than some of the buses, are another option. Visitors can also travel from Luang Prabang to Phongsali by boat; the Mekong cruise from Huay Xai to Luang Prabang is also a good choice. Huay Xai also serves as the entry and exit point for those traveling between Northern Laos and Northern Thailand.

For keys to symbols see back flap

Backpackers strolling through the main street, Vang Vieng

❶ Vang Vieng

Road Map B2. 90 miles (150 km) N of Vientiane. ⚐ 40,000. ⬛

Located on the banks of the Nam Song and surrounded by majestic limestone karst peaks, the town of Vang Vieng has always been a magnet for visitors to Laos. Initially a quiet place visited by a handful of visitors keen to enjoy the natural beauty of the area, Vang Vieng today is a bustling town that serves as the jumping-off point for various adventure sports in the vicinity. However, indiscriminate development in tourist infrastructure has robbed the town of its quaint feel, and its streets are now lined with concrete guesthouses and busy bars.

Nevertheless, the town attracts visitors who are keen to go rock climbing, abseiling, and spelunking in the karst mountains, which are a honeycomb of

caves – some with rivers running through them. Tubing is another option although mud volleyball, rope swings, and an endless supply of *lao lao*, a distilled rice spirit, offered by the riverside bars, are popular. Note that Vang Vieng has a growing reputation for safety issues and crime. Any adventure activities undertaken should be done so with careful consideration.

Environs

Located close to the Nam Song, just across from the Vang Vieng Resort, **Tham Jang**, also known as Tham Chang, is one of the most easily accessible caves in Vang Vieng. Used as a bunker in the early 19th century, the cave is approached by a flight of stairs leading to its mouth. Visitors can follow the well-marked path within, and emerge at a second, higher entrance, which offers a fantastic view over the valley. It is also possible to swim in the spring at the mouth of the cave, and follow it for about 164 ft (50 m) inside.

Located some 5 miles (8 km) west of Vang Vieng, **Tham Phu Kham** is another interesting stop. Also known as Blue Lagoon, for the azure stream running in front of the cave, it is ideal for a refreshing

Entrance to the fascinating Tham Hoi, Tham Sang Triangle

dip. The cave is considered sacred by locals, and it houses several bronze images of the Buddha. The journey to Tham Phu Kham, passing stunning and majestic karst landscapes, can be made on foot, by bicycle, or even in a hired tuk-tuk.

The **Tham Sang Triangle**, a group of four caves, all within walking distance of each other, is located 8 miles (13 km) north of Vang Vieng and is a popular destination for daytrippers. The first of these caves, Tham Sang, gets its name from the elephant-shaped stalactite formations within. A clearly marked path from here leads through rice fields for less than a mile to the entrances of Tham Hoi and Tham Loup. Tham Hoi is a sacred cave with a large Buddha image at the entrance, while Tham Loup, the more attractive of the two, has impressive stalactite formations. The final stop is Tham Nam, meaning water cave, which is located 1,321 ft (400 m) south of Tham Hoi. Depending on the season, it is possible to wade into the cave or to rent a tube to go in. Visitors can complete the return journey to Vang Vieng on hired kayaks or tubes.

Elephant-shaped stalactite, Tham Sang

🛕**Tham Jang**
Open 8–11:30am & 1–4:30pm. 🎟

🛕**Tham Phu Kham**
Open 8:30am–4:30pm. 🎟

🛕**Tham Sang Triangle**
Open 8:30am–4:30pm. 🎟 🛶
including tubing or kayaking.

Caves around Vang Vieng

Key
▬▬ Major road
═══ Minor road

Tham Hoi
Ban
Tham Loup
Ban Na Dao
Tham Sang
Tham Nam
Phao Thao
Tham Pha Thao
Pak Pok
Tham Phu Kham
Ban Na Thong
Tham Non
Nam Song
13
Tham Jang
Vang Vieng
Na Duang
Vientiane 90 miles (150 km)

0 km   3
0 miles   3

For keys to symbols *see back flap*

Activities Around Vang Vieng

A varied landscape comprising steep mountains, limestone caves, and the robust Nam Song make Vang Vieng an ideal venue for those seeking adventure sports. While the ever-popular ride on a mountain bike is a great way to appreciate the scenery and provide a good workout, spelunking (cave exploration), and navigating steep trails and water channels deep inside these caves, has its own charms. Some visitors also seek the additional thrill of rock climbing. Floating down the Nam Song on a giant tube has also become inextricably linked to the Vang Vieng experience. Tubing, and related activities such as zip lining, giant swings, and mud volleyball, especially appeal to young travelers. However, those seeking less energetic activities can always go on long, relaxing, kayaking trips down the Nam Song.

Tubing, Vang Vieng's signature activity, takes place on hired inflatable tractor tire tubes which float down the Nam Song. The starting point lies 3 miles (5 km) north of town and the entire route is lined with noisy beer bars. Those not planning to stop at the bars can start farther upstream at the bridge to Ban Tham Sang.

Spelunking, or caving, is an exciting activity and a favorite of visitors to the area. There are numerous unexplored mountain caves here.

Rock climbing and rappelling can be undertaken near Tham Non, 2 miles (3 km) north of town. Here, routes for varying skill levels have been established and basic courses for novices are also available.

Mountainbiking is a great way to explore Vang Vieng. Cycling along Route 13 is easier since it is paved, but the trails on the west side of the Nam Song are idyllic, although demanding.

Zip lines usually start from one of the many riverside bars and include a hand grip attached to a pulley that slides down an inclined cable. Zip-liners cling on to the grip and let go at the other end to fall into the water.

Kayaking is possible not only on the Nam Song, but also on the rapids of the nearby Nam Ngum. It is also possible to kayak from Vang Vieng to Vientiane, a trip that is undertaken with the help of a tour operator such as Green Discovery (see p271).

Defused UXO, Mines Advisory Group's Visitor Information Center, Phonsavan

❷ Phonsavan

Road Map C2. 132 miles (220 km) SE of Luang Prabang. 🚹 50,000. ✈ 🚌 from Vientiane or Luang Prabang. 🛈 (061)-312-217.

Capital of Xieng Khuang province, Phonsavan was built after the Vietnam War ended in 1975. The former capital, Muang Khoun, like most of the province, was completely destroyed by heavy fighting. Chosen simply because of its proximity to an airport, today Phonsavan is mainly of interest as a jumping-off point for the Plain of Jars. However, there are a variety of other interesting sights. The **Mines Advisory Group's (MAG) Visitor Information Center**, is an enlightening place. Although the war memorabilia on display can be disturbing, there is a wealth of information including a video on the devastation wrought by cluster bombs and other ammunition. Visitors will also find the **Mulberries Silk Farm** an absorbing stop. A fair-trade company dedicated to enabling local villagers to revive the art of silk production, the farm not only grows mulberry bushes, but also spins its own silk, which is then made into garments and accessories.

The surrounding hilltops provide magnificent views of the town, hills, and plains. The two hilltop war memorials – the Lao War Memorial and the Vietnamese War Memorial – south of town, are worth a visit. The atmospheric Auberge de Plaine des Jarrres *(see p231)*, at the top of Phu Padaeng, is a good place to stop for a drink.

MAG
Main Street, Phonsavan.
Tel (023)-218-396 (Phnom Penh).
🌐 **maginternational.org/where-mag-works/Cambodia**

Mulberries Silk Farm
No 7 Road, Ban Li, Meuang Pek District. **Tel** (021)-263-371.
Open 8am–4pm Mon–Sat.
🌐 **mulberries.org**

❸ Sam Neua

Road Map C2. 132 miles (220 km) NE of Phonsavan. 🚹 35,000. 🚌 from Phonsavan. 🛈 (064)-312-567.

The capital of the northeast province of Hua Phan, Sam Neua lies nestled in a small valley that is often shrouded in fog. On clear days, however, the sparkling Nam Sam, which flows through this quiet town, is a pleasure to behold. The town usually plays host to visitors on their way to the nearby Vieng Xai caves, or to those heading to the Vietnamese border crossing, 48 miles (80 km) to the east at Nam Xoi.

Sam Neua is famous for the intricacy of the handwoven textiles produced here. These can be found in the market close to the river, or at the homes of the weavers themselves. Visitors can be directed to the weavers' homes by the town's excellent local tourist information office, located on the main street.

❹ Vieng Xai

Road Map C2. 20 miles (32 km) E of Sam Neua. 🚌 from Sam Neua. **Taxi** from Sam Neua. 🛈 Kaysone Phomvihane Memorial Cave Tour Office, (064)-314-321. **Open** 9am–4pm daily. 🎧 📷 tours leave at 9am & 1pm.

Tucked away among the karst mountains of the Annamite Mountain Range near the Vietnamese border, this isolated valley initially served as the shelter and hiding place for Pathet Lao leaders, including Kaysone Phomvihane and Prince Souphanouvong, during the Vietnam War (1954–75). The caves in the valley were used not just as their homes, but as communication centers, hospitals, and small factories. Also used as a secret military area, it was the location of prison camps where key members of the former regime, notably the royal family, were incarcerated. These caves are now open to visitors. It is also possible to visit another huge cave nearby where mass political rallies, and musical and theatrical performances from friendly Socialist countries were held.

The caves are best visited as a day trip from Sam Neua on the obligatory guided tour, which includes excellent oral histories delivered via audio headsets. Visitors with enough time, however, can stay overnight in any one of the local guesthouses, and explore the quiet back roads of this spectacular and pristine valley on rented bicycles.

Visitors entering a cave, Vieng Xai

❺ Plain of Jars

Scattered across more than 50 separate sites, the curious stone jars that give the area its name, have puzzled archaeologists since the 1930s. Hewn from several types of local stone, they range in height from 18 in to 9 ft (50 cm to 3 m). Research here discovered human remains and burial offerings, which date the jars back to about 2,500 years. These give credence to the theory that the jars were in fact funerary urns, although other theories posit that they were used for grain or wine storage. Seven of these sites, now cleared of UXO (Unexploded Ordnance), are open to the public.

VISITORS' CHECKLIST

Practical Information
Road Map C2. 6 miles (10 km) SW of Phonsavan. 🛈 Phonsavan (061)-312-217. **Open** 8am–4pm daily. 🐾 🚫 🔌 🖥
Note: visitors must pay heed to warning signs and stay on the marked paths.

Transport
🚖 **Taxi** from Phonsavan.

Site 1 (Thong Hai Hin), containing 331 jars, is spread across a hillside. It also has the largest discovered jar, which local legend describes as the wine cup of the mythical king Khun Cheum, who is said to have freed locals from oppression.

An old Russian tank, damaged by extensive bombing during the war, can also be visited during a tour of these sites.

Locator Key
- Sites open to the public
- ▨ Area illustrated

Key
- ▬ Major road
- ▬ Minor road
- = = Dirt track

0 km 1
0 miles 1

Site 2 (Hai Hin Phu Salato) has a collection of 93 jars, which lie on two adjacent wooded hillsides. The highlight here is a jar with a marking resembling a frog. From this site it is possible to make trips to a nearby Hmong village.

Site 3 (Hai Hin Lat Khai)
An attractive site located at the top of a hill offering scenic views, Site 3 lies on the outskirts of Ban Xieng Di, inhabited by the Phuan ethnic group. Nearby is a Buddhist temple and a stupa damaged during the war.

Bomb Craters
Some sites, such as Site 1, are located near spots where heavy fighting took place during the Vietnam War, and large bomb craters are still visible here.

For keys to symbols *see back flap*

Boats moored by the shores of the Nam Song River in Vang Vieng ▶

Chinese-built concrete bridge spanning the Nam Ou, Nong Khiaw

❻ Nong Khiaw

Road map B1. 78 miles (126 km) NE of Luang Prabang. 🚩 6,000. 🚌 from Luang Prabang. 🚤 from Luang Prabang or Muang Ngoi.

The town of Nong Khiaw straddles the Nam Ou, split by an impressively tall bridge built by Chinese engineers in 1976. Most travelers arrive here from Luang Prabang by boat or road – the new, well-surfaced Route 13 runs parallel to the river most of the way and offers picturesque views.

The Tham Pha Tok caves, located 2 miles (3 km) east of the town, where villagers hid from B-52 bombers during the Vietnam War (1954–75), attract many visitors. The village of the Khamu ethnic group, a short distance east along the same route, is also a popular destination among visitors. Another wonderful option for those who want to relax is to sit on the balcony of a riverside

guesthouse and admire the mountain scenery. On longer stays, adventure seekers can also opt for trekking and mountain-bike excursions. The staff at guesthouses can arrange such activities for their patrons.

❼ Muang Ngoi

Road map B1. 20 miles (32 km) NE of Nong Khiaw. 🚩 2,000. 🚤 from Nong Khiaw or Muang Khua.

A sleepy village, Muang Ngoi nestles on the east bank of the Nam Ou. Owing to its location on a small plain, it is suited for growing rice in an otherwise mountainous area. Inaccessible by road, it has no electricity, and no cars – factors that contribute to its charm. Local attractions, apart from the calm and the scenery, include a few caves in a forested area that can be reached by fording a mountain stream about 3 miles (5 km) east of

the village. The caves are best explored in the company of a local guide.

❽ Muang Khua

Road map B1. 67 miles (107 km) N of Muang Ngoi. 🚩 20,000. 🚌 from Luang Prabang. 🚤 from Nong Khiaw or Hat Sa.

Farther upstream on the Nam Ou lies the bustling riverside town of Muang Khua. With precipitous mountains on either side of the river, Muang Khua resembles Nong Khiaw, but the atmosphere is much less placid – a steady stream of goods-laden trucks from Vietnam pour into the town, which is a busy commercial center. To escape the hustle and bustle, visitors can take a quick walk across the wooden suspension bridge spanning the Nam Phak (a tributary of the Nam Ou) to visit the local temple, Wat Srikkhounmoung. This interesting temple has *Ramayana*-based bas-reliefs and statues reflecting the syncretic nature of Lao Buddhism. It also has a temple bell that has been fashioned from an American cluster bomb casing.

From Muang Khua, a road leads 40 miles (60 km) east to the border post at Tai Xang, which is an international crossing, allowing all nation-alities to enter and leave Laos from here. Across the border lies Dien Bien Phu, where the 1954 battle that ended the French presence in Southeast Asia was

Boats docked by the riverside, Muang Khua

fought. However, it is impossible for visitors to cross the border into Vietnam from here without obtaining a visa in advance.

Environs

A sparsely populated riverside village in Phongsali province, **Hat Sa** seems to be perpetually shrouded in mist. There are no real sights here and still no regular supply of electricity, although limited accommodation options are available. It is from here that buses leave for Phongsali after the trip up the Nam Ou. The adventurous can continue farther north by boat to the remote village of Ou Tai, where the mountain scenery is said to be the most striking in the area.

Hat Sa
56 miles (90 km) N of Muang Khua. from Muang Khua.

Rice fields near the village of Ou Tai, north of Hat Sa

Fresh produce for sale at the morning market, Phongsali

9 Phongsali

Road map B1. 240 miles (386 km) N of Luang Prabang. 10,000. from Udomxai. from Nong Khiaw.

At 4,290 ft (1,430 m), the town of Phongsali is the highest provincial capital in Laos, giving it an agreeable climate in summer, but making it less than comfortable during the misty winter. Reached only via a rough 10-hour drive from Udomxai, or a two day boat trip from Nong Khiaw, the town is off the tourist track. The province is home to 22 ethnic minorities, the largest being a Sino-Tibetan group called the Phunoy. The **Phongsali Provincial Museum of Ethnic Minority Cultures** in the heart of the town documents these groups. Visitors could also take a stroll through the cobblestone roads crisscrossing the Phunoy village to the nearby morning market, which is great for people-watching. On the northeast edge of the town, **Phou Fa**, or Sky Mountain, has a stupa at the top reached by climbing 400 steps.

Environs

Located 9 miles (4 km) southeast of town on the road to Udomxai is **Ban Komaen**, where a 400-year-old tea tree stands in the midst of a modern plantation. Local teas are also available for tasting. Farther afield, to the northeast of the province, trekking in the **Phu Den Din National Protected Area (NPA)**, which covers 506 sq miles (1,310 sq km), is spectacular.

Phongsali Provincial Museum of Ethnic Minority Cultures
Ban Sansary, Muang Phongsali, Khoueng Phongsali

Open 7:30–11:30am & 1:30–4:30pm Mon–Fri. **Closed** Sat–Sun.

Phou Fa
NE of town center.

The Chinese Connection

Phongsali could easily be confused with a town in China – the people, language, and even street signs have more in common with China than Laos. Indeed, Phongsali is much easier to reach by road from China than Laos, and the border, now open to Lao and Chinese nationals only, is a mere 42 miles (70 km) away. The Chinese influence here began during the Vietnam War when the Chinese established a consulate in Pathet Lao-liberated territory, which still survives as the Phou Fa Restaurant (*see p231*). Today, however, the influence is strictly commercial; Laos imports Chinese goods such as toys, clothing, and manufactured food products, and many Chinese have established tea gardens here. In fact, the species of tea that grows in the wild here has its origins in the neighboring Chinese province of Yunnan. It is used to produce compressed blocks of the fermented Pu-erh tea that improves, and increases in value, with age.

A woman of the Phunoy tribe picking tea leaves

⓾ Luang Nam Tha

Road map B1. 124 miles (200 km) NW of Luang Prabang. 📍 35,000. ✈ from Vientiane. 🚌 from Huay Xai, Muang Sing, or Luang Prabang. 🛈 Provincial Tourism Office, (086)-211-534 or (020)-5871-2226. Note: boat tours on the Nam Tha between Huay Xai and Luang Nam Tha (Jun–Feb). 🅦 **luangnamtha-tourism.org**

This provincial capital was the scene of fierce fighting during the Civil War, and the current town is actually the result of recent construction – the original town, a few miles south, was razed to the ground by bombing. Happier times reign today, and Luang Nam Tha has emerged as an important center of ecotourism.The town is located within the boundaries of the Nam Ha National Protected Area and attracts adventure seekers for activities such as trekking, boating, and cycling. The town itself, often shrouded in mist until afternoon, is pleasant, with good restaurants, a small night market, as well as the **Luang Nam Tha Museum**, which houses various local artifacts, including ethnic clothing and ceramics.

Environs
For a taste of semirural village life, visitors can head to the prosperous villages on the opposite bank of the Nam Tha, reached by crossing a bamboo footbridge over the river.

Extensive terrace farming, Nam Ha National Protected Area

Another interesting destination is **That Phum Phuk**, a gilded stupa which sits atop a hill overlooking the valley. The original stupa was destroyed by aerial bombing.

🏛 **Luang Nam Tha Museum**
Behind Kaysone Monument.
Open Mon–Thu 8:30am–11:30am, Fri 1:30pm–3:30pm. 🗺

That Phum Phuk
4 miles (6 km) SE of Luang Nam Tha. 🗺

⓫ Ban Nam Di

Road Map B1. 4 miles (6 km) E of Luang Nam Tha. 📍 500.

Located just off Route 1 on the road to Luang Prabang, the village of Ban Nam Di is known for the unique paper made by the Lanten people. This paper is not only used to hold their Taoist religious texts,

but has also become a source of income as a handicraft item. Visitors can also stop at an attractive waterfall, a short distance from the village.

⓬ Nam Ha National Protected Area

Road map A1. 10 miles (16 km) W of Luang Nam Tha. 🗺 🖼
🅦 **ecotourismlaos.com**

One of the 20 National Protected Areas (NPAs) established by the Lao National Tourism Authority with assistance from UNESCO, this protected area covers 859 sq miles (2,224 sq km) and extends all the way to the Chinese border. The project aims to protect the environment by using sustainable ecotourism as a means to supplement villagers' incomes, and to deter them from taking part in activities that can harm the environment.
The forest cover here is largely first growth and the area is a watershed for four rivers, notably the Nam Ha, which gives the NPA its name. The Nam Ha NPA is rich in both flora and fauna. A large variety of animals, such as clouded leopard, tiger, gaur, a muntjac species, Asian elephant, as well as 228 bird species, can be found here. Tour agencies in Luang Nam Tha are active participants in the project and a couple of them offer a variety of tours in the NPA, ranging from one-day trips to several-day excursions, which can be undertaken on foot, by kayak, or bicycle.

A busy fresh goods market, Luang Nam Tha

Minorities of Northern Laos

Northern Laos, mainly home to the Lao Sung, or Highland Lao, has the highest percentage of ethnic minorities in the country. These communities include the Hmong, Akha, and Mien. However, the Thai Lue, a Lowland Lao people, also live here. Each of these groups is easily distinguished by their unique, brightly-colored attire, elaborate jewelry, and distinct language. Proud upholders of their cultures, the Lao Sung have complex religious beliefs and cultural practices, which include stories passed from one generation to the next, systems of kinship dictating norms of marriage, and a complicated system of taboos. The Highland Lao are as culturally different from each other as they are from the Lowland Lao. The best place to meet members of these minorities is usually the local market, where they come to sell their produce, particularly medicinal and edible plants collected in the jungle.

Hmong embroidery is unique, with tribal histories often woven into the cloth.

Hmong are a group of Sino-Tibetan people found across Southeast Asia. They assisted the Americans during the Lao Civil War and their relationship with the Communist authorities is strained.

A Hmong village consists of a cluster of about 20 huts. The huts, with dirt floors, thatched roofs, and no windows, are usually located adjacent to main roads.

Akha are easily distinguished by the elaborate silver head dress worn by their women. Their religious beliefs are a mix of animism and ancestor worship, and they speak a Tibeto-Burmese language.

Akha women are skilled weavers and also do needlework. They can often be spotted walking the streets of Luang Nam Tha and Muang Sing, hawking their handi-crafts to passersby.

Clothing of the Mien includes a maroon boa-like collar extending downward.

Mien are also known as the Yao. They practice Taoism and use a form of Chinese characters to write their religious texts. Mien women are distinguished by their black turbans.

Thai Lue are considered a Lowland Lao people. They are Buddhists, and known for their unique style of temple architecture, characterized by elaborate wooden or alloy fretwork.

Lanten are a sub-group of the Mien. A Chinese term, Lanten refers to their use of indigo dyes. They are best-known for their paper-making skills.

⓭ Muang Sing

Located on a broad river-fed plain northwest of Luang Nam Tha, Muang Sing was an important Thai Lue principality until the late 1800s. It was later occupied by the French but slipped into obscurity after their departure. Today, however, the town is experiencing a revival in its fortunes. The opening of the border with China, only 5 miles (8 km) to the north, has helped to invigorate the local economy, and garlic is now a major cash crop. There are few transport facilities, although tuk-tuks ply the roads, and a bus terminal has been set up.

Thongs adorning the inside of Wat Luang Ban Xieng Jai

🏛 Muang Sing Exhibition Museum

Northern left corner of Route 17.
Open 9am–4pm Mon–Fri. 🖼

Housed in the former home of a local prince, the well-proportioned wooden structure of Muang Sing Exhibition Museum is as impressive as the exhibits within. The museum focuses on the ethnic minorities of the area, such as the Hmong, Lolo, and Akha, with displays of clothing, musical instruments, religious artifacts, and tools used in their daily lives. Upstairs, there are panels explaining the history of Muang Sing and the work of archaeologists who uncovered the original dimensions of this once walled city. The staff, when available, usually runs a video program, which shows in vivid detail the town's intriguing past.

🏛 Wat Luang Ban Xieng Jai

Off Route 17, behind the Muang Sing Exhibition Museum.
Open 8am–3pm daily.

Located just behind the museum, this *wat* is among the most popular religious sights in town. It attracts hordes of worshipers, especially early in

Elegant wood-carved facade of Muang Sing Exhibition Museum

Muang Sing Town Center

③ Former French Garrison
① Muang Sing Exhibition Museum
② Wat Luang Ban Xieng Jai
④ Wat Nam Kaew Luang

For keys to symbols *see back flap*

the morning, when it is quite lively. The *wat's* architectural style is typically Thai Lue, with silver-painted filigree fretwork on the edges of the *sim's* exterior, and colorful *thongs* (long prayer flags) hanging inside.

🏛 Former French Garrison
Off Route 17, W of Kaysone Memorial.
🚉

Once an important military base for Moroccan and Senegalese troops, this garrison is among the last few remnants of the French Colonial era in Muang Sing. Now converted into a Lao Army base, its crumbling brick ramparts are all that remain of what was once a strategic point where the spheres of French, English, and Chinese influence met. There may be other remnants of French presence within the walls of the garrison, but its premises are off limits for visitors. In fact, visitors who

Naga-headed eaves decorating the columns at Wat Nam Kaew Luang

linger too long are hurried along by soldiers, and photography is strictly prohibited.

🏛 Wat Nam Kaew Luang
Off Route 17, near the beginning of the road to Xieng Kok.
Open 8am–3pm daily.

Situated on the southern edge of town, this Buddhist temple sits in a tree-filled compound and houses two beautiful *sims*. The *wat's* monks' quarters, built in the Thai Lue style, were formerly a *wihan* (assembly hall).

Multistory tree house with a zip line at The Gibbon Experience

⓮ Bokeo Nature Reserve

Road map A1. 68 miles (110 km) SW of Muang Sing. **Tel** (084)-212-021. Taxi 🚕 📷 🌐 gibbon experience.org

Covering 475 sq miles (1,230 sq km) of mixed deciduous forests, Bokeo Nature Reserve is home to endangered animals such as the black-crested gibbon, migrating populations of wild buffalo, elephants, and several species of birds.

The only way to visit the preserve is through **The Gibbon Experience**, which offers a unique adventure travel opportunity. As part of two- or three-day tours, visitors stay in the Bokeo Nature Reserve in multistory tree houses that serve as the base camp. These are reached by an exhilarating zip line. The elusive black gibbon, and a wide variety of flora and fauna, can be observed on day treks before returning to the base camp for the night. The site lies deep within the jungle and is accessed by a three-hour drive from Huay Xai, followed by a one-hour trek, which can be demanding. Visitors are advised to carry water and insect repellent.

A shy black crested gibbon, Bokeo Nature Reserve

⓯ A Boat Tour on the Mekong

An ideal way to soak up the beauty of Northern Laos is on a boat trip along the Mekong River. The tour offers stunning views of the surrounding landscape, including wooded mountains bordering the river, huge boulders jutting out from below the rapids, and unhurried views of bucolic country life – the tending of vegetable gardens, fishing, weaving, and even wild elephants stopping by for a drink. Although chartered speedboats are available along the tour route, these are usually not safe. Instead, visitors can take the comfortable cruise offered by Luang Say Mekong Cruises. The cruise makes an overnight stop at Pak Beng.

⑧ Huay Xai
The last town in Laos before the border crossing to Thailand, Huay Xai is usually the starting point for boat tours entering Laos from Thailand. The town, with shops selling precious and semiprecious gemstones, is the gateway for The Gibbon Experience (see p185).

Key

— Major road

═ Minor road

= = Untarred road

■ ▪ International border

⑦ Ban Huay Sanei
The French once established a gold-mining operation in this village. Even today, villagers can be seen panning for gold here.

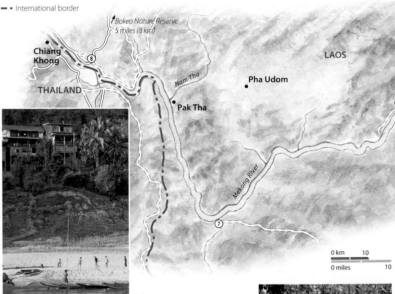

Bokeo Nature Reserve
5 miles (8 km)

Chiang Khong

⑧

THAILAND

Nam Tha

Pak Tha

Pha Udom

LAOS

⑥

Mekong River

⑦

0 km   10

0 miles   10

⑥ Pak Beng
A small town located on a steep hillside, Pak Beng is the midway resting point between Huay Xai and Luang Prabang. Popular sights in town include the pleasant Wat Sim Jong Jaeng, with a simple but refined *sim*. There is also an interesting morning market at the top of the hill.

⑤ Hong Sa
An isolated town, Hong Sa is the elephant capital of Laos. Primarily used for logging, the elephants are also available for safaris, lasting for one or several days, through the surrounding jungle. The nearby Thai Lue village of Vieng Kaew offers excellent textiles and other handicrafts.

② Pak Ou Caves

Located at the base of a towering limestone cliff, the Pak Ou Caves have been venerated, since pre-Buddhist times, as the home of river spirits. It became customary to "retire" Buddhist images here, when new offerings to various *wats* left no space for older or damaged images.

Tips for Drivers

Starting Point: Luang Prabang
Duration: 2 days
Visitor Information: Luang Say Mekong Cruises, 50/4 Sakkarin Rd, Ban Wat Sene, Luang Prabang; **Tel** (071)-252-553
Ⓦ **luangsay.com**

③ Had Tur

A picturesque Thai Lue village built on stilts, Had Tur is well-known for its woven silk fabrics and is an ideal stopover for visitors keen to purchase local handicrafts.

① Ban Xang Hai and Ban Thin Hong Villages

Nestled along the Mekong River, the villages of Ban Xang Hai and Ban Thin Hong are famous for *lao lao (see p221)*, the home-made spirit produced from sticky rice. They are also referred to as the "whiskey villages."

Lao Elephant Festival

Once known as the Kingdom of a Million Elephants and the White Parasol, Laos is among the few Asian countries where this mammal is still found in large numbers. Nevertheless, elephants continue to be endangered and the Lao Elephant Festival is aimed at increasing awareness of the need to protect this noble beast. This two-day festival usually includes traditional *baci sukhuan* ceremonies *(see p126)*, prayers by monks, elephant shows, as well as lectures on conservation. The event is organized by the NGO Elefantasia.

④ Ban Baw

Settled over 600 years ago by members of three different ethnic tribes – Lao Loum, Thai Lue, and Shan – Ban Baw is also renowned for the brewing of *lao lao*. The village women are skilled weavers of cotton and silk textiles and sell their handiwork at reasonable prices.

Monks and spectators at the Lao Elephant Festival

CENTRAL AND SOUTHERN LAOS

Lying between the Mekong and the Annamite Mountain Range, Central and Southern Laos appeals for its rich culture, history, and natural beauty. While "Mekong towns" such as Pakse and Thakhek, and the Khmer-built Wat Phu Champasak, highlight the region's architectural brilliance, the temperate Bolaven Plateau and the pristine Si Phan Don are still isolated and relatively unexplored.

Central and Southern Laos has not only been molded by a number of civilizations and cultures that have settled here from time to time, but also by its geography. The transport and food sources afforded by the mighty Mekong encouraged many civilizations, notably the Champa, Chenla, and Khmer empires, to flourish along its banks from the 5th century AD onward. The French settled the three major towns of Thakhek, Pakse, and Savannakhet during the early 20th century, leaving behind a distinct cultural imprint. At the same time, the Vietnamese entered the country from the east across the narrow band of land between the South China Sea and the Mekong. The Vietnamese put down roots here, intermingling with the local population and contributing to the cultural melting pot that is Southern Laos.

The Mekong River has provided an efficient means of transport and trade with neighboring countries such as Thailand and Vietnam. Despite this, much of the region, except for the three main towns along its banks, was off most tourist itineraries due to poor infrastructure. With the construction of the Friendship Bridge in 1994, however, there has been an increase in visitors, and today the region is slowly opening its treasures to the world.

Among the other attractions of the region are the mountainous Dong Natad and Dong Phu Vieng National Protected Areas, and the wetlands of the Xe Pian. The Bolaven Plateau, with its French-era coffee plantations, and the World Heritage Site of Wat Phu Champasak are also gaining popularity. The Si Phan Don, or Four Thousand Islands, is another interesting diversion.

Sunset over the Mekong near Si Phan Don

◄ Buddha statues in the Shiva Lingam Sanctuary, Wat Phu Champasak

Exploring Central and Southern Laos

The main attractions of the region lie in the south, and the riverside towns of Thakhek, Savannakhet, and Pakse serve as ideal starting points for exploring these sites. The cave networks of Tham Kong Lo and Mahaxai, best visited from Thakhek, are a great draw for adventure seekers. But it is the ancient Khmer ruins of Wat Phu Champasak that remain the highlight of the region. The Si Phan Don archipelago is also becoming a popular destination. The southeast is dominated by the beguiling Bolaven Plateau with its refreshing waterfalls and a host of ethnic minority villages. The National Protected Areas (NPAs) of Dong Natad and Dong Phu Vieng present a great opportunity to interact with Laos's ethnic minorities.

Typical market selling fresh fruit and vegetables, Pakse

Key

— Major road
= Minor road
=== Untarred road
– – Dirt track
▬ International border
— Provincial border
△ Peak

Sights at a Glance

Towns and Cities
❶ Thakhek
❻ *Savannakhet pp194–5*
❿ Pakse
⓫ Champasak

Places of Worship
❷ That Sikhot
❼ That Ing Hang

Museums and Galleries
⓭ Wat Phu Champasak Museum

Historical Sites
⓬ *Wat Phu Champasak pp198–9*
⓮ Ho Nang Sida and Hong Tha Tao
⓰ Wat Tomo

Islands and Beaches
⓯ Don Daeng
⓳ *Si Phan Don pp202–3*

National Parks and Preserves
❽ Dong Natad National Protected Area
❾ Dong Phu Vieng National Protected Area
⓲ Xe Pian National Protected Area

Areas of Natural Beauty
❸ Mahaxai Caves
❹ Kong Leng Lake
❺ Tham Kong Lo
⓱ Bolaven Plateau

Crossing the Mekong River on a boat near Champasak

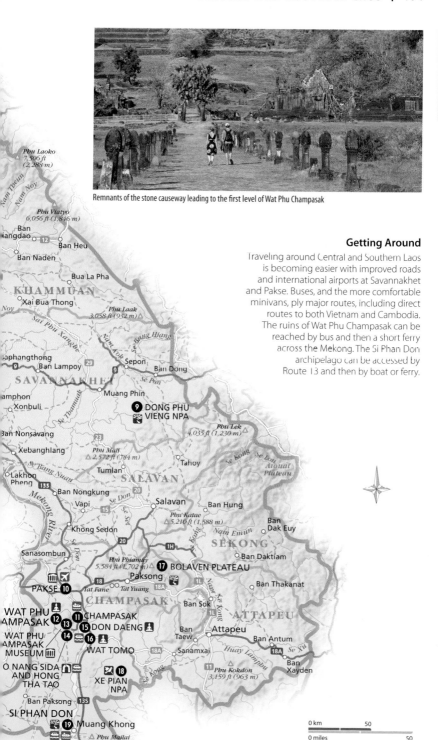

Remnants of the stone causeway leading to the first level of Wat Phu Champasak

Getting Around

Traveling around Central and Southern Laos is becoming easier with improved roads and international airports at Savannakhet and Pakse. Buses, and the more comfortable minivans, ply major routes, including direct routes to both Vietnam and Cambodia. The ruins of Wat Phu Champasak can be reached by bus and then a short ferry across the Mekong. The Si Phan Don archipelago can be accessed by Route 13 and then by boat or ferry.

Colonial-style fountain in the central town square, Thakhek

❶ Thakhek

Road map D3. 220 miles (350 km) S of Vientiane. 🏔 70,000. 🚌 🚏 ℹ Vientiane Rd (051)-212-512. 🎏 Boun That Sikhot (Feb).

Capital of Khammuan province, Thakhek was settled by the French in the 1920s. Although there are no major tourist attractions here, it remains a pretty settlement surrounded by majestic karst mountains and the meandering Mekong River. Inevitably, Colonial influence on the town is still visible in its buildings, the central town square and fountain, and wide avenues. An attractive tree-lined esplanade along the river is ideal for enjoying the cool breeze. Thakhek is an excellent resting point for visitors traveling by land to various places in Southern Laos. It is also a cross-over point for travelers to and from the neighboring countries of Thailand and Vietnam.

Thakhek is a convenient base from which to organize trips to the fascinating caves, waterfalls, and soaring limestone mountains of the **Phu Hin Pun National Protected Area**. This spectacularly beautiful preserve, covering an area of 610 sq miles (1,580 sq km), was established in 1993 and is home to a number of endangered species, such as the Douc langur, Francois's langur, Assamese macaque, 43 species of bat, sooty babbler, and limestone leaf warbler. Visitors can also take advantage of the exciting adventure and ecotourism facilities in Thakhek, which include trekking and

kayaking. These trips can be organized by visitors on their own or through tour operators, such as Green Discovery whose office is located in the Inthira Hotel Sikotabong *(see p215)* on Chao Anou Road. The local tourism office is also helpful. The NPA can be reached by tuk-tuk.

🗺 **Phu Hin Pun National Protected Area**
3 miles (5 km) N of Thakhek. **Tel** (021)-212-251. 🆆 ecotourismlaos.com

❷ That Sikhot

Road map D3. 4 miles (6 km) S of Thakhek. **Open** 8am–6pm daily. 🎏 Boun That Sikhot (Feb).

Formally known as Pha That Sikhotabong, this stupa and the adjacent *wat* (temple) are located on a site that dates from the Khmer principality of Sri Khotabura. The Khmer ruled this area from the 6th to the 10th centuries AD. The site was restored and reconsecrated by the famous Lao King Setthathirat in the 16th century. The unique lotus bud-shaped stupa is of considerable religious significance to the Lao people, and pilgrims visit from across the country to attend the annual fair, Boun That Sikhot, which is held in February. The stupa's riverside location makes it a pleasant place for people to visit at sunset.

Kayakers on the Mekong

Sprawling grounds housing the lotus bud-shaped stupa of That Sikhot and its adjoining *wat*

Footbridge leading to the Buddha Cave, Mahaxai Caves

❸ Mahaxai Caves

Road map D3. Off Route 12 miles (8 km) E of Thakhek. **Open** 8:30am–4:30pm daily. 🖼 ✏

A few miles east of Thakhek, the landscape along Route 12 begins to change with sheer karst formations looming on both sides of the road. These cliffs are riddled with caves, several of which are quite impressive, and all a cool respite from the heat of the day. The first of these, 5 miles (8 km) east of Thakhek, is **Buddha Cave**, known locally as Tham Pa Fa. This cave is popular with locals who come to venerate the 229 Buddha statues here – some of the statues are 500 years old. Another 4 miles (6 km) ahead, to the right of Route 12, lies **Tham Xiang Liab**. This cave is about 656 ft (200 m) long and emerges in an isolated valley with pools ideal for swimming. Among the last of the caves, **Tham Nong Aen** lies farther ahead and is famous for the constant flow of cool air from its depths. The caves can be reached by tuk-tuk from Thakhek.

❹ Kong Leng Lake

Road map D3. 30 miles (48 km) N of Thakhek. **Open** 8:30am–4:30pm daily. 🖼 ✏

This isolated lake, over 21 ft (70 m) deep in the center, lies in the foothills of the Phu Hin Pun NPA. Depending on the weather, the lake is either an emerald green or deep blue in color.

The Ho Chi Minh Trail

Named by the Americans, the Ho Chi Minh Trail is a vast system of parallel trails, roads, bridges, and a diesel pipeline, which was used by the North Vietnamese Army to transport troops and material to its forces during the Vietnam War (1954–75). A major point of entry into Laos was the Mu Gia pass, via which Route 12 now enters Vietnam. Tours are available from Lak Sao, 126 miles (202 km) north of Thakhek. Visitors can see war debris, including the remains of Russian surface-to-air missiles used to defend the trail from bombing. However, be aware that Unexploded Ordnance (UXO) still remains a problem here.

Aerial view of the Ho Chi Minh Trail through Laos

Sacred to locals, the lake is believed to be inhabited by spirits capable of ringing a gong on full moon nights, thus giving the lake its name, which means "evening gong." Fishing is not allowed here and swimming has been restricted to certain areas.

The best way to visit the lake is as part of an organized trek from Thakhek, which also includes visits to local villages and other caves.

❺ Tham Kong Lo

Road map C3. Off Route 9 miles (13 km) N of Thakhek. 🚌 **Open** 8:30am–4:30pm daily 🖼 📷 ✏

A visit to the Tham Kong Lo, a magnificent creation of nature, is the highlight of any trip into the karst highlands of Central Laos. This dramatic cave is entered on a motorboat, from the downstream end of the Nam Hin Boun, which runs for 4 miles (6 km) through the cave. The ride into the cave includes a stop at a hidden valley located on the upstream end, and the entire trip takes about 2 hours. Once back, visitors can enjoy a swim at any one of the large pools located close to the entrance, or can buy some great picnic food from vendors stationed here.

Tham Kong Lo has become popular, especially with locals, since the construction of the 24-mile (40-km) long paved road from the junction with Route 8. Decent guesthouses in the area also make this an excellent overnight trip from nearby Thakhek.

Visitors at the entrance to the magnificent Tham Kong Lo

❻ Savannakhet

Savannakhet's rarely used official name, Muang Kaysone Phomvihane, refers to its status as the birthplace of Laos's Communist patriarch, Kaysone Phomvihane, whose childhood home is located in the town center. Much of the activity in this small, bustling town is due to the bridge from neighboring Thailand and the road connecting it to the Vietnamese border. Fortunately, the town's expansion has not affected its old Colonial charm. The downtown area is dotted with several historic buildings, a Taoist temple, and St. Theresa's Catholic Church, all of which are best visited on a rented bicycle.

Buddha images being made in the factory at Wat Sainyaphum

🏛 Chao Mahesak Shrine

Tha Hae Rd. **Open** 8am–5pm daily.
Built under the shade of a huge bodhi tree on the riverside, the Chao Mahesak Shrine is a highly revered religious landmark. Locals come here to pay respects to a diverse pantheon of deities and spirits, including Chao Mahesak, who is mythically linked to the town's founding. A statue of the deity can be found in front of this elevated shrine. Inside, elaborate statues depict Chao Mae Kuan Yim, the Chinese Goddess of Mercy, as well as some Taoist deities. Fortunetellers offering their services to locals are a common sight here, and the smell of burning incense is all pervasive.

🏛 Wat Sainyaphum

Tha Hae Rd. **Open** 8am–5pm daily.
Lying across the street from the Chao Mahesak Shrine, and occupying a full block, is Wat Sainyaphum, the largest Buddhist temple in town. It is a pleasant complex constructed in a wide variety of architectural styles showing European as well as Chinese influences. Several parts of the building are adorned with bas-reliefs of mythical animals. A small factory toward the riverside entrance of the temple, where cement images of the Buddha are cast, painted, and consecrated, is an interesting

Colonial buildings overlooking the main square, Savannakhet

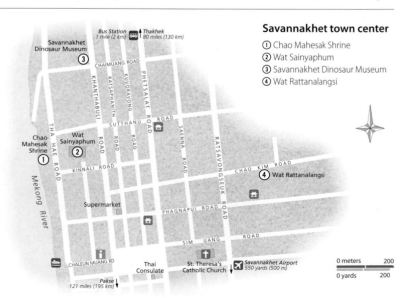

Savannakhet town center

① Chao Mahesak Shrine
② Wat Sainyaphum
③ Savannakhet Dinosaur Museum
④ Wat Rattanalangsi

For keys to symbols *see back flap*

place to stop. Visitors can also explore the large school close by, where monks are taught the precepts of Buddhism.

🏛 Savannakhet Dinosaur Museum

Khanthabuli Rd. **Open** 8am–noon & 1pm–4pm daily. 🚫 📷

Another interesting stop, the Savannakhet Dinosaur Museum, displays fossilized remains of a large brontosaurus and other specimens discovered in the province. Visitors can take guided tours of the museum accompanied by curators who were present at the digs where the fossils were found. They not only explain the importance of these specimens, but also provide information about other paleontological sites in the Savannakhet area.

🏯 Wat Rattanalangsi

Chao Kim Rd. **Open** 8am–5pm daily.
Situated in a pleasant tree-filled complex, Wat Rattanalangsi was built in 1951. The temple exhibits several examples of the syncretic inclusion of Hindu icons that characterize Lao Buddhist temples, such as a statue of Brahma, the God of Creation. The three-level gilded drum-and-gong-tower at the back of the compound is striking, as is the 45-ft (15-m) long Reclining Buddha.

Exhibits on display at the Savannakhet Dinosaur Museum

Devotees kneeling outside the stupa, That Ing Hang

❼ That Ing Hang

Road map D4. 10 miles (16 km) NE of Savannakhet. **Open** 7am–6pm daily. 🚫 🎎 That Ing Hang Festival (Dec full moon).

Of great religious significance to the Lao people, That Ing Hang is related to both the 10th-century Khmer empire of Sri Khotabura and King Chao Fa Ngum's return from Cambodia in the 14th century. The stupa was rebuilt several times and in its present form is an attractive four-tiered edifice with a lotus bud-shaped pinnacle. The complex is surrounded by a covered gallery containing 329 identical images of the Buddha. Women are not permitted into the inner sanctum surrounding the stupa. That Ing Hang can be reached by tuk-tuk from Savannakhet.

❽ Dong Natad National Protected Area

Road map D4. 10 miles (16 km) NE of Savannakhet. **Taxi** ℹ️ Savannakhet Eco-Guide Unit, Ratsaphanith Rd, (041)-214-203. 🚫 📷
🌐 savannahkhet-trekking.com

Among Laos's smallest NPAs, Dong Natad is easily accessed from Savannakhet. One of the highlights of any visit to this NPA, besides the verdant forest and several pristine lakes, is the opportunity to interact with locals who have inhabited this area for hundreds of years. Living in harmony with the environment, they earn their livelihood from non-timber forest products such as wild honey, edible insects, rattan, medicinal plants, and *nang* oil from dipterocarps, which is used as fuel.

It is possible to visit the area in a tuk-tuk on a day trip from Savannakhet or, alternatively, arrange a homestay in one of the villages in the forest. Cycling and trekking are both options, and visitors can either explore the area on their own, or engage the services of a guide from the Savannakhet Eco-Guide Unit.

❾ Dong Phu Vieng National Protected Area

Road map D4. 110 miles (180 km) E of Savannakhet. **Taxi** ℹ️ Savannakhet Eco-Guide Unit, Ratsaphanith Rd, (041)-214-203. 📷
🌐 savannahkhet-trekking.com

This remote NPA is home to a small Mon-Khmer ethnic minority called the Katang, who even today remain unaffected by modernization, steeped as they are in their own distinct culture and belief systems. It is possible to visit this area as part of a tour organized by the Savannakhet Eco-Guide Unit, which has established treks in close cooperation with the local people. The demanding trek begins at Muang Phin on Route 9 heading toward Vietnam. Visitors spend a couple of nights in the Katang villages, and the journey culminates with a boat trip on the Se Bang Hieng River.

Trekkers walking the forest trail through the Dong Natad NPA

For hotels and restaurants see p215 and pp232–3

Finely carved stone lintel at the Champasak Provincial Museum, Pakse

⑩ Pakse

Road map D5. 140 miles (230 km) S of Savannakhet. 🚗 90,000. ✈ 🚌 ℹ Provincial Tourism Office, Thanon 11 Rd, (031)-3121-2021.

Located at the confluence of the Don and Mekong rivers, Pakse, capital of Champasak province, was founded by the French in 1905. The Colonial Art Deco-style architecture of Pakse's downtown area, with several high-rise buildings, makes it more urban than the other towns along the Mekong. The town has become particularly busy after the completion of a Japanese bridge across the Mekong just south of town, which has enabled brisker trade with Thailand.

Although Pakse serves as a jumping-off point for sights such as Wat Phu Champasak and Si Phan Don *(see pp202–3)*, the town has several attractions of its own. The Dao Heuang Market, situated close to the bridge, is a huge complex rivaling Vientiane's Talat Sao *(see p144)*, where local textiles and produce, such as coffee from the Bolaven Plateau *(see p200)*, are on offer. Another interesting sight is the Champasak Palace Hotel on the corner of Route 13 and Road 1. It was built as a palace for Chao Boun Oum Na Champasak, a prince who held ceremonial sway in the area until the Communists seized power in 1975. Although the prince never really lived here, the former palace remains a popular attraction. The most interesting stop, however, is the **Champasak Provincial Museum**, which has some

excellent Khmer lintels taken from sites throughout the province. Visitors will also find walking along the riverfront esplanades a pleasurable experience.

🏛 **Champasak Provincial Museum**
Route 13. **Open** 8–11:30am & 2–4pm Mon–Fri. 🐾

⑪ Champasak

Road map D5. 21 miles (34 km) SW of Pakse. 🚗 3,000. 🚌 from Pakse. 🚌 from Ban Muang. **Taxi** from Pakse. ℹ Champasak Provincial Tourist Office, Thanon 11 Rd, Pakse, (031)-3121-2021.

A small town on the west bank of the Mekong River, Champasak was once the royal capital of the Na Champasak principality, which ruled much of Southern Laos. Popular due to its proximity to the majestic Wat Phu Champasak ruins to the south, and as a jumping-off point for Don Daeng, Champasak today is a sleepy town with the only remnants of royalty being two Colonial-style royal residences located just south of the fountain in the center of town. Due west of these buildings lies Wat Thong, the temple where the town's sovereigns performed religious rites, and where their cremated ashes now lie. The town is a pleasant place in which to relax after a tiring day at Wat Phu. It also has a variety of accommodation options that range from guesthouses to the upscale River Resort *(see p215)*.

⑫ Wat Phu Champasak

See pp198–9.

⑬ Wat Phu Champasak Museum

Road map D5. 5 miles (8 km) S of Champasak. **Taxi** from Champasak. **Open** 8:30am–4:30pm daily. 🐾 🐾 🖳 vatphou-champassak.com

Housed in a modern building situated close to the entrance of the Wat Phu complex, this museum has excellent exhibits telling the story of this ancient temple, as well as those of the other Khmer sites in the area. The museum is well lit, and all

A sprawling Colonial villa en route to Champasak

the exhibits are captioned in English. The statuary on display includes a stone figure of Nandi, the sacred bull and the mount of Shiva; an elaborate and well-preserved statue of Vishnu, the Protector of Creation, one of the gods in the Hindu pantheon; a Garuda, the eagle mount of Vishnu, and Ganesha, the elephant god. Amid this impressive display of Hindu iconography also stands an elegant 8th-century Dvaravati image of the Buddha, since the pre-Angkorian Khmers were followers of both Hinduism and Buddhism. The museum also contains an excellent collection of sandstone lintels, with intricate stone carvings, recovered from the private collection of Prince Boun Oum, and brought here for safekeeping.

A statue at Wat Phu Champasak Museum

Another interesting piece is the carved stone water spout (see p199) that originally carried holy water to the central Shiva lingam in the uppermost temple of Wat Phu. Pride of place in this museum, however, is given to the artistically unimpressive, but historically significant, 5th-century Sanskrit inscription that was found at Wat Luang Gau, near the town of Champasak. This stone inscription contains a clear mention of the original founder of the stunning Wat Phu Champasak – a Cham king named Devanika – thus laying to rest any doubts about the origins of the temple.

⓮ Ho Nang Sida and Hong Tha Tao

Road map D5. 1 mile (2 km) S of Wat Phu Champasak. 🚗 from Champasak.

Although not as magnificent or significant as the Wat Phu complex, the two Khmer sites of Ho Nang Sida and Hong Tha Tao are an interesting side trip to any visit to Wat Phu. Located

south of Wat Phu, they are accessed by turning left just before the two main galleries on the first level of the complex. The first, Ho Nang Sida, dates to the 10th century and is venerated by locals. A tree growing through the center of this crumbling shrine is festooned with Buddhist prayer flags put up by devotees who come here to pray. A mile farther south lies the site of Hong Tha Tao, which was once a rest house for travelers venturing to and from the ancient capital of Angkor. Although neither of these sites are of much architectural interest, they are quite atmospheric and certainly worth a visit.

⓯ Don Daeng

Road map D5. 0.5 miles (1 km) E of Champasak. 🚌 from Pakse. 🚌 from Ban Muang. 🚲

An island located in the middle of the Mekong River, across from Champasak, Don Daeng has recently emerged as a popular destination for visitors keen to experience life along the Mekong. The island is ringed by

Riverboats anchored at a pier on Don Daeng

eight separate villages, which are connected by an unpaved track. Sights around the island include the beautiful Wat Ban Boung Kham, situated on the southwest coast. The wat was built over a former Khmer shrine, indicating the island's history.

Visitors will find adequate accommodation facilities at the community guesthouse in the village of Ban Hua Daeng, located on the northern edge of Don Daeng. There is also the luxurious La Folie Lodge (see p215), a mile south, on the west coast. Don Daeng provides easy access to the forested precincts of Wat Tomo (see p200) nearby.

Ancient, crumbling ruins of the atmospheric Ho Nang Sida

⑫ Wat Phu Champasak

Named a World Heritage Site by UNESCO in 2001, Wat Phu, meaning Mountain Temple, is located in the foothills of the Lingaparvata Mountain, now known as Phu Phasak. Sacred to at least three different cultures, the temple is believed to have been revered by the Champa Empire during the 5th–8th centuries. Most of the present edifices, however, are pre-Angkorian, built around the beginning of the 9th century. In more recent times, the Lao Buddhist kingdom of Lan Xang converted the Hindu temples into structures honoring their own faith.

Crocodile Stone
The crocodile was a divine being for the ancient Khmers, and this stylized carving on a flat stone clearly dates from that period. The stone's function remains unclear.

Main Temple Lintels
Intricately carved lintels above the 12 entrances to the main temple depict Hindu and Buddhist deities.

Carving of Holy Trinity
Behind the main temple sanctuary is a bas-relief in stone depicting the Hindu holy trinity.

Elephant statue

Holy spring

Main Temple
The uppermost part of the complex, the main temple, houses the altar where the Shiva lingam once stood.

★ Shiva Lingam Sanctuary
Located in the innermost part of the main temple, the Shiva *lingam* sanctuary now houses a large Buddha statue and several smaller icons. It is regularly visited by devotees with offerings.

KEY

① **The Yoni**, a symbol of fertility, is the female counterpart of the Shiva *lingam*.

② **Relief of Shiva and Uma riding Nandi**

③ **Khmer Dvarapala**

Holy Spring
This underground spring once fed a channel that delivered holy water to the Shiva *lingam* via a stone spout. The spout is now on display in the Wat Phu Champasak Museum.

Champa-lined Stairs
The steep staircase leading to the upper levels is lined with pretty champa trees. These trees bear the *dok champa* blossoms, the national flower of Laos.

Khmer Dvarapala
A stone statue, clad in Buddhist robes, stands guard over the inner sanctum of the temple. According to local lore it portrays the legendary founder of Wat Phu.

★ Nandi Pavilion
This smaller pavilion, dedicated to the sacred bull Nandi, the mount of Shiva, stands close to the worship pavilion. The statue of Nandi, however, is now in the museum.

Half-buried statues

Stone causeway

To Champasak 5 miles (8 km) To Wat Phu Champasak Museum see pp196–7

0 meters 50
0 yards 50

★ Worship Pavilions
Two impressive pavilions, notable for their detailed bas-reliefs, are in the process of being restored. Experts believe that they served as separate worship facilities for men and women.

Visitors on a coffee plantation tour in the town of Paksong

16 Wat Tomo

Road map D5. 30 miles (48 km) S of Pakse. 🚌 from Champasak or Don Daeng. **Open** 8am–5pm daily. 🎫

Lying on the east bank of the Mekong River, a short distance south of Wat Phu Champasak (see pp198–9), the Khmer ruins of Wat Tomo, also known as Ou Muang, date from the 9th century. This wat was built in honor of Rudrani, the wife of Shiva, the God of Destruction. The temple is constructed of laterite, and while the best lintels are now in the Champasak Provincial Museum (see p196), some artifacts still remain, including a unique mukhalinga, which is an ornately carved lingam (phallic-like symbol). Situated in a shady forest of tall trees, the wat makes an excellent day trip from the town of Champasak or Don Daeng. It is also accessible by land from the east side of the Mekong River. In fact, when the water level is high, boats can come within 100 ft (30 m) of the temple,

otherwise it is a 15-minute walk from the river in the dry season.

17 Bolaven Plateau

Road map E5. 47 miles (78 km) E of Pakse. 🚌 **Taxi** from Pakse. **Open** 8:30am–4:30pm daily. 🎫 🎫

The French Colonialists found the temperate climate and rich soil of the Bolaven Plateau particularly suitable for habitation and cultivation. They planted the area with coffee, cardamom, and vegetables. This region can be explored from the town of Paksong – local coffee can be tasted here – which lies 14 miles (23 km) south of the plateau. Bolaven literally means Home of the Laven, which is the largest ethnic group that lives here. Besides the Laven, this region is home to many ethnic minorities such as the Alak and the Katu. The plateau was the site of intense battles during the Vietnam War (1954–75) and some areas, especially the Attapeu province, remain uncleared of UXO (Unexploded Ordnance). Today, the area is renowned for its waterfalls. Among the more popular are Tat Fane, a 360-ft (120-m) high cascade, and the 120-ft (40-m) high Tat Yuang, which is great for swimming. Visitors who wish to explore the area further can stay at the Tadlo Lodge (see p215), which is close to a couple of waterfalls. Treks to minority villages can be arranged from here as well.

Traditionally dressed Laven

Lush greenery surrounding a viewpoint, Bolaven Plateau

18 Xe Pian National Protected Area

Road map D5. 30 miles (48 km) S of Pakse. 🚌 from Pakse. ℹ Visitor Information Center (031)-212-177. 🎫 🎫

Beginning roughly at Wat Tomo and continuing south to the Cambodian border, Xe Pian National Protected Area covers an area of 1,000 sq miles (2,600 sq km). It sustains a variety of wildlife, including the tiger, Asiatic black bear, banteng, wild ox, gibbon, hornbill, and crane. The area is best explored from the Kingfisher Ecolodge (see p215), located near the village of Kiet Ngong at the northeastern corner of the NPA. It is possible to arrange treks deeper into the NPA from here. Elephant treks to Phu Asa, an interesting flat-topped mountain nearby, can also be arranged.

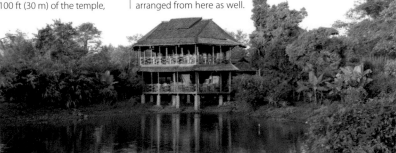

Charming Kingfisher Ecolodge, Xe Pian National Protected Area

For hotels and restaurants see p215 and pp232–3

Wildlife of Southern Laos

The geographical features of Southern Laos make it a particularly rich area in terms of wildlife. The Bolaven Plateau, with its sparse human habitation and cool climate, sustains a variety of wildlife, while the steep cliffs and caves in the limestone karst formations found throughout Southern Laos attract several kinds of animals. They provide secure habitats for birds as well as smaller mammals. Indeed, it is in this part of the country that several species, once thought extinct, have been rediscovered. Notable among them are the Laotian rock rat and the spindlehorn. Even larger mammals such as bears, elephants, and a variety of primates, often victims of poachers, have relatively large populations here.

Mammals

The region is home to a plethora of mammalian species ranging in size from the Asian elephant to the humble squirrel. Several species, such as the lesser panda and the pygmy slow loris, are unique to Laos.

The Indochinese tiger, a magnificent feline, has been relentlessly hunted for its skin and bones, driving it to the brink of extinction. It is believed to number less than 100 in the wild in Laos.

Asiatic black bears are distinguished by a white crest on the chest. These shy creatures survive in the remote regions of southeastern Laos.

Golden fur distinguishes the female.

The spindlehorn sports long, curving horns. A forest-dwelling bovine, it resembles an antelope and was identified in 1992 in Vietnam.

Yellow-cheeked crested gibbons engage in elaborate mating songs and live over 50 years in the wild. Adult males are black with golden cheeks, while females are golden.

Birds

More than 700 species of birds are found in Laos including such magnificent creatures as the Sarus crane. While indiscriminate hunting has put a few species on the endangered list, many are prolific breeders and their populations are, in fact, increasing.

Hornbills are characterized by a large and often colorful beak. More than 50 species of hornbill have been discovered. These birds prefer to nest in small caves in the limestone karst.

Purple-hued plumage

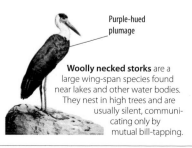

Woolly necked storks are a large wing-span species found near lakes and other water bodies. They nest in high trees and are usually silent, communicating only by mutual bill-tapping.

The Sarus crane, at a height of 6 ft (2 m), is the world's tallest non-migratory flying bird. It is distinguished by the red plumage on its head, and has a wing span of 8 ft (2.4 m).

⓳ Si Phan Don

Located between Champasak and the Cambodian border, Si Phan Don, or Four Thousand Islands, is an inland archipelago comprising thousands of islands, islets, and sand bars. The entire area covers a distance of some 30 miles (50 km) along the Mekong River from the northern tip of the largest island, Don Khong, to the massive Khon Phapeng Waterfalls in the south. These islands are inhabited by villagers who continue to lead a self-sufficient lifestyle, fishing and growing their own rice and other crops. However, the area's isolation from the outside world has changed since tourism has brought in more visitors and improved roads have connected the archipelago to Pakse. Three of the main islands are already on the electricity grid, and a few of the islands have accommodation facilities.

★ Don Khong
Lush green fields and hills dot the landscape of Don Khong. The best way to explore the island is on a bicycle or motorcycle since the roads are in good condition. This island has several good hotels centered around Muang Khong.

Map labels:
Ban Hua Khong ①
Mekong River
Don Hinyai
Don Khong
Tham Phu Khiaw
Muang Saen Nua
Kampong Sralau
LAOS
Ban Ha
Ban Thaphao
Ban Loppadi Cl

0 kilometers 5

0 miles 5

KEY

① **The residence of Khamtay Siphandone**, former president of the Lao PDR, is located near the village of Ban Hua Khong, at the northern end of Don Khong. The house is usually unoccupied and visitors are free to explore the grounds.

② **Don Det** can be reached either by a scenic two-hour boat ride from Don Khong or a quick trip from the mainland village of Ban Nakasong. The island's inexpensive accommodation facilities, coupled with its easy-going pace, attract many visitors.

Muang Khong
The main town on Don Khong, Muang Khong serves as a ferry port for boats arriving from the mainland. Local attractions include Wat Muang Khong, which has impressive *naga* statuary and the interesting Tham Phu Khiaw.

Irrawaddy Dolphins

Found in the waters of the Mekong River between Don Khon and the Cambodian border, the Irrawaddy dolphin (*Orcaella brevirostris*) is considered sacred by the Lao people. They never intentionally fish or trap this species, although destructive fishing techniques, such as gill netting, have reduced their numbers drastically. Trips to see the dolphins are organized from Don Khon.

Distinct box-shaped snout of the Irrawaddy dolphin

VISITORS' CHECKLIST

Practical Information
Road Map D5.
81 miles (135 km) S of Pakse.
🏞 Khon Phapeng Waterfalls.

Transport
🚌 from Pakse to Don Khong and Ban Nakasang. 🛥 between islands. 🛥 between Don Khong & Don Det and Don Det & Don Khon; not available during the dry season.

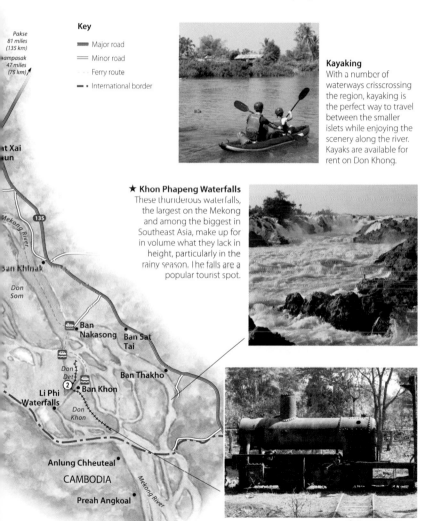

Key

- 🟫 Major road
- ═ Minor road
- ⋯ Ferry route
- ━ ▪ International border

Pakse
81 miles
(135 km)
ampasak
47 miles
(75 km)

at Xai
aun

Mekong River
135

San Khinak

Don Som

🛥 Ban Nakasong   Ban Sat Tai

🛥
Don Det   Ban Thakho
2
Li Phi   🛥 Ban Khon
Waterfalls
Don Khon

Anlung Chheuteal
CAMBODIA
Mekong River
Preah Angkoal

Kayaking

With a number of waterways crisscrossing the region, kayaking is the perfect way to travel between the smaller islets while enjoying the scenery along the river. Kayaks are available for rent on Don Khong.

★ Khon Phapeng Waterfalls

These thunderous waterfalls, the largest on the Mekong and among the biggest in Southeast Asia, make up for in volume what they lack in height, particularly in the rainy season. The falls are a popular tourist spot.

★ French Railway

Built by the French in the early 20th century, this 7-mile (12-km) long railway helped cargo ships to circumvent the two mighty waterfalls blocking their passage upstream on the Mekong River. Remnants of this project can still be seen today.

For keys to symbols *see back flap*

TRAVELERS' NEEDS

WHERE TO STAY

Accommodations in both Cambodia and Laos vary widely, from basic guesthouses to restored Colonial villas serving as boutique hotels. Luxury international chains, however, are mostly confined to larger towns and cities such as Siem Reap, Phnom Penh, and Sihanoukville in Cambodia, and Luang Prabang and Vientiane in Laos. A wide variety of mid-range accommodation options are also available. These establishments offer both air-conditioned and fan-cooled rooms, with the former being more expensive. Homestays are also becoming increasingly popular, especially in Laos. They not only present an opportunity to contribute directly to the community, but are also an excellent way to experience authentic rural life. Serviced apartments are another option, offering the freedom of your own space with the benefits of hotel service. The accommodation listings in this guide *(see pp210–15)* are arranged by area, and cater to a range of different budgets.

The tastefully decorated lobby of the Raffles Hotel in Phnom Penh, Cambodia

Hotel Grading

There is no official grading system for hotels in Laos. In Cambodia, the government is urging hotels to be formally classified on a scale of one to five stars, but so far only 18 percent of hotels have been rated. Price is therefore usually the best indicator of what to expect. Accommodations range from basic to luxury. Even at the low end of the market, rooms are usually spotlessly clean.

Luxury Hotels

Several international hotel chains, such as Raffles *(see p210)*, InterContinental and Sofitel have representation in major cities such as Phnom Penh and Siam Reap, and offer the same quality of facilities and service they provide in other parts of the world. While Luang Prabang and Vientiane also have their fair share of international hotels, these cities also have a wide variety of boutique hotels, such as The Belle Rive Hotel *(see p214)* in Luang Prabang.

The international hotels, in several cases, offer menus and interiors designed by people of global repute. Most hotels also have a busy events calendar with performances during the evening, such as traditional dance, and other events during the day.

Boutique hotels, on the other hand, offer a more specialized service with accommodations often in atmospheric, lovingly restored French villas. They are smaller in size, with fewer rooms, but will pay more attention to detail. Siem Reap, in particular, is experiencing a growth in this sector, although the term "boutique" is often loosely applied. Fortunately for visitors, due to increasing competition, such establishments may reduce their prices. There are some beautiful rooms in good boutique hotels that can be reserved for a reasonable rate.

Resort Hotels

Resort hotel chains have been quick to establish themselves in Cambodia, given its extraordinary archaeological treasures and pristine coastline. The coastal town of Sihanoukville *(see pp108–9)*, in particular, is home to a number of resort hotels. The Sokha Beach Resort *(see p212)* is a typically lavish resort, which offers a private beach, two swimming pools, tennis courts, a children's club, and the chance to relax in a world-class spa.

External facade of a popular boutique hotel in Luang Prabang, Laos

◀ Brightly colored parasols on display at a street market in Luang Prabang

The tranquil gardens of the Knai Bang Chatt resort in Kep, Cambodia

Resort hotels are also becoming increasingly popular in Laos, particularly in Luang Prabang, and in parts of Central and Southern Laos. With investors keen to tap into the untouched beauty of this country, many more resorts are likely to appear in the near future.

Guesthouses and Mid-Range Hotels

Guesthouses are usually family-run in both countries and can offer good value for the budget traveler. It is best to research extensively before making a reservation as some places can be extremely basic, particularly in rural areas. The majority of guesthouses, however, offer a simple fan-cooled room with a private or shared bathroom. They are usually thoughtfully furnished, with friendly service at reception. Guesthouses are also great places to meet other travelers and exchange tips. Indeed, they may be the only option available for travelers in the more remote areas of Cambodia and Laos.

Prices at mid-range hotels, on the other hand, start at around US$20 and may go up to as much as US$100, with a huge difference in the type of facilities available and services on offer. While some mid-range hotels are tastefully designed and may offer a pool, excellent food, and service, the less expensive ones may barely justify the price. It is therefore advisable to take a good look around before settling on one.

Laos usually offers better value, both in guesthouses and mid range hotels. The quality of service provided, and the facilities on offer are, on the whole, slightly better than in Cambodia.

Budget Hotels

Budget hotels are functional, inexpensive, and only slightly better than a guesthouse in terms of decor and furnishings. Unfortunately, service in these establishments can leave much to be desired, and hygiene is often only an afterthought. Although these hotels usually have fairly large rooms (sometimes even with a balcony), as well as modern amenities such as cable TV, there is not much to recommend such places except for the price. As a rule, rooms without any windows are cheaper.

A no-frills budget hotel on a quiet street in Vientiane, Laos

Budget hotels are usually used for Khmer business trips, and visitors must always carefully scrutinize these establishments because some of them double up as brothels.

Homestays

The concept of staying with a friendly local family, usually a member of an ethnic minority group, to enjoy the opportunity to discover their lifestyle, is particularly popular in Laos. Homestays are also gaining ground in Cambodia. They are especially common in remote areas such as the Ratanakiri and Mondulkiri provinces. Although such stays may not be as comfortable as a stay in a hotel or resort, they are an enchanting way to experience authentic rural life. Board and lodging is generally shared with the host family, and visitors may also be able to participate in a few daily activities.

Laos, with its large number of ethnic minorities, offers a varied homestay experience. However, when staying with a local family, visitors should remember to follow certain rules of etiquette, which include always eating the food offered, never littering the surroundings, and also refraining from giving sweets or medicine to the children. Companies such as **Airbnb** and **Homestay** have revolutionized homestays and attracted a wide range of new hosts, often with international outlooks.

Elegant interior of a spacious bedroom in The Apsara, Luang Prabang

Rental Apartments

Those who do not wish to stay in a hotel or resort, and for whom homestays are not an option, can always rent their own apartment. An increasing number of these are serviced, which means they offer hotel-like amenities, but with greater freedoms and often much lower price tags. The Internet is by far the best place to look for rental apartments in Cambodia and Laos. Companies such as **HomeAway**, **Airbnb**, **Cambodia Yellow Pages**, and **Immo Laos** offer a wide a range of properties for rent. Advertisements for rooms for rent also appear on bulletin boards, usually at restaurants, cafés, and bars, or in the classified section of local weekly newspapers, or at the back of popular publications. *Paisai? What's On?*, for instance, is a free monthly magazine, widely available in Vientiane, which also publishes lists of properties for rent.

Prices

Cambodia and Laos offer a wide range of accommodations, with varying prices. The least expensive among them are usually the budget hotels where a room with a fan and a private bathroom can be had for as little as US$4, with the better options costing up to US$20. Mid-range options cost anywhere between US$20 and US$100 with the higher-end range offering not only a good location, but also modern amenities such as a swimming pool, air-conditioning, and cable TV. Breakfast is usually included in the room rate.
The most exclusive boutique hotels, however, will cost well over US$100.

Reserving

Travelers visiting the most popular areas during the peak season, between November and February, may find all

places, especially high-end hotels and international resorts, completely booked. It is therefore recommended to reserve a room in advance, especially if staying in cities such as Siem Reap and Luang Prabang, to avoid any last-minute problems.
All the major hotels in both Cambodia and Laos have their own websites, as do several mid-range hotels. Guests can always contact these establishments online, and several of them also have online reservation options. Hotels are also widely represented on www.booking.com, a website that guarantees the lowest rates available and doesn't add on extras like tax or booking rates.
The official **Tourism of Cambodia** website offers assistance with online reservations and can help in finding the right hotel. **The Laos Hotel and Guesthouse Booking Service** is also well run and has a comprehensive website that can be used to make bookings.

Taxes

Most major hotels in Cambodia levy 10 percent government tax, 2 percent accommodation tax, and an additional 5 per cent service charge. In Laos, there is normally a 10 percent government tax and a 10 percent service charge. All of these charges will be detailed in the check, but reserving through a tour operator is a good way of ensuring a discount on rates

Visitors arriving at a guesthouse on Serendipity Beach, Sihanoukville

and taxes. Mid-range hotels will usually include tax and service charge costs in the price.

Bargaining

Asking for a discount is usually a good idea, especially for those who are staying for more than one night at a hotel. Rates will decrease with every extra couple of nights. Bargaining is common in both these countries, and visitors need not shy away from asking for a reduction. It is polite to stop bargaining when a mutually agreeable price has been reached, especially when the other person has stopped dropping his figures.

Most guesthouses, on the other hand, have low prices to begin with, and visitors should refrain from asking for any discount, although many guesthouse owners will be happy to offer a cheaper rate for a guest who is planning to stay for a longer duration. As a rule, less desirable, smaller rooms will be available for considerably lower rates.

Tipping

Gratuities are not usual in Cambodia or Laos, and tipping is not an essential part of their culture. Therefore, unless someone has been particularly helpful, visitors should not feel in any way obliged to tip. That

An inexpensive hotel advertising its services, Sihanoukville

said, both Cambodia and Laos are economically developing countries, and tips are often a good way of supplementing salaries if a visitor is particularly pleased with the service provided. US$1 is usually considered adequate.

Facilities for Children

Expensive, upscale hotels, equipped with modern amenities such as swimming pools, tennis courts, and table tennis facilities, usually have a family room and other facilities to keep children occupied. Most other hotels, however, will not provide any special facilities for families traveling with children.

Children under the age of 12 years are usually allowed to stay in a hotel free of charge.

DIRECTORY

Homestays

Airbnb
w airbnb.com

Homestay
w homestay.com

Reservations

The Laos Hotel and Guesthouse Booking Service
w laos-hotel-link.com

Tourism of Cambodia
w tourismcambodia.com

Rental Apartments

Cambodia Yellow Pages
w yellowpages-cambodia.com

HomeAway
w homeaway.com

Immo Laos
w immo-laos.webs.com

Cots and highchairs are usually available in upscale accommodations but they are not generally found elsewhere.

Recommended Hotels

The accommodation options featured in this guide – listed by area and then by price – have been selected across a wide price range for their unique appeal, excellent facilities, or value for money. They have been divided into a number of categories to help you to make the best choices for your trip, from luxury international hotels to budget guesthouses, and from chic city-center boutique hotels to basic rooms in stunning rural areas.

When choosing the very best accommodation for your stay, look out for hotels marked DK Choice in this guide. They may be set in beautiful surroundings or in a historically important building. They might offer excellent value or exceptional service. Whatever the reason, the DK Choice label guarantees an especially memorable stay.

A swimming pool in a luxury hotel with stunning views of the surrounding mountains

Where to Stay

Cambodia

Phnom Penh

DK Choice

PHNOM PENH:
Mad Monkey Hostel $
Hostel **City map** E4
St 302
Tel (023)-987-091
Ⓦ madmonkeyhostels.com
A perenially popular hostel with a buzzing rooftop bar and great facilities, including a TV room, a pool table, an ATM, and a laundry room. Choose between shared dorms and private rooms (private bathrooms are available). Guests are also offered guided tours of the area.

PHNOM PENH: SLA Boutique
Hostel $
Hostel **City map** D2
St 174
Tel (023)-997-515
Ⓦ slahostel.com
A super-clean, very modern hostel located south of the Central Market. Mixed and single-sex dorms are available, as are private rooms with shared facilities.

PHNOM PENH: Anise Hotel $$
Basic **City map** D4
St 278
Tel (023)-222-522
Ⓦ anisehotel.com.kh
Staff will do everything possible to help you make the most of your stay at this conveniently located family-run hotel. Rooms are spacious, with high ceilings.

PHNOM PENH: Billabong $$
Basic **City map** D2
St 158
Tel (023)-223-703
Ⓦ thebillabonghotel.com
Set in an idyllic tropical garden with a large salt-water swimming pool, Billabong offers chic, modern rooms that are spotlessly clean.

PHNOM PENH: Blue Lime $$
Boutique **City map** E2
St 19z
Tel (023)-222-260
Ⓦ bluelime.asia
Located down a quiet street behind the National Museum *(see p52)*, this small hotel has a lovely shared pool. Decor is artistically modern and minimalist, with plenty of concrete.

PHNOM PENH:
Frangipani Villa 90s $$
Boutique **City map** D5
St 71
Tel (023)-727-569
Ⓦ frangipanihotel.com
Restored according to the 1960s style of New Khmer Architecture, Frangipani Villa 90s has a lovely garden and a good restaurant serving Khmer and Western food. The staff go out of their way to ensure you have a pleasant stay.

PHNOM PENH: Golden
Gate Hotel $$
Basic **City map** E3
St 278
Tel (023)-721-161
Ⓦ goldengatehotels.com
Close to the Independence Monument, this hotel offers bright, air-conditioned rooms for a great price. There is also a free same-day laundry service.

PHNOM PENH: TeaHouse $$
Boutique **City map** D3
St 242
Tel (023)-212-789
Ⓦ theteahouse.asia
A smart hotel with comfortable, modern rooms and a lovely outdoor pool area. The highlight is the tea lounge, which serves a tempting array of more than 30 different types of tea.

PHNOM PENH: The Quay $$
Boutique **City map** E2
Sisowath Quay
Tel (023)-224-894
Ⓦ thequayhotel.com
Sleek and stylish, The Quay blends minimalist decor with an eco-conscious ethos. The hotel's Chow restaurant serves good Asian fusion cuisine.

Plush communal seating area at Raffles, Phnom Penh

Price Guide
Prices are based on one night's stay in high season for a standard double room, inclusive of service charges and taxes.

$	up to $20
$$	$20 to 100
$$$	over $100

DK Choice

PHNOM PENH: Raffles $$$
Luxury **City map** D1
Rukhak Vithei Daun Penh, off Monivong Blvd
Tel (023)-981-888
Ⓦ raffles.com
Opened in 1929, this opulent Art Deco-style building has several chic suites. The gardens are beautifully landscaped, the spa is excellent, and the staff are very attentive. As you might expect, prices are high.

Angkor

SIEM REAP: Ivy Guesthouse $
Guesthouse **Road map** C6
West of Pokambor Ave, near the river
Tel (012)-800-860
Ⓦ ivy-guesthouse.com
An intimate travelers' guesthouse with pretty gardens, hammocks, and pleasant rooms – all just a pleasant five-minute walk from the center of town.

SIEM REAP: Rosy Guesthouse $
Guesthouse **Road map** C6
74, Phum Slor Kram
Tel (063)-965-059
Ⓦ rosyguesthouse.com
An excellent budget guesthouse in an attractive old villa, with Wi-Fi, TVs, and DVD players in all rooms (air conditioning is optional).

SIEM REAP: Angkor
Vattanakpheap Hotel $$
Basic **Road map** C6
Route 6
Tel (063)-969-222
Ⓦ angkorvattanakpheaphotel.com
The simple hotel rooms here are brightened up by framed pictures and colorful scatter cushions. Even the cheapest rooms come with satellite TV and a bathroom.

SIEM REAP: Babel $$
Guesthouse **Road map** C6
Wat Bo Rd
Tel (063)-965-474
Ⓦ babel-siemreap.com
A good-value guesthouse with spotless white rooms and large

bathrooms. The pleasant tropical gardens are the perfect place to relax after a long day's sightseeing.

SIEM REAP:
Ei8ht Rooms Guesthouse $$
Guesthouse   **Road map** C6
Steng Thmey Village
Tel (063)-969-788
 ei8htrooms.com
Designed with flashpackers in mind, this hotel offers clean rooms, a relaxing roof terrace, and a free pick-up service from the airport.

SIEM REAP: Maison 557 $$
Boutique   **Road map** C6
Wat Bo St
Tel (089)-280-830
W maison557.com
With elegant rooms set around tropical gardens, this small hotel provides an intimate place for rest and relaxation. There is an inviting swimming pool, and staff are happy to put you in touch with knowledgable local guides.

SIEM REAP:
MotherHome Guesthouse $$
Guesthouse   **Road map** C6
Wat Bo Village
Tel (063)-760-302
W motherhomeguesthouse.com
An immaculately presented guesthouse, which offers free airport transfers and bike hire. You'll get five-star service here for a fraction the price.

SIEM REAP: Mysteres
d'Angkor $$
Boutique   **Road map** C6
235 Phum Slorkram
Tel (063)-963-639
W mysteres-angkor.com
A tranquil, French-run boutique hotel with tastefully decorated rooms and a lovely decked pool area surrounded by lush gardens.

SIEM REAP: The River Garden $$
Boutique   **Road map** C6
11 Phoum Treang
Tel (063)-963-400
W therivergarden.info
A peaceful oasis near the temples of Angkor. The rooms are quirky and colorful, with great views of the hotel's tropical gardens and the gorgeous pool area.

SIEM REAP: Shadow of
Angkor I $$
Guesthouse   **Road map** C6
353, Pokambor Ave
Tel (063)-964-774
W shadowofangkor.com
A river-view guesthouse in an old French Colonial building close to the Old Market. Rooms are clean and simple with white walls.

A bright, colorful room at The River Garden, Siem Reap

SIEM REAP: Hanuman Alaya $$$
Boutique   **Road map** C6
5 Krom 2
Tel (063)-760-582
W hanumanalaya.com
Situated away from the hustle and bustle of Siem Reap, this intimate hotel is beautifully decorated with antiques and local handicrafts. The swimming pool area, set in a pretty garden dotted with statues, is divine.

DK Choice

SIEM REAP: Shinta Mani
Club $$$
Luxury   **Road map** C6
Junction of Oum Khum and 14th St
Tel (063)-761-998
W shintamani.com
Conveniently located in the heart of the French Quarter, and set in a magnificently restored Colonial mansion, this opulent hotel hosts art exhibitions, and provides vocational training to underprivileged youths.

SIEM REAP: Sojourn
Boutique Villas $$$
Resort   **Road map** C6
Treak Village Rd
Tel (012)-923-437
W sojournsiemreap.com
Dotted around a lovely pool with a swim-up bar, the pretty bungalows at Sojourn Boutique Villas provide the perfect retreat from the busy city.

SIEM REAP:
Tara Angkor Hotel $$$
Luxury   **Road map** C6
Charles de Gaulle Rd
Tel (063)-966-661
W taraangkorhotel.com
A grand hotel with two restaurants, a spa, and a super-sized swimming pool. Rooms are decadent without being over the top, and the hotel runs its own cooking classes.

SIEM REAP: Unique Boutique $$$
Boutique   **Road map** C6
West of the center, off Route 6
Tel (063)-964-748
W uniqueboutiquecambodia.com
Supremely spacious, contemporary rooms decorated with local art and stylish furniture. Family friendly rooms and suites set over two floors are also available.

SIEM REAP: Viroth's Hotel $$$
Boutique   **Road map** C6
St 23
Tel (063)-761-720
W viroth-hotel.com
The fresh, contemporary rooms here are finished in cream linen and set around an exquisite salt-water pool. Traditional-style massages are available, and there is a breezy rooftop terrace to relax on.

Northern Cambodia

BAN LUNG: Lakeside Chheng
Lok Hotel $
Resort   **Road map** E6
Central Ban Lung
Tel (012)-957-422
This large hotel is a bit of an eyesore, but it is pleasantly located on the lake at the edge of the town center. The most basic rooms are fan-cooled; others have air-conditioning. The on-site restaurant is excellent.

BAN LUNG: Treetop Guesthouse $
Guesthouse   **Road map** E6
Phum No.1, Laban Seak Commune
Tel (012)-490-333
W treetop-ecolodge.com
A cheap yet comfortable option located in beautiful countryside near Ban Lung. Rooms are in wooden bungalows on stilts, and have mosquito nets, tasteful linen, and private bathrooms.

For more information on types of hotels *see pp206–7*

BAN LUNG: Terres Rouge Lodge $$
Resort   Road map E6
Beside Boeng Kansaign Lake
Tel (012)-770-650
W ratanakiri-lodge.com
The comfortable rooms here are decorated with pretty handicrafts and antiques. The hotel restaurant and lounge are great to relax in, and the lush grounds are home to birds of paradise.

DK Choice

BATTAMBANG: La Villa $$$
Guesthouse   Road map C6
Pom Romcheck 5 Kom
Tel (017)-411-880
W lavilla-battambang.net
Housed in a 1930s French Colonial mansion, this gorgeous guesthouse is beautifully decorated with Art Deco-style features and antique furniture. Dinner, served in the atrium, is a delightful experience. If possible, request one of the rooms upstairs as they are larger with private reading areas.

KRATIE: River Dolphin Hotel $
Basic   Road map D6
Sangkat Orrussey
Tel (072)-210-570
W riverdolphinhotel.com
A relaxed hotel offering small, budget rooms, and more comfortable options with their own balconies. There's also a good on-site gym and a lovely pool for guests to use.

KRATIE: Santepheap Hotel $$
Basic   Road map D6
Preah Soramarith Rd
Tel (072)-971-537
A long-running establishment in a peaceful location near the river. Rooms are basic, but spacious and fairly clean, with either air-conditioning or a fan.

DK Choice

SEN MONOROM: Nature Lodge $
Resort   Road map E6
Comka Tai Village, Spean Meanchey Commune
Tel (012)-230-272
W naturelodgecambodia.com
Nature Lodge lives up to its name with blissfully peaceful surroundings, simple cabins, and friendly staff who believe in eco-friendly principles. Nightly bonfires, hammocks, and tree-houses are among the other attractions of this fantastic place.

STUNG TRENG: Golden River Hotel $
Basic   Road map D6
Kandal Village
Tel (012)-980-678
W goldenriverhotel.com
It is no great architectural beauty, but this hotel has lavishly decorated interiors, and rooms come equipped with plasma TVs, refrigerators, and big bathtubs.

Southern Cambodia

KAMPOT: Rikitikitavi $$
Guesthouse   Road map C7
South end of Riverside Rd
Tel (017)-306-557
W rikitikitavi-kampot.com
Located in a great riverside spot, these stylish rooms have attractive Oriental fittings, and small but well-appointed private bathrooms.

KEP: Tree Top Bungalows $$
Resort   Road map C7
St 33, Thmey Village
Tel (012)-515-191
W keptreetop.com
A dozen quirky-looking wood-and-thatch bungalows built on stilts, allowing great views of the sea. The resort is on a large grassy plot of land and has a restaurant serving delicious Khmer food.

KEP: Knai Bang Chatt $$$
Resort   Road map C7
Phum Thmey, Sangkat Prey Thom
Tel (036)-210-310
W knaibangchatt.com
Unquestionably the most upscale address in Kep, this resort has modernist Le Corbusier-style villas set in lush grounds by the seashore. Facilities include an infinity pool and a first-class spa.

KOH KONG TOWN: Asian Hotel $
Basic   Road map B7
1 Village, Sangkat Smach MeanChay
Tel (035)-936-667
W asiankohkong.com
Large harborfront hotel with panoramic views. Rooms are large and come with TVs and private bathrooms. Family rooms and river-view rooms cost extra.

KOH KONG TOWN: Oasis Resort $$
Resort   Road map B7
1 mile (2 km) N from the town center
Tel (016)-331-556
W oasisresort.netkhmer.com
Peaceful retreat with family-sized, air-conditioned bungalows set around a lovely infinity pool. The resort has a DVD library and pool table, and staff offer excellent travel advice.

The pleasant pool area at Sokha Beach Resort, Sihanoukville

KOH RONG: Broken Heart Guesthouse $$
Guesthouse   Road map C7
Koh Rong
Tel (095)-775-165
W bhgh.info
These very basic bungalows offer a back-to-nature experience on a stunning stretch of beach on Koh Rong. Life here revolves around swimming, snorkeling, and sunsets.

SIHANOUKVILLE: Cloud 9 Bungalows $$
Resort   Road map C7
Serendipity Beach
Tel (098)-215-166
W cloud9bungalows.com
These wooden bungalows cling to the hillside, enjoying sweeping views over Occheuteal Beach *(see pp108–9)*. Local textiles add a splash of color to the rooms.

DK Choice

SIHANOUKVILLE: Sahaa Beach Resort $$$
Resort   Road map C7
Otres Beach 1
Tel (070)-218-607
W sahaabeach.com
Close to the beach, Sahaa has 16 bungalows arranged around a handsome outdoor pool. Sleeping spaces are cool and chic, and there is a restaurant serving freshly grilled fish, among other dishes.

SIHANOUKVILLE: Sokha Beach Resort $$$
Resort   Road map C7
St 2 Thnou
Tel (034)-935-999
This huge hotel complex has rooms and suites, plus a few villas on a wonderful private beach. There are also two pools and a childrens' playground.

Laos

Vientiane

CENTRAL VIENTIANE: Vientiane Backpackers Hostel $
Hostel **City map** B3
13 Nokeo Koummane Rd
Tel (020)-974-842-27
W vientianebackpackershostel.com
The big dorms here are about as basic as it gets, but the location is great. Laundry services and bike rentals are also available.

DK Choice

CENTRAL VIENTIANE:
Auberge Sala Inpeng $$
Guesthouse **City map** A4
063 Inpeng Rd
Tel (021)-242-021
W salalao.com
These well-tended, traditional-style bungalows are set around a pretty garden, providing a peaceful escape from the bustle of Vientiane's streets. A delicious breakfast is served up on the bungalows' big verandas each morning. Best of all are the staff, who speak excellent English and go above and beyond to ensure that you enjoy your stay.

CENTRAL VIENTIANE:
Day Inn $$
Basic **City map** C3
59 Pangkham Rd
Tel (021)-223-847
W day-inn-hotel.com
Painted bright yellow, this long-running hotel offers great-value rooms close to some of the city's best bars and restaurants. The public areas feel a little dated but they are all kept clean and tidy.

CENTRAL VIENTIANE: Mandala Boutique Hotel $$
Boutique **City map** D5
Ban Simuang, near Wat Simuang
Tel (021)-214-493
W mandalahotel.asia
This former school is a slight walk from the center, but it has blissfully peaceful gardens and elegantly decorated rooms.

CENTRAL VIENTIANE:
Moonlight Champa $$
Guesthouse **City map** C3
13 Pangkham Rd
Tel (021)-264-114
W moonlight-champa.com
Spotlessly clean, stylish rooms at great prices for the central location. Wi-Fi and TV are included in the price and discounts are offered for longer stays.

CENTRAL VIENTIANE:
Vayakorn Inn $$
Boutique **City map** B3
19 Hengbounnoy St
Tel (021)-215-348
W vayakorn.biz
Expect polished wooden floors, bright rooms, and a lobby full of objets d'art at this charming small hotel. It's situated on a quiet street, but close to plenty of great restaurants.

CENTRAL VIENTIANE:
Dhavara Hotel $$$
Luxury **City map** B3
25 Manthalath Rd
Tel (021)-222-238
W dhavaraboutiquehotel.com
A short walk from the river, this pretty hotel has spacious rooms that are smartly decorated in a Colonial style, with paneled walls and antique-style furniture.

CENTRAL VIENTIANE:
Salana Boutique $$$
Boutique **City map** B3
Chao Anou Rd
Tel (021)-254-250
W salanaboutique.com
One of the most desirable places to stay in downtown Vientiane, this boutique hotel has beautifully styled rooms decked out with lots of colorful Lao silk.

DK Choice

CENTRAL VIENTIANE:
Settha Palace Hotel $$$
Luxury **City map** C3
6 Pangkham Rd
Tel (021)-217 581
W setthapalace.com
Decorated with French-style furniture, this landmark hotel gives visitors a taste of Colonial-era Vientiane. The palm-shaded pool is sublime, and an excellent breakfast is served in the hotel's restaurant, which offers superb French and Lao dishes.

GREATER VIENTIANE:
Heuan Lao Guesthouse $
Guesthouse **City map** E5
Off Samsenthai Rd, near Wat Simuang
Tel (021)-216-258
This friendly, old-fashioned guesthouse is set among lush gardens and offers basic rooms. Located a pleasant walk or bike ride from the center, and close to Wat Simuang.

GREATER VIENTIANE:
Green Park Boutique Hotel $$$
Resort **City map** E5
248 Khou Vieng Rd
Tel (021)-264-097
W greenparkvientiane.com
The rooms at this relaxed resort are set among tranquil frangipangi gardens. There's also a spa on site and a delightful swimming pool area.

Luang Prabang

CENTRAL LUANG PRABANG:
The Apsara $$
Boutique **City map** D3
Kingkitsarat Rd
Tel (071)-254-670
W theapsara.com
The rooms in this converted rice warehouse have stunning views of the river, and are tastefully decorated in a pretty, Colonial-inspired style. The on-site bar has an impressive wine list.

CENTRAL LUANG PRABANG:
Le Bel Air $$
Resort **City map** D4
1 Old Bridge Rd
Tel (071)-254-699
W lebelairhotels.com
Airy, timber-framed rooms and bungalows are set in expansive gardens at this peaceful resort, just a 20-minute walk south of the center. The resort can arrange free bike rentals for guests.

Lush gardens surround the Colonial-style buildings at Settha Palace Hotel, Central Vientiane

For more information on types of hotels see pp206–7

CENTRAL LUANG PRABANG:
Lotus Villa Laos $$
Independent   **City map** D3
Kounxoa Rd, Ban Phone Huang
(near Wat Nong)
Tel (071)-255-050
W lotusvillalaos.com
Terra-cotta tiles and wooden
shutters give a sense of rustic
charm to this small hotel, housed
in a pretty, Colonial-style building.

CENTRAL LUANG PRABANG:
Villa Chitdara $$
Guesthouse   **City map** D3
Khounxua Rd
Tel (071)-254-949
W villachitdara.com
Lush gardens and a quiet location
make this a perfect choice for a
relaxing stay. The elegant rooms
have large balconies, some with
good views of the alms procession,
which passes right by the villa.

CENTRAL LUANG PRABANG:
Villa Lao Wooden House $$
Guesthouse   **City map** C4
Ban Wat Nong
Tel (071)-260-283
W laowoodenhouse.com
This attractive guesthouse is just a
short walk from the Night Market.
All rooms have air-conditioning
and pleasant balconies to relax on.

DK Choice

CENTRAL LUANG PRABANG:
Amantaka $$$
Luxury   **City map** D3
Kingkitsarat Rd
Tel (071)-860-333
W amanresorts.com
This former French hospital has
been converted into the epitome
of understated luxury. Many of
the suites have private pools,
and the spa is world-class.
The hotel also has a boutique
and an art gallery featuring
handicrafts made by local artists.

CENTRAL LUANG PRABANG:
The Belle Rive Hotel $$$
Boutique   **City map** D2
Khem Khong
Tel (071)-260-733
W thebellerive.com
This hotel occupies a series of
magnificent Colonial buildings
dating from the 1920s. Many of
the rooms have four-poster beds.

CENTRAL LUANG PRABANG:
Hotel de la Paix $$$
Luxury   **City map** C6
Ban Mano
Tel (071)-260-777
W hoteldelapaixlp.com/
A Colonial prison-turned-luxury-
resort, this place boasts some of

the city's smartest rooms.
There is also a popular bar area
and a restaurant serving first-
class Lao food.

CENTRAL LUANG PRABANG:
Mekong Riverview Hotel $$$
Luxury   **City map** D2
Mekong Riverside Rd, Xieng Thong
Tel (071)-254-900
W mekongriverview.com
As the name suggests, a number
of the lavishly furnished rooms
here have views of the Mekong
River. Personal touches abound,
most notably wine receptions
hosted by the Swedish owner.

CENTRAL LUANG PRABANG:
Satri House $$$
Luxury   **City map** B4
057 Photisarat Rd
Tel (071)-253-491
W satrihouse.com
Located in a quiet residential
area near Wat That Luang
(see p167), this opulent hotel
was once the home of a Lao
prince. Rooms are furnished
with antiques, and surrounded
by pretty gardens dotted with
pools and fountains.

DK Choice

GREATER LUANG PRABANG:
La Residence Phou Vao $$$
Luxury   **City map** B2
3 PO Box 50
Tel (071)-212-530
W belmond.com
Dominating a hilltop on the
southern edge of the city,
this hotel is an oasis of calm,
with a peaceful ambience,
refreshing infinity pools,
efficient service, and mouth-
watering food. Views of the city
and mountains are superb.
Prices, inevitably, are high.

A sumptuous room furnished with antiques
at Satri House, Central Luang Prabang

Northern Laos

HONG SA: Jumbo Guesthouse $
Guesthouse   **Road map** B2
Behind the Central Market
Tel (020)-5685-6488
W lotuselephant.com
Elephant rides and longer trekking
trips are available at this homely
guesthouse, run by an English-
and German-speaking owner.

HUAY XAI: Thaveesinh Hotel $$
Guesthouse   **Road map** A2
Riverfront road
Tel (084)-211-502
A basic guesthouse in a fantastic
central location. There is a good
mixture of twin and double
rooms; all have air-conditioning
and private showers. The staff
here are very helpful.

LUANG NAM THA: Zuela $
Guesthouse   **Road map** B1
Just off Route 3
Tel (020)-220-638-88
W zuela.asia
In a quiet spot in the town
center, Zuela is the best choice
for budget travelers. The brick
and wood buildings have relaxed
seating areas, and there is a good
restaurant serving Lao and
Western food.

MUANG KHUA: Nam Ou
Guest House $
Guesthouse   **Road map** B1
Next to the boat landing
Tel (088)-210-844
An old favorite with regular
visitors to Muang Khua, Nam Ou
Guest House offers extremely
basic facilities at wallet-friendly
prices. The adjoining restaurant
serves simple meals.

MUANG NGOI:
Lattanovongsa Guest House $
Guesthouse   **Road map** B1
Just up from the boat landing
Tel (020)-223-624-44
Clean bungalows with private
bathrooms, surrounding a
pleasant garden. Meals are
usually served in the large dining
room, which is quirkily decorated
with old bomb shells.

MUANG SING: Phou lu II $
Guesthouse   **Road map** A1
Down a dirt track, west of the
main road
Tel (086)-400-012
W muangsingtravel.com
Arranged around a pretty
garden, these bamboo-thatched
bungalows (both double and
twin rooms are available) are
simple but welcoming. Treks
can also be reserved here.

NONG KHIAW:
Nong Kiau Riverside $$
Guesthouse   Road map B1
Ban Nong Khiaw
Tel (071)-810-004
w nongkiau.com
Nong Kiau Riverside has large
bungalows offering spectacular
views of the surrounding
mountains. Trekking, kayaking,
mountainbiking, and rock climbing
can all be arranged here.

PAK BENG: Luang Say Lodge $$
Resort   Road map A2
1 mile (3 km) west of the boat landings
Tel (081)-212-296
w luangsay.com
Luxurious, all-wood bungalows
overlooking the water. The on-
site restaurant puts on excellent
cultural shows to entertain passing
tourists who arrive on river cruises.

PHONGSALI:
Viphaphone Hotel $
Basic   Road map B1
On the main road through town
Tel (088)-210-111
Very basic but fine for a night or
two, Viphaphone Hotel offers
rooms with private bathrooms.
Rooms are large, with good views.

PHONSAVAN:
Kong Keo Guesthouse $
Guesthouse   Road map C2
650 ft (200 m) north of Route 7
Tel (055)-211-354
A great option for budget travelers.
Simple rooms with private
bathrooms, and a sociable outdoor
bar area set around a fire pit.

SAM NEUA: Xayphasouk Hotel $
Basic   Road map C2
*South of the monument, on the road
to the bus station*
Tel (020)-557-666-44
This hotel offers the best rooms in
town, and is one of the few places
that is kept warm during the cold
winter. Free Wi-Fi and helpful staff,
though little English is spoken.

DK Choice

**VANG VIENG: Riverside
Boutique Resort** $$$
Resort   Road map B2
*Along the Nam Song river, just
south of the center*
Tel (023)-511-726-8
w riversidevangvieng.com
An exclusive luxury hotel, with
prices to match. The subtly
styled rooms here are set around
a gorgeous turquoise pool.
Views of the limestone karsts on
the other side of the river are
superb. The resort's restaurant is
an unbeatable spot for breakfast.

Central and Southern Laos

BOLAVEN PLATEAU:
Tadlo Lodge $$
Resort   Road map E5
Overlooking Tad Hang
Tel (031)-214-184
On a hill overlooking a spectacular
series of waterfalls, these private
bungalows are the most luxurious
option on the plateau.

DK Choice

CHAMPASAK:
The River Resort $$$
Resort   Road map D5
*2 miles (3.5 km) north of
Champasak, on the Mekong*
Tel (086)-885-117-0
w theriverresortlaos.com
A sensational luxury resort along
a peaceful stretch of the Mekong
River. It offers sleek, modern
bungalows that are separated
by verdant rice paddies. There is
an inviting infinity pool and an
excellent waterfront restaurant.

DON DAENG:
La Folie Lodge $$$
Resort   Road map D5
NW coast of Don Daeng
Tel (020)-5553-2004
w lafolie-laos.com
Across the river from Wat Phu
Champasak, this luxurious resort
has 12 secluded duplex bungalows
and a stunning pool.

DON DET: The Last Resort $
Resort   Road map D5
*On the west side of the island,
around 2460 ft (750m) from town*
A truly unique eco friendly resort
with accommodation in thatched
wigwams set around a pretty
garden with a fire pit. There is
also an open-air movie theater
and morning pilates classes.

DON KHONG:
Sala Done Khone $$
Resort   Road map D5
Northern edge of the island
Tel (031)-260-940
w salalao.com
Choose from stylish rooms in the
main building – a pretty French-
era Colonial bungalow – or opt for
a floating studio, with a balcony
just inches above the water.

PAKSE: Champasak Grand $$
Business   Road map D4
Next to the Japanese Bridge
Tel (031)-255-111
w champasakgrand.com
Modern rooms with superb
views over the river. The hotel

Modern bungalows line the Mekong River
at The River Resort, Champasak

complex is a bit of a walk from
the center, but has a pleasant
outdoor pool and a gym.

**SAVANNAKHET: Daosavanh
Resort & Spa** $$
Resort   Road map C4
Tha He Rd, south of the hospital
Tel (041)-252-188
w daosavanh.com
Sprawled along the main river
road, this is Savannakhet's best
hotel. There is a lovely outdoor
pool surrounded by fruit trees,
and the resort has its own spa.

THAKHEK: Inthira $$
Basic   Road map D3
Chao Anou Rd
Tel (051)-251-237
w inthirahotels.com
Comfortable rooms in a converted
shophouse just off the town
square. The restaurant serves
great Lao and Western dishes, and
staff are happy to arrange tours.

**THAM KONG LO: Sala Kong
Lor Lodge** $
Resort   Road map C3
4 miles (7 km) SE of Tham Kong Lo
Tel (020)-556-451-11
w salalao.com
These riverside bungalows
are a great place to relax amid
thick forests and luscious green
surroundings. The management
can provide boats for visiting
the famous caves nearby.

**XE PIAN NPA: Kingfisher
Ecolodge** $$
Resort   Road map D5
Ban Khiet Ngong
Tel (020)-557-263-15
w kingfisherecolodge.com
Near the Phu Asa mountain,
this lodge offers accommodation
in stilted bungalows or cheaper
"eco" rooms. Elephant treks and
mountain-bike rides can also
be arranged for guests.

For more information on types of hotels *see pp206–7*

WHERE TO EAT AND DRINK

The cuisines of Cambodia and Laos share many similarities with those of their neighboring countries, especially Thailand. At the same time, both countries have dishes that are distinctly Cambodian or Lao such as *amok* (fish cooked in coconut milk) and *laap* (meat salad), respectively. French Colonialists contributed to the cuisines of these two nations, evident from the roadside stalls and bakeries that sell baguettes and croissants. Parisian-style cafés are also common in urban centers. A variety of international cuisines are served at upscale restaurants in major cities such as Phnom Penh, Siem Reap, Vientiane, and Luang Prabang. From street vendors and barbecues on the beach to swanky cafés and restaurants in upscale hotels, the food choices in Cambodia and Laos are varied, as are the prices.

Plush dining area of the Hotel De La Paix, Luang Prabang

Restaurants

The service at restaurants in upscale hotels in Phnom Penh, Siem Reap, Vientiane, and Luang Prabang is as flawless as diners might find in the West, and may even be better in some cases. In contrast, the average Khmer and Lao restaurant is an informal affair offering a balance of rice, vegetables, and meat. Visitors will also find Chinese, Vietnamese, and Indian influences in spring rolls, spare ribs, and curries, thanks to Cambodia's mid-way location between the three countries. Fish features heavily in Cambodian food, no doubt due to the presence of the Tonlé Sap, which is teeming with fish. *Prahoc*, a fermented fish paste, which is also found in Laos, is used to flavor many dishes. The average Lao and Khmer meal might consist of a soup, followed by a fish or meat dish, and salad. Rice is eaten with everything and often on its own; it can be found in rice noodle soup, rice porridge, and as an accompaniment to almost every dish. Sticky rice is one of the main staples of Lao food, and it is often sold in bamboo tubes by the roadside. Both countries have plenty of Gallic food on offer due to their French Colonial past, the most common items being the baguette and pâté. There are also many French cafés and restaurants in all the major cities, where the steaks are tender, the tarts delicious, and the wines first class. Western fast-food chains and cuisine have also become popular with the increasing numbers of Western visitors: in some places, pizza is as likely to feature on the menu as local *amok*.

Street Food

Eating a quick snack from a street vendor is a wonderfully Khmer and Lao pastime, and the snacks are usually delicious. From fried crab, snake, frog, tarantula, beetle, cricket, *amok*, noodles, and meat to sugarcane, jackfruit, melon, rambutan, coconut, mangosteen, and crepes, there is a wide variety of food available on street corners, both in the provinces and in the cities. Bear in mind that the best time to visit a vendor for breakfast is early in the morning between 6:00–8:30am when the food is freshly cooked. It is best to go to a stall that seems busy, attracting people from every strata of society – a crowded stall is a sure sign that the food is good. Another promising sign to look out for is more than one family member working the stall, since that means it is popular and generates enough work for the other members of the family. It is best to avoid consuming fruit smoothies with ice even if they look delicious. In most cases unpurified water will have been used to make the ice, and consuming it may cause or lead to stomach ailments.

Variety of street food on offer in Battambang

Various tropical fruit for sale in the local market, Luang Prabang

Vegetarian Options

Both countries have an abundance of fruit, which is available on every street corner. Stir-fries and rice dishes with vegetables are very common, although it is likely that they will have been prepared in pans that have been used to cook meat. In more upscale restaurants in the cities, however, this might not be the case.

Avoiding meat in the provinces is harder because the average Lao and Khmer does not understand the concept of vegetarianism. In Phnom Penh, Siem Reap, Vientiane, and Luang Prabang strict vegetarians can head to one of the many Indian restaurants where the hosts will be more sympathetic to the idea of a pure vegetarian meal. Luang Prabang offers the best vegetarian cuisine and the most discerning menus of all four cities. Western-run restaurants are more than likely to provide authentic vegetarian dishes, and are usually careful about the way they should be cooked. Those vegetarians who are not overly strict about their dietary habits and can tolerate fish sauce will have no problem finding a satisfying meal.

Beer

The most popular Cambodian beverage is Angkor Beer, which is produced in Sihanoukville. In Laos there is Beerlao, which is delicious and even cheaper than Angkor Beer. There are many other international beers available, from Heineken to Tiger.

Eating Customs

Unlike the West, most meals in Cambodia and Laos are not served in a succession of dishes. If visitors order three separate dishes they will all arrive at the same time, or as and when they are cooked. Meals are a social event in both countries and a chance for families and friends to catch up. Individual bowls are arranged around a central platter of dishes and everyone shares each other's dish.

In the average restaurant, be it in the market or on the street, visitors can expect to use chopsticks or cutlery. Visitors must use the communal spoon to serve food into their bowls, not their own implements. The common practice is to hold one's bowl to the mouth, and spoon the food in with the chopsticks in the other hand. When using chopsticks, do not leave them together in the bowl pointing upward as this is a symbol of death. It is normal for a host to offer a guest more food than he would to his own family members – this must not be turned down. It is also good etiquette not to finish everything on the plate. Finally, the host should always be the first to sit down and taste the food.

Prices

Fast food from street vendors accompanied by a fruit shake will cost no more than a few dollars. Cambodian, Lao, and Western restaurant prices are usually reasonable unless visitors choose one of the

upscale restaurants in the urban centers. Budget travelers may find Cambodia slightly more expensive than Laos, but if they avoid beer and wine and stick to street stalls and cheap restaurants that serve basic dishes, they can get by for as little as US$10 per day.

Tipping

Although tipping is not expected in the same way as it is in the West, it is very much appreciated. If service is good, a small tip of US$1 is almost equivalent to half a day's wages for some, and can go a long way in supplementing a salary.

A popular brand of beer in Laos

Recommended Restaurants

The restaurants listed in this guide are among the best in Cambodia and Laos. They have been chosen for their reliably good food, location, service, and value. The listings cover a variety of eateries, from simple cafés to fine dining restaurants. Whether you are looking to try traditional dishes such as *amok, laap,* or crispy tarantulas, or you are simply craving Western food and desperate for a burger, the following pages offer plenty of choice.

Establishments labeled DK Choice have been selected because they are outstanding in some way. They may offer superb cuisine, a beautiful setting, exceptionally good value, or a combination of all of these.

Outdoor cafés surrounding Nam Phu Square, Vientiane

The Flavors of Cambodia

Cambodian food draws heavily on influences from Thailand, Vietnam, and China, while maintaining its own culinary tradition. Khmer meals are deliciously spicy and fragrant, with a characteristic sweetness derived from palm sugar, and sourness introduced by lime juice and tamarind. Fresh herbs and spices, including coriander, sweet basil, lemongrass, and fresh ginger are used judiciously. French influence is evident everywhere, typified by the ubiquitous roadside snack stalls selling crusty baguettes smeared with delicious pâté.

Sweet basil, lemongrass, and coriander

Skewers of barbecued frog at a food stall in Psar Nath, Battambang

Seafood and Fish

Fish is a key part of the Cambodian diet, including many freshwater species caught in the bountiful Tonlé Sap Lake, the wetlands around Takeo, and in the country's many rivers. Everything from huge catfish steaks to tiny tiddlers are available on Cambodian menus. On the coast, snapper and shellfish are popular, but perhaps Cambodia's most famous seafood dish is *K'damm mrek Kep*, or pepper crab, a specialty of the Kep region.

Curries and Soups

Khmer curries are delicately spiced although unlike their Indian and Thai equivalents, they have the consistency of soup. The classic Cambodian curry is *amok*, usually made with fish and featuring lots of turmeric. Almost every meal includes a *samlor* (soup) dish, which is often quite sweet and flavored with coconut and spices.

Durian   Mangosteens   Bananas   Pomelo

Limes   Rambutan

Selection of Cambodia's luscious tropical fruits

Cambodian Dishes and Specialties

Cambodian food has aroma, piquancy, and a zesty freshness that is addictive. Pungent and exotic, there is barely a dish (except, of course, desserts) that does not feature a seasoning of *prahoc* (fish paste) or *trey* (fish sauce). Rice is the main staple, and most meals are served with a bowl of steaming white or sticky rice,

Palm sugar

or noodles made from rice or wheat. Snacks include *num pang ang chia mui sach ko*, which is rounds of French bread baked with a spicy ground beef topping. You will also find *poat dot* (corn on the cob) and spring rolls (both vegetarian and with ground meat). Fast-food chains are everywhere in Phnom Penh and making their way to other cities as well. However, the toppings on a Cambodian "happy" pizza may include herbs you would not expect, so be careful.

Amok, Cambodia's most famous dish, is a mild, piquant coconut milk curry traditionally made with fish.

Vendors of meat, fruit, and vegetables at Psar Nath market

Salads

There are dozens of types of fresh salads available, with ingredients such as carrots, cucumber, green papaya, and unripe mango, often shredded or chopped. Thin strips of meat, fresh or dried shrimp, and plenty of fresh herbs may be added, and the dish is then laced with chopped peanuts. A popular dressing is *tirk trey chu p'em*, a sweet fish sauce with lime juice, a little chili, and garlic.

Fruits and Sweets

Tropical fruits are abundant. Mangoes and bananas (including small, red-skinned "fingers") are everywhere, with many unusual varieties not found in the West. The small, purple skinned *meangkhout* (mangosteen) with its subtle, sweet, and slightly sherbety flavor is a revelation. The hairy skin of the *sao meo* (rambutan) may be off-putting, but its fruit is succulent and reminiscent of a lychee; and the *salacca* (snake fruit) is sweet and slightly acidic in taste. The "king" of Cambodian fruits is, however, the *thouren*, the infamously smelly durian.

Cambodia's sweet desserts are an acquired taste, but rice pudding flavored with coconut and lime is delicious, as are bananas barbecued in their leaves and usually served with coconut sauce.

Freshly caught fish for sale at a market in Phnom Penh

Drinks

It is vital to stick to bottled water, but ice is usually safe in cities. Cafés in tourist areas may have espresso machines, but visitors will usually be offered a strong, local coffee. Khmers, however, like theirs with ice and condensed milk. Beer is inexpensive, with lager-style Angkor being the most popular brand. While local rice wine is cheap, wine from Australia and France is available in restaurants and supermarkets at reasonable cost.

AN EXOTIC MENU

Beetles *(kan te)* Fried dark green *kan te long* and *kan te touk* beetles (which look like cockroaches) are a popular Cambodian treat. Locals first remove the head and wings before devouring the bug.

Crickets *(jong-reut)* Demand for crickets grew in the Khmer Rouge years. They are usually deep-fried and enjoyed as an inexpensive, crunchy snack.

Eggs *(pong tea khon)* Boiled, fertilized duck and chicken eggs are served complete with the developed embryo.

Snakes *(bpoo-ah)* Small snakes are marinated and barbecued on bamboo sticks, *satay*-style.

Spiders *(a'ping)* Huge, deep-fried tarantula spiders are a specialty of Skuon, but eaten everywhere in Cambodia.

Cha kny'ey is a delicious, fragrant dish of chicken, stir-fried with plenty of ginger, black pepper, and a little chili.

K'damm mrek Kep, or Kep pepper crab, is soft-shelled crab and green peppercorns in a garlic-flavored sauce.

Bok L'hong salad mixes grated, raw papaya, basil, and peanuts. Dried shrimp and tomato are often added.

The Flavors of Laos

Green papaya, water buffalo skin, river moss, fish stewed in lime juice – at first reading, the culinary delights of Laos might seem a little daunting. It is, however, a case of a bite being worth a thousand words. While similar to the cuisine of neighboring Thailand, Lao food draws from its unique local ingredients and culinary traditions to offer flavors that are almost always spicy, though not necessarily fiery. Lemongrass, coriander, Kaffir lime, galangal, and chili peppers provide the base for a range of thrilling culinary experiences.

Fish sauce

Vegetables, spices, and fruit on sale in a market, Luang Prabang

Rice and Noodles

The mountainous geography of Laos dictates that sticky rice, which requires less irrigation than other varieties, is a staple here. Rolled into small balls and eaten with the fingers, it is the perfect accompaniment to many Lao dishes that are served as dips, or as a side dish with barbecued meat or fish. Sticky rice, which comes in black, white, or purple varieties, is commonly ground by the Lao people into a flour from which a variety of noodles and crispy cakes are made. It is also distilled into various types of alcoholic beverages. Standard paddy rice is also eaten on special occasions, and the French Colonialists introduced wheat, which is used to make both baguettes and Chinese-style wheat noodles.

Meat and Fish

Laos is a land that is criss-crossed by rivers, all of which are teeming with fish. Grilled, minced, eaten raw, or made into various dips and sauces, freshwater fish are a major protein source for the Lao. Poultry (the French imported turkey, which is popular) and pigs are domesticated, but the Lao also have a real taste for wild game. Boar and deer are

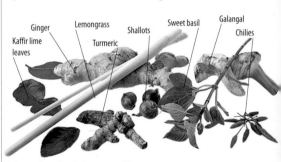

Ginger
Lemongrass
Shallots
Sweet basil
Galangal
Kaffir lime leaves
Turmeric
Chilies

Selection of typical Lao herbs, spices, and flavorings

Lao Dishes and Specialties

Luang Prabang is the home of Lao haute cuisine, and many esoteric specialties await the adventurous diner there. Vientiane has many dishes of French origin. Elsewhere, one can easily be content with standard Lao favorites. The most well-known is *laap* (meat salad), which can be made from any sort of meat or fish, either steamed, stir-fried, or simply "cooked" by being marinated, seviche-style, in spices. The green papaya salad *tam mak hung* is pounded in a mortar and pestle, mixing the piquant flavor of unripe papaya with spicy condiments. The Lao love to barbecue, and fresh chicken, pork, and fish skewers are readily available. The condiment of choice is *paa daek*, a fermented fish sauce, a richer cousin of the ubiquitous sauce found throughout Southeast Asia.

Rice noodles

Pho is a rich broth with rice noodles, vegetables, and meat. Originally Vietnamese, it is a favorite light Lao meal.

commonly served, but the menu extends to smaller creatures such as squirrels and field rats. Insects, including larvae, ant eggs, and bamboo worms, are very popular and a good source of protein. Needless to say, allparts of the animals are used – buffalo skin is a favorite condiment and snack, and offal is considered preferable to meat, with market prices reflecting this.

Vegetables and Fruit

Laos has a natural bounty of vegetables and fruits. From the rivers come an algae that is dried into sheets to form a delicious crispy snack called *kai paen*, which is eaten with a spicy chili dip called *jeow bong*. Papaya is used in the staple salad *tam mak hung*, and other tropical fruits are also plentiful. Wild mushrooms abound in the forests, while bamboo

Meats being grilled at a food stall beside the Mekong River

groves provide succulent shoots. The jungle is the source of the all-important sakan *(piper boehmeriaefolium)*, an aromatic vine used as a spice. Small riverside gardens cultivate delicate herbs.

Drinks

Unsweetened Chinese tea, usually served at room temperature, accompanies most meals. From France comes strong coffee, served Vietnamese-style with a steel filter over the cup. Lao beer is cheap and excellent, while stronger spirits include *lao lao*, a distilled rice spirit similar to schnapps in flavor and potency. Luang Prabang has its own rice wine, made from purple rice, called *lao gaam*, which is sweet and strong.

Enticing array of cooked dishes being served in a Lao street market

ON THE MENU

Baguette Sandwich Fillings can include meat, cheese, vegetables, or the local pâté.

Barbecue Chicken, pork, beef, or even buffalo, always well marinated, are served on a bamboo skewer.

Kai Paen This river algae, fried and served as a snack, is delicious with beer.

Khao Lam Sticky rice with coconut cream, steamed and sold in a bamboo tube, makes a good, filling snack.

Spring Rolls These are a popular Vietnamese import, served with a piquant dipping sauce. Try the uncooked variety for a change.

Yum Salad Watercress, lettuce, tomato, and boiled egg are served in a light mayonnaise sauce with peanuts. A mild, not spicy, dish.

Mok Pa uses pounded white fish blended with spices. The mixture is then wrapped in banana leaves and steamed.

Laap, the Lao national dish, is minced meat, poultry, or fish flavored with lime juice, onion, garlic, and mint.

Or Lam is a Luang Prabang specialty. Dried buffalo meat and skin are stewed with eggplant and spices.

Where to Eat

Cambodia

Phnom Penh

CENTRAL PHNOM PENH:
Blue Pumpkin   **$**
Café   **City map** E1
245 Sisowath Quay
Tel (023)-998-153
Bright and modern, this relaxed
bakery and patisserie overlooks
the river. It serves home-made
gelato, baked goods, coffee, fruit
shakes, sandwiches, and pasta.

CENTRAL PHNOM PENH:
Café Fresco   **$**
Café   **City map** E1
363 Sisowath Quay
Tel (093)-400-123
This air-conditioned café does a
good job of imitating a New York
deli, selling great subs and a good
range of fresh coffees. There is also
a pretty outside patio with seating.

CENTRAL PHNOM PENH:
Chiang Mai Riverside   **$**
Thai   **City map** E1
227 Sisowath Quay
Tel (011)-811-456
Popular with tourists and expats,
this long-established restaurant
serves tasty Thai food in a scenic
location near the waterfront.

CENTRAL PHNOM PENH:
Dosa Corner   **$**
Indian   **City map** E3
5E, St 51, near Wat Lanka
Tel (012)-673-276
More than 15 varieties of *dosa*
(South Indian crepes) are available
at this little Indian restaurant. There
are plenty of curries to choose
from and you can wash everything
down with a nice cold lassi.

CENTRAL PHNOM PENH:
Irina Russian House   **$**
Russian   **City map** E4
15, St 352
Tel (012)-833-524
For something a little different
from Khmer and Western
cuisine, this place is ideal.
It serves hearty goulash and
potatoes and, as you'd expect,
the vodka flows freely.

CENTRAL PHNOM PENH:
Kandal House   **$**
Pizza   **City map** E1
239 Sisowath Quay
Tel (012)-525-612
Worth a visit for its wood-fired
pizzas and home-made pasta,
Kandal House also runs a long

happy hour. The beer is cheap
and there are good views from the
river from the terrace. Inevitably,
it is popular with travelers.

DK Choice

CENTRAL PHNOM PENH:
Foreign Correspondents'
Club   **$$**
European   **City map** E2
363 Sisowath Quay
Tel (023)-724-014
There are far more tourists than
real journalists at this famous
club *(see p238)*, but the decor
and views from its superb third-
floor location overlooking the
river make this place definitely
worth a visit. Western food is
served here, including great
wood-fired pizzas and delicious
sundowners. Happy hour is
daily from 5–7pm.

CENTRAL PHNOM PENH:
Khmer Surin   **$$**
Khmer   **City map** D3
9, St 57, Boeung Keng Kang
Tel (012)-887-320
This well-run restaurant is very
popular with locals and NGO
workers. The interior has an
Angkorian decor with plenty
of plants. Try Khmer favorites
such as *lok lak* (slices of beef stir-
fried with oyster sauce and
green peppercorns).

CENTRAL PHNOM PENH:
K'nyay   **$$**
Vegan   **City map** D4
43, St 95, at The Terrace on 95
Tel (093)-665-225   **Closed** *Monday*
This totally vegan restaurant
serves standard Cambodian
dishes, with soy protein, taro root,

Atmospheric dining at Malis,
Central Phnom Penh

Price Guide

Prices are based on a three-course meal
for one person (excluding wine),
including tax and service.

$	up to $10
$$	$10 to 30
$$$	over $30

and sweet potatoes replacing
meat. The banana and jackfruit
curries are excellent, and even
the icecream is suitable for vegans.

CENTRAL PHNOM PENH:
Lazy Gecko Café   **$$**
European   **City map** F3
1D, St 258
Tel (078)-786-025
The Lazy Gecko Café serves tasty
international fare, and inspires
with its cheerful atmosphere.
This is a popular choice among
expats, who come for the
succulent roast lamb. Cambodian
dishes are also available.

CENTRAL PHNOM PENH:
Le Jardin   **$$**
Café   **City map** E3
16, St 360
Tel (011)-723-399
A real family café, Le Jardin lives
up to its name with peaceful
gardens, including a treehouse
for children to play in. There are
plenty of shaded areas in which
to enjoy the delicious breakfasts,
crepes, sandwiches, and coffees.

CENTRAL PHNOM PENH:
Pop Cafe da Giorgio   **$$**
Italian   **City map** E2
371 Sisowath Quay
Tel (012)-562-892
Italian-run, this excellent restaurant
is known for its authentic lasagne,
salads, and pasta dishes, all
freshly made and served up
in relaxed surroundings.

CENTRAL PHNOM PENH:
Le Rit's   **$$**
European   **City map** E3
71, St 240
Tel (023)-213-160
Le Rit's is operated by the charity
NYEMO, which protects women
and supports abandoned
children. It serves tasty European
and Asian cuisine in pleasant
indoor and outdoor settings.

CENTRAL PHNOM PENH:
Riverside Bistro   **$$**
European   **City map** E1
Corner of Sisowath Quay and St 148
Tel (023)-213-898
Set in an old Colonial building,
this restaurant-cum-bar offers
outdoor dining in comfortable

wicker chairs, plus views of the Tonlé Sap River. The food served here includes Khmer and Western dishes, though, as to be expected given the location, prices are a little on the high side.

DK Choice

CENTRAL PHNOM PENH:
Romdeng $$
Khmer **City map** D2
74, St 174, between sts 51 & 63
Tel (092)-219-565
Excellent Khmer food is served in this sophisticated villa setting. Most of the service staff are former street children, rescued and trained in the culinary arts by the local NGO Friends International. The food is based on traditional recipes using healthy local ingredients – crispy tarantulas are available to try if you are feeling brave enough.

CENTRAL PHNOM PENH:
Sam Doo $$
Chinese **City map** D2
56, Kampuchea Krom Blvd
Tel (023) 218 773
A popular Chinese restaurant serving Cantonese dim sum, spicy Sichuanese food, and classic Beijing duck until late into the night. Both food and atmosphere are authentically Chinese.

DK Choice

CENTRAL PHNOM PENH:
The Shop $$
Café **City map** E3
39, St 240
Tel (023)-986-964
The most delicious bakery-cum-deli in town, The Shop turns out tasty Western snacks, including delicious cakes, salads, fresh sandwiches, and refreshing fruit smoothies, as well as plenty of pastries. The sweet potato frittata with smoked salmon and cream cheese is particularly good. It is the perfect place for those who crave some home cuisine.

CENTRAL PHNOM PENH:
Sugar n Spice Café $$
Café **City map** E2
65, St 178
Tel (077)-657-678
An air-conditioned haven serving superb coffees, cakes, and salads. Sugar n Spice also has a more important purpose: giving women trafficked into the sex trade a new start in life. On the ground floor is a visitor center with information on the charity that runs the café.

A luxury setting for first-class cuisine at Topaz, Central Phnom Penh

CENTRAL PHNOM PENH:
Tom Yum Kung $$
Thai **City map** D4
10, St 278
Tel (023)-720 234
Some of the best Khmer and Thai dishes in the city are served at Tom Yum Kung. This is a small thatch-roofed place with simple decor and tasty curries. It is so popular that another branch has opened across town on St 432.

CENTRAL PHNOM PENH:
Dine in the Dark $$$
Fine Dining **City map** E2
126, St 19
Tel (077)-589-458
An unusual concept restaurant where, as the name suggests, guests dine in the dark, served by visually impaired staff. With no light, the focus is very much on the food – Khmer and Western flavors, mostly, plus delicious cocktails.

CENTRAL PHNOM PENH:
Malis $$$
Khmer **City map** E4
136 Norodom Blvd
Tel (012)-342-555
This sophisticated restaurant is set in gardens that have an Angkorian atmosphere. It is *the* place to experience Cambodian Royal cuisine at its best. Both traditional and modern interpretations of great classic recipes are available.

CENTRAL PHNOM PENH:
Shiva Shakti $$$
Indian **City map** E3
17, St 63
Tel (023)-213-062
Very good Mughal cuisine and stylish surroundings make this one of the best places for Indian food in Phnom Penh. The menu has more than 200 options to choose from. Try the exceptional tandoori chicken.

DK Choice

CENTRAL PHNOM PENH:
Topaz $$$
French **City map** E4
182 Norodom Blvd
Tel (012)-333-276
Chef Alain Darc presents classic French cuisine with hints of Southeast Asian fusion, such as lobster ravioli with green Kampot pepper. The steaks come highly recommended and there is always a great selection of good daily specials. There is also an excellent wine cellar, and a walk-in cigar humidor. De luxe dining in a first-class atmosphere.

Angkor

SIEM REAP: Blue Pumpkin $
Café **Road map** C6
Sivatha Blvd
Tel (063)-968-898
Blue Pumpkin is an air-conditioned haven that tempts its customers with an array of brownies, cakes, sandwiches, salads, fruit shakes, and ice creams in local flavors, such as star anise and cashew. The service is great here, and free Wi-Fi is available.

SIEM REAP: Bopha Angkor
Restaurant $
Khmer **Road map** C6
East side of Stung Siem Reap
Tel (063)-964-928
This traditional Cambodian restaurant serves curries, fried beef with ginger, and chicken and fish *amoks* (meat steamed in a savory coconut-based curry). Crepes, ice creams, and cocktails are also on offer. The restaurant is set in beautiful gardens, with a peaceful terrace overlooking the river.

For more information on types of restaurants see pp216–7

SIEM REAP: Butterflies Garden Restaurant $
Khmer **Road map** C6
535, St 25, near Wat Bo
Tel (063)-761-211
A tranquil location enhanced by tropical butterflies and a koi pond. The rich menu features Khmer and Western dishes, with many vegetarian options. The breakfasts are also good, with healthy smoothies and milkshakes to choose from.

SIEM REAP: Chamkar Restaurant $
Vegetarian **Road map** C6
Khum Svay Dangkum, Old Market area
Tel (092)-733-150
This sidewalk favorite is heaven-sent for strict vegetarians. Sweet potato curry, stir-fried egg plant medley, vegetarian oysters, and spring rolls all feature on the menu. There is strictly no MSG in any of the food.

SIEM REAP: Common Grounds $
Café **Road map** C6
719–721, St 14
Tel (063)-965-687
Clean, American-style café with modern amenities such as air-conditioning and fast Wi-Fi. Also on offer are excellent cakes, soups, salads, sandwiches, juices, coffees, and teas. All profits support NGO projects in Cambodia.

SIEM REAP: The Soup Dragon $
Vietnamese **Road map** C6
Old Market area
Tel (063)-964-933
This hole-in-the-wall eatery has bags of charm and is known for its Vietnamese food, particularly the *pho* (noodle soup) and fresh spring rolls. Open-air seating is available on two floors, but the rooftop area offers a cooler setting for dinner.

SIEM REAP: Amok Restaurant $$
Khmer **Road map** C6
Pub St, Old Market area
Tel (063)-965-407
This popular restaurant serves traditional Cambodian staples, such as *amok* (fish curry), *lok lak* (stir-fried beef in oyster sauce), and mango salads. There is a balcony overlooking the lively alley below.

SIEM REAP: Angkor Café $$
International **Road map** C6
Outside the main entrance of Angkor Wat
Tel (012)-946-227
The food is not extraordinary, but this café provides a handy place to eat before or after exploring the temples of Angkor. The cuisine is mainly Western, with a few reasonable Khmer dishes.

SIEM REAP: Cambodian BBQ $$
Barbecue **Road map** C6
The Passage, near Pub St
Tel (063)-965-407
Hidden down the passage running parallel to Pub Street, this place becomes hot in the evening with smoke rising from its cook-it-yourself barbecue dishes. Snake, crocodile, and ostrich meat help to make for a tasty – and very memorable – meal.

SIEM REAP: FCC Angkor $$
European **Road map** C6
Pokambor Ave
Tel (063)-760-283
Siem Reap's Foreign Correspondents' Club has more space than its counterpart in Phnom Penh (*see p238*), but lacks some of the charm. The building is set amid manicured lawns, beside a swimming pool. Dining upstairs is delightful, with an attractive bar and open kitchen.

SIEM REAP: Genevieve's Restaurant $$
International **Road map** C6
Sok San St
Tel (081)-410-783 **Closed** *Sunday*
Popular, very well-run restaurant that ploughs some of its profits back into the local community. Choose between Western-style fish and meat dishes, and flavor-packed Khmer soups and salads.

DK Choice

SIEM REAP: Haven Training Restaurant $$
Pan-Asian **Road map** C6
Sok San St
Tel (078)-342-404 **Closed** *Sunday*
Haven Training is a restaurant and training school for young people from Cambodia's orphanages. The restaurant has become one of the city's most popular places to eat, and with good reason. Edible delights include pork ribs, soba noodles with shrimp, and a banana flower salad. Refreshingly, the menu also has plenty of options for vegetarians.

SIEM REAP: Khmer Kitchen $$
Khmer **Road map** C6
The Passage, behind Pub St
Tel (063)-964-154
The ever-busy Khmer Kitchen offers simple, hearty food. The menu of Thai and Khmer staples features soups, stir-fries, curries, and spring rolls. Try the baked pumpkin or the *lok lak* (stir-fried beef). There is another Khmer Kitchen a short walk away, west of St 11.

Enjoy classic Cambodian cuisine in a lively, bright setting at Amok, Siem Reap

SIEM REAP: Little Red Fox Espresso $$
Café **Road map** C6
Hup Guan St, Kandal Village
Tel (016)-669-724
A diminutive, Australian-run coffee house and hair salon. The mixture of businesses may sound bizarre, but this place offers top-notch flat whites and espressos. The focus here is on locally sourced organic beans.

SIEM REAP: Le Malraux $$
French **Road map** C6
155, Sivatha Blvd
Tel (063)-966-041
With a leafy courtyard setting and Gallic haute cuisine, Le Malraux is a smart spot for dinner. Asian dishes are offered, too, but traditional French food is the real highlight. The service is excellent.

SIEM REAP: The Red Piano $$
International **Road map** C6
Pub St
Tel (092)-477-730
This charming restaurant is set in a lovely old villa, with sidewalk, indoor, and veranda seating. The food is predominantly Western, with plenty of pasta dishes and steaks on the menu. Angelina Jolie was a regular here during the filming of *Tomb Raider*.

SIEM REAP: Terrasse Des Eléphants $$
Khmer **Road map** C6
Sivatha Blvd, Old Market area
Tel (063)-965-570
A hotel restaurant, the Terrasse Des Eléphants is set in a Colonial-style building among gardens bursting with flowers. Khmer options include chicken *amok* and beef curry in coconut milk. The bar here is a great place to enjoy an evening cocktail.

SIEM REAP: The Touich
Restaurant $$
Southeast Asian   **Road map** C6
Toward the north of town, behind Wat Preah Enkosei
Tel (092)-808-040
This open-air restaurant receives rave reviews for its authentic Thai and Khmer meals. In addition to classics like fish *amok*, there are plenty of grilled dishes available.

SIEM REAP: Viroth's $$
Khmer   **Road map** C6
Wat Bo Rd
Tel (012)-826-346
This restaurant is renowned for its distinctive *amok* dishes and modern take on Khmer food. A regular crowd of discerning diners are drawn to the stylish garden terrace, and there is indoor seating in case of bad weather.

SIEM REAP:
Cuisine Wat Damnak $$$
Fine Dining   **Road map** C6
Wat Damnak village
Tel (077)-347-762
Housed in a pretty wooden building, this incredibly popular restaurant focuses on unusual local flavors. The tasting menu includes ingredients like frogs' legs, jack fruit, and wild cinnamon.

SIEM REAP:
The Dining Room $$$
French/Khmer   **Road map** C6
Park Hyatt, Sivatha Blvd
Tel (063)-211-234
On the ground floor of the Park Hyatt hotel, this upscale eatery fuses French cooking with traditional Khmer flavors. Dishes change with the seasons.

SIEM REAP:
Heritage Suites Hotel $$$
Khmer   **Road map** C6
East of the river, near Wat Polanka
Tel (063)-969-100
This restaurant at a top-end hotel offers a superb 'Khmer discovery' set menu, providing the chance to discover local flavors in exquisite surroundings. Live jazz and cocktails every Thursday.

SIEM REAP: Raffles' Apsara
Terrace $$$
Pan-Asian   **Road map** C6
Raffles Grand Hotel d'Angkor
Tel (063)-963-888
Raffles has several restaurants and bars, but the star is the Apsara Terrace. The sumptuous buffet dinner, served in a candle-lit garden setting, specializes in Asian barbeque and seafood. At 7:45pm a cultural show begins, featuring live traditional music, martial arts, and Apsara dancing.

Northern Cambodia

BAN LUNG: Gecko House $
European   **Road map** E6
South of Highway 78
Tel (012)-416-234
This place has a wide-ranging menu that caters to the Western palate. On offer are excellent breakfasts, pizzas, and pasta dishes. By night, Gecko House comes to life with a happy mix of locals and travelers.

BAN LUNG: Pteas Bay Khmer $
Khmer   **Road map** E6
Beside Boeng Kansaign Lake
Tel (097)-916-7221
With a gorgeous lakeside setting, this big, open-sided restaurant serves reliable, very fresh Khmer dishes. English-speaking staff will help you to navigate the menu. Breakfasts are also available.

BAN LUNG: Terres Rouge Lodge $
International   **Road map** E6
Beside Boeng Kansaign Lake
Tel (012)-770-650
The restaurant at Terres Rouge Lodge is surrounded by lush vegetation, in an old Colonial house. Sumptuous furnishings complement the menu, which includes French, Khmer, and Chinese flavors. There is also a good selection of cold beer, wine, and cocktails.

BAN LUNG: Treetop Ecolodge $
International   **Road map** E6
Phum No.1, Laban Seak Commune
Tel (012)-490-333
This place is an unusually rustic dining venue, more typical of Thailand or Laos. The treehouse-style, open-air restaurant and lounge is atmospheric, with great views. The menu changes regularly, but expect a good range of Cambodian and Western dishes. Free Wi-Fi is available.

BATTAMBANG: The Bungalow
Restaurant $
International   **Road map** C6
144 Kamakor, Svaypor
Tel (012)-916-123
The Bungalow Restaurant sells standard Western fare, such as burgers and pizzas, but it also offers fresh, traditional Khmer and Thai food. The coffee here is excellent, and the service is very quick and friendly.

BATTAMBANG:
Choco L'art Café $
Café   **Road map** C6
St 117
Tel (010)-661-617
Visitors with a sweet tooth should head to this chilled-out café with pretty artworks displayed on the walls. The place specializes in tasty cakes, fresh baguettes, and hot drinks. Try the home-made hot chocolate served in huge cups.

> ## DK Choice
>
> ### BATTAMBANG:
> **Coconut Lyly** $
> Khmer   **Road map** C6
> *St 111*
> **Tel** (016)-399-339
> Simple but freshly prepared, the rice and noodle dishes at Coconut Lyly are excellent value. Also available is a range of green mango salads and thirst-quenching fruit shakes. Cookery classes take place here twice daily.

BATTAMBANG:
Lonely Tree Café $
Mediterranean   **Road map** C6
St 121
Tel (053)-953-123
Spanish and Italian dishes feature on the menu at this café, which supports the work of an NGO. It is a cool, relaxed spot in which to sit back with a cold drink and a meal.

French Colonial decor and a beautiful setting at FCC Angkor, Siem Reap

For more information on types of restaurants *see pp216–7*

BATTAMBANG:
Lotus Bar & Gallery $
European **Road map** C6
St 2.5
Tel (092)-260-158
A combined bar and art gallery
that attracts plenty of creative
backpackers. As well as hosting a
wide range of events (everything
from poetry to visual arts), the
venue serves pizzas, sharing
platters, and more.

BATTAMBANG:
Sunrise Coffee House $
Café **Road map** C6
Near Psar Nath market
Tel (012)-953-426
Centrally located, this Western-
style bakery sells pancakes,
cookies, pastries, and pizzas,
as well as blended
coffees and teas. The breakfasts
are legendary.

DK Choice
BATTAMBANG: Jaan Bai
Restaurant $$
Pan-Asian **Road map** C6
Near Psar Nath market
Tel (012)-263-144 **Closed** *Monday*
This social enterprise, run by
the Cambodian Children's Trust,
serves up top-notch tapas-style
dishes. The menu includes
everything from dim sum to
curries. The focus is on organic,
locally-sourced ingredients.
The food is great value for
money, and the service and
atmosphere are excellent.

BATTAMBANG:
Pomme d'Amour $$
French **Road map** C6
St 2
Tel (012)-415-513
Just south of the Psar Nath
market, this excellent little
restaurant offers well-presented
fish, meat, and vegetarian dishes.
The French owner and his Khmer
wife provide wonderful service.

DK Choice
BATTAMBANG: La Villa $$
European **Road map** C6
Pom Romcheck 5 Kom
Tel (017)-411-880
The restaurant at this beautifully
restored guesthouse *(see p212)*
has a cool, air-conditioned
interior with a glass roof and
tiled floors. Diners can also eat
in the courtyard or on the
terrace. The menu features
many delicious French-inspired
dishes, and a wide choice of
barbecue-grilled meats.

KOMPONG CHAM:
Mekong Crossing $
International **Road map** D7
Preah Bat Sihanouk St
Tel (012)-432-427
A firm favorite with locals and
travelers, this retro-feel café is
festooned with old movie posters.
The food is tasty and fresh, and
ranges from comfort food such
as sandwiches and burgers to
Khmer dishes like fish *amok*.

KOMPONG CHAM:
Smile Restaurant $$
Southeast Asian **Road map** D7
St 7
Tel (019)-977-09
Started by the non-profit
organisation Buddhism for Social
Development Action, Smile
Restaurant gives orphans and
vulnerable children a new start
in life. There is a wide range of
options on the menu, from
spring rolls and fish soups to
freshly baked baguettes.

KRATIE: Red Sun Falling $
International **Road map** D6
Rur Preah Suramarit
Tel (012)-476-528
A little restaurant with a pleasant
mural and second-hand book
stall. At night, it becomes a
bubbling cauldron of travelers
studying maps and drinking
cheap beer. The Western and
Asian food is good enough to
attract local NGO workers.

KRATIE: Le Tonle $$
Khmer **Road map** D6
St 3
Tel (072)-210-505
Part of a not-for-profit tourism
training center, this restaurant is
staffed by disadvantaged local
youths. The Khmer food, served
in a garden setting, is some of
the best in Kratie.

Delicious food is dished up for an excellent
cause at Epic Arts Café

Southern Cambodia

DK Choice
KAMPOT: Epic Arts Café $
Café **Road map** C7
East of the old market
Tel (092)-922-069
A small café with a good
reputation and ethos – all
of its profits aid disabled
Cambodians. It offers a
Western menu, featuring
bagels, omelettes, and mezes,
and also bakes great cakes
on the premises. Prices are
reasonable and there is free
Wi-Fi for all customers.

KAMPOT: Café Espresso $$
Café **Road map** C7
*Down the sidestreet near
Epic Arts Café*
Tel (092)-388-736 **Closed** *Monday*
An Australian-run café that roasts
and sells regionally grown coffee.
Even if caffeine is not your thing,
it is worth dropping by for a bite
to eat – the excellent breakfasts
and burgers will keep you full
for hours.

KAMPOT: Ellie's $$
Café **Road map** C7
St 726
Tel (096)-309-2300
Freshly made smoothies, cakes,
and light lunches make Ellie's
a popular daytime hangout.
The healthy salads and sand-
wiches served here are delicious,
and there are plenty of board
games available to play.

KAMPOT: La Java Bleue $$
French **Road map** C7
*Corner of 726 St and Phoum
Ouksophear*
Tel (097)-517-0023
Fresh swordfish and barracuda
are grilled on the wood-fired
barbecue at this guesthouse's
popular restaurant. Succulent
steaks are also available, and
there is a very good selection
of wines and cheeses – a rarity
in these parts.

KAMPOT: Mea Culpa $$
Pizzeria **Road map** C7
44 Sovansokar
Tel (012)-504-769 **Closed** *Monday*
The best pizzeria in Kampot,
this restaurant uses a wood-fired
oven and imported Italian
ingredients, including mozzarella
and pepperoni. The garden
setting is superb, the service
is excellent, and there is also
an extensive cocktail menu.

KAMPOT: Rikitikitavi $$
International   **Road map** C7
South end of Riverside Rd
Tel (017)-306-557
The restaurant at Rikitikitavi
(see p212) enjoys great river
views. Feast on Western dishes
such as fish and chips, or choose
one of the Khmer specials. Grilled
meat and vegetarian-friendly
alternatives are also available.

KAMPOT: Rusty Keyhole $$
International   **Road map** C7
Riverfront Rd
Tel (012)-679-607
This bustling bar-restaurant
is known for serving the best
ribs in the country; the marinade
recipe is a closely-guarded secret.
There are plenty of other tasty
Western and Asian dishes on
the menu, and there is a popular
happy hour at sunset.

KEP: Holy Crab $$
Seafood   **Road map** C7
Crab market
Tel (097)-632-3456
Located down by the water and
with great views, this seafood
joint is best-known for its flavor-
packed crab dishes, but it also
serves up tasty tiger prawns,
squid, and vegetarian options.

KEP: Kep Lodge $$
International   **Road map** C7
Pepper St
Tel (092)-435-330
Set well back from the beach,
this large, open-sided hotel
restaurant is an enjoyable place
for a Cambodian-style salad
or some Western food (Swiss
dishes such as rösti appear
on the menu). For dessert,
try the home-made mango
or papaya ice cream.

KEP: Sailing Club $$$
Pan-Asian   **Road map** C7
Shoreside
Tel (036)-210-310
An upscale seafront restaurant
with stylish lighting and a pleasant
lounge vibe. The creative pan-
Asian menu features Western,
Khmer, and Japanese dishes,
plus plenty of seafood. Outdoor
seating is on a patio, surrounded
by a large garden.

KOH KONG: Café Laurent $$
European   **Road map** B7
Riverfront Rd
Tel (016)-373-737
An air-conditioned restaurant on
the waterfront with smart modern
decor and a large outdoor terrace.
Great pasta, salads, and pizzas,
and a tempting selection of ice
creams. The coffee is excellent.

Rusty Keyhole, Kampot – a bar-restaurant famous for its delicious ribs

DK Choice

KOH KONG: Fat Sam's $$
International   **Road map** B7
Near the traffic circle
Tel (097)-737-0707
Western classics like hamburgers,
hot dogs, and schnitzels share
menu space with Asian soups
and salads at this expat-run bar-
restaurant. Known for its hearty
portions, Fat Sam's is a popular
spot for travelers, who come
for the friendly, bustling atmos-
phere – as well as for the food.

SIHANOUKVILLE: Dao of Life $$
Vegan   **Road map** C7
375 Ekareach St
Tel (097)-706-1144
This eco-minded café is heaven
for vegans and the health-
conscious, who come for the
cleansing juices and vitamin-
packed salads. The furniture
inside is reclaimed or recycled,
and the café regularly hosts
community events.

SIHANOUKVILLE:
Ernie's Burgers $$
American   **Road map** C7
Mithona St
Tel (098)-844-400   **Closed** *Monday*
Guests can build their own fish-,
chicken-, or beef-burger at Ernie's,
where unusual toppings include
beetroot, fried garlic, pineapple,
and hot chilis. Eat in the classic-
style diner or order your food
to go – the choice is yours.

SIHANOUKVILLE: Happa $$
Japanese   **Road map** C7
Serendipity Beach Rd
Tel (034)-934-380
A stylish thatched-roof restaurant
that serves up a tasty mix of
Japanese and Cambodian flavors.
Try the fresh fish and teppanyaki
dishes – there are seats under
cover and outside at the front.

SIHANOUKVILLE: Marco Polo $$
Italian   **Road map** C7
2 Thnou St
Tel (092)-920-866
A popular Italian joint, Marco
Polo is perfect for a pizza (made
in a wood-fired oven) or some
home-made pasta. Leave some
room for dessert, and a shot or
two of limoncello.

DK Choice

SIHANOUKVILLE: Sandan $$
Khmer   **Road map** C7
Sokha Beach Rd
Tel (034) 452-4000
Run by an NGO that helps street
children, Sandan is a popular
spot serving fresh Cambodian
cuisine as well as inventive
dishes such as pork ribs with
five spice and Coca-Cola. There's
also a delicious selection of
cocktails, and occasional dance
performances. Members of staff
speak excellent English and are
very friendly and helpful.

SIHANOUKVILLE: Starfish $$
Café   **Road map** C7
7 Makara St
Tel (012)-952-011
A café with a cause, Starfish has a
lovely garden and serves Western-
style breakfasts and lunches, with
plenty of vegetarian choices.
Profits benefit medical and
development work in Cambodia.

SIHANOUKVILLE:
Lemongrass Restaurant $$$
Japanese   **Road map** C7
2 Thnou St
Tel (034)-935-999
This restaurant at Sokha Beach
Resort *(see p212)* is one of the
classiest places for dinner in
Sihanoukville, with Japanese-
inspired interiors, sea views,
and a menu that includes
fresh sushi and sashimi.

For more information on types of restaurants *see pp216–7*

Laos

Vientiane

CENTRAL VIENTIANE:
Antique Café $
Café **City map** B3
Upstairs at Indochina's Handicrafts
on Setthathirat Rd
Tel (021)-223-528
This tiny café above an antique
shop is full of old clocks, medals,
and paintings. There is only space
for a couple of people at a time,
but it is a lovely atmospheric spot
for an iced Lao coffee.

CENTRAL VIENTIANE:
Common Grounds $
Café **City map** B4
Chao Anou Rd
Tel (021)-255-057 **Closed** *Sunday*
Family friendly café with an
enclosed play area outside. The
cookies and cakes are extremely
tempting, but if you need
something more substantial there
are healthy wraps and salads.

CENTRAL VIENTIANE:
Lao Kitchen $
Traditional Lao **City map** B3
Heng Boun Rd
Tel (021)-254-332
Set in an open-air shop front,
Lao Kitchen is the perfect place
to get acquainted with Lao food.
The house special is a fresh-
tasting chicken *laap* (minced
chicken salad), but regional
dishes like spicy, Pakse-style
sausages are also available.

DK Choice

CENTRAL VIENTIANE:
Little House $
Café **City map** B4
Manthatulath Rd
Tel (020)-5540-6036
Japanese run, this beautiful little
coffee house is set back from
the road amid leafy gardens.
The coffee, sourced from the
Bolaven Plateau, is sublime
(choose to have it hot or
with ice). The home-made
chocolate truffles are divine.

CENTRAL VIENTIANE:
Noy's Fruit Heaven $
European **City Map** B3
Heng Boun Rd
Tel (030)-996-0913
As well as turning out simple
Western breakfasts, Noy's offers
great ice-cold smoothies packed
with fresh fruit – perfect if you
have been wandering around
town in the heat of the afternoon.

CENTRAL VIENTIANE:
Scandinavian Bakery $
Bakery **City map** 3
Northern edge of Nam Phu
Tel (021)-215-199
This long-running, Scandi-style
bakery near the fountain sells
huge sandwiches, traditional
Swedish cakes, and refreshing
lemonade. There is a handy
noticeboard by the entrance
advertising details of local events.

CENTRAL VIENTIANE:
Chokdee Café $$
Belgian **City map** B4
Fa Ngum Rd
Tel (021) 263 847
This Belgian bar and restaurant
draws in expats and travelers
with its *moules frites* (look out
for the special offers). As you
might expect, there is an
extensive list of imported beers,
including plenty of strong
brews from Belgium.

DK Choice

CENTRAL VIENTIANE:
JoMa Bakery Café $$
Café **City map** B4
Setthathirat Rd
Tel (021)-215-265
This long-running café still
makes the best coffee and
breakfasts in town, as well as
great pastries and sandwiches.
The space is air conditioned,
with newspapers to read,
and a strong Wi-Fi connection.
There are two other branches
across town, but this is the
most central.

CENTRAL VIENTIANE:
Khop Chai Deu $$
Western/Asian **City map** B3
54 Setthathirat Rd
Tel (021)-263-829
Situated in a Colonial-era villa
next to the Nam Phu fountain,
this lively restaurant is the top
evening venue for visiting
foreigners and expats. There is an
extensive menu of good Lao and
international dishes, and a wide
range of cocktails and beers.

CENTRAL VIENTIANE:
Makphet $$
International **City map** B3
Behind Wat Ong Teu, south of
Setthathirat Rd
Tel (021)-260-587 **Closed** *Sunday*
Established to help former street
kids, Makphet trains its students
in English language, cooking, and
restaurant operations. The Lao
food here is excellent – fresh,
traditional ingredients are given
a tasty modern twist.

Enjoy huge sandwiches and Swedish cakes at
the Scandinavian Bakery, Central Vientiane

CENTRAL VIENTIANE:
Sticky Fingers $$
European **City map** B4
François Nginn Rd
Tel (021)-215-972 **Closed** *Monday*
This Australian-run bar serving
decent Western food has built
up a loyal following among
the city's expats. Head to Sticky
Fingers on Wednesday or Friday
evenings, when all the cocktails
are half-price.

CENTRAL VIENTIANE: Swedish
Pizza & Baking House $$
Scandinavian **City map** B3
Chao Anou Rd
Tel (021)-254-041
In need of a revamp but with a
good choice of mouthwatering
pastries and sweet treats, this
Swedish-style bakery also offers
proper sit-down meals. Try the
meatballs served with lingon-
berries and mashed potatoes.

CENTRAL VIENTIANE:
La Terrasse $$
European **City map** B3
Nokeo Khumman Rd, near Wat Mixai
Tel (021)-218-550 **Closed** *Sunday*
Super steaks, plus decent pizzas,
red wine, and salads. The prices
here are slightly lower than at
other European restaurants in this
part of Vientiane. The covered patio
area is a lovely spot from which
to watch the world go by.

CENTRAL VIENTIANE:
La Vendome $$
French/Lao **City map** B3
In Paeng Rd, behind Wat In Paeng
Tel (021)-216-402
Tucked away on a small lane
behind Wat In Paeng, this place is
a long-standing Vientiane favorite
that serves reasonably priced
French and Lao food, and pizza
from a wood-fired oven. It can
get busy, but the service is good.

CENTRAL VIENTIANE:
Via Via $$
Italian/Asian **City map** B4
Nokeo Koummane Rd
Tel (020)-28-177-932 **Closed** *Saturday*
Very popular with the tourist crowd, Via Via spills out onto the sidewalk, its tables loaded with Italian-style pizzas. Wine is available by the jug and there are some decent Lao dishes on offer, too. This is a great place to meet new people.

CENTRAL VIENTIANE:
La Belle Epoque $$$
French/Lao **City map** C3
6 Pangkham Rd, inside the Settha Palace Hotel
Tel (021)-217-581
Refined French and Lao food is offered at La Belle Epoque, the elegant dining room inside the Colonial-era Settha Palace Hotel *(see p213)*. Prices for the food (such as foie gras, duck, and seared salmon) are high by Vientiane standards, but they are more than justified by the elegant setting.

GREATER VIENTIANE:
Jamil Zahid $
Indian **City map** B3
Off Khoun Boulom Rd
Tel (030)-990-9456
Very cheap, very tasty Punjabi curries served up in a shed-like restaurant toward the west side of the city center. The eccentric owner might try to take your picture with his digital camera, but do not be alarmed – he seems to do it with everyone.

GREATER VIENTIANE:
Ray's Grille $
American **City map** A3
17/1 Sihom Rd, west of the gas station
Tel (020)-5896-6866 **Closed** *Saturday*
This tricky-to-spot place (look for the whiteboard menu out front), makes magnificent philly cheese steaks dripping with cheddar. Mexican food is also available – it is all served up from a simple food cart, with seating in a narrow shop behind.

GREATER VIENTIANE:
Le Silapa $$
French **City map** A5
88, Setthathirat Rd
Tel (021)-219-689
Adorned with original artworks, Le Silapa is a small, intimate restaurant. It serves delectable French dishes such as seared salmon steak in red wine and grilled shallot sauce, and is a big favorite among Vientiane's expat community.

GREATER VIENTIANE:
The Spirit House $$
Western **City map** B3
105 Fa Ngum Rd
Tel (021)-243-795
With an enviable location beside the Mekong River, The Spirit House is a great place for a drink at sunset. There's a wide selection of cocktails and spirits. If you are hungry, burgers, sandwiches, and salads are also available.

Luang Prabang

CENTRAL LUANG PRABANG:
Lao Lao Garden $
Western/Lao **City map** D3
Phou Si Rd, Ban Aphai
Tel (020)-766-611-84
Built on the side of a hill, this restaurant has a terraced garden setting. It has many barbecue options, both Lao and Western. Expect DJs and dancing after dark.

CENTRAL LUANG PRABANG:
Nisha $
Indian **City map** C4
Kitsalat Rd
Tel (020)-9826-6023
This back-to-basics Indian eaterie attracts a steady stream of backpackers with its tasty curries and cold beer. There are also plenty of meat-free dishes available on the menu.

CENTRAL LUANG PRABANG:
Riverside Barbecue $
Barbecue **City map** C3
Souliyavongsa Rd
Tel (020)-559-999-45
A classic *sin dad* (Lao barbecue) place down by the Mekong River, where punters cook their own fish, meat, soup, and vegetables over tabletop barbecues. One price per-person covers as much food as you can eat – just go early because it tends to get busy.

CENTRAL LUANG PRABANG:
Tamnak Lao $
Traditional Lao **City map** D3
Sakkarin Rd, Ban Wat Sene
Tel (071)-252-525
Also known as the Three Elephants, Tamnak Lao serves great Lao food at reasonable prices. Try the steamed fish with local herbs. The Western and Thai dishes on offer are also good.

CENTRAL LUANG PRABANG:
Le Banneton Café and Boulangerie $$
Café **City map** D3
Sakkarin Rd, opposite Wat Sop
Tel (020)-546-491-89
Close to the row of temples toward the end of the peninsula, this café makes a welcome refreshment stop for weary tourists. The pastries and sandwiches are superb.

> **DK Choice**
>
> **CENTRAL LUANG PRABANG:**
> **Blue Lagoon Restaurant** $$
> Western/Asian **City map** D3
> *Ban Choumkhong*
> **Tel** (020)-592-525-25
> The Blue Lagoon has an elegant setting in the middle of town and offers thoughtfully presented Lao and European dishes. Fare includes imported steak, beef stroganoff, and some delicious gourmet desserts. There is also an excellent wine list.

CENTRAL LUANG PRABANG:
Café Toui $$
Café **City map** D3
Sisavangvatthana Rd
Tel (020)-565-767-63
The good-value taster meals at this small Lao-run café allow diners to try several Lao dishes at once – pork *laap* (minced meat with lime juice and mint) and *mok pa* (steamed fish) to name just two.

The elegant dining room at La Belle Époque, Central Vientiane

For more information on types of restaurants *see pp216–7*

CENTRAL LUANG PRABANG:
Dyen Sabai $$
Traditional Lao   City map D3
Ban Phan Luang, across the Nam
Khan from the center
Tel (020)-551-048-17
Cosy bamboo huts complement
the inventive menu here,
which includes unusual options
such as Mekong "seaweed",
local sausages, and a minty
laap. The traditional Lao
barbecue is excellent.

DK Choice

CENTRAL LUANG PRABANG:
L'Etranger Books & Tea $$
Café   City map D4
Ban Aphay
Tel (071)-212-880
Whether you are looking for a
new holiday read or just fancy
relaxing with a cup of jasmine
tea, this café in a second-
hand bookstore is a lovely
place to spend time. It also
serves light meals, milkshakes,
and smoothies, and hosts
regular free movie nights.
A laid-back, homely place
with very friendly staff.

CENTRAL LUANG PRABANG:
Hive Bar $$
American   City map C4
Ban Aphay
Tel (020)-599-953-70
For some time, Hive has been a
popular bar in Luang Prabang's
(admittedly rather limited)
drinking scene. It also offers
hearty meals based around
smoked meats – ribs and
chicken wings, mostly.

CENTRAL LUANG PRABANG:
The House $$
Belgian   City map C4
Ban Aphay
Tel (071)-255-021
A Belgian-French restaurant with
its own boules court and beer
garden, where you can slurp
your way through some
refreshingly different Belgian
beers. There's a good selection
of Flemish food, but Lao dishes
are also available.

CENTRAL LUANG PRABANG:
JoMa Bakery Café $$
Café   City map B4
Chao Fa Ngum Rd
Tel (071)-260-920
Located in an air-conditioned,
Colonial-style two-story house,
JoMa serves excellent coffee,
pastries, and sandwiches. If you
are looking for something more
substantial, the pasta dishes are
also delicious.

DK Choice

CENTRAL LUANG PRABANG:
Tamarind $$
Traditional Lao   City map D3
Koun Xoa Rd
Tel (020)-7777-0484
This is one of the best places in
town to try authentic Lao food.
Tamarind specializes in tasting
platters, with dishes like herbed
fish steamed in banana leaves.
The service is excellent, and, if
you like what you try, staff offer
cookery classes and can teach
you how it is done.

CENTRAL LUANG PRABANG:
Utopia $$
Western/Asian   City map C4
Ban Aphai, on the Nam Khan
Tel (020)-238-817-71
Spectacularly positioned, this
restaurant has a large vaulted
ceiling and an open-air pagoda,
which is surrounded by smaller
dining areas overlooking the
river. Western and Lao food is
served on low tables surrounded
by comfortable cushions.

CENTRAL LUANG PRABANG:
Apsara $$$
Asian fusion   City map D3
Kingkitsarat Rd, Ban Wat Sene
Tel (071)-254-252
Located in the lobby of the hotel
of the same name, this restaurant
overlooks the Nam Khan river.
The carefully crafted dishes
combine elements of Indian,
Lao, and Malaysian cuisine.

CENTRAL LUANG PRABANG:
L'Elephant $$$
French/Lao   City map D3
Ban Wat Nong, diagonally opposite
the School of Fine Arts
Tel (071)-252-482
Lao, French, and fusion dishes,
made using vegetables and herbs
from the restaurant's own garden.

Fine dining in a pretty setting at Nagas,
Central Luang Prabang

The decor is elegant, with white
napkins and polished brass,
complemented by Lao antiques.

CENTRAL LUANG PRABANG:
Nagas $$$
Traditional Lao   City map C3
Sakkarin Rd
Tel (071)-260-777
Situated in the hotel of the same
name, Nagas is an upscale restau-
rant focusing on traditional Luang
Prabang cuisine. Try the delicate
laap with sliced Mekong fish.

CENTRAL LUANG PRABANG:
Nava Mekong $$$
Traditional Lao   City map C3
44/03 Suvannakhamphong Rd, Ban
Wat Nong
Tel (071)-260-319
Dine aboard a teakwood cargo
boat while cruising the Mekong
River. The Nava offers buffet-style
meals served with Lao specialties
such as Mekong fish.

CENTRAL LUANG PRABANG:
Tangor $$$
French/Asian   City map C3
Sisavangvong Rd
Tel (071)-260-761
Local, seasonal produce helps the
chefs at Tangor to create tongue-
tingling dishes that fuse together
the best elements of French and
Asian cuisine. As the busy tables
attest, this is one of the top
places to eat in Luang Prabang.

Northern Laos

HUAY XAI: Bar How $
Western/Asian   Road map A2
150 m north of the old ferry landing
Tel (020)-551-672-20
Hip music and lighting make this
place a firm favorite with backpackers – as do the cold beers,
cocktails, and reasonably priced
food. There are Lao and Thai
dishes, plus American-style food.

HUAY XAI: Dream Bakery $
Café   Road map A2
100 m south of the old ferry landing
A bright bakery selling very good
coffee from the Bolaven Plateau,
plus scrumptious croissants, cakes,
and pastries. A great spot for breakfast or a mid-morning snack.

HUAY XAI: Muang Nuea $
Traditional Lao   Road map A2
Saykhong Rd
Tel (020)-556-842-57
In the middle of town, Muang
Nuea is the top backpacker option
in Huay Xai, and a great place to
pick up the latest travel gossip.
Lao and Western dishes available.

DK Choice

LUANG NAM THA: Bamboo Lounge $
Italian **Road map** B1
Main street
Tel (020)-556-800-31
Run by New Zealanders, this community-focused place serves great wood-fired pizzas and pasta dishes (gluten-free options are available). It also serves sandwiches, cocktails, and great coffee.

LUANG NAM THA: The Boat Landing $
Traditional Lao **Road map** B1
6 km south of the center
Tel (086)-312-398
A rustic restaurant in a beautifully tranquil setting, serving good-quality food from the northern part of Laos. The Akha ginger chicken soup is good, as are the fresh fruit juices.

LUANG NAM THA: Manikong Bakery $
Western **Road map** B1
Opposite the Night Market
Tel (020)-223-544-46
The perfect spot for breakfast, this bakery lures in early risers with fried eggs, bacon, toast, and freshly made croissants.

LUANG NAM THA: Manychan $
Western/Asian **Road map** B1
Route 3
Tel (086)-312-209
The food at this popular guest-house is a cut above the usual tourist-oriented places. Great steaks, pizzas, and Lao food, plus freshly baked bread.

LUANG NAM THA: Minority $
Southeast Asian **Road map** B1
Just off the main road
Tel (020)-299-8224
Minority is a simple-looking restaurant, but is easily the best place to sample traditional recipes from tribes across the region.

MUANG KHUA: Nam Ou $
Traditional Lao **Road map** B1
Above the boat landing
Tel (088)-210-844
Travelers flock to this terrace restaurant by the river, where bowls of noodles and fish-based dishes are available for a few dollars each.

MUANG NGOI: Ning Ning $
Western/Asian **Road map** B1
Near the boat docks
Tel (020)-388-0122
Located on the small lane leading to the boat dock, Ning Ning

A khan tok (pedestal tray) of delicious Lao cuisine

serves good Lao and Western food. Do not miss the river fish dishes here – they are superb.

MUANG SING: Tai Lu $
Southeast Asian **Road map** A1
Route 17
Tel (081)-212-375
An attractive Colonial shophouse serving authentic renditions of native cuisine. Spicy vegetable dips, which are eaten with balls of sticky rice, feature heavily.

NONG KHIAW: Deen Restaurant $
Indian **Road map** B1
Ban Sop Houn
Vegetable and meat curries, accompanied by home-made naans and chapattis and a choice of lassi or cold beer. This is a lovely place to watch the world go by on a breezy evening.

NONG KHIAW: Delilah's $
Café **Road map** B1
Main street, north side of the bridge
Tel (020)-543-956-86
A popular breakfast hangout among travelers, this place sells basic baguettes, omelettes, and strong coffee. There is also a good menu of daytime and evening food, including delicious desserts.

PAK BENG: Khop Chai Deau $
Indian **Road map** A2
Facing the river
Tel 020-517-170-68
Specializing in north Indian curries, this restaurant also offers Western food, including pizza. It is lively in the evenings with travelers trading tales of boat trips on the Mekong.

PAK BENG: Sabaidee $
Traditional Lao **Road map** A2
Facing the river
River views, big tables, and very good Lao food make this the most popular option for tourists

staying overnight in Pak Beng. Try the deliciously minty water buffalo *laap*

PHONGSALI: Phou Fa Restaurant $
Lao/Chinese **Road map** B1
NW of the town center
Tel (020)-556-953-15
This fortress-like restaurant was the Chinese consulate during the Lao Civil War. The Lao and Chinese food on offer is good, and views from the terrace beer garden are superb. It's a steep climb to get to the restaurant.

PHONSAVAN: Nisha $
Indian **Road map** C2
Route 7, near Bamboozle
Tel (020) 982-660-23
Rough around the edges, this dusty, shack-like Indian restaurant serves tasty curries. In the mornings, the banana roti makes a nice alternative to noodle soup.

PHONSAVAN: Auberge de Plaine des Jarres $$
French/Lao **Road map** C2
Phou Phadaeng Hill
Tel (020)-551-722-82
This lodge on a hill overlooking the town offers classic French food as well as Lao dishes. It also has a cosy fireplace in the winter, when much of the town is left shivering.

DK Choice

PHONSAVAN: Bamboozle $$
Western/Lao **Road map** C2
Route 7
Tel (030)-952-3913
Decorated with bamboo, this friendly joint serves tasty Western dishes like hamburgers, plus very cheap and filling noodle soups. A percentage of the restaurant's profits help local kids to learn English.

For more information on types of restaurants *see pp216–7*

PHONSAVAN: Craters $$
Western   **Road map** C2
Route 7
Tel (020)-780-5775
Do not let the old bomb casings and weaponry put you off – this traveler's café is a safe bet for Western breakfasts, club sandwiches, and the like.

SAM NEUA: Chittavanh Restaurant $
Lao/Vietnamese   **Road map** C2
Near the Nam Sam, between the bridge and the market
Tel (064)-312-265
On the first floor of a guesthouse of the same name, this restaurant is large by Sam Neua standards. Locals like the tasty Lao and Vietnamese food, and Chinese workers like the drinks, which flow freely by night.

SAM NEUA: Dan Nao Muang Xam $
Western/Asian   **Road map** C2
Route 6
Tel (020)-288-028-87
A family run restaurant near the river serving cornflakes and fried eggs for breakfast, and tasty pork and chicken soups for dinner.

VANG VIENG: AMD Restaurant $
Southeast Asian   **Road map** B2
Main river road, south of the hospital
Tel (020)-553-012-38
A bit of a trek from the town center, but the food – including an irresistably tangy *tom yam* soup – is worth the effort. This is a small, family owned business that has earned a loyal following.

VANG VIENG: Organic Mulberry Farm $
Café   **Road map** B2
2 miles (3 km) north of town
Tel (023)-511-220
The birthplace of Vang Vieng's tubing craze is a surprisingly sleepy spot, offering drinks and snacks based around organic ingredients grown on the farm.

VANG VIENG: River Spirit $$
Western/Asian   **Road map** B2
Ban Sabai Bungalows, main river road
Tel (023)-511-070
Part of a hotel complex, this restaurant presents Lao and Thai dishes in a waterfront setting. The extensive menu offers plenty of choice, from spring rolls to steaks.

VANG VIENG: Whopping Burger $$
American   **Road map** B2
Town center, next to Central Climbing School
A chic little burger bar run by Japanese expats. As the name

suggests, the burgers are pretty hefty – try the "sumarai", which comes with chunky fries.

Central and Southern Laos

CHAMPASAK: Champasak With Love $
Café   **Road map** D5
North of the traffic circle
Tel (030)-926-5926
A fresh and funky place with its own riverside terrace and a tree swing. It makes a pleasant change from some of the town's older restaurants.

CHAMPASAK: Inthira Restaurant & Bar $$
Western/Asian   **Road map** D5
On the main road through Champasak
Tel (031)-511-011
There is a great atmosphere at this restored Chinese shophouse. The chefs, trained in Vientiane, turn out a wide variety of tasty Western and Lao dishes.

DK Choice

CHAMPASAK: The River Resort $$$
Western/Asian   **Road map** D5
2 miles (3.5 km) north of Champasak, on the Mekong
Tel (086)-885-117-0
Overseen by a Thai chef, the restaurant at this luxury resort has unbeatable views over the river. Locally sourced vegetables and herbs are complemented by imported meats. The Lao, Thai, and European dishes here are all beautifully presented.

DON DAENG: La Folie Lodge $$
French/Asian   **Road map** D5
NW coast of Don Daeng
Tel (030)-5553-2004
Accessible only by boat, this makes an interesting excursion for dinner. The food is excellent, and includes classic French dishes and a good dessert menu.

DK Choice

DON DET: Crazy Gecko $$
Western/Asian   **Road map** D5
Sunrise side, south of Don Det Bungalows
A laidback riverfront restaurant with a terrace full of tropical plants. It has perhaps the island's most varied menu, with dishes such as a lightly spiced pumpkin burger and tasty Lao soups.

Spectacular views from The River Resort, Champasak

DON KHON: Seng Ahloune $
Western/Asian   **Road map** D5
Just east of the bridge
Tel (031)-260-934
Very close to the old French bridge and popular with tour groups, this large restaurant, which also has bungalows for overnight stays, offers tasty Western, Lao, and Vietnamese dishes.

DON KHON: Sunset Paradise Guesthouse $
Western/Asian   **Road map** D5
East of the bridge, at the far end of the path
Staff at this guesthouse speak good English, and serve cheap Western and Asian food on a wooden terrace right on the river's edge. It is the easternmost guesthouse on the main riverside path.

DON KHONG: Pon's River Guest House $
Western/Asian   **Road map** D5
150 m north of the ferry landing
Tel (020)-222-700-37
One of several guesthouses with simple restaurants overlooking the water, Pon's is a safe bet for decent fried rice, sandwiches, fruit salads, pancakes, and other backpacker staples.

PAKSE: Daolin $
Western/Asian   **Road map** D5
At the junction of Route 13 and No. 24 Rd
Tel (020)-557-331-99
A large, open-sided restaurant on a busy junction in the city center, which offers noodle dishes and cheese baguettes at knock-down prices. The local coffee is good, and excellent ice cream sundaes are also available.

DK Choice

PAKSE: Viengsavanh Seendard $
Barbecue   **Road map** D5
Just south of No. 46 Rd
Tel (031)-212-388
An insanely popular barbecue place that draws in a mostly local crowd with its delicious cook-it-yourself meals. Order a *sin dad* "set", including raw meat, fresh lime, salad, dips, and instant noodles, and enjoy the lively atmosphere as you cook.

PAKSE: Dok Mai $$
Italian   **Road map** D5
No. 24 Rd, south of Route 13
Tel (020)-980-086-52
Unusually for an authentic Italian restaurant, Dok Mai does not serve pizza. However, it is still worth visiting to try the excellent pasta dishes, drizzled with extra virgin olive oil.

PAKSE: Le Panorama $$
Western/Asian   **Road map** D5
On the top floor of Pakse Hotel
Tel (031)-212-131
Up on the roof of the long-running Pakse Hotel, this is a romantic spot for dinner. The Asian and European dishes are good, and the setting is incredible, with views for miles around.

DK Choice

PAKSE: Na Dao $$$
French   **Road map** D5
North of the Champasak Grand on No. 16W Rd
Tel (031)-255-558
By far the best restaurant in Pakse, Na Dao offers fine French dishes, including divine rib-eye steaks and duck dishes. The impeccable service is the best in southern Laos, and the wine list is excellent.

SAVANNAKHET: Hompha VIP $
Bar   **Road map** C4
Latsavongseuk Rd, on northern edge of the New Market
Few Westerners venture into this busy beer garden, which often has live music, but those who do tend to end up chatting and drinking with the locals. The papaya salad is brutally spicy.

SAVANNAKHET: Café Chai Dee $$
Café   **Road map** C4
Latsavongseuk Rd
Tel (030)-500-333-6
Travel books are available to borrow at this relaxed café, which sells delicious fruit shakes and a good mix of Western and Japanese dishes at reasonable prices.

SAVANNAKHET: Lin's Café $$
Café   **Road map** C4
Latsaphanit Rd, just north of the town square
Tel (020)-998-816-30
Lin's Café serves spring rolls, organic salads, and home-made vegetable curries. Upstairs, there is a small exhibition on the history of the region.

SAVANNAKHET: Dao Savanh $$$
French   **Road map** C4
On the northwestern side of the town square
Tel (041)-260-888
For elegant French cuisine in Savannakhet, look no further than this beautifully restored Colonial house on the main square. The set menu, featuring an excellent beef *bourguignon*, is very good value, and the outside terrace is delightful.

TAT LO: Café Em $
Café   **Road map** D5
On the road to the falls
Tel (020)-563-346-37
Organic, freshly roasted Arabica beans from the Bolaven Plateau are ground and served at this pretty outdoor coffee shop. The breakfast, with honey pancakes, is a great way to start the day.

THAKHEK: Orlasone Fusion $
Barbecue   **Road map** D3
Chao Anou Rd, north of the junction with Vientiane Rd
Tel (020)-552-224-09
At this open-air grill, fresh slivers of beef, pork, seafood, and even liver are delivered raw for diners to cook on tabletop barbecues, and to dip in deliciously spicy sauces. This place is extremely popular with locals.

THAKHEK: Song Fang Khong $
Thai   **Road map** D3
Kouvolavong Rd, just north of the square
Tel (020)-540-333-50
This restaurant serves authentic dishes from Thailand, just a short distance away on the other side of the Mekong. Dishes include decent papaya salads, prepared by the Thai chef. It is a small place, so you may have to wait a while for your food.

THAKHEK: The Kitchen at the Inthira Hotel $$
Western   **Road map** D3
Chao Anou Rd
Tel (051)-251-237
Located in front of the hotel of the same name, this restaurant serves everything from pizza to Lao food, and excellent breakfasts as well. The bar makes excellent cocktails.

THAM KONG LO: Sala Kong Lor Lodge $
Western/Lao   **Road map** C3
4 miles (7 km) SE of Tham Kong Lo
Tel (020)-556-451-11
The restaurant serving these quaint riverside bungalows dishes up competent Asian and Western meals, but the real highlight is the spectacular setting, with jungle and mountain scenery as far as the eye can see.

XE PIAN NPA: Kingfisher Ecolodge $
Lao/Italian   **Road map** D5
Ban Khiet Ngong
Tel (020)-557-263-15
The open-sided, two-story restaurant at this ecolodge serves a good mix of Lao and Italian pasta dishes. Views over the water are superb and the service is excellent. There is also a good bar selling Beerlao and local spirits.

Delectable beef *bourguignon* at Dao Savanh

SHOPPING IN CAMBODIA

Cambodia is a shopper's paradise with expensive, upscale boutiques and malls sharing space with noisy markets and street stalls. Over the last 15 years, successful jewelry designers and painters, who grew up overseas, have returned, adding to the country's burgeoning arts and crafts sector. Atmospheric markets offer a wide variety of ceramics, silk *kramas* (scarves), curios, silverware, statuary and carvings, brass rubbings, and paintings. Cambodian silk is prized all over the world and shoppers can strike some great bargains in markets where prices are flexible and friendly haggling is the norm. Those looking for more exclusive purchases will not be disappointed in the stylish shops that proliferate the shopping districts of major cities.

Opening Hours

Most shops in the cities open at 7:30am and close by 8pm, but supermarkets are open until 10pm. Shops also close for a couple of hours for lunch from 11am. Markets in Phnom Penh and Siem Reap operate from sunrise to sunset and are best visited after the morning rush. Some markets also shut for public holidays. All shops and markets are open through the week and on the weekends.

How to Pay

Cash is the most readily accepted means of payment with most upscale stores also accepting credit cards. The US dollar is accepted throughout the country, and many premium shops often quote prices in dollars rather than the local riel. Areas along the eastern border, close to Thailand, also accept the baht.

Haggling is part of Khmer culture and happens everywhere – with vendors, tuk-tuk and *moto* drivers, in local markets, hotels, and shops – but it is unlikely to be the norm in upscale

Visitors browsing through the merchandise, Russian Market

establishments. If bargaining is done in the right manner – with a friendly and calm disposition – you can catch yourself a real steal. Remember that prices are inflated to begin with, and the vendor expects you to bargain.

Rights and Refunds

As a general rule, once sold, goods are not taken back. In malls, however, where certain items come with a warranty, exchange or refund is possible. Similarly, boutiques owned by foreigners may be more willing to take back damaged goods.

Department Stores and Malls

Increasingly popular in Phnom Penh and Siem Reap, department stores and malls offer stiff competition for traditional markets. The capital has three malls, the newest of them being the **City Mall**. **Sovanna**, a department store, and **Sorya**, the oldest and most Western-style mall are located south of the Central Market. Siem Reap's plush **Museum Mall** and **Angkor Trade Shopping Mall** are home to stylish boutiques, electronic shops, and eateries.

Shopping Streets and Districts

Phnom Penh's Street 178, running parallel to the road near the National Museum, is known for its sculpture shops and art galleries. There are also a number of handicraft artisans here, as well as silk boutiques. Nearby, Sisowath Quay has a

Store selling antique figurines and other carvings, Psar Chaa

rich selection of boutiques, galleries, and bookshops. The charming Boeung Keng Kang area, long considered the foreigner's quarter, has many shops, massage spas, and elegant silk boutiques.

Quality boutiques have also blossomed all over Siem Reap, particularly in the old French Quarter, with a wide range of jewelers, tailors, picture galleries, artisans, and shops specializing in luxury home decor. While these shops are not cheap, they reflect the excellence of their artists, many of whom are widely respected outside the country.

Markets and Street Vendors

The best places to shop and experience an authentic slice of Cambodian life is in one of its markets. The bustling bazaars of Phnom Penh include the **Russian Market**, **Central Market**, and **Psar Russei**. Siem Reap's well-known markets include **Psar Chaa**, next to the old French Quarter, and the **Angkor Night Market**, which is replete with jewelry stalls, food vendors, and handicrafts, as well as a thatched bar.

Arts and Crafts

Produced all over the country, Cambodia's arts and crafts include a wide variety of finely wrought silver, gems, *kramas*, wood-carvings, stone sculptures, and antiques. **Apsara Art Gallery** has a range of contemporary Southeast Asian art, while **Asasax Art Gallery** celebrates the unique paintings of its contemporary artist Asasax. Silk products can be bought at **CYK Handicrafts**, an NGO, or **Couleurs d'Asie**. **Artisans d'Angkor** make wood and stone carvings worth buying. Visitors can also head to **Mekong Quilts**, for quilts made by rural women.

Clothing

Apart from traditional clothes, Cambodia also offers a wide

Swatches of silks on display at Artisans d'Angkor

variety of designer garments in outlets such as **Bliss**, which also tailors clothes. Visitors can use similar services at **Cherry Blossom Boutique** and **Tom and Alice Tailor**. Attractive T-shirts, sold at **Mulberry Boutique** and **Bambou Company Indochine**, make for memorable souvenirs. Yet another great place to pick up stylish clothes is **Pich Reamker Shop**.

Ceramics and Lacquerware

Traditional Khmer lacquerware continues to flourish today through organizations such as

Artisans d'Angkor, where visitors can not only observe the process of making lacquerware, but can also buy the finished product. **The National Center for Khmer Ceramics Revival** is another organization from where visitors can pick up beautiful souvenirs.

Counterfeit Goods

Cambodians selling silverware or other silver artifacts in markets are more often than not hawking poor quality products or fakes. If a silver product, for instance, does not weigh much in your hand, it is likely to have a low silver content and should not be priced very high. Visitors should be wary of traders claiming to sell original artifacts from Angkor. This is not only illegal, because it robs the country of its heritage, but it is also likely to be fake.

DIRECTORY

Department Stores and Malls

Angkor Trade Shopping Mall
Pokambor Ave,
Old Market area,
Siem Reap.
Tel (063)-766-766.

City Mall
Monireth Blvd,
Phnom Penh.
City Map B3.
Tel (023)-223-083.

Museum Mall
Next to Angkor National
Museum, Siem Reap.
Tel (063)-966-616.

Sorya
Sts 63 and 154,
Phnom Penh.
City Map D2.
Tel (023)-210-018.

Sovanna
Building 307–309, St 271,
Phnom Penh.
City Map B5.
Tel (017)-333-199.

Markets

Angkor Night Market
Off Sivatha Blvd, Siem
Reap. **Tel** (092)-654-315.
W angkornight
market.com

Central Market
N of St 63, Phnom Penh.
City Map D2.

Psar Chaa
French Quarter, Siem Reap.

Psar Russei
Between Charles De
Gaulle Blvd and St 182,
Phnom Penh.
City Map C2.

Russian Market
S of Mao Tse Toung Blvd,
Phnom Penh.
City Map B5.

Arts and Crafts

Apsara Art Gallery
170A, St 450,
Phnom Penh.
Tel (012)-867-390.

Artisans d'Angkor
Off Sivatha Blvd, near Old
Market, Siem Reap.
Tel (063)-963-330.
W artisansdang
kor.com

Asasax Art Gallery
192, St 178, Phnom Penh
City Map D2. **Tel** (023)-
217 795, (012)-877-795.

Couleurs d'Asie
St 240, Phnom Penh. **City
Map** D3. **Tel** (023)-221-075.

CYK Handicrafts
67, Sothearos Blvd, Phnom
Penh. **City Map** F3.
Tel (023)-210-849.
W cyk.org.kh

Mekong Quilts
49, St 240, Phnom Penh.
City Map D3.
Tel (023)-219-607.
W mekong-quilts.org

Clothing

**Bambou Company
Indochine**
Lucky Mall, Sivatha Blvd,
Siem Reap.
Tel (063)-966-822.

Bliss
St 240, Phnom Penh.
City Map D3.
Tel (023)-215-754.

**Cherry Blossom
Boutique**
St 10, Siem Reap.
Tel (012) 320-568.

Mulberry Boutique
On corner of sts 51 and
278, Phnom Penh.
City Map E3.
Tel (016)-222-750.

Pich Reamker Shop
Museum Mall, Siem Reap.
Tel (012)-876-863.

Tom and Alice Tailor
153, St 278, Phnom Penh.
Tel (012)-796-286.

Ceramics and Lacquerware

**The National Center
for Khmer Ceramics
Revival (NCKCR)**
Charles De Gaulle Blvd,
Siem Reap. **Tel** (063)-210-
004. For free pick up call
(017)-843-014.
W khmerceramics.com

SHOPPING IN LAOS

In recent years, shopping venues in Laos have increased both in number and variety. Goods on offer range from handwoven rice baskets, commonly found in wet markets, to splendid silk clothing and souvenirs in fancy boutiques. Luang Prabang's Night Market is well known for excellent, locally woven textiles, clothing, and bags. Fair-trade companies help villagers to market their goods, although buying direct from a street vendor benefits the local economy. Items, particularly handicrafts, from neighboring countries such as Thailand and Vietnam also find their way here. As a rule, it is best to visit a number of shops selling the same product before going ahead and buying it. Visitors should not expect shopping malls in Laos, nor guarantees or certificates of authenticity.

Stalls selling goods made by ethnic minorities, Night Market, Luang Prabang

Markets and Street Vendors

Every town in Laos has a local market, which is always worth a visit. There are several different markets, some selling dry goods such as textiles and clothing, and others selling fresh, local produce. While these markets usually cater to locals and do not have much variety for a visitor, they are good places to find authentic local products. Street markets catering to foreign visitors are often set up in the evening and usually offer products made by Laos's ethnic minorities. Luang Prabang's Night Market, set up along Sisavang Vong Road, is quite popular. In Vientiane, similar markets, such as Fa Ngum Quay by the river and Talat Sao, sell a variety of products from across the country.

Bargaining

There are no fixed prices in Laos, but the biggest margin for bargaining is in goods for sale in local markets and boutiques. Bargaining must be done with a smile, and buyers should be prepared to walk away as they are sure to find the same thing elsewhere. It is always best to have an idea of an item's price before bargaining. It is also not worth bargaining for small sums since the kip, when converted, is worth very little.

Textiles

Laos's handwoven silk and cotton textiles are beautiful, and can be priced quite exorbitantly at times. Each province has its own unique style, with those from Hua Phan in the northeast considered the most delicate. Lao textiles can be tailored into Western-style garments, but they look best in traditional shapes such as a long skirt. Older pieces should be avoided as they are fragile. The geometric appliqué work carried out by members of the Hmong community on everything, from bedspreads to bedroom slippers, is also attractive and relatively less expensive since it is not hand-woven. In Luang Prabang, **Kopnoi** and **Ock Pop Tok** are good sources for innovative designs. **Carol Cassidy Lao Textiles** and **Satri Lao Silks**, in Vientiane, make textiles in more traditional forms.

Antiques

Since fakes abound, it is best to leave the purchase of antiques to experienced buyers who are able to discern an original from a reproduction. Buyers should

Variety of handwoven silk garments on display at a shop, Ban Xang Khong

Baskets and other goods made of bamboo and rattan, Luang Prabang

avoid anything of a religious nature since it may have been stolen from a temple; besides, exporting religious art is illegal in Laos. True antique objects such as porcelain, especially from China, musical instruments, jewelry, wood-carvings, and bronze statues are generally illegal to buy and export without a permit. Items such as bank notes, stamps, coins, or medals associated with the previous regime are more likely to be authentic. The best source for buying antiques in Luang Prabang is **Phatana Boupha Antique House**. **Tha Vee Souk** also has an impressive collection of original antiques.

Visitors to Vientiane can head to **Indochina Old House** or **Mandalay Furniture**.

Handicrafts

The Lao people are expert weavers of baskets, which they make from both rattan and bamboo. The *tip khaw* (woven rice baskets), used for storing sticky rice, are inexpensive and attractive. Laos is renowned for its wood-carvings, which are also worth considering, although visitors should check the quality of them very carefully. Another indigenous product is *sa* paper, which is produced from the bark of mulberry trees. This paper is used to craft beautiful lanterns and other decorative items, which make great souvenirs. Lacquered parasols, made from bamboo, and ceramics are also considered good buys. The upscale **Caruso Lao** in Luang Prabang does fantastic work in carved wood, and **Blue House** has great *sa* paper creations. Shops in Vientiane worth visiting include **Phai Exclusive Crafts**, which sells a wide collection of traditional crafts, and **T'shop Lai Gallery**, with its unusual handicraft items.

Jewelry

Gold and silver jewelry is readily available in the markets of Laos, often sold in brightly lit, red-colored shops. Both are usually sold by weight, with an additional charge depending on the workmanship of the item. Gold is almost always the 24-karat variety with a dull luster popular in Asia, but there are varying qualities of silver with no fixed standard.

Among the best buys are jewelry pieces made by ethnic communities, which though usually rough, are quite unique. Probably the most attractive item is the silver belt, which looks best paired with the traditional *pha sin* wraparound skirt worn by Lao women.

Few gemstones of quality are mined in Laos, so unless you are an expert at recognizing these, avoid buying them. In Luang Prabang, **Naga Creations** is considered to be the place to go to for modern creations, but **Thithpeng Maniphone Silversmiths** is a master silversmith of traditional jewelry of high quality. **Bari Gems & Jewelry** and **Saigon Bijoux**, in Vientiane, offer diverse collections of tempting pieces.

Gemstone-studded earring

DIRECTORY

Textiles

Carol Cassidy Lao Textiles
Ban Mixay, Vientiane.
City Map B3. **Tel** (021)-212-123. ⓦ laotextiles.com

Kopnoi
Across Ban Aphay Primary School, Luang Prabang.
City Map C4.
Tel (071)-260-248.

Ock Pop Tok
Ban Wat Nong, Luang Prabang. **City Map** D2.
Tel (071)-212-597.
ⓦ ockpoptok.com

Satri Lao Silks
Setthathirat Rd, Vientiane.
City Map B4.
Tel (021)-219-295.
ⓦ satrilao.laopdr.com

Antiques

Indochina Old House
Setthathirat Rd, Vientiane.
Tel (021)-212-579.

Mandalay Furniture
Francois Ngin Rd,
Vientiane. **City Map** B4.
Tel (021)-218-736.

Phatana Boupha Antique House
Across from Wat Visounarat, Luang Prabang. **City Map** D4.
Tel (020)-55-570-658.

Tha Vee Souk
Sisavang Vong Rd, Luang Prabang. **City Map** C3.
Tel (071)-260-624.

Handicrafts

Blue House
Sakkarin Rd, Luang Prabang. **City Map** D3.
Tel (020)-58-754-990.

Caruso Lao
Sakkarin Rd, Luang Prabang. **City Map** D3.
Tel (071)-254-574.
ⓦ carusolao.com

Phai Exclusive Crafts
03/01 Thongtoum St, Thongtoum, Vientiane.
City Map B3.
Tel (021)-214-0804.

T'shop Lai Gallery
Behind Wat Inpaeng, Vientiane. **City Map** B3.
Tel (021)-223-178.
ⓦ laococo.com/tshoplai.htm

Jewelry

Bari Gems & Jewelry
Samsenthai Rd, opposite Asian Pavilion Hotel, Vientiane. **City Map** C3.
Tel (021)-212-680.

Naga Creations
Sisavang Vong Rd, Luang Prabang. **City Map** C3.
Tel (020)-777-5005.

Saigon Bijoux
Samsenthai Rd, Vientiane.
City Map C3.
Tel (021)-214-783.

Thithpeng Maniphone Silversmiths
Ban Wat That, Luang Prabang.
City Map B4.
Tel (071)-212-925.

Entertainment in Cambodia

The country's entertainment industry was destroyed by the Khmer Rouge. However, since the late 1970s, Cambodia has steadily recovered, producing a new generation of contemporary artists and a Thai-Chinese influenced pop music scene. Cinema is also making a steady, if slower, return to form. More traditional arts, such as the *apsara* dance, closely linked to the artistic zenith of Angkor, are being heavily promoted. Contemporary and traditional music can be heard across the capital and smaller cities, while Cambodia's top new wave of musicians often perform at restaurants situated across the Japanese Bridge in Phnom Penh.

Dancers performing the traditional *apsara* dance, Cambodia

Information and Reserving Tickets

The city guides published by Canby Publications provide up-to-date information on the best bars, clubs, and musical and theatrical events taking place in Phnom Penh, Siem Reap, and Sihanoukville. These guides are also free of charge. The daily English-language newspaper *The Phnom Penh Post* is a useful city guide. *Bayon Pearnik*, a free monthly magazine, also contains listings for local events and places to eat. Reserving tickets in advance is not common in Cambodia, but most tour agents and hotels can easily do this for you.

Traditional Dance, Theater, and Film

Cambodia's traditional music and dance has seen a poignant return to form. The **Sovanna Phum Arts Association** stages traditional dancing and puppet theater every Friday and Saturday at 7:30pm. Traditional and folk dances can also be seen at the **Apsara Arts Association** every Saturday at 7:30pm. Films are screened at **Cinema Lux** and **Centre Culturel Français**.

Contemporary Music, Nightclubs, and Bars

The capital has a wide range of bars, cafés, and nightclubs. Live music enthusiasts have a couple of options, including the **Art Café** with its blues nights and classical Khmer music, and **Miles**, a rooftop jazz café. Performances of Khmer pop music take place in a number of the large, new hotels in Phnom Penh. **Green Vespa** is a down-to-earth, Irish-owned bar with a friendly atmosphere. Visitors seeking contemporary chic can head to the **Fly Lounge**, which has a cocktail lounge and a boutique pool. On the other hand, the **Foreign Correspondents' Club** has a friendly, yet sophisticated Colonial ambience. **Sharky's Bar** is one of the city's older sports bars with pool tables and a great bar. Siem Reap also has a range of bars and elegant watering holes. **Molly Malone's** is a typical Irish bar selling Guinness for thirsty visitors while **Miss Wong** trades on the nostalgia of 1920s Shanghai. **Angkor What?** has loud music to match its effusive atmosphere. **The Elephant Bar** at Raffles Grand Hotel d'Angkor is the epitome of style and elegance.

DIRECTORY

Traditional Dance, Theater, and Film

Apsara Arts Association
71, St 598, Phnom Penh.
Tel (023)-990-621.
🌐 apsara-art.org

Cinema Lux
44 Norodom Blvd, Phnom Penh. **City Map** E2.
Tel (012)-343-498.

Centre Culturel Français
218, St 184, Phnom Penh.
City Map D3.
Tel (023)-213-124.
🌐 ccf-cambodge.org

Sovanna Phum Arts Association
111, St 360, Chamkarmon, Phnom Penh.
Tel (023)-987-564.
🌐 shadow-puppets.org

Contemporary Music, Nightclubs, and Bars

Angkor What?
Pub St, Siem Reap.
Tel (012)-490-755.

Art Café
84, St 108, Phnom Penh.
City Map D1.
Tel (012)-834-517.

The Elephant Bar
Raffles Grand Hotel d'Angkor, Siem Reap.
🌐 raffles.com

Fly Lounge
St 148, Phnom Penh.
City Map E2.

Foreign Correspondents' Club
363 Sisowath Quay, Phnom Penh.
City Map E2.
Tel (023)-210-142.
🌐 fcccambodia.com

Green Vespa
95 Sisowath Quay, Phnom Penh. **City Map** E1.

Miles
310, St 113, Phnom Penh.
City Map C4.
Tel (011)-698-470.

Miss Wong
Passage (behind Pub St), Siem Reap.
Tel (092)-428-332.

Molly Malone's
Pub St, Siem Reap.
Tel (063)-963-533.
🌐 mollymalonescambodia.com

Sharky's Bar
126, St 130, Phnom Penh.
City Map E1.
Tel (012)-228-045.
🌐 sharkysofcambodia.com

Entertainment in Laos

The entertainment scene in Laos is fairly sedate since the government strictly regulates both closing times and the content of performances. There was a time when any music considered modern or foreign was prohibited. Since 2003, however, when the government relaxed its stance, Lao pop has emerged with a number of home-grown artistes. Vientiane has the widest choice of entertainment venues, followed by Luang Prabang. In smaller towns, things get very quiet after sunset. Performances of Lao classical music and dance, along with Lao folk music are staged in the capital and Luang Prabang, giving visitors a glimpse into Lao culture.

Visitors enjoying the laid-back atmosphere of a popular bar, Laos

Information

A free local monthly pocket-sized magazine called *Pai Sai*, found in hotels and restaurants in Vientiane, publishes listings of music, sports, drama, and film events. Visitors can even receive a daily SMS from the magazine with updates, provided they have a Lao SIM card for their cell phone. The government-owned *Vientiane Times* has a limited but useful selection of upcoming events, as does the monthly magazine *Society Lifestyle*. Other than this, small posters on lampposts around the tourist areas of Vientiane and Luang Prabang can be quite informative regarding upcoming events.

A musician playing a Sol

Traditional Dance and Theater

Both the classical culture represented by the *Phra Lak Phra Lam* (the Lao version of the Hindu epic, *Ramayana*), and the popular culture of Lao folk music, with its hypnotic rhythms, are interesting options. Performances of the *Phra Lak Phra Lam* can be seen at the **Lao National Opera Theater** in Vientiane, as well as in Luang Prabang at the **Royal Ballet Theater** within the grounds of the National Museum Complex. Folk music is also staged at these venues, but for a taste of the real thing, travelers should try to visit a temple fair, where audience participation, in the form of the *lam wong* dance, takes the performance to another level.

Films and Art Exhibitions

Although DVDs have spelled the end of movie theaters in Laos, foreign films are still shown by the cultural arms of certain embassies such as the **French Center**, and those of Japan, and Germany, but subtitles are not always in English. It is also worth visiting the **ITECC**, a local trade and convention center. Art exhibitions are found in embassy cultural centers, and there are plenty of private galleries in Vientiane and Luang Prabang displaying the work of Lao artists.

Contemporary Music, Clubs, and Bars

Vientiane and, to some extent, Luang Prabang have a growing nightlife. Although travelers tend to stick to hotel clubs, the **Wind West** has good live music. The biggest club, **Marina Disco**, also has a bowling alley. The **Khop Chai Deu** restaurant in Vientiane also has live music. In Luang Prabang, hotel cocktail lounges surpass clubs, although **The Hive** offers more upbeat music and an ethnic fashion show.

DIRECTORY

Traditional Dance and Theater

Lao National Opera Theater
Khun Bulom Rd, Vientiane.
City Map B3. **Tel** (021)-260-300.

Royal Ballet Theater
National Museum Complex,
Luang Prabang. **City Map** C3.
Tel (071)-253-705.

Films and Art Exhibitions

French Center
Lan Xang Avenue, Vientiane.
City Map D3. **Tel** (021)-214-764.

ITECC
Khampheng Muang Rd,
Vientiane. **City Map** B5.
Tel (021)-415-477.

Contemporary Music, Discos, and Bars

The Hive
Across Wat Aphay, Phou Si Rd,
Luang Prabang.
City Map D3.
Tel (071)-212-880.

Khop Chai Deu
Setthathirat Rd, Vientiane.
City Map B4. **Tel** (021)-223-022.
🌐 khopchaideu.com

Marina Disco
Luang Prabang Rd, Vientiane.
City Map A5. **Tel** (021)- 216-978.

Wind West
Luang Prabang Rd, Vientiane.
City Map A5.
Tel (021)-200-777.

OUTDOOR ACTIVITIES AND SPECIAL INTERESTS IN CAMBODIA

With its natural heritage of rivers, lakes, mountains, and a pristine coastline, Cambodia offers a wide choice of activities. While eco-trekking is developing in the northern wilderness, the western provinces offer wonderful camping excursions in safari-style tents, coupled with trekking among ancient ruins. The beaches of the south are perfect for snorkeling, diving, deep-sea fishing, sailing, and windsurfing.

Rolling hills and paddy fields also present superb opportunities for cyclists. Ornithologists and marine life enthusiasts can enjoy exploring the natural wonders of the Tonlé Sap Lake, which attracts a rich variety of endangered waterbirds. Those seeking a more relaxed holiday will not be disappointed by the meditation sessions and massages offered at upscale spas.

Diving and Snorkeling

Cambodia's fresh and clear waters, home to moray eels, barracuda, scorpion fish, lion fish, parrot fish, octopus, reef shark, dolphins, and whales, are a haven for divers. The seaside resort of Sihanoukville is perhaps the best place to undertake these trips, ideally between October and June, when underwater visibility is between 33–82 ft (10–25 m). With their rich, coral-encrusted reefs, the islands of Koh Rong Samloem and Koh Koun, lying a short distance from Sihanoukville, are among the best-known dive sites in Cambodia. Those with more time can venture farther out to Koh Tang, Koh Prins, and Condor Reef. There are several dive centers in Phnom Penh, including a number of authorized PADI (Professional Association of Diving Instructors)

centers. All of these centers organize trips of varying lengths, for different levels of experience. Those not keen on diving can ask centers to arrange day-long snorkeling trips.

Among the better-known centers are **Scuba Nation**, which pioneered diving in the country, **Angkor Dive**, Cambodia's first conservation-based dive center, **Eco Sea Dive**, and **The Dive Shop**.

Sailing, Kitesurfing, and Fishing

Watersports are very popular in Cambodia, and Sihanoukville, which has access to four great beaches, is the hub of all water-based activity. Kitesurfing, a relatively new and still evolving sport in the country, is offered by **Hurricane Windsurfing** on Otres Beach. It is one of the few places from where you can hire kitesurf boards. **Otres Beach 1 @ QueenCo Palm Beach** rents out catamarans and offers sailing lessons. A number of reliable outfits such as **Sankeor**, **Sun Tours**, and **Trade Winds Charters** also offer fishing of

barracuda and marlin in the deep sea. Fishing trips can last for one or several days, and rates are reasonable.

Sailing in Sihanoukville

Kayaking

Sea-kayaking is still finding its feet in Cambodia with only a few places offering kayaks for rent. Otres Nautica and **The Golden Sunset**, both on Otres Beach, can organize boat tours to neighboring islands. It is also possible to kayak without too much effort from Otres Beach to nearby Koh Chaluh. It is advisable to use plenty of sunscreen and to wear a hat.

Trekking and Elephant Riding

The best place to trek is undoubtedly in the remote regions of the northeast, namely Ratanakiri's Virachey National Park. Here, one- and three-day treks are organized by the **Virachey National Park Headquarters**. The undulating alpine hills of Mondulkiri also provide exciting trekking and elephant-riding trails. **Hanuman Tourism**'s trekking tours take in mountain lakes and some minority villages of the northeast, and also include elephant rides. In the south, both Ream and Bokor national parks offer

Snorkeler with a whale shark, Sihanoukville

one-day treks to the Cardamom Mountains with their picture-perfect waterfalls. Both parks are accessible from Koh Kong.

Tour organizers in Siem Reap also organize treks to remote Angkorian temples. **Terre Cambodge**, for instance, runs three-day safaris, on foot or by elephant, to isolated temples.

It is best to use the services of an experienced guide for these trekking trips and never venture alone, since UXO (Unexploded Ordnance) continues to pose a threat.

Braving a tough trail through the thick forests of northeast Cambodia

Zip Lining

Not for the faint hearted, zip lining is a popular adventure activity. **Flight of the Gibbon** runs zip line canopy tours inside Angkor Park. Tours include lunch, a shuttle service from Siem Reap, and a chance to see gibbons in their natural habitat.

Cycling

Cambodia's flat terrain is perfect for cycling and many travelers bring their own bikes. Mountainbiking in Ratanakiri and Mondulkiri provinces is particularly popular owing to challenging roads, bounteous countryside, and the rugged appeal of the area. A number of companies specializing in motorcycle and bicycle tours, including **Pepy Ride** and **Terre Cambodge**, organize regular excursions in these areas.

Cyclists, however, should be careful of rash driving by locals, unexpected obstacles in the form of cattle or children running across roads, and UXO on fresh or unexplored terrain. It is also better to bring your own supply of inner tubes and other spares as these are not readily available, especially for expensive foreign bicycle models.

Golf

Long associated with the Khmer elite, golf has been popular in Cambodia for many years. While major cities such as Siem Reap and Phnom Penh have some good courses, **Cambodia Golf**

and Country Club, situated some distance from Phnom Penh off Highway 4, was the country's very first course. **Phokeethra Country Club** is Siem Reap's first international standard 18-hole golf course. **Angkor Golf Course**, also in Siem Reap, has been rated by the Professional Golfers' Association of America (PGA), and is equally popular.

Bird-Watching

Cambodia is an ornithologist's paradise, thanks to the Tonlé Sap Lake and the host of migratory birds that nest there each year. These include the milky stork, black-headed ibis, gray-headed fish eagle, spot-billed pelican, and greater and lesser adjutants. These birds depend on the nutrient-rich water of the lake. The Prek Toal Bird Sanctuary, located in the heart of the Tonlé Sap Biosphere Reserve, is known to be the most important breeding ground for globally threatened large waterbirds in Southeast Asia. The biosphere, which covers an area of 120 sq miles (311 sq km), is best visited

View of Hole 13, Angkor Golf Course, Siem Reap

during the dry season when the water recedes and there are large numbers of migratory birds. Day trips can easily be arranged by your hotel or guesthouse in Siem Reap, as can overnight stays at the **Prek Toal Environment Research Station**, which is superb for viewing the birds at sunrise and sunset. In cooperation with the locals, **Sam Veasna Center**, based in Siem Reap, organizes full- and half-day trips to remote places such as Chepp, to see birds such as the Saurus crane and giant and white shouldered ibis.

Martial Arts

Kbach kun pradul, better known as kickboxing, is very popular across the country. Although a Thai might disagree, kickboxing in its purest form is said to have its roots from Khmer fighters. For thousands of years, senior figures in the military were expected to be proficient in martial arts, the oldest of which is *bogotao*. Unfortunately, this martial art is all but obsolete today with only one local, an octogenarian, still alive with knowledge of this form. Many martial arts masters were also prosecuted under the Khmer Rouge. Since the end of the regime, efforts have been made to restore these ancient traditions. Kickboxing events are held regularly in Sihanoukville and Siem Reap, but most notably at the **Phnom Penh National Olympic Stadium**. Those interested in learning the art can visit **Paddy's Fight Club and Gym**, also in Phnom Penh, which is renowned for its excellent training sessions.

Cooking Courses

Cambodian cuisine is fast becoming popular with international visitors who are keen to take back some of its culinary secrets. You can enrol in **Cambodia Cooking Class** in Phnom Penh, or in **The River Garden Guesthouse** and **Le Tigre De Papier** in Siem Reap, which also offer cooking classes.

Cooking class in progress at Le Tigre De Papier, Siem Reap

Spas

Once a byword for refinement, comfort, and panache under the French Colonialists, traditional spa treatments are regaining popularity in the country. Developers keen to cater to increasing numbers of visitors are restoring antique Gallic villas and turning them into chic spa boutiques, providing excellent service. There are several such spas in both Phnom Penh and Siem Reap where you can not only enjoy a relaxing spa treatment but also taste the finest of wines. The treatments at **Spa Indochine** at Hotel De La Paix in Siem Reap are well regarded as are those at **Amara Spa** in Phnom Penh. Those on a tighter budget can try the **Seeing Hands Massage**, where the masseurs are blind.

DIRECTORY

Diving and Snorkeling

Angkor Dive
Serendipity Beach, Koh Rong, Sihanoukville.
Tel (096)-224-5474.

The Dive Shop
Serendipity Beach Rd, Sihanoukville. **Tel** (034)-933-664. ⓦ diveshopcambodia.com

Eco Sea Dive
Serendipity Beach, Sihanoukville. **Tel** (012)-654-104. ⓦ ecoseadive.com

Scuba Nation
Mohachai Guesthouse, Serendipity Beach Rd, Sihanoukville.
Tel (012)-604-680.
ⓦ divecambodia.com

Sailing, Kitesurfing, and Fishing

Hurricane Windsurfing
Otres Beach, Sihanoukville.
Tel (017)-471-604.

Otres Beach 1 @ QueenCo Palm Beach
Otres Beach, Sihanoukville.
Tel (034)-633-8484.

Sankeor
Victory Beach, Sihanoukville. **Tel** (099)-905-430.

Sun Tours
Sihanoukville. **Tel** (016)-396-201. ⓦ suntours-cambodia.com

Trade Winds Charters
Snookeys Restaurant and Bar, Sihanoukville.
Tel (034)-677-3444.

Kayaking

The Golden Sunset
Golden Sunset Beach Restaurant, end of Otres Beach, Sihanoukville.
Tel (012)-812-087.

Trekking and Elephant Riding

Hanuman Tourism
12, St 310, Phnom Penh.
City Map C4. **Tel** (023)-218-396. ⓦ hanumantourism.com

Terre Cambodge
Hup Guan St, Siem Reap.
Tel (077)-448- 255.
ⓦ terre cambodge.com

Virachey National Park Headquarters
Department of Environment, Ban Lung, Ratanakiri.
Tel (077)-965-196.
ⓦ virachey ecotourism.blogspot.com

Zip Lining

Flight of the Gibbon
Angkor Park. **Tel** (096)-999-9101. ⓦ treetopasia.com/cambodia-holiday/angkor

Cycling

Pepy Ride
PO Box 93220, GPO Siem Reap. **Tel** (063)-690-5465.
ⓦ pepycambodia.org

Golf

Angkor Golf Course
Kasekam village, Siem Reap. **Tel** (063)-767-688.
ⓦ angkor-golf.com

Cambodia Golf and Country Club
Sang Kreach Tieng, St 222, Phnom Penh.
City Map D3.
Tel (012)-811-778.
ⓦ cambodiagolf.net

Phokeethra Country Club
Angkor Wat, Siem Reap.
Tel (063)-964-600.
ⓦ phokeethra golf.com

Bird-Watching

Prek Toal Environment Research Station
Osmose Tonlé Sap, Siem Reap. **Tel** (012)-832-812.
ⓦ osmose tonlesap.net

Sam Veasna Center
552, Group 12, Wat Bo, Siem Reap.
Tel (063)-963-710.
ⓦ samveasna.org

Martial Arts

Paddy's Fight Club and Gym
63, St 294, Phnom Penh.
City Map D5.
Tel (012)-217-877.
ⓦ paddysgym.com

Phnom Penh National Olympic Stadium
Blvd Samdech Preah Sihanouk, Phnom Penh.
City Map C3.

Cooking Courses

Cambodia Cooking Class
67, St 240, Phnom Penh.
City Map E3. **Tel** (012)-524-801. ⓦ cambodia-cooking-class.com

The River Garden Guesthouse
113 Mondul, 111 Phoum Treang, Siem Reap.
Tel (063)-963-400.
ⓦ therivergarden.info

Le Tigre de Papier
La Residence, Siem Reap.
Tel (012)-265-811.
ⓦ angkor-cooking-class-cambodia.com

Spas

Amara Spa
Sisowath Quay, Phnom Penh. **City Map** E1.
Tel (023)-998-730.

Seeing Hands Massage
77Eo, Sothearos Blvd (St.), Phnom Penh.
City Map D1.
Tel (092)-260-910.
ⓦ seeinghandmassage.com

Spa Indochine
Hotel De La Paix, Sivatha Blvd, Siem Reap.
Tel (063)-966-000.

OUTDOOR ACTIVITIES AND SPECIAL INTERESTS IN LAOS

With its stunning landscape and remote getaways, Laos is any adventure traveler's dream destination. Visitors can choose from a variety of itineraries, which include trekking, cycling, kayaking, and elephant riding, in a single day. Many prefer focused trips, especially for trekking – the most popular activity here. It is not necessary to join a tour either – those keen to go cycling or kayaking can import their own gear and set off independently. Those looking for relaxing pastimes will find plenty of activities to fill their days – from cooking courses to traditional techniques of weaving and dyeing. Laos is one of the few places where visitors can take a course in elephant tending. Studying with a master mahout, visitors can learn the basics of feeding, bathing, controlling, and taking care of these incredible beasts.

Trekkers negotiating a path through the wilderness in Luang Nam Tha

Trekking

The Lao government has established 20 National Protected Areas (NPAs), some of which are open to trekkers. Tour companies employ the services of local guides, and trekkers usually spend the night at a local village. Such community-based tourism, an excellent way to pump money into local communities and involve them in environmental protection, is being increasingly encouraged. While trekking is possible throughout the country, certain areas, such as the Nam Ha National Protected Area, have earned a reputation for being particularly diverse and fascinating. Treks are organized by **Vientiane Orchidées**, based in Vientiane, and **Green Discovery** and the **Nam Ha Eco-Guide Unit**, which have offices in Luang Nam Tha.

Cycling

With its low vehicular traffic and spectacular scenery, Laos is an ideal destination for cycling. Mountain bikes are particularly suitable, since most of the best routes still include unpaved sections. Local tour operators offer either one-day rides or several-day tours, but serious cyclists usually arrive with their own bikes and set out independently. Particularly popular is the route from the northern port of entry at Huay Xai on the Thai border to Luang Prabang, a several-day ride through mountains and forests involving some serious climbs. From Luang Prabang, Route 13 extends farther south to Vang Vieng, Vientiane, and eventually to the Cambodian border. These are demanding rides, but if things get too arduous, it is always possible to continue the rest of the way on a bus. For fully supported countrywide tours, **Spice Roads**, in Thailand, is by far the best operator. In Luang Prabang, **Tiger Trail** organizes trips lasting a day or longer. The website www.biking-laos. com is also useful.

Kayaking and Rafting

The many rivers in Laos also provide great opportunities for kayaking and rafting. It is possible to undertake this independently, although taking advantage of local knowledge, logistical support, and equipment is recommended. All major rivers are navigable, and the areas east of Thakhek in Khammuan province receive particularly good reviews. The Green Discovery office in Thakhek provides all necessary information. It also has an office in Luang Prabang.

Kayakers beginning their journey on the Nam Song, Vang Vieng

An adventure sports enthusiast trying an exciting zip line over a waterfall in the forests of southern Laos

Spelunking and Rock Climbing

The limestone karsts of Laos offer world-class opportunities for spelunkers. Except for those who are experts, spelunking is best undertaken with the help of a local guide because it can be very dangerous. Besides this, many caves still remain relatively unexplored and are known only to locals. Vang Vieng is regarded as the national center for this activity since the caves here are superb and well explored. Experienced spelunkers can also try the area around Phu Hin Pun NPA in Khammuan province, which is deemed to be the best in the country.

The karst formations of Laos also lend themselves well to rock climbing. Again, the area around Vang Vieng has the most activity. Here, dozens of bolted and mapped routes of varying difficulty await the climber. Some climbing also takes place around Luang Prabang. **Green Discovery** and **Adam's Rock Climbing School** in Vang Vieng organize spelunking and rock-climbing tours. The website www.laos-climbing.com is also worth looking at.

Zip lining

Not as physically demanding as other outdoor adventures, zip lining can be a lot of fun. Typically, zip lines run above the jungle canopy and provide a great way to spend a day. The most popular zip line tour is offered by **Flight of the Nature** at the Tat Sae Waterfalls near Luang Prabang. Flight of Nature also offers elephant trekking. At Nam Lik, between Vang Vieng and Vientiane, there is another zip line. Those who prefer a longer, more thrilling experience with excellent zip line facilities and the opportunity to spy on the elusive Laotian black gibbon, should try **The Gibbon Experience**, near Huay Xai. The place also provides night stays in a fascinating treehouse deep within the jungle.

Elephant Activities

Riding an elephant has now become an almost mandatory part of a visit to Laos. Tours are available throughout the country, particularly in the north. For those interested in gaining a deeper knowledge of the subject, *mahout* courses teach the basics of tending to these giant mammals. Courses are usually offered in Luang Prabang by **Elephant Village** and the **Mahout Lodge**. An alternative is a multi-day safari through the jungles of Sainyabuli province, usually starting from the town of Hong Sa and finishing at the Mekong River. This safari is offered by the well-known **ElefantAsia**.

Cooking Courses

A great way for visitors to gain insight into the culture and traditions of the country, cooking courses are usually a full day affair, and begin with a visit to the market to buy ingredients. This is followed by the actual hands-on cooking of the meal, and finally enjoying the fruits of your labor. For true aficionados, however, several-day courses are usually a better choice. Luang Prabang is the best place to try out your culinary skills. Courses are offered by the **Tamarind Cooking School** and the **Tamnak Lao Restaurant**. **Villa Lao Guesthouse** also runs several good cooking courses.

Textile Courses

The hand-woven textiles of Laos are an important aspect of the country's culture. Visitors can

Visitors undergoing *mahout* training at a camp near Mohout's Tomb

enrol in courses that explore the traditional arts of silk-weaving and dyeing. But these are not vocational training classes; rather they confer an appreciation for the skill and the patience this ancient art requires. Course attendees are able to keep a sample of their own work. Courses are offered at the workshops of **Ock Pop Tok** in Luang Prabang, and **Houey Hong Vocational Training Center for Women**, an NGO working to reinvigorate traditional skills among local women, in Vientiane.

Spectators enjoying a match of *kataw* in the evening

Spectator Sports

There are two unique sports worth looking out for in Laos. The first, *kataw*, is better known as *sepak takraw*, and is similar to volleyball, but it allows only the use of the feet and head. The ball is made from rattan, and is half the size of a volleyball. Informal matches are usually held in temple compounds in the evenings, but for serious competition, contact the **Lao Kataw Federation**.

Muay lao, or Lao boxing, differs from Western versions of the sport in that the feet are also used. Matches are held at the **Sok Sai Boxing Stadium**. It is also hard to miss the games of *pétanque*, a French legacy, played by the roadside in the evenings throughout Laos.

DIRECTORY

Trekking

Green Discovery
Route 7, Luang Nam Tha.
Tel (021)-223-022.
w greendiscovery
laos.com

Nam Ha Eco- Guide Unit
Behind the Night Market, Luang Nam Tha.
Tel (020)-9944-0084.
w namha-npa.org

Vientiane Orchidées
642/37, Ban Phonethong Tchomany, Vientiane.
Tel (021)-560-444.

Cycling

Spice Roads
14/1-B Soi Promsi 2, Sukhumvit, Bangkok, Thailand. Tel +66 (0) 2 381 7490. w spiceroads.com

Tiger Trail
Sisavang Vong Rd, Luang Prabang. **City Map** C3.
Tel (071)-252-655.

Spelunking and Rock Climbing

Adam's Rock Climbing School
Route 13, N of Wat Kang, Vang Vieng.
Tel (020)-501-0832.

Green Discovery
Route 13, next to Xayoh Restaurant, Vang Vieng.
Tel (023)-511-230.

Zip lining

Flight of the Nature
Tat Sae Waterfalls, Luang Prabang.
Tel (020)-434-8748.
w flightofthenature.com

The Gibbon Experience
Main road, S of Sabaidee Guest House, Huay Xai.
Tel (084)-212-021.
w gibbon experience.org

Elephant Activities

ElefantAsia
Ban Khunta, Vientiane.
City Map A5.
w elefantasia.org

Elephant Village
Xieng Lom village, Luang Prabang.
Tel (071)-212-311.
w elephantvillage-laos.com

Mahout Lodge
Ban Nonsavath (near Mouhot's tomb), Luang Prabang. **City Map** C3.
Tel (071)-254-547.
w mahoutlodge.com

Cooking Courses

Tamarind Cooking School
Kounxoa Rd, opp Wat Nong, Luang Prabang.
City Map C3
Tel (071)-213-128.
w tamarindlaos.com

Tamnak Lao Restaurant
Sakkarin Rd, across from Villa Santi, Luang Prabang.
City Map D3.
Tel (071)-252-525.
w tamnaklao.net

Villa Lao Guesthouse
Near Northern Bus Station, Vientiane.
City Map A4.
Tel (021)-242-292.
w villa-lao-guesthouse.com

Textile Courses

Ock Pop Tok
Next to L'Elephant Restaurant, Ban Wat Nong, Luang Prabang.
City Map C3.
Tel (071)-212-597.
w ockpoptok.com

Houey Hong Vocational Training Center for Women
Lane 19, Houey Hong village, Vientiane.
Tel (021)-560-006.
w houeyhongcentre.com

Spectator Sports

Lao Kataw Federation
National Stadium, Vientiane. **City Map** C3.
Tel (020)-569-4355.

Sok Sai Boxing Stadium
Thong Khan Kham Rd, Vientiane.
Tel (021)-212-459.

SURVIVAL
GUIDE

PRACTICAL INFORMATION

Both Cambodia and Laos are rapidly developing tourist destinations. New and improved road networks and better facilities have made access possible even to the remote parts of these countries. Old Colonial villas in cities such as Siem Reap, Phnom Penh, Vientiane, and Luang Prabang have been restored as trendy boutique hotels, while restaurants in even the most isolated places are beginning to offer a variety of cuisines. Unlike Laos, tour operators in Cambodia, with a few exceptions, have been slow to develop. However, savvy customer-focused companies, specializing in ecotourism and sightseeing in and around Angkor, are now burgeoning. Laos, on the other hand, is regarded as an ecotourism blueprint for the developing world, with vast protected areas open for responsible trekking companies.

Colorful umbrellas lining the seafront at Occheuteal Beach

When to Go

Cambodia and Laos are both tropical countries and generally all hot year round. The temperature during the hot season, from March to May, usually exceeds 40°C (104°F), and exploring temples, especially in Cambodia, can be an unpleasantly humid affair. A few mountainous regions in Laos, however, have cool weather throughout the year.

It is possible to visit during the rainy season, from July to September, since the downpours usually last only a few hours in the late afternoon, and visitors can make the most of deserted beaches and archaeological ruins; besides, accommodations are cheaper and easily available. However, most unpaved roads are washed away by flooding and heavy rain during this time.

The best time to visit is during the cool season, from October to January, soon after the monsoon, when both countries glimmer with verdant paddy fields, wooded mountains, and a welcome breeze that caresses the land. The ideal months are December and January. By mid-February the temperatures are already rising.

What to Take

Although most necessary items can be bought in major cities such as Siem Reap and Luang Prabang, as well as the capital cities of both countries, it is best to bring your own supply of important items. Wide-brimmed hats are highly recommended, as is a good quality sunscreen. For those planning trekking trips in the remote Cardamom Mountains or Northern Laos, a sturdy pair of walking boots is a must, as is insect repellant. Dengue and malaria are quite common in both these countries and a mosquito repellent as well as anti-malaria pills are strongly recommended. Those traveling during the rainy season can buy rain ponchos in most towns. For the cooler months, a sweatshirt is usually advisable because the evenings can be chilly, especially in the north.

Visas and Passports

It is essential to have a visa when entering Cambodia by land, air, or sea. A tourist visa is usually issued for short stays. Visitors disembarking at Siem Reap and Phnom Penh airports, or entering Cambodia by land, automatically receive this one-month visa at borders. This can be applied for in advance, since the formalities are minimal and the visa is processed surprisingly swiftly. Those applying for a visa on arrival should carry a passport-sized photograph, otherwise they will be charged an additional fee (although it is quite nominal). Those planning to extend their stay by a couple of months should apply for a business visa, which can be extended for long periods with multiple entries; tourist visas provide the option of extending the stay only once, and for a single month.

Trekkers interacting with a local guide during a trek in Luang Nam Tha

◀ Bicycles available for rent in Vientiane

Those overstaying their visa are usually charged an additional fee for each extra day.

The cost of a visa to Laos depends on the visitor's nationality and can be acquired on arrival at Vientiane, Luang Prabang, and Pakse airports, as well as the land borders at Nong Khai, Chiang Khong (on the Thailand-Laos border), and Savannakhet. Visitors must bring along two passport-sized photographs, since there are no provisions for getting one taken there. Visa extensions are painless affairs and cost a few dollars for every extra day up to a maximum of 30 days. The immigration office in Vientiane is well equipped to handle visa proceedings, although this can also be done through a travel agency.

Immunization

Medical facilities in Cambodia and Laos are not very dependable. Visitors suffering from a serious injury, or from an illness that requires specialized treatment, may need to be evacuated to neighboring Thailand for help. Getting immunized against some of the widespread diseases is therefore advisable. These include Hepatitis A and B, tuberculosis, typhoid, yellow fever, polio, diptheria, tetanus, and Japanese B encephalitis. Malaria can be a problem in remote parts of these countries, but taking a dose of prophylactics during the stay is not required unless traveling to such areas.

Medical treatment for foreign visitors in Cambodia and Laos is expensive and visitors need to have medical insurance, while ensuring that their travel documents are on hand in the event of an emergency.

Customs Information

Customs regulations in both Cambodia and Laos are relatively relaxed compared with neighboring countries. Visitors can officially enter and exit both countries with one bottle of

spirits, a carton of 200 cigarettes, as well as a moderate amount of perfume or aftershave. Cigarettes in both Cambodia and Laos are quite inexpensive and a carton of 200 usually costs around US$10. However, the authorities are quite tough on the import of drugs, guns, and pornography. A maximum of US$10,000 in cash can be brought into the countries.

Tourist Information

There are very few tourist offices in Cambodia apart from those in cities such as Phnom Penh and Siem Reap. The staff in the tourist offices in Phnom Penh are usually not very helpful and may not always be fluent in English. While the best source of information is usually the local listings guide or the hotel information desk, visitors can also consult the helpful **Canby Publications** website for the latest offerings. Siem Reap has plenty of tourist offices that can help visitors to plan their itinerary to the temples of Angkor, but even here, the best source of information is usually a hotel or even a busy guesthouse.

Tourist information in Laos, however, is easier to come by with the helpful **Lao National Tourism Administration**, which has offices in most major cities. The staff is usually eager and helpful, and will have brochures and other handy information about trekking and other activities, although they

Travelers outside a tour agency in Huay Xai, Laos

may not be very fluent in English or other languages.

Admission Charges

Most museums, zoos, and botanical gardens in Cambodia and Laos charge an entry fee between US$1–5. Entry to the countries' active *wats* is usually free. However, it is customary to make a donation toward the upkeep of the temple.

Entrance tickets to Angkor, and the National Museum and Silver Pagoda

Time and Calendar

Cambodia and Laos are 7 hours ahead of Greenwich Mean Time (GMT), 15 hours ahead of Pacific Standard Time (PST), and 12 hours ahead of Eastern Standard Time (EST). Although the Western Gregorian calendar is used for official and commercial purposes in these countries, the lunar calendar is still used for religious purposes, and for calculating the dates of festivals.

Measurements

Both countries have been using the metric system since the Colonial era.
Imperial to Metric
1 inch = 2.54 centimeters
1 foot = 30 centimeters
1 mile = 1.6 kilometers
1 ounce = 28 grams
1 pound = 454 grams
1 US quart = 0.947 liter
1 US gallon = 3.6 liters

Metric to Imperial
1 millimeter = 0.04 inch
1 centimeter = 0.4 inch
1 meter = 3 feet 3 inches
1 kilometer = 0.6 mile
1 gram = 0.04 ounces
1 kilogram = 2.2 pounds
1 liter = 2.1 pints

Two-prong electric plugs used in Cambodia and Laos

Electricity

The electric current for both Cambodia and Laos is 220 volts. While flat, American-style pins and French-style rounded pins are most commonly used, multi-prong plugs are also in use. It is advisable to buy a multi-purpose adaptor beforehand. Power cuts are the norm, and visitors should ensure that they keep a flashlight handy by the bed, or in their pocket.

Facilities for the Disabled

Unfortunately, Cambodia and Laos are ill-equipped for disabled travelers, with unkept pavements, poor quality roads, high curbs, and crowded buses. Although much of Cambodia is flat and major tourist attractions such as Angkor Wat (see pp70–71) are easily accessible by wheelchairs, the more remote provinces can prove to be quite a challenge, since hotels are not usually equipped with elevators, nor are there any toilet facilities for the disabled. Laos is even more difficult with its mountainous roads and lack of facilities for the disabled.

Facilities for Children

Khmer and Lao people love children, be it their own or other peoples. Children can expect to be treated with affection wherever they go. However, facilities for children leave a lot to be desired anywhere far from major hotels and capital cities. Separate beds and highchairs are available only in upscale establishments, and there are no special meals for children. Hired cars rarely have seats for strapping infants, and parents need to be especially vigilant

about letting children walk the streets unattended in the capitals – tuk-tuk drivers can be careless and accidents are not uncommon. Despite these shortcomings, there is enough to keep children amused and occupied. The Phnom Tamao Wildlife Rescue Center (see p61) in Phnom Penh, for instance, and the city's many swimming pools offer enough opportunities for fun. Alternatively, boat trips down the Mekong River are enjoyed by most children, as are visits to the ancient Angkorian ruins such as Ta Prohm (see pp82–3). An aerial view of Angkor Wat from a hot air balloon would also be appealing to most kids. This can be followed by shadow puppets at the Sovanna Phum Arts Association (see p238) in Phnom Penh.

Provinces such as Ratanakiri have waterfalls and offer elephant rides, which make for many lasting memories. In the south, there are plenty of gently shelving beaches, including Otres (see p109), which are child-friendly, although parents need to keep a watch since the current can get dangerously strong at times.

In Laos, Xieng Khuan (see p148) is a quirky place; children love the variety of statues. Vientiane also offers several opportunities for a refreshing swim with its many clean swimming pools. For children who enjoy the outdoors, trekking in the north is an excellent option. A visit to the Tat Kuang Si Falls (see p169) in Luang Prabang is a

A family enjoying a meal at a restaurant in Phnom Penh

wonderful experience, as are the resident sun bears rescued from poachers. Elephant rides can also be organized in Luang Prabang, and children often enjoy the magical Night Market (see pp158–9) with its authentic Oriental feel and delectable food.

Language

Khmer is the official language of Cambodia, spoken by almost 90 percent of its population, while the official language of Laos is Lao. Used since the 7th century AD, Khmer script appears similar to Thai but is in fact much older, originating in India. It is not an easy language to learn, but its non-tonality makes it easier than Thai or Vietnamese. English is widely spoken in most major hotels, restaurants, and tour offices. French is also spoken by the older generations, a hangover from the days of French Colonialism.

Sign outside a temple in Laos

Photography

Among Southeast Asia's most photographically rewarding countries, Cambodia and Laos offer visitors abundant opportunities to take good pictures. However, there is certain etiquette to be followed when photographing monks – photographers must seek their permission before capturing them on camera and never get in their way. Followers of animism may not react well to having their portrait taken as they believe it steals a part of their soul. Recent measures to protect children from Western pedophiles have also raised awareness and suspicion. Visitors should be careful of photographing children.

Western-standard hardware, from tripods to digital cameras, is available in major cities such as Phnom Penh, Siem Reap, Vientiane, and Luang Prabang, as are memory cards and batteries. With the growing popularity of digital photography, film rolls are no longer widely available. Printing of photographs is easy

Shooting panoramic views from Mt Phou Si

and quite inexpensive, especially in Cambodia, where shops and Internet cafés will readily burn a CD or DVD for a charge.

Etiquette

Cambodians and Lao are very polite and placid people. Cambodians can get easily offended, but more often than not, they will refrain from confrontation. It is best to bear a few things in mind when interacting with the locals.

The traditional greeting in both countries is offered by pressing the hands together as if in prayer and bowing slightly, and it is polite to return the greeting in the same way. Losing one's temper is seen as a loss of face, indeed Lao people use the term *jai yen* (cool heart) to describe their preferred state of equilibrium. The fastest way for a foreigner to exacerbate any situation is to lose his or her temper, and such behavior should be avoided.

When entering a temple, visitors must remove their hat and shoes, and turn their feet away from any sacred statue when sitting down. Visitors must also be appropriately dressed in a long-sleeved shirt or T-shirt; women should avoid showing too much skin when entering a *wat*. The top of the head is regarded as the repository of the soul, and visitors must avoid touching anyone, child or adult, on the head.

Visitors to Laos should take special care to respect the allowed atmosphere of calm while observing the morning almsgiving ceremony (*tak bat*). Flash photography is not allowed, and it is best to maintain an appropriate distance.

Visitors at a temple, sitting with feet facing away from Buddha statues

Sunbathing in bikinis is considered offensive, except in Southern Cambodia where it is viewed as acceptable. Lastly, when offered a drink or something to eat, it is polite to take at least a sip or a bite to prevent the host from losing face.

Responsible Travel

Owing to their slow rate of development, Cambodia and Laos are not yet in a position to consider carbon emissions as an environmental priority. Less polluting fuels, such as gasohol and Liquid Petroleum Gas (LPG), have not yet found their way into these countries, which use benzene and diesel to power vehicles. Hopefully, the many hydroelectric dams being built, especially in Laos, will provide a cleaner source of fuel in the future.

There are, nevertheless, a few choices that an informed traveler can make to lessen the ecological impact of a trip. In general, shared transport, such as buses or ferries, emit less carbon per person than private vehicles. When renting a motorcycle, visitors should avoid the highly polluting two-stroke engine bikes. Water transport, such as the speedboats that ply the Mekong River are not only dangerous, but also polluting and should be avoided. Visitors should consider hiring a bicycle for long excursions and walking for shorter distances.

DIRECTORY

Embassies

Australia
16B, National Assembly St, Phnom Penh.
City Map E3.
Tel (023)-213-470.
Nehru Blvd, Ban Phonxai, Vientiane.
City Map D3.
Tel (021)-413-600.
w **cambodia.embassy. gov.au**

China
156 Mao Tse Toung Blvd, Phnom Penh.
City Map C5.
Tel (023)-720-920.

Ban Wat Nak, Vientiane.
City Map A5.
Tel (021)-315-105.

France
1 Monivong Blvd, Phnom Penh. **Tel** (023)-430-020.
Setthathirat Rd, Vientiane.
City Map D4.
Tel (021)-215-258.

Germany
76–78, St 254, Phnom Penh. **City Map** D3.
Tel (023)-216-381.
Sok Pa Luang Rd, Vientiane.
City Map A5.
Tel (021)-312-111.

Thailand
196 Norodom Blvd, Phnom Penh. **City Map** E5.
Tel (023)-726-306.
Kuvoravong Rd, Vientiane.
City Map E2.
Tel (021)-212-373.

UK
27, St 75, Phnom Penh.
Tel (023)-427-124.

USA
1, St 96, Phnom Penh.
City Map D1.
Tel (023)-728-000.
That Dam Rd, Vientiane.
City Map C3.
Tel (021)-267-000.

Tourist Information

Canby Publications
w **canbypublications. com**

Lao National Tourism Administration
Lan Xang Ave, Chanthabuli, Vientiane.
City Map D3.
Tel (021)-212-248.
w **tourismlaos.org**

Personal Health and Security in Cambodia

Cambodia is a relatively safe country to travel in. The primary dangers visitors might face are posed by pickpockets, motorcycle thieves, or crafty tuk-tuk drivers overcharging them. Visitors should refrain from wearing flashy jewelry and from using expensive gadgets in public. Healthcare facilities are quite poor, except in main cities, and visitors should ensure that their health insurance makes provision for a medical evacuation.

One of several pharmacies in and around the center of Siem Reap

General Precautions

The days of impoverished, war-torn Cambodia, especially in Phnom Penh, are long over. Even though there is a concentration of arms in the capital, it rarely affects foreigners. Visitors should keep an eye out for pickpockets, con artists, and purse-snatchers. It is also advisable to take a licensed taxi at night to avoid getting mugged. Visitors should also be wary of the fact that prostitution is on the rise, and the country has one of the highest incidences of HIV infection in Southeast Asia.

Cambodia is one of the most mined countries in the world, with UXO (Unexploded Ordnance) still scattered in the remote northeast, and Khmer Rouge-laid mines in the west around Battambang and Pailin. Visitors should exercise caution in these areas, use a guide, and never stray from marked paths.

A general travel insurance, which covers theft, accident, and illness is also vital.

Police

Cambodia has a limited number of tourist police in cities that are frequented by foreigners, such as Phnom Penh, Siem Reap,

and Sihanoukville. Tourist police officials speak English but can be reluctant to fill in insurance details should you suffer theft or other criminal offences. Visitors should be careful in cities such as Sihanoukville, where gun mugging and pickpocketing are common after dark. In remote areas, where tourist police officials are not available, contact the regular police station.

Medical Facilities

Standards of hygiene are not always high in Cambodia, and the most common ailment contracted by travelers is diarrhoea, which affects 30–50 percent of visitors within the first couple of weeks. It is best dealt with by resting and drinking plenty of water. Diseases such as giardiasis and amoebic dysentery, contracted through food, can be prevented by washing hands before each meal and avoiding roadside eateries. Water-borne diseases such as typhoid and cholera are not uncommon either; it is advisable to avoid consuming tap water or ice.

Over exposure to the sun can be prevented by wearing a hat, taking breaks while sightseeing, and drinking plenty of water.

Mosquito bites are another nuisance. Most mosquitoes do not carry malaria or dengue, but visitors should exercise caution by using a mosquito net or repellent.

The **International SOS Medical Center** in Phnom Penh, and the **Royal Angkor International Hospital** and **Angkor Hospital for Children** in Siem Reap are equipped to handle minor health problems such as an upset stomach or a fever. The **Royal**

DIRECTORY

Emergency Numbers

Fire Service
Tel (063)-760-133 or 118.

Police
Tel (011)-997-296 or 117.

Tourist Police
Tel (012)-942-484 (Phnom Penh).
Tel (012)-402-424 (Siem Reap).

Medical Facilities

Angkor Hospital for Children
Achar Maen St, Siem Reap.
Tel (063)-963-409.
w angkorhospital.org

International SOS Medical Center
161, St 51, Phnom Penh.
City Map D2. **Tel** (023)-216-911.

Royal Angkor International Hospital
Airport Rd, Siem Reap.
Tel (063)-761-888. w royal angkorhospital.com

Royal Phnom Penh Hospital
888 Russian Confederation Blvd, Phnom Penh. **Tel** (023)-991-000. w royalphnompenhhospital.com

Phnom Penh Hospital in Phnom Penh is well equipped with modern facilities and staff speak English. In case of serious illness or injury, however, visitors should head to Bangkok. World Nomads (www.worldnomads. com) can evacuate you from the country to better facilities. It is advisable to visit a private clinic rather than provincial hospitals, which are usually under-equipped. Antibiotics and anti-malaria medication can be bought over the counter in most pharmacies in urban areas.

Visitors wearing hats to escape the scorching heat

Personal Health and Security in Laos

Visitors to Laos do not need to worry about safety, but a few general precautions should be taken to avoid petty crime such as pilfering and purse snatching in larger towns. Traveling on public transport is safe. Food is also generally safe, although bottled water is a must. UXO still poses a problem, but only in the most remote areas. However, medical facilities are quite poor and visitors should have traveler's insurance that includes medical evacuation.

Street food, best avoided by those with a delicate stomach

General Precautions

Violent crime against visitors is unheard of in Laos, but theft is not. It is best to keep an eye on your baggage, especially when using public transport, and to look out for purse snatchers who operate in pairs on motorcycles. Ideally, large sums of money should be kept in the hotel safe, and visitors should be wary of bystanders when changing money or using an unguarded ATM.

Although UXO continues to pose a problem, statistically, the chances of a visitor suffering injuries caused by this is quite low. Nevertheless, it is best to stick to marked paths or to follow guides closely in rural areas. Visitors are also cautioned to never pick up anything that remotely resembles a grenade.

Drug trafficking is another danger visitors need to be wary of. Foreigners are often approached as potential customers for illegal drugs, but they should be aware that the Lao government is anxious to ensure that the country is not known as a drug tourist destination. Those found dealing in drugs

usually face severe penalties, and the government has no qualms about prosecuting foreigners.

Visitors should also take precautions against accidents on roads. Sidewalks in Vientiane, in particular, have large holes. Speedboats on the Mekong River are also best avoided because they can be dangerous.

Police

A lingering suspicion about foreign spies still prevails in the country, and visitors must not take pictures of soldiers or military bases. Although attempts to pull scams on foreigners are not common, visitors need to take care of their own safety since police officials in Laos do not speak English, and may not be very helpful if anything goes wrong.

Laos does not have any designated tourist police officials. In case of a mishap with a foreign national, a local English teacher is usually called on to translate.

Medical Facilities

The most common ailments that affect visitors are usually food or water-borne diseases such as diarrhea, mild dysentery, or intestinal parasites.

DIRECTORY

Emergency Numbers

Ambulance
Tel 195.

Fire Service
Tel 190.

Police
Tel 191.

Medical Facilities

Aek Udon Hospital
Udon Thani, Thailand. **Tel** (042)-342-555. W **aekudon.com**

Mahosot International Clinic
Fa Ngum Rd, Vientiane.
City Map C4. **Tel** (021)-214-022.

US Centers for Disease Control
W **cdc.gov**

UK Department of Health
W **doh.gov.uk**

These illnesses are usually not serious and can be treated locally. In case of a serious infection, however, visitors should head to a hospital or medical center in a larger city. A wide range of imported medicines is available at pharmacies in Vientiane.

Foreign visitors report good care for minor medical matters at the **Mahosot International Clinic** in Vientiane, but a serious illness is best addressed across the border in Thailand. The **Aek Udon Hospital** in Udon Thani, Thailand, about 50 miles (80 km) from Vientiane, can dispatch an ambulance to Laos. For information on any current disease outbreaks or recommended vaccinations, foreign nationals should consult the websites of the **US Centers for Disease Control**, as well as that of the **UK Department of Health**.

Typical police vehicle, common in the streets of Vientiane

Banking and Currency in Cambodia

Travelers should carry a fair amount of riel or US dollars at all times. The US dollar is readily accepted in supermarkets and shops, and prices are given in both US dollars and riel. ATMs are common in Phnom Penh, Sihanoukville, and Siem Reap but absent in rural areas. Visitors must be aware that there are no banks near Cambodian land borders. Visa and MasterCard are accepted in upscale restaurants, boutiques, hotels, and travel agents. A pre-loaded currency card is also a good way to pay with minimal risk. The exchange rate hovers at 4,000 riel to a US dollar.

Banks and Banking Hours

Cambodia's leading banks e **Cathay United Bank**, **Acleda Bank**, **Cambodia Commercial Bank**, **Cambodia Asia Bank**, and **Canadia Bank**. **ANZ Royal Bank** is the most well-known international bank. All these banks have an ATM presence across the major cities, and withdrawing money from them is safe and efficient. Foreign banks charge a minimum of US$4 for cash withdrawals, with the exception of Canadia Bank. All ATMs have a cash withdrawal limit of US$250 per day.

While timings can vary from bank to bank, most remain open Monday to Saturday from 7:30 to 11:30am, and from 2 to 5pm or 6pm. Bureau de change in international chain hotels are usually open throughout the weekend.

Changing Money

The Thai baht is often accepted in towns such as Poipet and Battambang. However, travelers should bear in mind that the riel is not accepted or changed in Thailand. The US dollar can be used everywhere, but getting change for higher denomination notes can prove difficult unless it is in a top hotel or restaurant. Banks may refuse to change US dollar notes with a slight rip or tear. However, this is not the case with ragged riel notes. Changing any non-dollar currency will result in a poor exchange rate; however, money-changers in the markets will offer better rates. Markets usually operate from around 6am until sundown. Western Union and Moneygram money transfer services are represented by a number of banks such as Cambodia Asia Bank. Changing money with black market operators waiting at borders yields a very poor conversion.

Credit and Debit Cards

Visa and **MasterCard** are accepted by hotels, airlines, and upscale restaurants, as is **JCB** and, to a lesser extent, **American Express**. However, shops, restaurants, and hotels in smaller towns do not accept credit cards and it is best to carry the local currency or US dollars to make payments. Using a credit or debit card often means a 3 percent charge on the spot.

Credit card advances are available at Battambang,

Western Union counter at Cambodia Asia Bank, Phnom Penh

Phnom Penh, Sihanoukville, Siem Reap, Kampot, and Kompong Cham. All banks, apart from Canadia Bank, which offers free advances, levy a US$5 charge.

Traveler's Checks

Traveler's checks are no longer in common use. Few stores or restaurants will accept them, and banks may charge a hefty commission to exchange the cheques for cash, which may make changing small sums of money uneconomical. A pre-loaded currency card is a good alternative. These cards can be loaded with money before traveling and used like debit cards abroad. Money is converted into the local currency at the current exchange rate wherever the card is used. As the card is not directly connected to a bank account, it minimizes the risks of fraud.

Currency

The official unit of currency in Cambodia is the riel (KHR), however, the US dollar is the de facto currency, and the one travelers will find most useful to carry. The riel cannot be exported, so it

must be spent or exchanged before leaving the country. 500 and 1,000 riel notes are the most convenient denominations to have when paying for tuk-tuk rides. There is no coinage in Cambodia, only notes.

Bank Notes

The riel comes in denominations of 100, 200, 500, 1,000, 2,000, 5,000, 10,000, 20,000, 50,000, and 100,000.

5,000 riel

100 riel

10,000 riel

500 riel

20,000 riel

1,000 riel

50,000 riel

2,000 riel

100,000 riel

Banking and Currency in Laos

The unit of currency in Laos is the kip, although the US dollar and the Thai baht are widely accepted, and at times prices for more expensive items are quoted in dollars. Financial services in Laos are efficient and easily available, at least in major towns. Travelers rarely encounter problems while changing currency, cashing traveler's checks, getting a cash advance on a credit card, or when using an ATM. With an exchange rate hovering at about 8,000 kip to a US dollar, many visitors to the country will feel like multi-millionaires. Even small purchases can seem more expensive than they actually are. It is best to keep both kip and dollars on hand while traveling around Laos.

Money exchange counter, Banque Pour le Commerce Exterieur, Lao

Banks and Banking Hours

Most banks in Laos are open Monday to Friday from 8:30am to 3:30pm. The bank most foreigners will deal with is the government-owned **Banque Pour le Commerce Exterieur Lao (BCEL)**, which has numerous red and yellow streetside exchange kiosks. These are open from morning until night, and can be used for all standard exchange transactions. Apart from BCEL the best local bank is **ANZ Laos**, which is a joint venture between ANZ, International Finance Corporation, and Vientiane Commercial Bank. In addition to the Thai-owned **Bangkok Bank** and **Siam Commercial Bank**, a few small privately owned Lao banks, such as **Phongsavanh Bank**, also offer useful services for travelers. Thai banks are a better choice for transactions other than exchanging money, since the Lao banks are geared more toward catering to the needs of the local population.

Changing Money

Although the US dollar and the Thai baht are the most commonly traded currencies, all major international currencies are exchangeable in Laos. In addition to banks, there are also private money changers. Gold shops in small towns, or the biggest store in a village, often exchange money, but these are cash transactions only. Rates change daily and are posted. However, it is best to change enough money before

Entry to Phongsavanh Bank, Vientiane

DIRECTORY

Banks

ANZ Laos
33 Lan Xang Avenue (across Talat Sao), Vientiane. **City Map** D3.
Tel (021)-222-700. **W** anz.com

Bangkok Bank
Khun Bulom Rd, Vientiane.
City Map C3. **Tel** (021)-213-560.
W bangkokbank.com

Banque Pour le Commerce Exterieure Lao (BCEL)
1 Pangkham Rd, Vientiane.
City Map B4. **Tel** (021)-213-200.
W bcellaos.com

Phongsavanh Bank
147 10 Samsenthai Rd, Vientiane.
City Map B3. **Tel** (021)-711-522.
W phongsavanhbank.com

Siam Commercial Bank
117 Lan Xang Avenue, Vientiane.
City Map C3. **Tel** (021)-213-501.
W scb.co.th

Credit Cards

MasterCard
Tel 001-636-722-7111.

Visa
Tel 001-303-967-1096.

Visitors withdrawing money from an ATM, Luang Prabang

embarking on any trips through smaller towns and provinces. Visitors should be aware that the kip is not convertible into other currencies outside Laos.

ATMs and Credit Cards

Both BCEL and ANZ Laos have Automatic Teller Machines (ATMs) in major towns, although the rate is about 7 percent less favorable than other exchange transactions. Added to it is a fixed transaction fee of about 50,000 kip. This is in addition to a foreign transaction fee that most US and European banks charge. Debit cards and bank cards using the Cirrus or Plus systems should work in Laos, but if they are not accepted in ATMs, making a cash withdrawal from an exchange counter or a bank is a good alternative. Credit cards such as **MasterCard** and **Visa** are most readily accepted in major hotels, upscale boutiques, and restaurants. In all other places, they are grudgingly accepted and a service charge of 3 percent is often added. Travelers who encounter any

credit card-related problems can call the home company for assistance.

Traveler's Checks

Since ATMs accepting all major credit cards are becoming more common, traveler's checks are becoming less popular, but they can be exchanged at Lao banks, and the rate is in fact better than ATM-based transactions. Upscale hotels will also exchange them, but most merchants will not. If traveler's checks are lost in Laos, a collect call to a

representative office abroad will suffice to have replacement checks sent via courier.

Currency

The currency of Laos is the Lao kip, abbreviated as LAK. Denominations are displayed in Arabic numerals on one side of the notes only. All notes bear the portrait of Kaysone Phomvihane, and the 20,000 and 50,000 kip notes are both red. It is better to pay with small bills when buying from vendors because they often lack sufficient change.

Bank Notes

The kip comes in denominations of 500, 1,000, 2,000, 5,000, 10,000, 20,000, and the fairly recent 50,000 kip note. Coins are not in use.

5,000 kip

500 kip

10,000 kip

1,000 kip

20,000 kip

2,000 kip

50,000 kip

Communications and Media in Cambodia

Cambodia's communication facilities have improved vastly over the past few years. Cell phones and laptops are a common sight. It is easy to make a call, and 4G Internet is fast and cheap in Phnom Penh and Siem Reap. Most hotels and cafés have Internet or Wi-Fi access. Major newspapers are available across Siem Reap and Phnom Penh. The postal system is also fairly reliable, although it is advisable to use a courier service for valuables.

An Internet café offering several facilities, Phnom Penh

International and Local Telephone Calls

Cambodia uses the GSM mobile telephone system, and cell phone coverage is strong in most parts of the country. Phone cards are usually a good way of making a local or international call. They can be used in phone kiosks on the street or in hotel lobbies. Personal cell phones automatically connect to a local network but calls can prove to be fairly expensive. Calls placed from hotel rooms can also be exorbitant because a surcharge is applied over and above the cost of the call. Using a pre-paid SIM card with a local number on your cell phone is usually a good option, but using Skype from an Internet café is usually the cheapest.

If dialing from a local SIM card-operated cell phone or if using a card phone, replace the 001 country code with 007, for cheaper rates. Numbers starting with 01 or 09 are cell phone numbers.

Internet Facilities

Internet connections are widely available in most hotels, mid-range guesthouses, as well as in bars, restaurants, and cafés.

Siem Reap and Phnom Penh boast excellent cafés with Internet, good menus, and air conditioning. Broadband is widely available, though it can be slow, with many customers on the same line. Free Wi-Fi is now becoming a standard feature in many tourism venues.

Postal Services

Cambodia's postal system is fairly reliable. Post offices are open from 7am–7pm but closed on Sundays. There is also a *poste restante* service at the main post office in Phnom Penh. Letters and postcards take one to two weeks to reach countries outside of Asia, although the service is usually inexpensive. Valuable items should preferably be sent by courier companies such as **DHL**, **TSP Express Cambodia**, and **UPS**, which operate in Siem Reap and Phnom Penh.

Newspapers and Magazines

There are two major English-language newspapers in Cambodia – *The Cambodia Daily*, which carries a good summary

Streetside kiosks selling newspapers and magazines, Phnom Penh

of local and international affairs, and the excellent *The Phnom Penh Post*, published on weekdays, which carries local and international articles. *Time*, *Newsweek*, *The Bangkok Post*, and *Herald Tribune* are all sold in Phnom Penh, Sihanoukville, and Siem Reap, and in other major cities. A number of glossy magazines, published periodically, offer a calendar of upcoming events. *Phnom Penh Asia Life Guide* has colorful features on food and drink, shopping, and fashion. *Touchstone Magazine*, which features restaurant reviews, is also popular. The free periodicals published by Canby Publications, which include maps, local features, temple guides, and restaurant and hotel listings, are very useful for visitors.

Television and Radio

While Cambodia ranked 85th among 180 countries in the press freedom index released by Reporters Without Borders in 2008, it slipped a number of places to reach the 144th position in 2014. There have been repeated incidents of journalists and their families being harassed or murdered after highlighting issues of corruption and illegal logging.

Most hotels have cable TV where you can access BBC or CNN news, as well as sports channels covering major events. Among the radio channels, most people prefer the BBC World Service to state-run channels.

Communications and Media in Laos

Laos has kept abreast of the latest developments in communications, in particular the use of the Internet and cell phones. Barring remote areas, cell phones are widely used. Public phones are not common and few venture to the Lao Telecom offices. The postal system is outdated and it is better to use international courier companies. Cable TV is available in most hotels, and international newspapers arrive regularly, albeit a few days late.

DIRECTORY

Courier Services

DHL
031, Nongno St, Ban Wattay Noy, Vientiane. **City Map** D4.
Tel (021)-214-868.

FedEx
Lan Xang Ave, Vientiane.
City Map D4. **Tel** (021)-223-278.

Ocher-colored mailbox, typically seen throughout Laos

Popular brand of phone card and cell phone SIM used in Laos

International and Local Telephone Calls

Although the offices of Lao Telecom can make overseas calls for visitors, it is better to use either a VOIP system, available in Internet cafés, or to bring along a cell phone. Laos uses the GSM system, so those who have an unlocked tri-band phone can simply buy a local SIM card from any cell phone shop or street kiosk. This will allow visitors to make and receive calls locally and internationally. Those whose phones are locked can consider using the service provider's roaming system, which is usually good enough for staying connected, although the service is expensive and does not permit making or receiving local calls. When making a local

call in Laos, the city code must be inserted before the phone number.

Internet Facilities

Internet cafés abound in Laos. Their prices are moderate and connection speeds are generally adequate for checking e-mail and surfing the Internet. Wi-Fi is also a common feature in numerous hotels, cafés, and restaurants in Vientiane, as well as in Luang Prabang. However, the service is rarely free of charge. Those traveling with a laptop or smart phone will find Wi-Fi more convenient than using an Internet café.

Postal Services

The Lao postal system is not always reliable and visitors should avoid using it, especially for mailing valuables or other important items. A safer alternative is to use a courier company such as **DHL** or **FedEx**, which also have domestic operations, although the service is usually expensive. Travelers who are continuing

on to Thailand or Vietnam could consider mailing their packages from those countries.

Newspapers and Magazines

The government-published English-language *Vientiane Times* is the most commonly available newspaper in Laos. Although Communist in its leanings, it offers an insider's view of the country. Besides vernacular publications, there is also the popular French-language *Le Renovateur*. Some international publications are available at large bookstores in Vientiane, Luang Prabang, and in hotel shops. There are also a few cultural magazines such as *Vannasin Magazine* and *Sinxay Weekly*, which are published in Lao, and *Wattanatham (Culture) Magazine*, which is published in both English and Lao.

Television and Radio

The government controls the television and radio channels and there are no programs in English. The satellite systems found in hotels vary widely, and often focus on Thai programs. However, there is usually some English-language news, as well as financial and sports coverage.

Variety of stationery, books, and publications at Monument Books, Vientiane

TRAVEL INFORMATION IN CAMBODIA

The most convenient way of reaching Cambodia is by air from Bangkok. Connections are short, and there are a number of carriers servicing Phnom Penh from Bangkok's Suvarnabhumi International Airport (Bangkok's Don Muang Airport serves Phnom Penh and Siem Reap). The country's internal air transport system is reasonably well developed with regular flights between major towns. Remote provinces such as Ratanakiri, however, are no longer serviced by air. Visitors can also enter Cambodia by bus, or ferry from Laos, Thailand, or Vietnam. Traveling within the country varies from easy to grueling, depending on the roads. While many highways have been greatly improved, making journeys by bus fairly comfortable, reaching remote places may not always be a good experience. For commuting within cities, visitors can choose from tuk-tuks, motos, and taxis.

Shops and cafés inside Phnom Penh International Airport

Arriving by Air

There are two major airports: Phnom Penh International Airport and Siem Reap-Angkor International Airport, which operate flights from Ho Chi Minh City, Vientiane, Kuala Lumpur, Doha, Singapore, Manila, Seoul, Shanghai, and most major cities in the US, UK, and Australia. International carriers, such as **Thai Airways**, **Bangkok Airways**, **Vietnam Airlines**, **Eva Airways**, **Air Asia**, **Lao Airlines**, **Malaysia Airlines**, **Qatar Airways**, and **Cathay Pacific**, operate flights from Cambodia. Jetstar serves Singapore, and Cebu Pacific flies to Manila – reservations for both these airlines can be made online only. Flying from the US takes more than 20 hours, while flying from Europe takes around 13 hours.

Air Fares

The cost of flying to Cambodia varies depending on the airline, season, and travel agent used. Fares are usually high during holidays and the cool season (Nov–Feb), when the country receives most of its visitors. However, air fares fall considerably during the rainy season (Jun–Oct). Visitors are advised to reserve tickets well in advance.

Arriving by Land or Water

There are at least 12 border crossings into Cambodia from Thailand, Vietnam, and Laos. The most popular crossing from Thailand is Arayprathet to Poipet. Due to recent trouble with Thailand over the ownership of Prasat Preah Vihear temple (see pp96–7), however, the northeastern border is sometimes closed. Veun Kham to Dom Kralor from Laos, and Moc Bai to Bavet from Vietnam are also used regularly. These places are accessible only by road since none of the borders are linked by a rail service. Improved highways have now

A Bangkok Airways plane standing at Siem Reap-Angkor International Airport

Tuk-tuks waiting outside Phnom Penh International Airport

cut journey time significantly. Travel by water is becoming increasingly rare with few waterways linking the borders.

On Arrival

Cambodia provides the facility of visa on arrival, though it can also be applied for in advance. An e-visa can be obtained from the website http://www.mfaic.gov.kh/evisa. Visitors are handed an immigration form in-flight, which must be presented on arrival, along with a passport-sized photograph. The process takes some time since, along with the visa application, there is fingerprint scanning and health forms to complete. The visa fee can be only paid in cash in US dollars, and a one-month business visa is slightly more expensive than a tourist visa. At Siem Reap and Phnom Penh airports, visitors automatically receive a one-month visa. Note that on arrival in Cambodia visitors should have at least six months left on their passport before it expires.

Getting to and from Airports

Departures and arrivals are handled with courtesy and efficiency at international airports, although visitors must be prepared for security checks during arrival and departure. Tuk-tuks and air-conditioned taxis can be hired from outside the terminal at both airports. Taxis and minibuses can also be organized in advance from upscale hotels. While the journey time from Siem Reap's

airport to the town center is 10–15 minutes, traveling through Phnom Penh's over-crowded streets can take up to an hour.

Green Travel

While travel around Cambodia is becoming increasingly convenient with improved road networks and a growth in the transport infrastructure, it is far from eco friendly. Many cars and mopeds still use leaded fuel, which is sold on the roadside in second-hand plastic and glass bottles, because unleaded fuel is expensive. Added to this, cities such as Phnom Penh are crowded with numerous outdated, polluting vehicles.

Visitors, however, can help by taking measures such as avoiding excessive use of air conditioning in the car – especially during the cool season, using bicycles or walking for sightseeing trips wherever possible, and careful disposal of litter. When participating in activities such as eco-trekking, visitors should check the credentials of the company

they are considering using, including details of how long they have been operating, how they contribute to the local community, and what they do to minimize their carbon footprint.

DIRECTORY

Arriving by Air

Air Asia
179, St Sisowath, Phnom Penh.
Tel (023)-890-035. **w** airasia.com

Bangkok Airways
61A, St 214, Phnom Penh.
City Map D3. **Tel** (023)-426-624.
w bangkokair.com

Cathay Pacific
168 Monireth Blvd, Phnom Penh.
City Map B3. **Tel** (023)-424-300.
w cathaypacific.com

Eva Airways
11-14B, St 205, Phnom Penh.
City Map B4. **Tel** (023)-210-303.
w evaair.com

Lao Airlines
111 Sihanouk, St 274, Phnom Penh. **City Map** D3. **Tel** (023)-222-956. **w** laoairlines.com

Malaysia Airlines
35–37 Samdech Pan, St 214, Phnom Penh. **City Map** D3. **Tel** (023)-426-688. **w** malaysiaairlines.com

Qatar Airways
Tel (023)-963-800.
w qatarairways.com

Thai Airways
294 Mao Tse Toung, St 245, Phnom Penh. **City Map** B4. **Tel** (023)-890-292. **w** thaiairways.com

Vietnam Airlines
41 Samdech Pan, St 214, Phnom Penh. **City Map** D3. **Tel** (023)-215-998. **w** vietnamairlines.com

Visitors cycling out of the eastern gate, Angkor Thom

Getting Around Cambodia

Transportation is finally coming of age in Cambodia, after years of stagnation. The last few years have seen major investment in roads and highway networks, with water-resistant surface roads connecting major towns such as Phnom Penh, Siem Reap, Sihanoukville, and Battambang. Boat travel is often very slow, although enjoyable, so it is not recommended for visitors on a short trip. The internal airways network is also quite efficient, although visitors traveling to remote locations will have to make use of local transportation such as a bus service, or rent a car and driver. Driving alone, however, can be quite challenging, especially in the provinces, where few locals speak English, and road signs are in the Khmer script.

New long-distance bus offering comfortable, efficient travel

Domestic Airlines

Cambodia is served by two domestic airlines – **Cambodia Angkor Air**, in collaboration with Vietnam Airlines, and **Bayon Airlines**, which is Chinese owned. Cambodia Angkor Air offers flights to Sihanoukville, Siem Reap, Phnom Penh, and Ho Chi Minh City; Bayon Airlines connects Phnom Penh, Siem Reap, and Sihanoukville.

Plane Tickets, Fares, and Reservations

Tickets can be purchased at the airlines' reservation offices at the airport, in their offices in Phnom Penh, online, or through a reputable tour agent. Agents are often able to obtain discounts on ticket prices, especially on long-distance flights. Prominent agents such as **Exotissimo** and **Hanuman Tourism** are located in Phnom Penh, while others, including **All Concierge Services** have offices in Siem Reap. Some

of the larger hotels will also be happy to deal with your onward travel at no extra cost. A one-way ticket from Phnom Penh to Siem Reap will usually cost under US$100. Tickets may not be easily available during Christmas, major festivals, or at any time during the peak season from November to February. Visitors are therefore advised to reserve their flights well in advance during these times. Ticket prices generally drop during lean periods, especially in the months of February, June, and October.

Buses

Bus journeys have improved immeasurably, with newer air-conditioned buses and vastly upgraded roads on major routes. As a result, travel time between places such as Siem Reap and Battambang has more than halved. Among the principal bus companies that

operate decent services out of the capital are **Phnom Penh Sorya Transport Company**, which runs services to Sihanoukville, Siem Reap, Bangkok, Battambang, and other provincial towns, and **Mekong Express**, which follows similar routes, but offers greater luxury. For remote places, it is necessary to rent a car with a driver or catch a local minibus, which can be uncomfortable, dangerously overcrowded, and have constricted seating space. It is usually advisable to hire a minibus and driver if there are sufficient passengers. Buses and minibuses take regular breaks en route.

Bus Tickets and Fares

Tickets can be bought through tour agents, organized from your hotel, or on arrival at the bus terminus – from where most buses operate. If traveling on a busy route, such as Phnom Penh to Siem Reap, it is advisable to make reservations in advance as buses fill up very quickly. Bus fares are usually very reasonable.

Renting a Car or Motorbike

Renting a motorbike is a great way to see the country, and if you are an experienced rider, it can be a terrific way to tackle the roads in isolated regions such as Mondulkiri and Ratanakiri. Motorbikes also have the advantage of allowing travelers to move at their own pace, as well as to interact with locals.

Counter at a travel agency selling bus tickets, Phnom Penh

Motorcycles for rent outside a dealer's office in Kep

However, bikers must keep in mind that traveling this way may not always be a pleasant experience, especially since many of the roads in remote areas, barring the highways, are in very poor condition. Locals often speed along the wrong side of the road, especially on hairpin bends, and riders also need to keep an eye out for wandering livestock and children running across their path.

Renting a car is generally quite easy and affordable, but recommended only if you plan to take a local driver who knows the road and the locations of temples and other sights. Driving on one's own is not advisable for visitors who do not speak the local language. However, should you wish to do so, bear in mind that driving without a local license may warrant a fine from the Cambodian police.

Boats and Ferries

Cambodia's many rivers offer a great way to travel from one place to another while observing the fantastic wildlife, as well as local cultures en route. Travel companies such as **Angkor Express** offer boat trips between Siem Reap and Battambang, which usually take around 5 to 8 hours. Boat tours between Phnom Penh and Siem Reap can take up to 5 hours. Although both routes take in the Tonlé Sap

Lake, the latter is less rewarding as there is little to see except vast expanses of water.

Travelers coming from Laos now have the option of the rocket boat, which can be a dangerous way to travel due to rocks hidden below the surface of the river, particularly during the wet season. These longtail boats ply the route between the Lao border and Cambodia's Stung Treng, but in the dry season, when the river is low, the route can be fraught with danger. In Laos, similar vessels have met with accidents that have killed people every year. If traveling on these boats, visitors must carry earplugs because the noise from the engines can be deafening. They must also never agree to travel when the light is fading and visibility is poor. Sun block and a hat are essential, especially if traveling on the roof.

DIRECTORY

Domestic Airlines

Bayon Airlines
CEIB Building, La Russia Blvd,
Khan Semsok, Phnom Penh.
City Map B1. **Tel** (023)-231-555.

Cambodia Angkor Air
206A, Preah Norodom Blvd,
Phnom Penh. **City Map** E5.
Tel (023)-666-6786.
w cambodiaangkorair.com

Buses

Mekong Express
87 Sisowath Quay, Phnom Penh.
City Map E1. **Tel** (023)-427-518.

**Phnom Penh Sorya
Transport Company**
Corner of Sts 217 and 67.
City Map D2. **Tel** (023)-210-359.
w ppsoryatransport.com

Boats and Ferries

Angkor Express
Beside the Titanic Restaurant,
Sisowath Quay, Phnom Penh.
City Map E1. **Tel** (012)-789-531.

Travel Agencies

All Concierge Services
051, Stung Thmei Village, Siem
Reap. **Tel** 855-89-855-855.

Exotissimo
66 Norodom Blvd, Phnom Penh.
City Map F2. **Tel** (023) 218-948.
w exotissimo.com

Hanuman Tourism
310, St 12, Phnom Penh.
City Map E4. **Tel** (023)-218-396.
w hanumantourism.com

Tourists crossing the Tonlé Sap Lake on a ferry, Chong Kneas

Local Transportation

The last five years have seen some rapid development in Cambodia, with improved road networks and better transportation facilities. However, this has also led to an increase in traffic, and jams are common in major cities such as Phnom Penh and Siem Reap, particularly in the morning and evening. The quickest way of getting around bigger cities is on *motos* (motorcycle taxis), which weave effortlessly through congestion. Leisurely *cyclos*, motorized tuk-tuks, and metered taxis are also readily available.

Visitors enjoying the sights of Phnom Penh from a tuk-tuk

Getting Around Phnom Penh

A small city, Phnom Penh is easy to travel around despite the absence of a local bus system. Perhaps the most charming means of navigating the city streets is on a *remorque-moto*, better known as the tuk-tuk. Another gentle, albeit time-consuming way of getting through the traffic is the *cyclo*, tried by most visitors to the city. A *cyclo* can easily accommodate two to three passengers, and is pedaled by the driver who sits at the back. While a ride on a *cyclo* may not cost much, tuk-tuk drivers often hike their prices for foreigners, particularly if they see them exiting an expensive hotel. It is recommended that visitors negotiate prices before taking the ride.

Those keen to explore the city at their own pace can also rent a bicycle for the purpose. Bicycles are usually available at most guesthouses for a few dollars per day. Cyclists, however, are advised to be careful, when riding, of the heat and pollution in larger cities. Motorcycles are another way to explore the city, but riders must wear helmets. Riders should also possess a local license, or they run the risk of being stopped by the police and fined a few dollars.

Buses and Minibuses

Although there is no centralized bus service in Cambodia yet, the country is well served by buses heading to all provinces. These buses, run mostly by private operators, are usually air-conditioned and cover most major towns. Minibuses also operate in the provinces and are an inexpensive, if overcrowded, way to get around. Visitors are advised to reserve tickets in advance to ensure a seat.

Metered Taxis

Metered taxis are available in Phnom Penh. **Global Taxis** is the only official metered taxi service, running air-conditioned, modern cars at reasonable prices. Although a certain minimum amount is charged to all visitors, the service is usually quite inexpensive. Upscale hotels, guesthouses, and most travel agents can also arrange for taxis, especially if renting one for the entire day, or for traveling long distances. There are also non-official taxi drivers eager to ferry visitors, though sometimes they are hard to spot. It is essential to settle on a price before getting into these cars in order to avoid disagreement or arguments later on.

Rules of the Road

Owing to rapidly increasing traffic and little concern for safety, driving in large cities such as Phnom Penh and Siem Reap is quite a dangerous proposition. Rules are seldom followed, and pedestrians have no right of way.

Metered taxis operated by different companies in Phnom Penh

Group of visitors on an organized tour of Ta Prohm, Siem Reap province

While driving in Cambodia is on the right-hand side of the road, there are few traffic lights at junctions and most vehicles do not follow traffic rules. Drivers must be careful not to turn left on a "No left turn" sign, and to use headlights at night. Pedestrians should remain vigilant when crossing roads. The ideal way to do this is to walk at a regular pace with purpose, ensuring that drivers can see you and swerve around you accordingly.

Renting a self-drive car, especially in Phnom Penh, is not advisable. If an accident occurs, foreigners will find the local police difficult to deal with, and they are likely to run into problems with bureaucracy and the language barrier. Besides, traffic police officials in the capital, although lax with locals, are quite strict with foreigners.

If traveling on a motorcycle, drivers must wear a helmet. Although this rule is hardly followed by locals, foreigners are fined for the same offense.

Organized Tours

Considering the number of sights worth visiting, not just in and around Phnom Penh and Siem Reap, but also other major towns in Cambodia, taking an organized tour is usually a great idea. These range from one- to several-day trips. Besides being convenient, they are often less time-consuming,

and usually work out to be less expensive. As a rule, the more people there are in a group, the cheaper the individual price will be. At the same time, prices for the same trip can vary a lot, so visitors should ask in several offices before settling for any one agent, in order to get the best deal. There are several good tour companies in Phnom Penh, mostly around the Sisowath Quay area, as well as in Siem Reap. Companies such as **Exotic Angkor Travel** in Siem Reap, and **Diethelm Travel** in Phnom Penh, are great for package tours and cover all major sights in and around these towns. They are also helpful for organizing flight reservations, accommodation facilities, and transportation.

Road sign in Kampot

Hanuman Tourism, among the best known in the business, and **Hola Travel**, based in Phnom Penh, also organize comprehensive tour packages for visitors. **Sun Tours** arranges unique one and two-day boat cruises to the verdant islands off Sihanoukville.

Cruise taking visitors on a trip to the Sihanoukville Islands

TRAVEL INFORMATION IN LAOS

Most visitors arrive in Laos by air. Since there are no direct flights into the country from Europe or the Americas, many travelers make the final leg of their trip via Bangkok, which has the highest number of connecting flights to Laos. Lao Airlines, the national carrier, serves eight cities within the country. There are also international air connections from China, Vietnam, Malaysia, and Cambodia. There are 15 border crossings open from all the countries bordering Laos with the exception of Myanmar. The road network connecting Laos to its neighbors is rapidly improving, and the roads are plied by modern buses and minivans. Boat travel is an interesting option, particularly on the wide and navigable Mekong River. Within the towns and cities metered taxis are a convenient mode of transportation.

Arriving by Air

Wattay International Airport in Vientiane has flights to and from Bangkok in Thailand, Ho Chi Minh City in Vietnam, Phnom Penh and Siem Reap in Cambodia, Kuala Lumpur in Malaysia, and Kunming in China. The international airport at Luang Prabang serves Bangkok, as well as Hanoi and Siem Reap. Pakse International Airport has flights to Bangkok, Siem Reap, and Phnom Penh. **Lao Airlines** has the most flights in and out of the country, followed by **Thai Airways**, **Vietnam Airlines**, **China Eastern Airlines**, and **Air Asia**. Other airlines include Bangkok Airways with flights to Vientiane and Luang Prabang, and Nok Air from Bangkok to Udon Thani.

Lao Airlines plane stationed on the tarmac, Savannakhet Airport

Air Fares

The cost of traveling to Laos by air fluctuates depending on the season. Fares can double during the peak season. Most of the discount flights from Europe and the US via Bangkok. Online travel companies and travel agents can assist travelers in finding the best deals.

On Arrival

Upon arrival two official forms need to be filled out – a visa application form and an immigration form. These forms are distributed on all flights landing in Laos. Visitors can apply for a visa at the port of entry with a passport-sized photograph and the completed forms, along with a fee. The fee varies with nationality, and payment is always in foreign currency, usually US dollars. The formalities required are minimal and generally involve only a stamp in the passport. Visas can also be applied for in advance. The immigration form that is placed in the passport is an important document and must be kept safe as losing it can result in a fine. Customs checks are cursory, although the standard limits on the import of alcohol and tobacco should be observed.

Getting to and from Airports

The three international airports in Laos are located fairly close to the cities they serve, and as a result there are no shuttle bus services between the airports and the cities. However, taxi tickets are sold within the arrivals terminal in Vientiane. In Luang Prabang and Pakse, tuk-tuks are readily available outside the airport. Hotels usually offer pick-ups from

Arrival terminal, Pakse International Airport

airports for a small fee. Upscale hotels, however, offer free airport transfer for all guests.

Arriving by Land

Laos has 15 international land-border crossings. The main crossing from Thailand is via the Friendship Bridge from the Thai town of Nong Khai to Tha Deua in southern Laos, linked to the capital by bus and rail. The boat crossing from the Thai town of Chiang Khong in Chiang Rai province to Huay Xai in Bokeo province allows travelers to cruise down the Mekong River to Luang Prabang. Another crossing in Mukdahan province leads to the town of Savannakhet via the Friendship Bridge. A crossing near Loei in Thailand leads to the Lao village of Nam Heuang; however, no visas are issued here. There is a crossing from the Thai town of Chong Mek to Vang Tau, which is 27 miles (43 km) from Pakse, where visas are available on arrival.

The border between Laos and Cambodia is also open. Boats and minibuses operate between Stung Treng and the crossing in Laos. The immigration point at Vueng Kham in Laos may or may not issue visas on arrival. Visitors need to check with travel agents in Phnom Penh.

A Lao visa is available on arrival at all the border crossings from Vietnam. There is a remote entry point at Bo Y, about 60 miles (100 km) east of Attapeu town. Buses and taxis ply the route. The Vietnamese village of Lao Bao is connected to Dan Savan in Laos, a popular crossing. From here a good road leads to Savannakhet, 140 miles (230 km) west. Buses originating in Da Nang ply the route regularly. The crossing from Cau Treo to Nam Phao puts the traveler within striking distance of the beautiful Phu Hin Pun National Protected Area. The border crossing at Nam Can into Nam Kahn can be used to reach the Plain of Jars, which is a 5-hour bus journey farther west. From Tay Trang a crossing leads to Sop Hun, which is 36 miles (60 km) southwest of the town of Muang Khua. Buses to Muang Khua originate in Dien Bien Phu in Vietnam.

A crossing from the Chinese town of Mohan leads to the village of Boten in Luang Nam Tha province. Public transport is available to the provincial capital, Luang Nam Tha.

Green Travel

The Lao National Tourism Administration, working in conjunction with foreign governments and NGOs, has been seriously promoting the country as an ecotourism destination. The Lao people are being educated about the

Pick-up car, Lao Plaza Hotel

DIRECTORY

Arriving By Air

Air Asia
 airasia.com

China Eastern Airlines
Luang Prabang Rd, Vientiane.
City Map A5. **Tel** (021)-212-300.
 flychinaeastern.com

Lao Airlines
2 Pangkham Rd, Vientiane.
City Map B4. **Tel** (021)-212-051-54. laoairlines.com

Thai Airways
Luang Prabang Rd, Vientiane.
City Map A5. **Tel** (021)-222-527.
 thaiair.com

Vietnam Airlines
Lao Plaza Hotel, Samsenthai Rd, Vientiane. **City Map** C3.
Tel (021)-217-562.
 vietnamairlines.com

advantages of sound environmental practices, in order to preserve the resources that attract visitors. Preserving the environment will, in turn, be economically beneficial for them as opposed to slash and burn agriculture, logging, and trapping wildlife. Community-based treks, which promote village homestays, and involve villagers by renting them as guides, are popular.

However, old practices still persist. Visitors should steer clear of items such as deer, often featured on restaurant menus, and wildlife products such as tooth necklaces, bags made from animal skins, and alcohol containing snakes.

Passengers waiting at the terminal, Wattay International Airport, Vientiane

Getting Around Laos

Road conditions in Laos have improved, but dirt roads are still common in remote areas, and road repairs are never immediate. The Russian flat-bed truck with wooden seats and a zinc roof has given way to double-decker, air-conditioned buses. Minivans are also popular, and more comfortable and faster than buses. The *songthaew* (literally meaning two rows) is common in rural areas. Due to the improved road network, boat travel is less common, although still possible, and necessary, in some areas. Laos's only railway ends just after crossing the Friendship Bridge from Thailand. Two domestic airlines reach all the major cities in Laos.

Domestic Airlines

Laos's national carrier, **Lao Airlines**, has regular domestic flights between cities, such as Vientiane, Luang Prabang, Pakse, and Luang Nam Tha, covering most regions of the country. The destinations of Lao Airlines seem to change quite frequently, so it is best to check locally for the latest information. The company uses modern turbojet aircraft and has a good safety record. **Lao Central Airlines** is a privately owned airline based in Vientiane. It operates both domestic and international routes with a greater number of international services to Thailand, China, Vietnam, and Malaysia. The airline currently offers regular domestic flights between Luang Prabang and Vientiane, and uses Boeing 737-400 jets for both its international and domestic services.

Plane Tickets, Fares, and Reservations

While it is possible to purchase tickets at the offices of Lao Airlines, an efficient e-ticketing

Passengers waiting to buy tickets at a bus ticket counter in Savannakhet

service makes it much simpler for visitors to buy tickets on the company website and print them out at home. Many travel agents and hotels will also be happy to print these out for customers. Domestic airfares are usually less than US$100 per flight, but not all are direct. For example, flights from Luang Prabang to Pakse would entail a change at Vientiane. Lao Central Airlines flights can be reserved online or via a travel agent for a small fee. In the peak season,

from November to February, demand for flights exceeds supply, and it is advisable to reserve reasonably far in advance.

Buses

A wide variety of buses ply the roads of Laos. These range from the sleek, new air-conditioned VIP coaches that ply Route 13 along with the international routes, to the rattletrap blue-and white- government-run buses that serve the environs of Vientiane and other cities. There are also a variety of mid-range options to choose from. As a rule, the longer and more well-traveled the route, the better the vehicles serving it will be. Travelers should find out about the kind of vehicle they are boarding in order to avoid arduous road journeys. A local bus will probably stop at every village, while an express bus will make fewer stops. Ascertaining this is not always easy, although the fare is usually the best indication of the quality of the ride.

Bus Tickets and Fares

Most long-distance buses depart from a station located on the outskirts of town rather than from city-center bus stations. Additionally, most major cities have two or more bus stations, depending on the direction and distance of travel. For example, Vientiane has three bus stations: the **Southern Bus Station** on Route 13 situated on the southern edge of town, the **Northern Bus Station** en route to the airport, and the Talat Sao Bus Station in the center of town for short journeys and trips to Thailand. Luang Prabang makes do with two bus stations – a northern and a southern bus terminal.

It is worth making a trip to the bus station on the day before a long journey in order to buy a ticket. This will allow travelers to see the types of buses that are available as well as to obtain the most accurate information on departure times. If time does not permit this, it is also possible

Air-conditioned, double-decker VIP luxury bus

to buy VIP bus tickets from travel agents. However, travelers must be specific about their requirements in order to avoid misunderstandings about the types of buses and departure times.

Minivans and Songthaews

Air-conditioned minivans are an excellent way for small groups to travel. They are usually designed to take about 10 passengers, and seats are sold individually. However, it is possible for travelers to charter the vehicle, often at a negotiable price, and also to arrange rest or sightseeing stops en route at their convenience. Minivans run between all major cities and also stop in the city centers, thereby avoiding the inconvenience of suburban bus stations.

At the other end of the midsized vehicle spectrum lies the *songthaew*, which is basically a pick-up truck fitted with two benches. Passengers usually sit facing each other on or on the roof of the vehicle. These are a common sight in rural Laos because they ply the routes between cities, and are used for short-to-medium distance trips in rural areas. They are usually tightly packed with passengers and their belongings. *Songthaew* follow fixed routes and stop whenever a potential passenger flags them down, or when someone wishes to disembark. These vehicles are generally slower and dustier compared with buses, but they are an excellent way to observe local life in rural Laos.

Visitors riding rented motorcycles, a convenient mode of transport

Renting a Car or Motorcycle

Most rental cars come with a driver, although self-drive options are available – neither is particularly cheap. Cars can be rented from **Avis** and **Sixt**, but driving within cities can be dangerous because of darting motorcycles, stray cattle and water buffaloes, and pedestrians. Once out of town, the relative lack of traffic makes it less of a challenge, especially for those used to driving. Renting a motorcycle is quite popular, especially in Vientiane, from companies such as **Jules Classic Bikes.** Travelers should rent motorcycles only if they have prior riding experience. It is advisable to wear long pants, and shoes instead of sandals.

Boats and Ferries

The improved road network in Laos has resulted in a reduction in the number of riverboats that

DIRECTORY

Domestic Airlines

Lao Airlines
2 Pangkham Rd, Vientiane.
City Map B4. **W** laoairlines.com

Lao Central Airlines
Souphanonvong Rd, Vientiane.
W flylaocentral.com

Bus Stations

Northern Bus Station
Evening Market Rd 12, Vientiane.
City Map A4. **Tel** (021)-260-094.

Southern Bus Station
Dongdok Rd, Vientiane.
City Map D4. **Tel** (021)-740-521.

Car and Motorcycle Rental

Avis
Setthathirat Rd, Vientiane.
City Map B3. **Tel** (021)-223-867.

Jules Classic Bikes
Phonpapao Rd, Vientiane.
Tel (020)-5951-1295.

Sixt
Wattay Airport, Vientiane.
City Map A4. **Tel** (021)-513-228.

once carried travelers along scenic if slow routes on the Mekong and other rivers. However, boats still ply the upper Mekong, the Si Phan Don region (*see pp202–3*), and the Nam Ou in Northern Laos. The Luang Say Mekong Cruise from Luang Prabang to Huay Xai (*see pp186–7*), or vice versa, remains the highlight of many a visitor's trip to Laos. Mekong riverboats are large wooden-hulled motor launches with a roof to protect passengers from the sun, and are capable of carrying dozens of passengers. The so-called speedboat is a light, narrow, shallow-draft vessel with a huge gimbal-mounted engine. These operate on the upper Mekong, but are dangerous and should be used only in emergency situations. Riverboats on the Nam Ou are smaller and faster versions of the Mekong cruisers, and chartering one is a viable option, especially if traveling in a group. Small motorized pirogues are used to travel between the islands in the Si Phan Don region.

Massive wooden riverboat plying the scenic Mekong River

Local Transportation

Laos lacks a reliable intra-city public transportation system that travelers can realistically use. There are shared tuk-tuks that ply fixed routes in Vientiane, but destinations are not written in English and this can be a handicap for travelers without knowledge of the local language. Moreover, tuk-tuk drivers often quote exorbitant fares and can be difficult to deal with, especially in Vientiane. It is better to use metered taxis, which are easily available in the capital and are often cheaper than tuk-tuks. Motorcycles and bicycles are also good options, but walking is sometimes the easiest way to explore a particular region.

Getting Around Vientiane and Luang Prabang

Given the absence of public transportation, and the extortionate fares charged by tuk-tuk drivers, many visitors find themselves happier getting around Vientiane and Luang Prabang on foot or on a bicycle. While Vientiane consists of a fairly large urban and suburban sprawl, the area where most visitors will spend their time is in fact quite small. The areas lying between the Mekong River and Samsenthai Road, and between Lan Xang Avenue and Chao Anou Road are only about a mile (2 km) from one end to the other, and can be covered on foot. In Luang Prabang, the peninsular Old Town is about the same size as central Vientiane and can also be explored on foot. However, Luang Prabang is better suited to bicycles than Vientiane, since

Bicycles available for rent on the roadside, Vientiane

there is less vehicular traffic on the roads. It is easy to rent motorcycles in both Vientiane and Luang Prabang, and they are a good option for those with some experience on these machines. Visitors should not attempt to learn to ride a motorcycle while in Laos because traffic conditions are challenging and medical facilities are basic. Motorcycle rental shops usually ask for a copy of your passport; an international driving permit is technically required but rarely asked for. Warnings to use the extra lock supplied and to park in designated motorcycle parking areas, where an attendant is on duty, should be taken seriously. Motorcycle theft is rife in Vientiane, and the renter will be held responsible if this happens. Travelers should also inspect the condition of the vehicle (brakes in particular), and check for any damage, even small scratches, which should be noted on the contract in order to avoid being charged for this damage later.

Walking, however, is the best option and also provides visitors with a chance to interact with the locals while taking in the sights. It should be kept in mind, though, that the sun shines brightly most of the time so a hat and sun block are essential. Drinking plenty of fluids is vital and walkers should try to keep to the shade. Mornings and late afternoons are best for strolls.

Tuk-Tuks and Taxis

Since tuk-tuk drivers mainly serve foreign travelers, the ones in major tourist centers have also evolved into self-appointed guides offering tours of local sights, particularly those out of town, such as waterfalls. If travelers chance upon a reliable tuk-tuk driver, it is advisable to obtain his cell phone number and use his services regularly. Several types of tuk-tuk (see p144) ply the streets of Vientiane and other towns and cities. These three-wheeled vehicles are

Shared tuk-tuks lined up, waiting for passengers, Vientiane

Typical rush-hour traffic, Vientiane

usually brightly painted and can be useful to get between towns and bus stations, which are often located far from the town center. Most commonly, tuk-tuks are rented for one-way trips to a specific destination. They can also be used for a round trip with waiting time included. Travelers should expect a serious amount of bargaining before boarding. In Vientiane, metered taxi services, such as **TVCL**, offer air-conditioned, dust-free rides at reasonable prices. Older, unmetered taxis are also available, but travelers should settle on a price before boarding.

Tourist taxi logo

Rules of the Road

Observing local traffic etiquette is vital, even for pedestrians. In Vientiane, particularly, the once quiet streets are now filled with new cars, especially at rush hour. In provincial towns, motorcycles weave through the downtown thoroughfares without any consideration for road safety. Most riders are inexperienced, and many do not even have a license. Traffic rules are seldom followed, with the larger vehicles usually getting right of way. Pedestrian crossings are also ignored by drivers, although the recently installed stop lights are shown more respect, especially with a policeman ready to give chase and extract a fine from mis-creants. Although cars keep to the right side of the road, it is wise to look both ways while crossing a street, since motorcycles will go against the flow of traffic if it means a short cut. Only about half the motorcyclists on the road will use headlights after dark. Travelers will find it easier to get around once they are familiar with, and learn to expect, these local ways.

Organized Tours

Organized tours are available in all the major towns and cities of Laos. Single-day excursions and several-day trips are easy to reserve. In Vientiane and Luang Prabang, travelers can contact any one of the numerous tour operators, such as **Green Discovery**, **Exotissimo**, and **Diethelm Travel Laos**, while in other cities the local tourist office can provide information. These government-run services are excellent, and focus on trekking and community-based ecotours.

DIRECTORY

Taxi Service

TVCL
Tel (021)-454-168.

Organized Tours

Diethelm Travel Laos
Nam Phu Square,
Setthathirat Rd, Vientiane.
City Map C4.
Tel (021)-213-833.
Phu Vao Rd, Luang Prabang.
City Map B5.
Tel (071)-261-011.
w diethelmtravel.com

Exotissimo
Pangkham St, Vientiane.
City Map B4.
Tel (021)-241-861.
Khemkhong Rd, Luang Prabang.
City Map D2.
Tel (071)-252-879.
w exotissimo.com

Green Discovery
Setthathirat Rd, Vientiane.
City Map B3.
Tel (021)-251-524.
Sisavang Vong Rd, Luang Prabang.
City Map C3.
Tel (071)-212-093.
w greendiscoverylaos.com

In Vientiane, a typical itinerary would take in the Haw Phra Kaew (see p142), Wat Si Saket (see p143), the Patuxal, and the Talat Sao (see p144). In Luang Prabang, the National Museum Complex (see p158), Wat Xieng Thong (see pp162–3), the Santi Chedi (see p168), and sometimes a Mekong River cruise, are covered in a day.

River cruise boat on the Mekong River from the Thai border to Luang Prabang

General Index

Acknowledgments

Dorling Kindersley would like to thank the many people whose help and assistance contributed to the preparation of this book.

Main Contributors
Peter Holmshaw has lived in Asia for 25 years and now makes his home in Chiang Mai, Thailand where he raises his family, rides a mountain bike, and works in publishing.

Iain Stewart first visited Cambodia and Laos in 1991 as a backpacker. Now an author and journalist, he has written over 30 guidebooks to destinations as diverse as Ibiza and Indonesia. He lives in Brighton, UK.

Richard Waters has had a long association with Southeast Asia and writes for a number of British newspapers, magazines, and other guidebooks. He lives in the Cotswolds with his family.

Fact Checker Adam Bray
Proofreader Janice Pariat
Indexer Hilary Bird
Khmer and Lao Translations Andiamo! Language Services Ltd
Editorial Consultants Ros Belford, Claire Boobyer

Design and Editorial
Publisher Douglas Amrine
List Manager Vivien Antwi
Project Editor Michelle Crane
Junior Editor Vicki Allen
Editorial Assistance Adam Bray, Scarlett O'Hara
Project Art Editor Shahid Mahmood
Senior Cartographic Editor Casper Morris
Senior DTP Designer Jason Little
Senior Picture Researcher Ellen Root
Production Controllers Vicky Baldwin, Linda Dare

Revisions Team
Neha Dhingra, Caroline Elliker, Sumita Khatwani, Bhavika Mathur, Catherine Palmi, Marianne Petrou, Erin Richards, Joanne Stenlake, Stuti Tiwari, Steve Vickers, Laura Walker, Sophie Wright

Cartography Credits
Base mapping supplied by Kartographie Huber, www.kartographie.de and Lovell Johns Ltd, www.lovelljohns.com The maps on pages 46/47, 60/61 and 138/139 are derived from © www.openstreetmap.org and contributors, licensed under CC-BY-SA, see www.creativecommons.org for further details.

Additional Photography
Max Alexander; Edward Allwright; Jane Burton; Ian O'Leary; Bethany Dawn; Tim Draper; Christopher and Sally Gable; Steve Gorton; Frank Greenaway; Amisha Gupta; David Henley; Barnabas Kindersley; Dave King; Stephen Oliver; Jon Whitaker; Rough Guides: Simon Bracken, Tim Draper; Rob Shone; Michael Spencer.

Photography Permissions
Dorling Kindersley would like to thank the following for their assistance and kind permission to photograph at their establishments:
The Apsara Hotel; Artisans d'Angkor; The Battambang Provincial Museum; The Foreign Correspondents' Club; Khmer Ceramics Centre; Saun Kham at The Laos National Museum; Hab Touch at The National Museum of Cambodia; Raffles Hotels & Resorts; Santuk Silk Farm; The Traditional Arts and Ethnology Centre; Wat Ong Teu Mahawihan; Wat Pa Huak; Wat Si Muang; Wat Si Saket; Wat Xieng Thong; Xieng Khuan.

Picture Credits
Key: a-above; b-below/bottom; c-centre; f-far; l-left; r-right; t-top.

The publisher would like to thank the following individuals, companies, and picture libraries for their kind permission to reproduce their photographs:

123RF.com: Choosakdi Kabyubon 231tr, Chirasak Tolertmongkol 11cr.

Alamy Images: Prisma Bildagentur AG 54bl; age fotostock 227tr; AHowden - Cambodia Stock Photography 265tl; Alan Copson City Pictures 261br; Victor Paul Borg 183cra; G P Bowater 18cr; Jon Bower Cambodia 26clb; Thomas Cockrem 23ca; Ian Cruickshank 20cr;Danita Delimont 21tr, 137crb;David Myers Photography 28cl; David Noton Photography 220cla; DBImages 21cl; Adam Deschamps 81br; Dreamtours 169tc; Shaun Edwards 156br; F1online digitale Bildagentur GmbH 260b; Philip Game 195tc; David Gee 27cr, 185tr, 228tr; Mike Goldwater 177br; Micah Hanson 25tl, 25bl, 126cr, 181cl, 193br; Henry Westheim Photography 18fclb, 51br, 129bc, 234bl; Roger Hutchings 20clb; ImageBroker 127c, 212tr; ITPhoto 189b; Alistair Laming 33tr; Lonely Planet Images 155cra, 155bl; Neilsetchfield.com 92crb; Douglas O'Connor 221cl; Paul Gisby Photography 155br; Photos-12 23cr; Rick Piper 226bc; Robert Harding World Imagery 214bc; Bert de Ruiter 176bc; Yaacov Shein 125bl, 148bl; Michael Sparrow 219c; Dave Stamboulis 183bl; Stephen Frink Collection 119br; Bjorn Svensson 185bl; Travel Ink 126bl; Peter Treanor 61tr, 260cl; Ian Trower 200c; Tom Vater 263tl; Volvox Inc 203tl; Whitehead Images 183bc; Terry Whittaker 86tl, 185br, 201cla, 201br; Andrew Woodley 267b.

Jerry Alexander: 129c, 169b.

Amok Restaurant: 224tr.

Angkor Golf Resort: 241bc.

Angkor National Museum: 68b.

ardea.com: D. Parer & E. Parer-Cook 18cb; Masahiro Iijima 201c; Thomas Marent 18bl; M. Watson 18clb; Wardene Weisser 19bl.

Asian Explorers: Timothy Tye 73cla.

Anna Boyson: 195bl.

Bridgeman Images: View of the Ho Chi Minh Trail in Laos 193tr.

Cambodian Living Arts, A Program of the Marion Institute: Daniel Rothenberg 116bl.

Centre Culturel Français du Cambodge: 28bl, 28br.

Corbis: 13 / Matthew Wakem / Ocean 225br; Bettmann 135t; Michael Freeman 96clb; Kevin R. Morris 110bl; National Geographic Society / Gervais Courtellemont 57cra.

CPA Media: 132tr, 132c, 133tc, 133crb, 133bc, 134tc, 134clb, 134bc, 135br; Joe Cummings 38, 39bc, 40crb, 41crb, 41bl, 42ca, 128br; Oliver Hargreave 21bl, 128cl, 183cla; David Henley 39br, 40br, 45br, 127b, 132bc, 135crb.

Dreamstime.com: Xavier Allard 2-3; Angelo2319 150; Bjeayes 13br; Anan Bootviengpunth 13tl; Rthaiman72 15br; Pablo Caridad 138; Ionut David 178-179; Donyanedomam 64; Jackmalipan 12tc, 104; Lakhesis 11tl, 88, 146-147; Manjik 30-31; James Menges 210bc; Luciano Mortula 98-99; Oscar Espinosa Villegas 10bc, 14tc; Rodrigolab 204-205; Saaaaa 78-79; Alistair Thomas 12bl; Tortoon 15tl; Tuulijumala 14b.

Dutch Co & Co: Rik Hendriks 45cr, 241tr, 255br.

Elefant Asia: Yves Bernard 187br.

FLPA: Minden Pictures / Hiroya Minakuchi 19cb; Terry Whittaker 19fbr.

Getty Images: AFP Eric Feferberg 42bc/ Jimin Lai 43tr, 43cb/ Claude Juvenal 42clb/ Stringer 157c/ Stringer / Tang Chinn Sothy 43bc/ Tang Chhin Sothy 35cr, 35bl, 36bl; Hulton Archive / Alex Bowie 42cb; JTB Photo 122-123; Michael Nolan 58-59; Stringer / Tang Chhin Sothy 96br, 97cla; Luca Tettoni 164 165; Time Life Pictures / Larry Burrows 41tl; Ian Trower 46, Roger Viollet / Francoise De Mulder 43c;

Green Discovery Laos: 244t; Mr. Inthy Deuansavanh 149tr.

Peter Holmshaw : 194tr.

Hôtel de la Paix: 216cl.

Keith Kelly: 113br.

The Kobal Collection: Enigma/ Goldcrest 121br; Lawrence Gordon/ Mutual Film/ Paramount/ Bailey Alex 83bc.

Le Tigre de Papier: 242tc.

Lonely Planet Images: Rachel Lewis 218cla, 219tl, Aldo Pavan 221tr; Carol Wiley 22bl.

Marine Conservation Cambodia: 119crb.

Masterfile: Horst Herget 22cr; J. A. Kraulis 67tl; Robert Harding Images 23cla; Jeremy Woodhouse 135bc, 176tl, 201bl.

Monument Books & Toys Co., Ltd: 259bl.

Naturepl.com: Roberto Rinaldi 19br; Rod Williams 19ca, 19bc.

Photolibrary: Age fotostock / Eric Baccega 201cr/ Juan Carlos Munoz 32c/ Morales Morales 19cla/ R Matina 26tr; Asia Images RM / Gareth Jones 4br; Stefan Auth 72crb, 170; Juniors Bildarchiv 19clb, 201cb; F1 Online / Rozbroj Rozbroj 217tl; Hemis / Gotin Michel 24-25c; Per-Andre Hoffmann 55b; Imagebroker.net / Stefan Auth 181br; jspix 201cra; JTB Photo 29tr, 97tc; Jean Kugler 23tr; Lonely Planet Images / Juliet Coombe 47b/ Mark Kirby 105b/ Peter William Thornton 25cr; Mary Evans Picture Library 23clb; R Matina 87cl; Louis Meulstee 73cr; Oxford Scientific (OSF) / David Courtenay 19tc; Robert Harding Travel 37c; Still Pictures / Stuart Chape 18cl; The Travel Library / Paul Strawson 54tr, 85tr, 144cr; Ticket / Thien Do 56tr; WaterFrame - Underwater Images / Borut Furlan 18bc/ Franco Banfi 119bl.

The RiverGarden Siem Reap: 211tr.

Robert Harding Picture Library: Kay Maeritz 188.

Settha Palace Hotel: 213br, 229br.

Suntours Cambodia: 19cr, 44clb, 110cla, 111c, 240bl, 265br.

SuperStock: age fotostock / Chua Wee Boo 246-247, ImageBroker 114-115.

Thalias Co., Ltd.: Malis Restaurant 222bc, Topaz Restaurant 223tr.

The River Resort Laos: 215tr, 232tr.

Travel-Images.com: M. Torres 56bc.

Xe Plan National Protected Area: Phillipe Coste 200b.

Front Endpaper: Left: Dreamstime.com: Angelo2319 c; Pablo Caridad cr; Donyanedomam bc. **Photolibrary**: Stefan Auth tl.
Right: Dreamstime.com: Lakhesis c; Jackmalipan br; **Getty Images**: Ian Trower cr. **Robert Harding Picture Library**: Kay Maeritz tl.

Jacket Images Front: Robert Harding Picture Library: Bruno Morandi Main; DK Images: Rough Guides/ Tim Draper bl; Spine: **Robert Harding Picture Library**: Bruno Morandi

All other images © Dorling Kindersley
For further information see: www.dkimages.com

Special Editions of DK Travel Guides

DK Travel Guides can be purchased in bulk quantities at discounted prices for use in promotions or as premiums. We are also able to offer special editions and personalized jackets, corporate imprints, and excerpts from all of our books, tailored specifically to meet your own needs.

To find out more, please contact:
in the United States **specialsales@dk.com**
in the UK **travelguides@uk.dk.com**
in Canada **specialmarkets@dk.com**
in Australia **PCorporatesales@ penguinrandomhouse.com.au**

Phrase Book for Cambodia

Khmer or Cambodian is the language of the Khmer people and the official language of Cambodia. It is a widely spoken Austroasiatic language. Khmer has been considerably influenced by Sanskrit and Pali, especially in the royal and religious registers, through the vehicles of Hinduism and Buddhism. It is also the earliest recorded and written language of the Mon-Khmer family, predating Mon and, by a significant margin, Vietnamese. Khmer has influenced and also been influenced by Thai, Lao, Vietnamese, and Cham – many of which form a pseudo-sprachbund in peninsular Southeast Asia, since most contain high levels of Sanskrit and Pali influences. Additionally, during and after the French occupation, Khmer was strongly influenced by French. Hence, some of the medical, legal, and technical terminology is borrowed from it. The Khmer alphabet consists of 28 consonants and about 38 vowels. Unlike English, Khmer has a vowel for almost every sound, and is a phonetic language in both oral and written forms. It consists of long and short vowels with distinctive pronunciation. Unlike its Southeast Asian counterparts, Khmer does not have intonation.

Guidelines for Pronunciation

The consonants are pronounced as follows:

k	is equivalent to the French pronunciation of k
kh	is equivalent to the English pronunciation of k
c	is a sound that is between c and j in English
ch	is equivalent to the English pronunciation of ch
ng	is equivalent to the English ending sound of ng
ny	is equivalent to the Spanish pronunciation of ñ
t	is equivalent to the French or Spanish pronunciation of t
th	is equivalent to the English pronunciation of t
p	is equivalent to the French or Spanish pronunciation of p (bi-labial, nonfricative)
ph	is equivalent to the English pronunciation of p
អ	is a representation of a consonant that has a vowel-like sound. Unlike English, Khmer cannot begin any word with a vowel. Hence this consonant "អ" is used

Vowels are pronounced as follows:

/a/ or /aa/ is equivalent to the French or Spanish pronunciation of /a/. The single /a/ is short while the double /aa/ is long.

/i/ or /ii/ is equivalent to the French or Spanish pronunciation of /i/. The single /i/ is short while the double /ii/ is long.

/o/ or /oo/ as in "zone", "cone", or "bone". The single /o/ is short while the double /oo/ is long.

/u/ or /uu/ as in "tune", "soon", or "cube". The single /u/ is short while the double /uu/ is long.

/aw/ as in "saw" or "thaw"

/y/ or /yy/ is a sound that does not exist in the English language. It is made in the epiglottis; it is a high sound made in the back of the oral cavity.

/ɛ/ or /ɛɛ/ is equivalent to the short /a/ or /ă/ of the English language. The single /ɛ/ is short while the double /ɛɛ/ is long.

/uh/ as in "doctor", "master", or "pasture"

/u/ as in the English sound "schwa"

A single vowel is a short vowel using the glottal stop to distinguish it from the long vowel.
A double or two vowels make a long vowel.
Akhosa is any consonant that ends with (aw) while khoosa is any consonant that ends with (oo).
The former has a low sound while the latter is high.
Hence, the tones change depending upon which of the two consonants is used.

In an Emergency

Help!	ជួយផង!	Cuay phawng!
Fire!	ភ្លើងឆេះ!	Phluhng cheh!
Where is the... nearest hospital?	តើ មន្ទីរពេទ្យ យក ជិតនេះនៅ ឯណា?	Tau montii peet kbae nih nuv tii naa?
Call an ambulance!	សុំហៅ ឡានពេទ្យ	Som hau laan peet!
Call the police!	សុំហៅ ប៉ូលីស!	Som hau poolis!
Call a doctor!	សុំហៅ វេជ្ជបណ្ឌិត	Som hau wiceabawndit!

Communication Essentials

Hello!	សួស្ដី	Joom reapsooa!
Goodbye!	ជាសិនហើយ	Joom reapleah!
Yes	បាទ / ចាស	Baat / caas
No	ទេ	Tee
Please	សូម	Soom
Thank you	សូមអរគុណ	awkoon
No, thank you	មិនអីទេ	Min ey tee
I don't understand	ខ្ញុំមិនយល់ទេ	Khnyom min yul tee
I don't know	ខ្ញុំមិនដឹងទេ	Khnyom min dung tee
Sorry/excuse me	សូមអភ័យទោស!	Soom aphpheytoos
What?	អ្វី?	Aawey aawey?
Why?	ហេតុអ្វី?	Haet aawey?
Where?	នៅ ឯណា?	Nuv tii naa?
How?	ដៃ របៀប]ុណ្ណា?	Doay roobiab naa?

Useful Phrases

How are you?	តើ អ្នកសុខសប្បាយ ទេ?	Tau neak sok sabaay cia tee?
Very well, thank you – and you?	សប្បាយជាទេ អរគុណ ចុំអ្នកវិញ?	Sabaay cia tee awkun coh neak vinya?
What is this?	តើ នេះគឺអ្វី?	Tau nih cia aawey?
How do I get to...?	តើ ខ្ញុំអាចទៅ ១៦...?	Tau khnyom aac tuv ae...?
Where is the restroom/toilet?	តើ...នៅ ទៅកន្លែងណា? បន្ទប់ទឹក?	Tau...nuv tii kawnlaeng naa? bawntub tyk?
Do you speak English?	តើ អ្នកនិយាយភាសា អង់គ្លេសរឺទេ?	Tau neak niyiay phiasaa awngkles ryy tee?
I can't speak Khmer/Lao	ខ្ញុំនិនិយាយភា សាខ្មែរ / ឡាវទេ	Khnyom min niyiay phiasaakhmae/ liaw tee

Useful Words

woman/women	ស្ត្រី	satrey
man/men	បុរស	boraws
child/children	កុមារ	komaa
hot	ក្ដៅ ១	kdaw
cold	ត្រជាក់	trawceak
good	ល្អ	l-aw
bad	អាក្រក់	aakrawk
open	បើក	bauk
closed	បទិ	bet
left	ខាងឆ្វេង	khaang chweeng
right	ខាងស្ដាំ	khaang sdam
straight ahead	ខាងមុខ	khaang muk
near	ក្បែរនេះ	kbae nih

far	ឆ្ងាយ	chngaay
entrance	ផ្លូវចូល	phlow cool
exit	ផ្លូវចេញ	phlow cenya

Money

I want to change US$100 into 100 Cambodian/Lao currency.	ខ្ញុំចង់ប្តូរលុយ ១០០ដុល្លា ទៅក្នុង ១០០ លុយខ្មែរ/លាវ	Khnyom cawng bdoo luy muayrooy dollaa tuv knong luy khmae/ liaw.
exchange rate	តំលៃនៃការប្តូរ	dawmlay ney kaabdoo
I'd like to cash these traveler's checks.	ខ្ញុំចង់ប្តូរសែកទេសចរទៅជាលុយ	Khnyom cawng bdoo suek tesacaw tuv cia luy.
bank	ធនាគា	thooniakia
money/cash	លុយ / លុយសុទ្ធ	luy/ lut sot
credit card	កាតក្រេឌិត	kaatkreedit

Keeping in Touch

I'd like to make a telephone call.	ខ្ញុំចង់ប្រើទូរស័ព្ទ	Khnyom cawng prau tuurosap.
I'd like to make an international phone call.	ខ្ញុំចង់ទូរស័ព្ទចេញក្រៅប្រទេស	Khnyom cawng tuurosap cenya tuv prawteh.
cell phone	ទូរស័ព្ទដៃ	tuurosap day
public phone booth	ទីកន្លែងទូរស័ព្ទសាធារណរដ្ឋ	tii kawnlaeng tuurosap saathiaronaroad
address	អាសយដ្ឋាន	aasaythaan
street	វិថី	withey
town	ស្រុក	srok
village	ភូមិ	phuum

Shopping

Where can I buy…?	តើខ្ញុំអាចទិញ… ទីកន្លែង?	Tau khnyom aac tii kawnlaeng?
How much does this cost?	តើនេះមានតម្លៃប៉ុន្មាន?	Tau nih mian daw-mlay ponmaan?
I would like…	ខ្ញុំចង់…	Khnyom cawng…
Do you have…?	តើអ្នកមាន…?	Tau neak mian…?
Do you take credit cards?	តើអ្នកយកក្រេឌីកាតទេ?	Tau neak yook kreedit kaat ryy tee?
What time do you open/close?	តើពេលណាអ្នកបើកទ្វា របិទទ្វា?	Tau peel naa neak bauk twia ryy but twia?
How much?	តំលៃប៉ុន្មាន?	Dawmlay ponmaan?
expensive	ថ្លៃណាស់	thlay nah
cheap	ថោកណាស់	thoak nah
to bargain	តថ្លៃ	dawmlay
size	ទំហំ	tumhum
color	ពណ៌	poa
black	ពណ៌ខ្មៅ	poakhmau
white	ពណ៌ស	poasaw
red	ពណ៌ក្រហម	poakrawhawm
market	ផ្សា	phsaa
pharmacy	ឱសថស្ថាន	oasawtthaan
souvenir store	ហាងលក់អនុស្សាវរីយ៍	haang luk ahnuhsaawoorii
souvenirs	អនុស្សាវរីយ៍	ahnuhsaawoorii
lacquer painting	គំនូរក្រស់ណាទ៍មុក	kumnuu msahsankhuk
painting on silk	គំនូរនៅលើសូត្រ	kumnuu nuv luh soot
wooden statue	រូបចំលាក់	ruub cawmlak
silk scarf	កន្សែងបង់កសូត្រ	kawnsaeng bawng kaw soot

Sightseeing

beach	មាត់សមុទ្រ	moat sawmut
cave, grotto	រូងភ្នំ	roongphnom
festival	ពិធីបុណ្យ	pithii bon
forest	ព្រៃ	prey
island	កោះ	koh
lake	បឹង	bung
mountain	ភ្នំ	phnom
museum	សារមន្ទី	saamontii
pagoda	វត្ត	wat
river	ស្ទឹង	nam, stung
tourist office	ការិយាល័យទេសចរណ៍	kaariyaalay tehsacaw
travel agent	ភ្នាក់ងារទេសចរណ៍	phneak ngia tehsacaw

Transportation

When does the train for…leave?	តើរទេះភ្លើងចាកចេញ…ពេលណា?	Tau rootehphluhng caakcenya…peel naa?
A ticket to…please.	សូមទិញសំបុត្រទៅ…	Soom tinya… sawmbot tuv.
How long does it take to get to…?	តើត្រូវចំណាយពេលប៉ុន្មានដើម្បីទៅ…?	Tau trow cawmnaay peel ponmaan daumbey tuv…?
I'd like to reserve a seat, please.	ខ្ញុំចង់រក្សាកៅអីទុក	Khnyom cawng reaksaa kaw-ey tuk.
Which platform for the…train?	តើណាមួយគឺជាវេទិកាសំរាប់រទេះភ្លើង	Tau naamuay kyycia weetikaa sawmrab rooteh phluhng…?
Where is the bus stop?	តើវេទិកាសំរាប់បស់នៅទីណា?	Tau weetikaa sawmrab bus nuv tii naa?
Where is the bus station?	តើស្ថានីយបស់នៅទីណា?	Tau sthaanii bus nuv tii naa?
arrivals	ការមកដល់	kaamook dawl
train station	ស្ថានីយរទេះភ្លើង	sthaanii rootehphluhng
airport	វាលយន្តហោះ	wial yunhawh
bus station	ស្ថានីយបស់	sthaanii bus
ticket	សំបុត្រ	sawmbot
one-way ticket	សំបុត្រឯកទិស	sawmbot aektys
round-trip ticket	សំបុត្រត្រឡប់មកវិញ	sawmbot trawlawb niik winya
taxi	តាក់ស៊ី	taksii
car rental	ការជួលឡាន	kaacual laan
car	ឡាន	laan
train	រទេះភ្លើង	rootehphluhng
plane	យន្តហោះ	yunhawh
plane ticket	លិខិតយន្តហោះ	likhet yunhawh
motorcycle	ម៉ូតូ	mootoo
bicycle	កង់	kawng

Accommodations

Do you have a vacant room?	តើមានបន្ទប់ទំនេរទេ?	tau mian bawntub tumnee ryytee?
I have a reservation	ខ្ញុំចង់ធ្វើការបំរុងទុកជាមុន	Khnyom cawng thwuhkaa bawm-rong tuk cia mun
double/twin room	បន្ទប់សំរាប់មនុស្សពីរនាក់	bawntub sawrab moonuh pii neak
single room	បន្ទប់សំរាប់មនុស្សម្នាក់	bawntub sawrab moonuh mneak
hotel	សណ្ឋាគារ	sawnthaakia
guesthouse	បន្ទប់ទទួលភ្ញៀវ	bawntub tootual phnyiaw
air conditioning	ម៉ាស៊ីនត្រជាក់	maasin trawceak
bathroom	បន្ទប់ទឹក	bawntub tyk
passport number	លេខប៉ាស្ព័រ	leek pahboa

Eating Out

A table for two please.	តុសំរាប់ពីរនាក់	Toh sawmrab pii neak.
May I see the menu?	ខ្ញុំសុំមុំមើលបញ្ជីអាហារបានទេ?	Khnyom som muhl aahaa baan tee?
Can I have the check, please?	តើខ្ញុំអាចបានលិខិតលុយរឺទេ?	Tau khnyom bann likhut luy ryy tee?

Do you have any special dishes today?	តើ មានមុខអាហារពិសេ សរាប់ថ្ងៃនេះទេ?	Tau mian muk aahaa pises sawmrab thngay? nih ryy tee?
baguette	នំបុ័ង	num pang
beef	សាច់គោ	sac koo
beer	បេ ្យរ	bia
bottle	ដប	dawb
breakfast	ហាយព្រឹក	baay pryk
butter	ប៊រ	buh
chicken	សាច់មាន់	sac moan
chilli	ម្ទេស	mteeh
chopsticks	ចង្កឹស	cawngkus
coconut	ដូង	doong
coffee	កាហ្វេ	kaafee
crab	ក្ដាម	kdaam
dessert	បង្អែម	bawng aem
egg	ពងមាន់	poongmoan
fish	សាច់ត្រី	sactrey
fork	សម	sawm
fruit	ផ្លែឈើ	plaechuh
glass	កែវ	kaew
ice	ទឹកកក	tykkawk
ice cream	ការ៉េម	kaarm key
knife	កាំបិត	kambut
lime	ក្រូចឆ្មា	krooc chmaa
mandarin orange	ក្រូចឃ្លុកៗ	krooc tooc tooc
mango	ស្វាយ	swaay
meat	សាច់	sac
milk	ទឹកដោះគោ	tyk dawhkoo
mineral water	ទឹកសាប	tyk saab
mushrooms	ផ្សិត	phset
noodles	គុយទាវ	kuytiaw
onion	ខ្ទឹមបារាំង	khtum barang
papaya	ល្ហុង	lhong
pâté	សាច់ប៉ាតេ	sac paatee
pepper	ម្ទេស	mtees
pork	សាច់ជ្រូក	sac crook
prawn	បង្គា	bawngkia
restaurant	ភោជនីយដ្ឋាន	phooconiithaan
rice	អង្ករ/ បាយ	awngkaw/ baay
salad	សាឡាដ	saalad
salt	អំបិល	awmbel
soft drinks	ទឹកក្រូច	tyk krooc
soup	សុប	sub
spicy (hot)	ហិលណាស់	hel nas
sour	ជូ	cuu
soy sauce	ស៊ីអ៊ីវ	tyk sii-iw
spoon	ស្លាបព្រា	slaappria
stir-fried	ឆា	chaa
sugar	ស្ករ	skaw
tea	ទឹកតែ	tyk tae
vegetables	បន្លែ	bawnlae
water	ទឹកសាប	tyk saab
Western food	អាហារអាមេរិកាំង	aahaa aameerikang
wine	ស្រា	sraa

Health

I do not feel well	ខ្ញុំមិនស្រួលខ្លួន	khnyom min srual khluan
It hurts here	ឈឺកន្លែងនេ	chyy kawnlaeng
I have a fever	ខ្ញុំក្ដៅ	khnyom krun
I'm allergic to antibiotics	ខ្ញុំមិនទាស់ ថ្នាំរាំងមេរ៉ូក	khnyom min toas thnam rumngoab meerook
blood	ឈាម	chiam
blood pressure (high/low)	ឈាម (ឡើង/ចុះ)	chiam (laum/cos)
cough	ក្អក	k-awk
diabetes	ជំងឺទឹកនោមផ្អែម	cumngyy tyknoomph-aem
diarrhea	រាគ	riak

dizzy	វិលមុខ	wilmyk
doctor	គ្រូពេទ្យ	kruupeet
ear	ត្រចៀក	trawceak
flu	ជំងឺគ្រុនញាក់	cumngyy krun nyeak
food poisoning	ការពុលអាហារ	kaapul aahaa
headache	ការឈឺក្បាល	kaachyy kbaal
heart	បេះដូង	behdoong
hospital	មន្ទីរពេទ្យ	muntii peet
illness	ជំងឺ	cumngyy
injection	ការចាក់ថ្នាំ	kaa cakthnam
malaria	ជំងឺគ្រុនចាញ់	cumngyy krun canya
operate	ផ្ស្សវល	cuascul
prescription	សំបុត្រថ្នាំពេទ្យ	sawmbot thnam peet
temperature	ធាតុអាកាស	thiat aakas

Time and Day

minute	នាទី	niatii
hour	ម៉ោង	moang
day	ថ្ងៃ	thngay
week	អាទិត្យ	aatit
month	ខែ	khae
year	ឆ្នាំ	chnam
Monday	ថ្ងៃចន្ទ	Thngay can
Tuesday	ថ្ងៃអង្គារ	Thngay awngkia
Wednesday	ថ្ងៃពុធ	Thngay put
Thursday	ថ្ងៃព្រហស្បតិ៍	Thngay proohoas
Friday	ថ្ងៃសុក្រ	Thngay sok
Saturday	ថ្ងៃសៅរ៍	Thngay sau
Sunday	ថ្ងៃអាទិត្យ	Thngay aatit
What time is it?	តើម៉ោងប៉ុន្មានហើយ?	Tau moong ponmaan hauy?
8:30	ម៉ោងប្រាំបីកន្លះ	moong prambay kawnlah
10:15	ម៉ោងដប់ប្រាំនាទី	moong dawbpiipram niatii
12:00	ម៉ោងដប់ពីរ	moong dawbpii
morning	ព្រឹក	pryk
midday	ថ្ងៃត្រង់	thngay trawng
afternoon	ថ្ងៃរសៀល	thngay roosial
evening	ល្ងាច	lngiac
night	យប់	yub

Numbers

1	មួយ	muay
2	ពីរ	pii
3	បី	bey
4	បួន	buan
5	ប្រាំ	pram
6	ប្រាំមួយ	prammuay
7	ប្រាំពីរ	prampii
8	ប្រាំបី	prambey
9	ប្រាំបួន	prambuan
10	ដប់	dawb
11	ដប់មួយ	dawbmuay
12	ដប់ពីរ	dawbpii
13	ដប់បី	dawbbey
14	ដប់បួន	dawbuan
15	ដប់ប្រាំ	dawbpram
20	ម្ភៃ	muayphey
30	សាមសិប	saamseb
40	សែសិប	saeseb
50	ហាសិប	haaseb
60	ហុកសិប	hokseb
70	ចិតសិប	cetseb
80	ប៉ែតសិប	paetseb
90	កៅសិប	kawseb
100	មួយរយ	muayrooy
200	ពីររយ	piirooy
1,000	មួយពាន់	muaypoan
10,000	មួយម៉ឺន	muaymuhn
1,000,000	មួយលាន	muaylian

Phrase Book for Laos

Lao or Pasa Lao, the official language of Laos, is a tonal, generally monosyllabic language. Thus having good pronunciations and tonal sounds is essential for communication. It is a part of the Tai sub-group of the Sino-Tibetan group of languages, and its written form evolved from an ancient Indian script called Pali. Just like English, Lao is read from left to right and follows the subject-verb-object word order. In addition, most Lao letters are pronounced just like the sounds that exist in English. However, Lao differs from English in that it has little grammar, no plurals, few articles, and regularly omits the subject pronouns (I, he, she) when the context is understood.

Guidelines for Pronunciation

Lao consonants below have been divided into three groups according to the tone in which they are spoken. The consonants are pronounced as follows:

Aksone sung (high sounding consonant)

ຂ	**kh**	like 'c' in "cat" (aspirated)
ສ	**s**	like 'ss' in "hiss"
ຖ	**th/t**	like 't' in "top"
ຜ	**ph**	like 'p' in "pig" (aspirated)
ໝ	**m**	similar to 'm' in "mother"
ຫຼ	**l**	similar to 'l' in "long"
ຫວ	**w**	like 'w' in "weight"

Aksone kang (middle sounding consonant)

ກ	**k/g**	like 'k' in "skate" (unaspirated)
ຈ	**ch/j**	like 'ch' in "chop"
ດ	**d/t**	like 'd' in "dog"
ຕ	**t**	like 't' in "stab"
ບ	**b**	like 'b' in "bed"
ປ	**p**	like 'p' in "spit" (unaspirated)
ຢ	**y**	like 'y' in "yes"
ອ	**o**	like 'o' in "top"

Aksone tum (low sounding consonant)

ງ	**ng**	like 'ng' in "sing"
ຊ	**s/x**	like 'z' in "zoo"
ຍ	**nh/y**	like 'y' in "yes"
ຝ	**f**	like 'f' in "fan"
ມ	**m**	like 'm' in "mother"
ຣ	**r**	like 'r' in "room"
ລ	**l**	like 'l' in "love"
ວ	**v**	like 'v' in "vacant"
ຫ	**h**	like 'h' in "help"
ນ	**n**	like 'n' in "nice"

Lao vowels are pronounced as follows:

◌ິ	**i**	like 'i' in "nit"
◌ີ	**ii**	like 'ee' in "feet"
◌ະ	**a**	like 'u' in "gum"
◌າ	**aa**	like 'a' in "father"
ແ◌ະ	**ae**	like 'a' in "fat"
ແ◌	**e**	like 'e' in "fence"
ໄ◌	**eh**	like 'ai' in "bait"
◌ຸ	**u**	like 'u' in "fruit"
◌ູ	**ou**	like 'oo' in "mood"
◌າວ	**aw**	like 'aw' in "saw"
◌ຳ	**am**	like 'um' in "drum"
ໂ◌	**oe**	similar to the 'uh' in "huh"
ເ◌ຶ	**eu**	like 'eu' in the French "deux"

In an Emergency

Help!	ຊ່ວຍແດ່!	Suoy dae!
Fire!	ໄຟໃໝ້!	Fai mai!
Where is the nearest hospital?	ໂຮງໝໍໃກ້ສຸດຢູ່ໃສ?	Hong Mor Kai Sud Yu sai?
Call an ambulance!	ໂທຫາວິດຄົນສົ່ງຄົນເຈັບແດ່!	Towha lod khonsong khonchep dae!
Call the police!	ໂທຫາຕຳຫຼວດແດ່!	Towha tum luot dae!
Call a doctor!	ໂທຫາທ່ານໝໍແດ່!	Towha thanmor dae!

Communication Essentials

Hello!	ສະບາຍດີ!	Sabaidee!
Goodbye!	ລາກ່ອນ!	Lakhon!
Yes	ແມ່ນ	Maen
No	ບໍ່	Bauw
Please	ກະລຸນາ	Kaluna
Thank you	ຂອບໃຈ	Khobjai
No, thank you	ບໍ່, ຂອບໃຈ	Bauw, Khobjai
I don't understand	ຂ້ອຍບໍ່ເຂົ້າໃຈ	Khoy Bauw Khaojai
Sorry/excuse me	ຂໍໂທດ!	Khauwthod
What?	ແມ່ນຫຍັງ?	Maen yang?
Why?	ຍ້ອນຫຍັງ?	Yonyang?
Where?	ຢູ່ໃສ?	U sai?

Useful Phrases

How are you?	ເຈົ້າສະບາຍດີບໍ?	Jaw Sabaidee Bor?
Very well, thank you – and you?	ຂ້ອຍສະບາຍດີ, ຂອບໃຈ - ເຈົ້າເດ?	Khoy sabaidee, Khobjai – Jawdee?
How do I get to…?	ຂ້ອຍຈະໄປ...ໄດ້ແນວໃດ?	Khoychapai ....ai neo day?
Where is the restroom/toilet?	ຫ້ອງນ້ຳຢູ່ໃສ?	Hongnam u sai?
Do you speak English?	ເຈົ້າເວົ້າພາສາອັງກິດບໍ່?	Jaw Vaw Pasa Anggit Bor?
I can't speak Khmer/Lao	ຂ້ອຍບໍ່ສາມາດເວົ້າພາສາກຳປູເຈຍ/ພາສາລາວໄດ້	Khoy bor sa mart vaw pasa gampuchia/ pasa Lao dai.

Useful Words

woman/women	ແມ່ຍິງ	mae ying
man/men	ຜູ້ຊາຍ	phu xai
child/children	ເດັກນ້ອຍ	dek noy
open	ເປີດ	peurt
closed	ປິດ	pit
left	ຊ້າຍ	sai
right	ຂວາ	khuua
near	ໃກ້	kai (high falling short)
far	ໄກ	kai (mid – long)
entrance	ເຂົ້າ	khao
exit	ອອກ	ork

Money

I want to change US$100 into 100 Cambodian/Lao currency.	ຂ້ອຍຕ້ອງການປ່ຽນ 100 ໂດລາເປັນເງິນກຳປູເຈຍ/ເງິນກິບລາວ	Khoy tong kan pien neung hoy do la pen ngeun kampuchia/ngeun kip lao.
exchange rate	ອັດຕາແລກປ່ຽນ	aat ta laek pien
I'd like to cash these traveler's checks.	ຂ້ອຍຕ້ອງການແລກໃບເຊັກທ່ອງທ່ຽວເຫຼົ່ານີ້ເປັນເງິນສົດ	Khoy tong kan laek bai sek thong thieu nee pen ngeun sot.
bank	ທະນາຄານ	thanakhan
money/cash	ເງິນ/ເງິນສົດ	ngeun/ngeun sot
credit card	ບັດເຄດິດ	bat khe dit

Keeping in Touch

I'd like to make a telephone call.	ຂ້ອຍຢາກໂທລະສັບ	Khoy yark tow la sap.
cell phone	ໂທລະສັບມືຖື	tow la sap meu theu
public phone booth	ຕູ້ໂທລະສັບສາທາລະນະ	tu tow la sap sa tha la na

Shopping

How much does this cost?	ອັນນີ້ວລາຄາເທົ່າໃດ?	An nee la kha thao dai?
What time do you open/close?	ເຈົ້າເປີດ/ປິດເວລາຈັກໂມງ?	Jaw peurt/pit vei la chak moung?
size	ຂະໜາດ	kha nat
market	ຕະຫລາດ	ta lat
pharmacy	ຮ້ານຂາຍຢາ	han khai ya
souvenir store	ຮ້ານຂາຍຂອງທີ່ລະນຶກ	han khai khong tee la neuk

Sightseeing

cave, grotto	ຖ້ຳ	tham
lake	ໜອງ	nong
mountain	ພູເຂົາ	phu khao
river	ແມ່ນ້ຳ	nam
tourist office	ຫ້ອງການທ່ອງທ່ຽວ	hong kan thong thieu
travel agent	ຕົວແທນທ່ອງທ່ຽວ	tou thaen thong thieu

Transportation

A ticket to…please.	ເອົາປີ້ໄປ…. ໃຫ້ແດ່.	Aw pii pai … hai dae.
Where is the bus stop?	ບ່ອນຈອດລົດເມຢູ່ໃສ?	Bon chot lot mei u sai?
arrivals	ຂາເຂົ້າ	kha khao
airport	ສະໜາມບິນ	sa nam bin
one-way ticket	ປີ້ຂາໄປ	pii kha pai
round-trip ticket	ປີ້ໄປກັບ	pii pai kub
taxi	ລົດແທັກຊີ	lot taek xee
car rental	ການເຊົ່າລົດ	kan sao lot
plane ticket	ປີ້ຍົນ	pii nhon
motorbike	ລົດຈັກ	lot chak
bicycle	ລົດຖີບ	lot theep

Accommodations

Do you have a vacant room?	ເຈົ້າມີຫ້ອງຫວ່າງບໍ?	Jaw mee hong vang bor?
I have a reservation	ຂ້ອຍໄດ້ຈອງໄວ້ແລ້ວ	Khoy dai chong vai laeo
double/twin room	ຫ້ອງຕຽງຄູ່/ສອງຕຽງ	hong tieng khou/ song tieng
single room	ຫ້ອງຕຽງດ່ຽວ	hong tieng dieu
hotel	ໂຮງແຮມ	hoong haem
guesthouse	ເຮືອນພັກ	heuan pak
air conditioning	ເຄື່ອງປັບອາກາດ	kheuang pap aakard
bathroom	ຫ້ອງອາບນ້ຳ	hong arb nam
passport number	ເລກທີ່ໜັງສືຜ່ານແດນ	Leik tee nang su phan daen

Eating Out

May I see the menu?	ຂ້ອຍຂໍເບິ່ງເມນູໄດ້ບໍ?	khoy khor beung mei nu dai bor?
Can I have the check, please?	ກະລຸນາ ເອົາບິນໃຫ້ແດ່?	Ka lu na ao bin hai dae?
baguette	ເຂົ້າຈີ່ກ້ອນຍາວ	khao chii kon yao
beef	ຊີ້ນງົວ	xeen ngua
chopsticks	ໄມ້ຖູ່	mai thu
chicken	ໄກ່	gai
coffee	ກາເຟ	ka fei
crab	ປູ	pu
egg	ໄຂ່	khai
fish	ປາ	pa
fork	ສ້ອມ	som
fruit	ໝາກໄມ້	mark mai
meat	ຊີ້ນ	xeen
mineral water	ນ້ຳແຮ່	nam hae
milk	ນົມ	noom
noodles	ໝີ່	mee
pepper	ພິກໄທ	pik thai
pork	ຊີ້ນໝູ	xeen mou
prawn	ກຸ້ງ	kung
restaurant	ຮ້ານອາຫານ	han aa han
rice	ເຂົ້າ	khao

salt	ເກືອ	keua
spicy (hot)	ເຜັດ	fet
spoon	ບ່ວງ	boang
sugar	ນ້ຳຕານ	nam tan
tea	ຊາ	xaa
vegetables	ຜັກ	fak
water	ນ້ຳ	nam
Western food	ອາຫານຕາເວັນຕົກ	aa han ta ven tok

Health

I do not feel well	ຂ້ອຍຮູ້ສຶກບໍ່ສະບາຍ	Khoy hu seuk bor sa bai
It hurts here	ມັນເຈັບບ່ອນນີ້	Man cheb bon nee
I have a fever	ຂ້ອຍເປັນໄຂ້	Khoy pen khai
I'm allergic to antibiotics	ຂ້ອຍແພ້ຢາຕ້ານເຊື້ອ	Khoy pae ya tan xeua
blood pressure (high/low)	ຄວາມດັນເລືອດ (ສູງ/ຕ່ຳ)	khoam dun luot (sung/tum)
cough	ໄອ	i
diabetes	ເບົາຫວານ	bao wan
diarrhea	ຖອກທ້ອງ	thok thong
food poisoning	ອາຫານເປັນພິດ	aa han pen pit
headache	ເຈັບຫົວ	cheb hua
illness	ການເຈັບປ່ວຍ	kan cheb puoy
malaria	ໄຂ້ມາລາເຣຍ	khai ma la ria
prescription	ໃບສັ່ງຢາ	bai sang ya
toothache	ເຈັບແຂ້ວ	cheb khaeo

Time and Day

minute	ນາທີ	na tii
hour	ຊົ່ວໂມງ	xou mohng
day	ມື້	meuh
week	ອາທິດ	aa thit
month	ເດືອນ	deuan
Monday	ວັນຈັນ	Van chan
Tuesday	ວັນອັງຄານ	Van ang khan
Wednesday	ວັນພຸດ	Van phut
Thursday	ວັນພະຫັດ	Van pa hat
Friday	ວັນສຸກ	Van suk
Saturday	ວັນເສົາ	Van sao
Sunday	ວັນອາທິດ	Van aa thit
What time is it?	ເວລາຈັກໂມງແລ້ວ?	Vei la chak mohng laeo?
morning	ຕອນເຊົ້າ	ton xao
afternoon	ຕອນບ່າຍ	ton baii
evening	ຕອນແລງ	ton laeng
night	ກາງຄືນ	kang keun

Numbers

1	ໜຶ່ງ	neung
2	ສອງ	song
3	ສາມ	saam
4	ສີ່	sii
5	ຫ້າ	ha
6	ຫົກ	hok
7	ເຈັດ	jet
8	ແປດ	paet
9	ເກົ້າ	kao
10	ສິບ	sip
20	ຊາວ	xao
30	ສາມສິບ	saam sip
40	ສີ່ສິບ	sii sip
50	ຫ້າສິບ	ha sip
60	ຫົກສິບ	hok sip
70	ເຈັດສິບ	jet sip
80	ແປດສິບ	paet sip
90	ເກົ້າສິບ	kao sip
100	ໜຶ່ງຮ້ອຍ	neung hoy
1,000	ໜຶ່ງພັນ	neung pan
10,000	ສິບພັນ	sip pan
1,000,000	ໜຶ່ງລ້ານ	neung laan

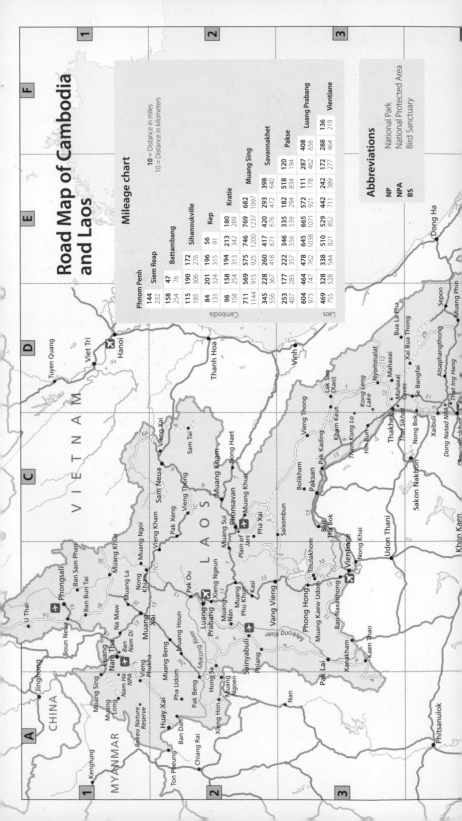

Road Map of Cambodia and Laos

Mileage chart

10 = Distance in miles
10 = Distance in kilometers

	Phnom Penh	Siem Reap	Battambang	Sihanoukville	Kep	Kratie	Muang Sing	Savannakhet	Pakse	Luang Prabang	Vientiane
Cambodia	**144** 232										
	158 254	**47** 76									
	115 185	**190** 306	**172** 276								
	84 135	**201** 324	**196** 315	**56** 91							
	98 158	**194** 313	**213** 342	**180** 289							
Laos	**711** 1144	**569** 915	**575** 925	**746** 1200	**769** 1237	**682** 1097					
	345 407	**228** 367	**260** 418	**346** 539	**420** 671	**293** 472	**120** 194				
	253 407	**177** 285	**222** 357	**335** 539	**417** 676	**182** 294	**293** 462				
	604 973	**464** 747	**478** 762	**665** 1071	**572** 921	**518** 834	**287** 462	**111** 178			
	469 755	**328** 528	**338** 544	**510** 821	**529** 852	**442** 711	**242** 389	**172** 277	**408** 656	**288** 464	**136** 219

Abbreviations

NP	National Park
NPA	National Protected Area
BS	Bird Sanctuary